FULL COURT
PRESS

Race, Rhetoric, and Media Series
Davis W. Houck, General Editor

FULL COURT PRESS

Mississippi State University, the Press, and the Battle to Integrate College Basketball

Jason A. Peterson

University Press of Mississippi / Jackson

www.upress.state.ms.us

The University Press of Mississippi is a member
of the Association of American University Presses.

First printing 2016
∞
Library of Congress Cataloging-in-Publication Data available

978-1-4968-0820-2 (hardback)
978-1-4968-0821-9 (ebook)

British Library Cataloging-in-Publication Data available

Contents

Acknowledgments

I would like to begin by acknowledging the contributions of the many journalists and athletes cited in this volume, some of which displayed great courage and foresight. Even now, I marvel at the conviction of many of the individuals featured in this book, and I thank them for making social progress a priority in the face of such adversity. Wilbert Jordan Jr., Perry Wallace, Joe Dan Gold, Dr. Douglas Starr, Jimmie McDowell, Joe Mosby, Rick Cleveland, and Bob Hartley all contributed to an overall understanding of the civil rights era, and the commentary offered by each validated my exploration into this topic.

I would also like to thank my friends and mentors David R. Davies and Brian Carroll. Both men were instrumental in my completion of this volume, and without their guidance and wisdom, I doubt I would have completed such a task. Also, in no particular order, I would also like to thank the following individuals for their assistance and guidance: Art Kaul, Gene Wiggins, Dan Fultz, Thomas Keating, Bob Frank, Curt Hersey, Diane Land, Kevin Kleine, Thomas Kennedy, Kim LeDuff, Cheryl Jenkins, Christopher Campbell, Ginger Carter Miller, Mary Jean Land, William Griswold, Louis Benjamin, Mazharul Haque, Bradley Bond, Louis Kyriakoudes, Willie Pierce, Betty Self, Jennifer Ward, John Wall, Andrew Sharpe, Pristina Armstrong, Jennifer Brannock, Cindy Lawler, and Xiaojing Zu.

On a personal note, I would like to thank my parents, William and Sandy Peterson, for fueling my thirst for knowledge over the years, and my brother, Billy Peterson, who jokingly doubted my sanity during my years as a journalist, yet never questioned my dreams and aspirations. He has remained a steady and supportive influence in my life and, for that, I will always be grateful.

Last, but not least, I would like to thank my wife and my two children. An endeavor of this magnitude would not be possible without their unconditional love, support, and encouragement. My wife has never questioned my desires to achieve this goal and lovingly followed me on a trek through the southern United States. She is my best friend and my biggest fan. There is no doubt that I would have been unable to complete such an arduous task without her. Joy, Addison, and Connor, this is for you. I love you.

FULL COURT
PRESS

Introduction

The civil rights era in Mississippi was a dark and violent time in our country's history. While the rest of the southern states moved on from the heated debate concerning the extent of states' rights and began to catch up with their northern brethren, Mississippi held firm in its believed right to segregate. Notions like equality and integration into the traditionally white customs and social structure of the Magnolia State were cast aside with vigor and rage. While the 1954 *Brown vs. Board of Education* decision was supposed to alleviate some of the dominance of Mississippi's white elite, the groundbreaking legal precedent only helped strengthen the foundation on which the Closed Society was built. Governor Hugh White responded to what has been called Mississippi's Second Reconstruction by continuing with his plan to develop segregated, white-only schools rather than integrating existing educational establishments.[1]

From the mid-1950s through the late 1960s, Mississippi's white-dominated caste system, dubbed the Closed Society by historian James Silver, permeated every segment of society and, for better or worse, had a profound influence on how whites and blacks in the state lived. The social and political atmosphere emphasized a belief in white supremacy through segregation, which was rationalized by an appeal to states' rights.[2] Historians have paid considerable attention to events in the civil rights era that either opposed the Closed Society or pointed out the horrific extent some would go to protect it, and that ultimately lead to the collapse of that white-dominated way of life. A key component of the Closed Society was the role of local journalism, which acted as an arm of organizations like the Citizens' Council and the Sovereignty Commission to protect the way of life that segregation had built. Journalists and editors, like the colorful yet spiteful Frederick Sullens and his protégé Jimmy Ward of the *Jackson Daily News*, opposed all threats to the Closed Society. Others, such as Hodding Carter of the *Delta Democrat-Times*, respected the notion of civil rights and would attempt to balance any debate with logic and reason. While these journalists and others addressed historical events like *Brown vs. Board of Education*, the integration of the University of Mississippi, the Civil Rights Acts of 1964, Freedom Summer, the Voting Rights Act of 1965, and the Civil Rights Act of 1968, there were events in local sports that fostered considerable debate in the press that would demonstrate the slow but progressive change in Mississippi journalism during the civil rights era and assist in the deconstruction of the Closed Society.

In 1955, after Jones County Junior College's football team lost to the integrated Tartars of Compton Junior College in the Junior Rose Bowl, the state's political elite banded together with the State College Board to create the unwritten law, a gentleman's agreement, that would keep Mississippi's athletic venues segregated and in compliance with the Closed Society.[3] The agreement, which never had any legitimate legal power, was nevertheless treated as law and punishable by the loss of state funding and scholarships.[4] After the creation of the unwritten law, Louisiana and Georgia attempted to institute legal standards to prevent integrated athletic competition, specifically in their home venues, but to no avail.[5] Despite the legal failures of other southern states, the unwritten law endured in Mississippi and was the only one of its kind in the South.

While the Magnolia State was covered in a veil of oppression, a surprising enemy of white supremacy emerged in the small college town of Starkville. Mississippi State University was at the forefront of the battle for equality in the state with the school's successful collegiate basketball program. When Mississippi State was granted university status in 1958, the Maroons won four consecutive Southeastern Conference championships from 1959 through 1963 and created a championship dynasty in the South's preeminent college athletic conference.[6] Despite its in-conference success, national prominence escaped the teams of James "Babe" McCarthy, as his teams never participated in the NCAA tournament and rarely ventured outside the South due to the unwritten law. In turn, the efforts of MSU went unnoticed by the national press, and invitations to the Maroons for a shot at national basketball glory were passed to the University of Kentucky and legendary coach Adolph Rupp.[7] However, in all four title-winning seasons, the press feverishly debated the possibility of an NCAA appearance for the Maroons, culminating in Mississippi State University's participation in the 1963 NCAA's National Championship basketball tournament, where they lost to the integrated Loyola of Chicago.

During the unwritten law's eight-year existence, the hardwood of Mississippi's college basketball courts brought forth multiple challenges to the Closed Society, all of which were debated with fervor and spite in the pages of Mississippi's newspapers. While the basketball teams from the University of Mississippi, the University of Southern Mississippi, and Jackson State College would all experience the repercussions of the unwritten law, it was Mississippi State that was the most frequent challenger of Mississippi's segregated athletic standard. Mississippi's editors and journalists overall expressed polarizing opinions on the merit of integrated athletics, which ultimately damaged the Closed Society's racial united front.

While James Meredith would become the first black student to enroll at the University of Mississippi in 1962, signaling the integration of Mississippi's colleges and universities, the state would not welcome blacks as basketball adversaries until 1967, when Perry Wallace integrated the SEC by playing for Vanderbilt University. A season later, Wilbert Jordan Jr. became the first collegiate black athlete at the University of Southern Mississippi when he walked on to the Southerners' freshman basketball squad. A new political ideology was sweeping through Mississippi, and the shackles of the Closed Society began to slowly loosen. Editors from across the state denounced the 1964 Civil Rights Act, which guaranteed that blacks and other minorities had equal access to all public facilities, including institutions of higher learning.[8] While Mississippi's journalists verbally lambasted the act, it also signaled a change in the way in which matters of race were covered in the press. Over time, the principles of the Civil Rights Act were accepted and integration arrived in Mississippi. The press reflected those ideological changes even in the area of sports, as when Jordan's addition to the Southern Miss roster went unnoticed by the local *Hattiesburg American*. While national occurrences such as the landmark *Brown vs. Board of Education* decision of 1954, the integration of Ole Miss, the Civil Rights Acts of 1964 and 1968, Freedom Summer, and the Voting Rights Act of 1965 are often viewed by media historians as major disruptions to the southern way of life and fatal blows leading to the eventual end of the Closed Society, cracks in the racial armor began to appear with every local challenge to the unwritten law.[9]

An examination of Mississippi newspapers during the eight-year existence of the unwritten law shows that the various challenges placed before the gentleman's agreement, specifically those posed by Mississippi State University, generated three primary responses from Mississippi's journalists. Reporters and editors either condemned or dismissed any threats to the unwritten law, voiced no opinion on the possibility of integrated competition and published little or no original material on the matter, or supported a venture into integrated play, more often than not only to better Mississippi's chance at a championship. For each expression of outrage, the press gave the unwritten law a degree of credibility as a vital and crucial part of Mississippi's white way of life, and helped enforce the segregated standard. Furthermore, the legitimacy of the unwritten law was perpetuated by the silence from Mississippi's sports writers, who typically hid in the comfortable confines of athletics and rarely addressed the racial controversy surrounding each of these challenges. While silence from the press can be taken to mean different things, Richard Iton argues that "intentional silences also have significance: to say nothing suggests acceptance of, or satisfaction with, existing arrangements, and implicitly represents the expression of a political preference."[10] Iton's perspective is easily applicable to the issue of race in Mississippi during the Civil Rights era. By failing to acknowledge the racial connotation of the various controversies involving MSU's basketball team, journalists in the state were validating both the unwritten law and the Closed Society, thus offering the state's dominant white ideology a sense of power. But as the years and the challenges mounted against the state's segregationist athletic standard, more journalists began to question the validity of the unwritten law and advocate integrated competition, culminating in MSU's 1963 entry into the NCAA tournament. After the elimination of the unwritten law in 1963, Mississippi's press returned to its conservative habits only to face the various social changes of the subsequent years, signaling the waning of the powerful Closed Society and ushering in a new era of equality. Little was written in the pages of Mississippi's newspapers when the SEC integrated in 1966, and only one reporter acknowledged Perry Wallace's first trek through the state as the conference's first black basketball player at Vanderbilt in 1967. Issues of race in sports did not generate the same level of reaction from journalists because, as Kurt Kemper argues, sports fandom during this time was based on the need for cultural identity and the search of reflective values.[11] The emergence of racial connotations in athletic endeavors, in this case MSU basketball, was ignored because it forced the Closed Society to question its own superiority and unity. Consequently, the sports scribes of the state found little news value in the pioneering presence of Jordan, of Coolidge Ball at Ole Miss in 1970, or of Larry Fry or Jerry Jenkins at Mississippi State in 1971, rarely identifying the athletes' skin color. The silence that once served the journalistic stalwarts of the Closed Society slowly became a nod to the social progress made by the members of the press, as the integration of sports was no longer a source of polarizing opinion from reporters and editors.

An examination of the work of the press in matters of sports and race can serve as a historical spyglass into the cultural and social values of the Magnolia State. It has long been established by scholars such as Walter Lippmann, Donald Shaw, Maxwell McCombs, Richard Letz, and Karla Gower that the press has a profound influence on public opinion and the interpretation of the news.[12] With that theoretical framework, it becomes clear that the reporters in Mississippi had considerable influence and power on their reading audience. Sociologist David Zirin describes sports as "keeping the average person from worrying about the things that matter in their lives" and serving as an area in which the ideas of our society can be presented and challenged. Sports, in essence, can reflect both the dominant ideas of a society and the struggles that lie beneath the surface.[13] Similarly, Kurt Kemper writes that people in a Cold War society often looked to sports for a sense of cultural distinctiveness and reflective values.[14] In the South, values like loyalty, honor, and segregation had significant meaning.[15] While Mississippians were looking to the MSU men's basketball team for reassurance of their own cultural distinctiveness, they instead faced questions regarding their own superiority and unity due to the various challenges to the unwritten law. Mississippi State, rather than projecting the cultural values of the Closed Society, rejected them with each one of these challenges, putting the press in a protective and influential position. Thus, the debate surrounding the issue of race and sports within the press was more about preserving the values of the Closed Society than it was about athletics or, in this case, Mississippi State basketball.

Though there are a number of credible and useful sources that deal with the press's coverage of race and the social impact and justification of the segregation of sports, the literature dealing with coverage of college sports in Mississippi is thin. The creation of the unwritten law and the subsequent challenges to the Closed Society from Mississippi college basketball occurred after the Supreme Court's decision in *Brown vs. Board of Education* and before the Civil Rights Act of 1964. Peter Levy writes that, from a political standpoint, rather than moving forward with the integration of schools after *Brown*, the "citadel of segregation and white supremacy" did the opposite. [16] Historian David Sansing writes that there was such a need for unity, unanimity, and conformity in Mississippi's Closed Society that the College Board and college officials deferred to the state's power structure on matters that threatened white Mississippi's way of life. [17] Along those lines, the idea of playing against an integrated team was a disturbing thought for many white southerners who grew up in the Closed Society. [18] Furthermore, in the vein of historians John Dittmer, Charles M. Payne, Emilye Crosby, Ted Ownby, and David R. Davies, a true understanding of the events of the civil rights movement in Mississippi is best gained by an understanding of local events. [19] While there was a level of attention paid to Mississippi State during its various attempts to enter the integrated NCAA tournament, the efforts of one of Mississippi's segregated institutions to violate the state's unwritten law was primarily a local story. Therefore, the reaction of state journalists and the very audiences they served was rooted in such a local context.

Despite *Brown*, Mississippi was gripped by the segregation rules of Jim Crow through the mid-1960s when the unwritten law enforced the segregation of athletics. [20] The press in Mississippi mirrored the political structure of the state, with some exceptions. Mississippi did not resort to censorship or violence to influence the press; rather the majority of the state's newspaper editors were white supremacists. [21] Historians such as Davies and Maryann Vollers have described how proponents of integration were typically met with a barrage of discontent and anger in the Magnolia State, usually fueled by coverage in the mainstream press. [22] Mississippi newspapers have been viewed by historian Julius Eric Thompson as falling into three predominant categories: the first was made up of the extremely conservative papers, such as the *Clarion-Ledger* and the *Jackson Daily News*, both owned by the segregationist Hederman family, and other papers such as the *Natchez Democrat*, the *Hattiesburg American*, the *Fayette Chronicle*, the *Tunica Times-Democrat*, and the *Pike County Summit Sun*.[23] According to Thompson, these papers have been labeled as some of the worst in the United States at the time because of their "dishonest treatment" of blacks and issues involving race.[24] The Hederman papers, in particular, often took the role of segregation proponents. According to a *Time* article in 1966, "The morning *Clarion-Ledger* and the afternoon *Daily News* indulge in more Yankee-baiting and race-baiting than any other paper in the South."[25] Bob Hederman published both the *Jackson Daily News* and the *Clarion-Ledger*, and his cousin Tom Hederman served as the editor of the *Clarion-Ledger*. With a combined circulation of about ninety thousand, the Hederman newspapers were the only dailies available statewide. According to historian John Dittmer, most Mississippians saw the world through the eyes of the Hedermans, who were extremely influential in other sectors of Mississippi society as well and "poured out a steady stream of invective against black activities and their white allies."[26] The Hedermans were unquestioning supporters of Governor Ross Barnett, had nothing but praise for the Citizens' Council, and were Mississippi's primary voice for segregation.[27] The tone of newspaper coverage in the state was set by the *Clarion-Ledger* and the *Jackson Daily News*.[28] While the work of known segregationist Jimmy Ward in the pages of the *Jackson Daily News* seemed to epitomize the racial outlook of the Hederman empire, some found the tone and content of these publications to be a reflection of the audience rather than the personal views of the Hederman family.[29] While the Hedermans also owned the *Hattiesburg American*, the openly segregationist publication was not considered "a white sheet" because it lacked the blatantly racist materials of its Jackson-based counterparts.[30]

A direct and more moderate competitor for the Hederman papers could be found in the *Jackson State Times*, which opened in 1954 and closed in 1962.[31] The *State Times* led a crusade against the Hederman empire, often speaking out against segregation and calling for temperance and reason when it came to issues of race, including the 1954 *Brown vs. Board of Education* decision.[32] According to James T. Sellers, the paper promoted "good, honest, and responsible government."[33] However, over time, the paper yielded to public pressure and began to mirror its Jackson-based fellows in its views on race.[34] Many historians have indicated that the only factor that kept the *State Times* from becoming a mirror image of the Hederman papers was the presence of J. Oliver Emmerich, editor of both the *State Times* and the McComb-based *Enterprise-Journal* and one of the few journalists who openly challenged the ideals of the Closed Society.[35] Although in the minority, some newspapers in Mississippi took a more moderate stance on race issues within the state. Editors such as Carter and Emmerich challenged the ideals and principles of the Closed Society.[36] Frequently pressured by other journalists and readers, these publications at times spoke out on race-related issues.[37]

Black newspapers also had remarkably different positions from their white counterparts on race. Conservative black newspapers in Mississippi, including the *Jackson Advocate* and the *Mississippi Enterprise*, were silent on many of the controversial issues involving race, fearing a backlash from the white segregationist power structure.[38] The most prominent black newspaper, the *Jackson Advocate*, was edited by Percy Greene, who advocated the right to vote for blacks, yet was on the payroll of the state's Sovereignty Commission—a government agency responsible for the monitoring of black activism in the state—and advocated only equal education rather than all-out integration.[39]

Despite the presence of Carter and Emmerich, in general Mississippi's newspapers and journalists worked for the good of the Closed Society. According to historian Joseph Atkins, journalists in the state were often selective about what they covered, choosing to print materials straight from the Citizens' Council rather than cover issues of racial strife.[40] Former Associated Press correspondent Douglas Starr agreed with Atkins's contention in a 2009 interview, saying that newspapers in the Magnolia State stayed away from topics that did not complement the Closed Society and would publish news-agency accounts on controversial issues to give the publication and its editors a scapegoat to blame in case there were any public objections to the coverage of a particular topic.[41] The same sort of approach was evident in coverage of the various challenges to the unwritten law and the segregation of Mississippi's collegiate sports.

The political and social fervor brought forth by the *Brown* decision could also be seen on the playing fields of Mississippi. During the 1950s, the white South firmly resisted any racial change. Conservative southern whites adamantly resisted efforts to eliminate discrimination, including in the areas of higher education and athletics.[42] At the time of the *Brown* decision, no university or college in the Atlantic Coast Conference or in the Southeastern Conference had integrated either its undergraduate student body or its athletic programs.[43] According to political scientist Renford Reese, the loss of the Civil War led to years of resentment on behalf of the South. Rivalries developed between the northern and southern teams, to the point that these battles were of a more passionate nature than their in-conference games. The South was slow to react to the *Brown* decision and often responded by enacting state laws prohibiting integrated competition.[44] The *Brown vs. Board of Education* decision caused many segregationists to see the playing fields as a vulnerability in the fight against race mixing. Once athletic venues began to welcome integration, there was a period of unrest, as there was no accepted method for discussing, understanding, and bridging racial divides, let alone agreement that such efforts were desirable. According to author Barry Jacobs, the weight of habit and custom worked against African Americans, as did an older generation of athletic officials in a position to ease their transition.[45]

Things began to change during the early 1960s with the federally enforced enrollment of James Meredith at the University of Mississippi. After the U.S. Supreme Court ordered Meredith's enrollment in September 1962, Barnett went on state television and vowed that "no school will be integrated in Mississippi while I am your governor. . . . We will not drink from the cup of genocide."[46] Despite the admission of Meredith to the Oxford-based university, advancement in the area of race was nonexistent in Mississippi. Charles M. Payne writes that during the 1960s, "Everything that took place in Mississippi took place against the state's long tradition of systematic racial terrorism. Without some minimal protection for the lives of potential activists, no real opposition to the system of white supremacy was possible."[47]

In the aftermath of Meredith's enrollment, the use of violence against blacks was replaced by the threat of economic reprisals, a tactic used throughout the duration of the unwritten law's existence.[48] Despite such racial landmarks as the integration of the University of Mississippi and the 1964 Civil Rights Act, Payne writes that there was still "a more or less tacit understanding in Mississippi that public officials would do all in their power to stop integration."[49] Not surprisingly, strategies used by whites to resist the civil rights movement changed as well. Historian Kenneth Andrews writes that the local variation in white resistance corresponded partially to the characteristics of the local social structure. White strategies developed through a process of tactical response to black mobilization, real or anticipated, and to the perceived successes of the civil rights movement.[50]

The State College Board was unwilling to accept many of the changes that were going on around them, despite the impending integration of the state's predominantly white institutions.[51] Despite the passing of the Civil Rights Act, social problems still existed in Mississippi. New York journalist Tom Johnson, who covered the July 1964 disappearance of Michael Schwerner, Andrew Goodman, and James Chaney in Philadelphia, described his experience in Mississippi in a chilling sentence: "I saw the hatred on [whites'] faces and knew they wanted to kill us."[52] Only time changed things in the South. By the late 1960s, more avenues opened for blacks in the southern states, and by 1968, almost 60 percent of blacks in Mississippi were registered to vote, signaling a new and almost alien era of equality in the state.[53]

While the work of the Mississippi press during the civil rights era has been examined in detail by the aforementioned authors, the coverage of sports and integration from within the Magnolia State has not been the subject of a major historical study. The integration of sports and the work of the press have been examined in great detail, especially Jackie Robinson's breaking of baseball's color barrier by signing with the Brooklyn Dodgers in 1947. Glen Bleske and Chris Lamb, who examined Robinson's debut in the major leagues from the perspectives of the white and black presses, found that the black press was much more aware of the social significance of Robinson's appearance in Major League Baseball, while white journalists failed to identify the historical context of the event.[54] William Simmons, who also examined press coverage of Robinson's groundbreaking introduction, notes the underwhelming level of attention from the white press and concludes that most Americans were unaware of how much racism was a part of the country's social and cultural values.[55] David K. Wiggins, who has written a number of books and scholarly articles on issues of race in athletics, expresses a similar sentiment, arguing that with the exception of "crime and scandal," white-owned and -operated newspapers traditionally gave limited coverage to activities that involved black Americans, especially in the realm of sports.[56] Kathryn Jay concurs, pointing out that while the national press covered the exploits of Robinson, journalists ignored that the majority of avenues in sports remained segregated and assisted with the continued segregation of both professional and college sports.[57] John Carroll and Charles K. Ross have similar observations on the integration of the National Football League, with both authors arguing that the white press ignored the presence and social significance of black athletes in the sport, especially that of Fritz Pollard, who was one of the first blacks to play professional football.[58] Even in Mississippi, the coverage of sports and the appearance of African Americans on the previous all-white playing fields before 1955 was an anomaly. For example, Hodding Carter, editor of the *Delta Democrat-Times*, was one of the few editors in Mississippi who published a photo of Olympic legend Jesse Owens on the front page of the paper, citing the newsworthy nature of Owens's accomplishments.[59]

Basketball serves as a convenient lens through which to look at the world of sports in Mississippi and the musings of its journalists. Challenges to the unwritten law only revealed themselves when Mississippi collegiate teams were having a degree of success. While the University of Mississippi won three football national championships in 1959, 1960, and 1962 under head coach John Vaught and quarterback Archie Manning, it played in the segregated Sugar Bowl in New Orleans, Louisiana, at the conclusion of each season, thus maintaining its all-white competition.[60] Ole Miss's baseball team proved to be equally successful, winning the SEC championship in 1959 and 1960, but typically ruled out in advance any thought of playing in the national title tournament.[61] While making history on the hardwood, Mississippi State was equally inept in football and baseball. The Maroons, later renamed the Bulldogs, did not win the SEC conference championship in football until 1965, almost two years after the demise of the unwritten law and a year before the SEC integrated.[62] MSU's football teams under head coaches Darrell Royal, Wade Walker, and Paul Davis went a combined 42–50–4 during this time period and made only one appearance in a bowl game, a 1963 berth in the Liberty Bowl in Philadelphia. The game, a 16–12 victory over North Carolina State, was overshadowed by threats of protests from the National Association for the Advancement of Colored People (NAACP) because of the state's unwritten law.[63] MSU's baseball team won the SEC championship in 1949 but did not win again until 1965, well after the elimination of the unwritten law.[64] Mississippi Southern College, now the University of Southern Mississippi, had similar success on the gridiron, as the Southerners of Thad "Pie" Vann won two United Press International college-division national championships, the equivalent of the modern Division II national championship. Much like Ole Miss and MSU, however, the Southerners played a segregated schedule.[65] Because of the success of Mississippi's universities on the hardwood, collegiate basketball in Mississippi was the sport more likely to produce conflict pertaining to the unwritten law.

With Mississippi State as the unwritten law's most frequent challenger, the events examined in this text include newspaper accounts of the then-Mississippi State College and the University of Mississippi's 1956 withdrawals from integrated basketball holiday tournaments; Mississippi State's challenges of the unwritten law in 1959, 1960, and 1962; MSU's 1963 acceptance and appearance in the NCAA National Championship Tournament, and the eventual integration of Mississippi State basketball with the 1971 additions of Larry Fry and Jerry Jenkins to the Bulldogs' roster. While some of the articles and work examined looked at other sports, specifically Jones County Junior College's football game with Compton Junior College, basketball and the plight of MSU are the primary sport of interest because the majority of incidents that challenged the unwritten law came from the Starkville-based Bulldogs.

The newspapers used in this volume include the Jackson-based *Jackson Daily News*, the *Clarion-Ledger*, the *Jackson State Times*, and the black *Jackson Advocate*. The *Meridian Star*, which politically fell into the same camp as the Jackson-based Hederman publications, was also examined. Other newspapers, such as the *Delta Democrat-Times*, the *Enterprise-Journal*, the *Vicksburg Evening Post*, and the *Daily Herald* in Biloxi were consulted to offer a counterpoint to the work of the Hederman empire. Hometown newspapers are also included in this examination, depending on the home base of each of the challenging colleges and universities. Those publications include the *Laurel Leader-Call*, the *Starkville Daily News*, and the *Hattiesburg American*. Each of these newspapers offered a distinct local perspective on the challenges to the unwritten law. Per historian Susan Weill, together the publications referenced above produced 207,579 issues per day on average from 1954 through 1964, or 70 percent of all daily newspapers distributed in the state, also making them logical subjects for

such an inquiry.[66] Additionally, the *Jackson Advocate* was considered Mississippi's predominant black newspaper and averaged between five and eight thousand issues per week.[67] Student newspapers at Mississippi State University, the
University of Mississippi, and the University of Southern Mississippi were also
consulted for a student perspective.

Each of these publications were examined for their news content, which
included articles on the aforementioned incidents in both the news and sports
sections, written by staff writers, editors, and wire-based journalists. While it is
conceivable that a number of publications would turn to wire articles for their
coverage of these incidents, a number of the accounts were edited by local editors and thus varied in content, length, headlines, and placement within the confines of the newspaper. These cosmetic differences at times offered significant
information about the editors' opinions and attitudes on issues of race. Much
like the use of wire material, letters to the editor also provided useful material
about both the opinion of the editor at each newspaper and its local audience.
Editorials and columns from editors, daily columnists, and sports reporters
were also examined and offered some of the more significant evidence used in
this book, as the opinion articles addressed more accurately the personal feelings of the editor or the reporter.

A segment of prominent Mississippi sports journalists appear in this text,
including Mississippi Sports Hall of Fame members Jimmie McDowell, sports
editor of the *Jackson State Times*; Carl Walters of the *Jackson Daily News* and the
Clarion-Ledger; Lee Baker, sports editor and writer for the *Jackson Daily News*,
the *Jackson State Times*, and the *Clarion-Ledger*; Billy Ray of the *Vicksburg Evening Post*; Billy "Sunshine" Rainey of the *Meridian Star*; Dick Lightsey of the
Daily Herald; Bill Ross of the Tupelo-based *Daily Journal*; Arnold Hederman of
the *Clarion-Ledger*; and Robert "Steamboat" Fulton of the *Clarion-Ledger* and
the *Meridian Star*. While most of the writers listed, such as Baker and Walters, wrote in a conservative fashion when it came to violations of the unwritten law, others such as McDowell and Ross were outspoken and advocated the
elimination of the gentlemen's agreement. News-based journalists and editors,
including Frederick Sullens and Jimmy Ward of the *Jackson Daily News*, columnist Tom Ethridge of the *Clarion-Ledger*, James B. Skewes of the *Meridian Star*,
Hodding Carter of the *Delta Democrat-Times*, and J. Oliver Emmerich of the
Enterprise-Journal and the *Jackson State Times* are also featured in this volume
and represent the dichotomy of ideological approaches when it came to issues
of race.[68]

This study begins with Jones County Junior College's participation in the
1955 Junior Rose Bowl, an overview of the implementation of the unwritten
law, and the first challenges posed to the gentleman's agreement by the then-
Mississippi State College and the University of Mississippi basketball teams.

State Representative R. C. McCarver's 1956 legal proposal banning college teams in Mississippi from participating in integrated competition was met with a degree of journalistic neglect, as few publications published an article on the proposal and even fewer expressed any opinion on the issue. The first chapter also examines the press coverage of the first challenges to the unwritten law, which were brought forth from Mississippi State and Ole Miss in a one-week period during the final days of December 1956 and and the first of January 1957. Like in Jones County in 1955, noteworthy journalists such as Frederick Sullens, Hodding Carter, and Carl Walters criticized Mississippi State for failing to stop the Maroons before they played an integrated University of Denver squad, thus violating the unwritten law.

The subsequent chapters look at the SEC-title winning season of Mississippi State and the furious debate in the press that surrounded the school's claim to an NCAA tournament bid. In 1959, 1961, 1962, and 1963, the Maroons and, later, Bulldogs of MSU dominated the Southeastern Conference, winning four conference basketball titles in five years. However, little was known about the Starkville contingent outside of the Southeast because of the school's refusal to participate in the national championship tournament. During each conference winning season, the legitimacy of the team's right to play for a national title was debated in the pages of Mississippi's newspapers. The sour musings of *Jackson Daily News* editor Jimmy Ward highlighted the opposition to the school's title hopes, arguing that such a venture would signal the deconstruction of the Magnolia State's segregated way of life. However, a degree of social progress could be found in Mississippi's sports sections as McDowell led a crusade against the unwritten law and supported the socially radical proposal of Mississippi State's participation in the NCAA tournament. Other sports reporters, such as Ray, Lightsey, Fulton, and Herb Phillips of the *Commercial Dispatch* would, over time, take up the fight with McDowell. The various in-season debates would culminate in 1963 when MSU accepted an invitation to play in the integrated NCAA tournament.

This text concludes with the decision by the State College Board to eliminate the unwritten law in 1963 and the integration of college basketball in the Magnolia State. By the time Mississippi State integrated its basketball team in 1971 with the additions of Fry and Jenkins, the press found their presence of little news value, as few publications identified the duo as black. With the socially and politically historic implications of the 1964 Civil Rights Act, journalists in Mississippi, ultimately and begrudgingly, accepted integration. Thus, the social outrage present in past accounts was absent in the coverage and reporting of the integration of these basketball teams. For the most part, the integration of these basketball teams was minimized and ignored, but less as a means of protecting the Closed Society and more in the vein of social progress.

   Overall, the press in Mississippi was reflective of the society it served, even when it came to sports. From the violent treatment of blacks in the 1950s, the threats of financial loss in the early 1960s, to the questionable climate of 1964 and the Civil Rights Act, Mississippi journalism went through an ideological metamorphosis, slowly transforming from an organ that minimized the rights of blacks and advocated outright racism, to an industry that, at least in appearance, covered the exploits of white and black athletes on equal footing. The coverage of the unwritten law and the integration of college basketball in Mississippi demonstrated the power of the white-dominated press and mirrored the ebb and flow of the political climate in the state. The work of the press as it pertained to the potential integration of Mississippi athletics was no different from the journalistic reaction to the threat of social integration, as stalwarts of the Closed Society, such as Sullens and Ward, attacked the offending colleges and universities with spite and contempt, while others, including Mississippi's sports press, sat in silence, ignoring the issue and therefore enforcing the unwritten law. As an agent in the socially tumultuous environment of the Magnolia State, the press helped protect the Closed Society and even extended its considerable influence and power into the realm of athletics. With the social changes discussed and the press reaction to the integration of sports, the coverage of athletics, and especially the aforementioned local challenges to the unwritten law, reflected the cultural changes that occurred in Mississippi from 1955 until the early 1970s.

Chapter 1

Sometimes, Even College Administrators Act Like Freshmen

During the 1950s, every facet of life in the Magnolia State, including sports, was considered segregated. In the aftermath of the *Brown vs. Board of Education* decision, Mississippi became an increasingly hostile and dangerous place. According to historian Michael Vinson Williams, "White Mississippians considered the *Brown* decision an all-out attack upon their way of life," and while paranoia infested the white residences of Mississippi, it was the black community that would pay the price.[1] By 1955, the Citizens' Council, which was formed in the aftermath of the *Brown* decision, grew to sixty thousand members statewide and had considerable influence in the areas of government, education, and newspapers.[2] Blacks were put in a subservient position to whites and, for the most part, lived in squalor.[3] If a member of the black community dared challenge the second class nature of their citizenship, they were typically met with deadly consequences. In 1955 alone, both the Reverend George Lee and Lamar Smith were murdered for attempting to register blacks to vote.[4] The subsequent murder of fourteen-year-old Emmett Till, together with the deaths of Lee and Smith, helped create an atmosphere of intimidation and fear that solidified the extreme approach many in the Magnolia State would use to protect the Closed Society.[5]

Within this increasingly hostile and dangerous environment, the football Bobcats of Jones County Junior College would embark on a brief journey in the December twilight of 1955 that would challenge the state's veil of white supremacy and usher in a new standard of segregation in sports. After finishing the season with a 9–1 record, head coach "Big" Jim Clark and his squad was rewarded with a trip to Pasadena, California, to play for the junior college national championship against the Tartars of Compton (California) Junior College. While most Mississippians were seemingly uninterested in the exploits of a junior college football team, the Bobcats became the bane of segregationists statewide when it was discovered that Compton fielded an integrated team.[6] While school officials and members of the Junior Rose Bowl selection committee were aware of the Tartars' integrated status, a number of Mississippi's more prominent journalists and politicians took issue with the

HINNY

Bob Howie of the *Jackson Daily News* penned a "Hinny" cartoon aimed at Mississippi State and Ole Miss's participation and withdrawals from the integrated Evansville Invitational Basketball Tournament and the All-American Holiday Tournament in December 1956. *Courtesy Bob Howie/Jackson Daily News.*

team's participation, arguing that a Junior Rose Bowl appearance for the Bobcats could be interpreted as a step towards integration and a threat to white supremacy within the state.[7]

For a two-week period in December 1955, what initially began as Jones County's innocent quest for gridiron dominance became one of the more highly contested issues in state newspapers. With the *Brown* decision still fresh in the minds of Mississippi's political and journalistic elite, most editors and reporters either protected the Closed Society and damned the JCJC contingent for its violation of Mississippi's traditions and way of life for a chance at championship glory, or turned a blind eye to the issue, expressing no opinion on the matter and thus seemingly supporting the segregated elite and the opposition to JCJC's championship efforts. Because of the perceived threat of integration, Mississippi's journalists either acted to create a negative view of the contest or depended on wire content and remained silent, negating the overall social importance of the issue to the news-reading audience. More often than not, the issue was overlooked or buried within the confines of newspapers in accordance with the protection of the Closed Society. By ignoring the issue, journalists ensured the audience's interest in the topic would be fleeting. It was this sort of journalistic neglect that would plague debates surrounding the validity of integration in Mississippi athletics for years to come.[8]

Perhaps no newspaper or journalist voiced more vehement objections than *Jackson Daily News* editor Frederick Sullens. One of the more racist representatives of Mississippi's journalistic past, Sullens often looked at issues of race as a personal vendetta and was an ardent supporter of the Citizens' Council.[9] The work of Sullens and the Hederman-owned *Jackson Daily News* epitomized the ideals and characteristics of Silver's Closed Society, and the debate involving Jones County was no different. While many of his journalistic peers on news desks and in sports sections remained silent, Sullens wrote with the tone of a religious zealot, calling JCJC's presence in the Junior Rose Bowl "a flagrant violation of the Southern way of life, a spineless surrender of the principles all true white Mississippians hold near and dear, and all those responsible deserve the sharpest rebuke it is possible to administer."[10] The editor openly cheered for JCJC to receive a "stinging defeat" and attributed the decision to "greed for gate receipts and a little fleeting fame."[11] Despite Sullens's imprecations, JCJC would play in the game, losing to Compton 22–13.[12]

While many historians have noted Sullens's venomous tone, his influence in the Closed Society was unparalleled. After he penned these comments and recommending that the State College Board cut funding from Jones County Junior College for their participation in the game, his work was picked up by the Associated Press and published in newspapers across the state, extending his racist reach even further.[13] The work of Sullens during the JCJC-Compton controversy demonstrated the power the press had in Mississippi and the extent to which the Closed Society had infiltrated its ranks. Because of Sullens's connections within the Closed Society, his commentary likely had a profound influence on the creation of the unwritten law months later.

The shadow cast by the loss of Jones County in the Junior Rose Bowl was considerable. On January 19, 1956, Mississippi newspapers reported that State Representative R. C. McCarver of Itawamba County had proposed a bill that would legally prohibit the state's collegiate teams from participating in integrated competition.[14] The political climate in Mississippi favored McCarver's proposal, as segregationist governor J. P. Coleman led the Magnolia State. Coleman was a graduate of the University of Mississippi who ran for governor in 1955 on the platform of quietly maintaining segregation in the state's colleges and universities. Coleman would later oppose the admission of James Meredith to his alma mater.[15]

Press coverage of McCarver's proposal was minimal. Both the *Jackson Daily News* and the *Clarion-Ledger*, considered two of the more racist journalistic representatives of Mississippi during the civil rights era, featured front-page accounts of the proposed law on January 19, 1956. The articles, which lacked a byline, cited Jones County participation in the Junior Rose Bowl as justification for McCarver's proposal. However, the *Clarion-Ledger's* account differed from its sister publication by mentioning that JCJC played in the game despite the objections of state politicians and journalists, and lost. The same article, minus the political reference, also appeared in the *Meridian Star*, an indication that the commentary was omitted by the editors of the *Star* or, the more likely scenario, added by an editor in the *Clarion-Ledger*.

Despite the fervor surrounding the JCJC Junior Rose Bowl appearance, very little was published overall about McCarver's proposed segregation law. Most of the newspapers in the state featured content from either the Associated Press or United Press and offered no commentary pertaining to the Junior Rose Bowl, often publishing a brief summary of the day's legislative happenings and identifying the potential law only by its docket number, HB 47.[16] Even United Press's Mississippi bureau chief John Herbers, who has been noted by historians for his groundbreaking coverage on the civil rights movement, neglected to make the proposal the focal point of his account, identifying it in the eleventh paragraph of his story, which was published in the January 19, 1956, edition of the *Delta Democrat-Times*.[17] Other noteworthy newspapers, such as the *Jackson State Times*, the *Commercial Dispatch*, the *Jackson Advocate*, and the *Hattiesburg American*, failed to publish anything on the potential law.

While the bill was introduced on the floor of the Mississippi House of Representatives, McCarver's proposed law made it no further. Undaunted, the political elite in the state banned together with the Board of Trustees for Institutions of Higher Learning, also known as the State College Board, in a private meeting to create a segregated standard in state collegiate athletics that would prevent a repeat of JCJC's challenge to the Closed Society.[18] The state and its educational institutions began to acknowledge the ban as the "unwritten law," a gentleman's agreement that all-white teams in the South would abstain from playing integrated teams from the North.[19] Any violation of the agreement would result in a one-year prison sentence for the offending school official, a fine of $2,500, and the loss of state funding.[20] While the law did not actually exist, Mississippi legislators and the State College Board enforced it anyway, threatening to withdraw funds from schools that violated the agreement.[21] Verifying the secretive nature of political dealing in the Closed Society, none of the newspapers examined in this volume published an article on the creation of the unwritten law. Furthermore, there is no record of the State College Board hearing the proposed gentleman's agreement and of its eventual acceptance. The first challenge to the unwritten law would emerge less than a year later.

It has long been customary for college basketball teams to participate in holiday tournaments in December. In the case of both Mississippi State College[22] and the University of Mississippi, the 1956 Evansville Invitational Basketball Tournament and All-American Holiday Tournament were to be barometers for the teams' upcoming Southeastern Conference schedules. The Maroons were led by standout center Jim Ashmore, who averaged 27.4 points per game, and Bailey Howell, who led the nation in rebounding and averaged 26.4 points per game. The State contingent had won six of its first seven games going into the Evansville tournament and was slated to play the University of Denver Pioneers in the first round on December 28, 1956. The Maroons defeated the Pioneers 69–65 behind the play of Howell, who scored twenty-two points. The Denver squad closed to 67–65 with eighteen seconds left, but Ashmore scored two of his twenty points in the final seconds to give the representatives from the Magnolia State the win. However, what appeared to be just another basketball game had great significance within the ideological borders of the Closed Society, as the Pioneers carried two blacks on their roster, Billy Peay and Rocephus Silgh, making the contest the first integrated game for Mississippi State in the school's history. Despite their presence, neither Peay nor Silgh had an impact on the outcome of the game. Silgh scored only two points and Peay did not play.[23] The repercussions of State's violation of the unwritten law were swift, both displaying the power of Mississippi's segregationist beliefs and setting the stage for the enforcement of the gentleman's agreement for years to come.

After the game, it was announced that the Maroons would leave the tournament before their game against Evansville College because of the integrated presence of the already defeated Pioneers.[24] Many newspapers were initially unaware of the integrated status of the Denver squad, as the *Jackson State Times*, the *Clarion-Ledger*, the *Delta Democrat-Times*, and the *Meridian Star* all published December 29, 1956, accounts of the victory without referencing Mississippi State's exodus. The *Clarion-Ledger* even published a photograph of Howell from the MSC-Denver contest, seemingly unaware that two black players wore Denver uniforms.

The state newspapers depended primarily on wire accounts from the Associated Press and United Press when it came to the coverage of the Maroons' exit from the tournament. The *Jackson Daily News* was the first newspaper to publish an article on the Maroons' history-making contest on December 29, 1956, proclaiming that "racial barriers broke down for a Southern school in athletic competition." MSC president Ben Hilbun told the unknown reporter that he was surprised by the presence of blacks at the tournament: "If we had known

It was Mississippi State President Ben Hilbun who was often shouldered with the burden of deciding the basketball team's fate when it came to playing integrated teams. Publicly, Hilbun told the press it was his decision for the Maroons to leave the integrated Evansville Invitational Basketball Tournament in 1956 and would make similar admissions during subsequent challenges to the unwritten law while Mississippi State was under his administration. *Courtesy Mississippi State University Libraries, University Archives.*

that the Denver team had Negroes, our team would not have been there to play the game." Head coach James "Babe" McCarthy, who would become a central figure in State's battles with the unwritten law, declined comment.

The rest of the state's newspapers seemed to get wind of MSC's tournament exit and published similar accounts on December 30, 1956. The *Daily News* would later claim that the Maroons won the contest "in spite of the presence of black players," making a clear editorial statement in the confines of a news article. Questionable editorial decisions continued to plague the Hederman-owned newspapers as both the *Daily News* and the *Clarion-Ledger* published an Associated Press article on MSC's withdrawal from the tournament on its front pages on December 30, 1956, and, in the process, presented an interesting dichotomy of race issues in the South. The first part of the article went into detail about the MSC-Denver contest and the Maroons' subsequent exit from Evansville. It was reported that MSC athletic director C. R. "Dudy" Noble made the decision to remove the team from the tournament, free of influence from the state legislature. "It has always been our policy that our teams would not compete with Negroes," Noble explained. "That's tradition with our institution. There is no rule here; it is just a matter of policy and tradition. It is the way we have always operated." However, in a stark topical switch, the article also discussed a dynamite explosion at the Citizens' Council headquarters in Clinton, Tennessee, in which no one was hurt. The peaceful withdrawal of the MSC contingent was balanced with the violent incident at the Citizens' Council headquarters, an organization to which both the editor and owners of the *Jackson Daily News* and the *Clarion-Ledger* belonged. From a journalistic perspective, it was clear that the two items had no business being in the same article. A similar article, without the mentions of the bombing, could also be found in the December 30, 1956, edition of the *Natchez Democrat*.

The *Jackson State Times* published a United Press article on MSC's exit from the Evansville Tournament, which led with Evansville Mayor Vance Hartke lashing out at MSC for leaving the tournament. "Basketball is a prime example of judging a man by his ability—not the color of his skin," Hartke told the reporter. "Someday, perhaps, we all will come before one great judge. I hope our Southern friends then learn what justice really is." The article also stated that MSC was called home by the school's administration although no MSC sources were represented in the account. In the December 30, 1956, edition of the *Meridian Star*, the MSC tournament story was covered in an article with the headline, "Maroons Quit Tournament; Negroes Play." The story, which included no byline, was in boldface type and identified the presence of "colored players in the tournament" as justification for State's exit. In an article on the front page of the December 30, 1956, edition of the *Vicksburg Evening Post* and the sports section of the *Clarion-Ledger*, much of the above-referenced information was repeated. However, Evansville College athletic director Don Ping was quoted by the Associated Press as saying, "We feel that all of the teams accepted the bids in good faith," insinuating that the integrated status of the tournament should not have been a surprise for the contingent from Starkville.

Noble's decision to withdraw MSC from the tournament was again featured in the December 31, 1956, edition of the *Clarion-Ledger* and indicated that Hilbun acted after he read about the black players in the press. The MSC president reiterated his position on the matter, telling the United Press in reference to playing mixed competition, "We've never done it before and we will never do it as long as I am in charge. The decision to withdrawal our team was automatic." Despite their unified front in the press, Hilbun did not get along with Noble and eventually fired the former Maroon hero and replaced him in 1959 with football coach Wade Walker.[25] In terms of the racial climate at MSC during Hilbun's tenure as president, historian Michael B. Ballard writes that the campus had "a stereotypical racial tinge to it," especially when it came to the treatment of black employees on campus, who were typically referred to as "uncles."[26] While Hilbun managed to avoid the discussion on integration with his retirement at the conclusion of the 1959–1960 school year, Ballard writes that, based on Hilbun's known views on issues of race, the former university president would not have handled the integration of Mississippi State very well.[27]

In the aftermath of the Maroons' withdrawal, the *Starkville News* failed to reference the incident in any subsequent coverage of the team. In a January 4, 1957, article on the squad's Kentucky road trip, the game against Denver was discussed in detail, as was the team's contest against Murray State. However, the integrated status of the Pioneers and the school's refusal to play Evansville College was never mentioned. Similarly, in the Associated Press's January 1, 1957, article on the team's surprising 91–80 loss to Murray State, the only reminder of the controversy of Evansville could be found in the article's lead: "In its first game since walking out of a basketball tournament, Mississippi State fell before a second half rally of Murray last night."[28] Other wire-based accounts made no mention of the Evansville walkout.[29]

Two years later, during the debate surrounding Mississippi State and its possible entry into the integrated NCAA tournament, Shelby Bailey, a member of the 1956–1957 Maroons, voiced his support for the Starkville contingent in the pages of the February 23, 1959, edition of the *Jackson State Times*. Bailey said of his experience playing against the integrated Pioneers, "I guarded one of them and it did not affect my feelings towards integration, nor did it affect any of our boys on the team. It only embarrassed us and Coach McCarthy in front of the people of Evansville and the other basketball teams and coaches represented there when we were forced to withdraw and come home."

Perhaps in a reactionary move to Mississippi State's decision to leave Evansville, the University of Mississippi also withdrew from the All-American City Basketball Tournament in Owensboro, Kentucky after it was discovered that their upcoming opponent, Iona College of New Rochelle, New York, featured guard Stanley Hill, who was black. Ole Miss athletic director C.M. "Tad" Smith told the Associated Press that it was his understanding that the tournament was not integrated. Smith's comments were featured in an article on the front page of the December 31, 1956, edition of the *Jackson Daily News* under the headline, "Mississippi Cagers Balk at Integration." While it is difficult to determine Smith's beliefs and views on integration explicitly, the Ole Miss alum was one of the individuals who met with Governor Ross Barnett and Chancellor J. D. Williams before James Meredith's application for admission was denied on September 20, 1962.[30] Time and the need to compete may have softened Smith's views on issues of race as the athletic director later helped recruit basketball star Coolidge Ball, the school's first black athlete, in the 1970s.[31]

In the pages of the *Daily News* and the *Clarion-Ledger*, it was reported that Ole Miss officials refused to play Iona unless Hill was held out of the game. Interestingly enough, Smith acknowledged to the anonymous AP writer the nonexistent legal nature of the gentleman's agreement. "There is not a written rule, only policy," he said. Williams reiterated Smith's contention on the unwritten law in a December 31, 1956, article from the *Delta Democrat-Times*, calling it "the policy of the school to maintain segregation so far as the team play is concerned inside or outside of the state." The University of Mississippi later claimed that it was guaranteed by officials that the tournament would be segregated and denied ever asking Iona College or tournament officials to prohibit Hill from playing. Smith told the United Press that he could not remember the individual's name that made the guarantee, only that "it was the tournament manager or director."[32] The UP reported that tournament chairman and Kentucky Wesleyan College professor Gus E. Paris "flatly denied" Williams's and Smith's claim that Ole Miss was promised that no blacks would play in the tournament.[33] "The question of Negroes was not discussed with the University of Mississippi officials and absolutely no guarantee was made that there would be no Negro players in the tournament," Paris told the United Press.

The actions of both MSC and Ole Miss drew praise of the state's political elite as per *Jackson Daily News* staff writer Phil Stroupe's December 31, 1956, article. "The colleges took the only honorable course they could," Sen. Earl Evans of Canton told Stroupe. "Their action will be heartily endorsed by the vast majority of people in Mississippi." Evans was identified as a member of the state Sovereignty Commission, an agency founded in 1956 to propagandize the segregationist position and monitor black activists.[34] Rep. George Oayne Cossar of Charleston said that the two schools should have made more of an effort to learn the specific nature of the two tournaments. The Ole Miss graduate was one of the original members of the Sovereignty Commission and was appointed by state Speaker of the House Walter Sillers, a segregationist.[35] Rep. Russell Fox, who was identified in the article as being pro-segregationist, said, "I approve of the withdrawal. We can compromise on method and manner, but never on principle. Officials at both institutions should be commended."[36] Fox was one of the sturdiest purveyors of the Closed Society in Mississippi's political circles. Described by journalist Bill Minor as "vicious," Fox was never shy about using his considerable political clout to manipulate legislation, especially in collaborations with fellow segregationist Sillers. Fox supported school equalization in 1954 as a means of keeping integration at bay and, as of 1955, stated publicly that maintaining segregation in the school system was the most important issue facing the state.[37] The article included a photograph of Hill with Iona Head Coach James McDermott.

In the editorials and columns that were published during this three-day time period, the overwhelming opinion from editors and reporters in the state was that the State College Board and officials at Mississippi State and Ole Miss failed in their duties to enforce the unwritten law and protect the Closed Society. From segregationist publications like the *Jackson Daily News* to the more progressive *Delta Democrat-Times*, editors expressed a degree of disappointment in these agencies for perpetuating the belief that issues of race were being governed inconsistently thus painting the Magnolia State in a weak and hypocritical light.

In a strange twist of irony, *Jackson Daily News* sports columnist Lee Baker almost predicted the historic events before they even happened. On December 26, 1956, Baker wrote in his column "Baker's Dozen," that MSC and Ole Miss "would get a chance to show their wares against teams that never could be met at home. . . . It's for the best they get this crack at outsiders from around the nation. No matter how they fare, they should come back wiser and tougher." Despite the accuracy of his commentary, it is not known if Baker was aware that the schools could and would participate with integrated teams. After his April 22, 2003, death at the age of 78, Baker was inducted into the Mississippi Sports Hall of Fame in 2004. The state Senate recognized Baker as "the first person in Mississippi sports media history to cover predominantly black colleges and high schools and one of the first writers in the South to give women's athletics full coverage."[38] However, an examination of his work throughout this volume found that Baker was, perhaps, unable or unwilling to speak out for athletic integration and often failed to acknowledge the larger social issue in his work. By the time Mississippi State participated in its first NCAA tournament in 1963, Baker appeared to have softened his stance on race relations and sports.

In the January 1, 1957, edition of the *Jackson Daily News*, Sullens used his daily editorial to address MSC and Ole Miss, defend the unwritten policy, and express outrage over the lack of consistency demonstrated. He wrote that everyone associated with college athletics in the state should "understand, once and for all, that they must not take part in games anywhere or under any circumstances where the opposing team has Negro players composing a part of the personnel" and that the unwritten law was "as irrepealable as the law of gravitation." Because of the considerable influence Sullens had in political circles in the Closed Society, his commentary on the unwritten law legitimized the gentleman's agreement to his audience. In a final nod to the fiascos, the January 3, 1957, edition of the *Daily News* devoted a Hinny cartoon by cartoonist and segregationist Bob Howie to MSC and Ole Miss. "Hinny" featured a donkey that often spoke in broken English and took editorial liberties with state political issues. In this particular cartoon, the donkey dribbled a basketball. In the caption, the donkey is quoted as saying, "If Hinny Were a Cager He'd be Cagey as he should and find out who he's playin' before he said he would!"

Delta Democrat-Times editor Hodding Carter also took both Mississippi State and Ole Miss to task for their failure to know about the integrated status of the individual tournaments beforehand. On January 3, 1957, Carter called both situations a "flagrant mishandling which has brought bad publicity on

Mississippi and harmed race relations." Carter was the only editor to point out that MSC actually played and defeated a team with blacks. Carter blamed the situation on school officials and the Board of Trustees for Institutions of Higher Learning. Unlike Sullens, Carter took the unwritten law to task, writing that college officials should have felt silly trying to enforce a segregated sports policy and that the unwritten law would eventually force the best athletes to stay away from the state. "Sometimes, even college administrators act like freshmen," Carter concluded. A Pulitzer Prize winner, Carter respected the notion of civil rights and often challenged the ideals and principles of the Closed Society.[39]

Vicksburg Evening Post sports editor Billy Ray commended the two universities for "keeping Southern tradition" in the December 31, 1956, edition of his column "Press Box Views."[40] Despite his support, Ray criticized the two teams for waiting so long to leave their respective tournaments and said he believed the schools knew that "colored players were on some of the teams competing" unless, he quipped, they were "color blind." Ray would later advocate the elimination of the unwritten law and Mississippi State's future participation in the integrated NCAA national championship tournament despite his self-professed status as a segregationist.

From the perspective of the student press, only the University of Mississippi's student newspaper, the *Daily Mississippian* of editor Ann Flautt published an article on either MSC's or Ole Miss's withdrawal. In a January 11, 1957, column on the dual exodus of Ole Miss and Mississippi State, Flautt placed the blame for both incidents on school officials, writing, "Realizing that it is the strong policy of our state institutions not to engage in sports activities with integrated schools, one has to wonder why a more defined investigation was not made of the schools invited to play in the tournament." Flautt argued that, by walking out, the schools provided more ammunition to the northern critics of the Magnolia State. "If we are to expect to meet success in our plans to maintain segregation in spite of the High Court's order, we are hardly taking concrete steps in that direction by constantly slapping the other sections of the nation," Flautt explained. "This is no way to win friends and influence people, but an effective means of turning the sentiment of the whole nation against the South."

Other columnists in the state, sports or otherwise, seemed to focus the bulk of their commentary on Mississippi State rather than Ole Miss. *Clarion-Ledger* sports writer and columnist Carl Walters questioned MSC's decision to play against Denver, even when it was evident that the team was integrated, before "withdrawing and disrupting the tournament."[41] The *Vicksburg Evening Post* of Louis P. Cashman also took MSC to task, calling the Maroons' participation and subsequent withdrawal "regrettable." The anonymous author, assumed to be Cashman, professed a belief in segregation before damning the team for its exit from the tournament. "We believe it best to remain aloof from situations which will precipitate drastic action," the editorial read. "By withdrawing, State has given the liberal-radicals some choice fuel to add to their flame and, instead of representing Mississippi properly, has directed all kinds of adverse publicity in our direction."[42] *Jackson State Times* editor Paul Tiblier wrote that MSU's withdrawal after playing the integrated Denver team was hypocritical and called for consistent rules and regulations from the State College Board to be put in place.[43] *Natchez Democrat* sports columnist Joe Mosby expressed a similar opinion on State's handling of the team's withdrawal and, in particular, with the actions of Noble, claiming that the MSC athletic director "goofed," citing the timing for the school's withdrawal considering the all-white contingent from Starkville had already played the integrated Denver team.[44] Mosby also doubted the claim that the team's exodus was Noble's idea alone, citing pressure from state legislators and added that had Noble refused to participate in the tournament in the first place, "It would of demonstrated Mississippi State's determination to uphold the traditions of segregation, even in the face of inevitable criticism from the north." Mosby would later muse about the actions of both MSC and Ole Miss, writing that both schools would be hard pressed to receive an invitation to play in another basketball tournament unless it was in the "deep, deep South."[45] Citing the negative attention both schools received from the incidents, Mosby wrote that Smith and Noble could have avoided their situations altogether if they had been taught "the old axiom of 'when in Rome, do as the Romans do,' and they should also be taught that nobody is making them go to Rome."[46]

While Mosby dedicated some of his work in 1957 to the topic, in hindsight, he said it was almost a non-issue for his audience. "I recall a newsroom conversation to the effect that college presidents and politicians need to shut up and let the players do their thing," he said in a 2009 interview. "It was not a major concern for our readers." Mosby, who would leave Mississippi sports reporting to run the news desk in 1957, said, at the time, he favored segregated athletics because "that was what we had and what I had grown up with. When times changed, I changed. As a boy, I played sandlot baseball with black kids. I enjoyed it. We went to separate schools, and I do not recall any talk of 'wish I could play at your school' or such."

While many of the newspapers in the state, despite their obvious ideological and political differences, noted the overall lack of unity on the enforcement of the unwritten law, only Carter of the *Democrat-Times* called the law into question. During the introduction of the potential law in January 1956, few, if any, newspapers commented on the proposal. In many of the articles, the proposal was an afterthought, as if the majority of Mississippians had already accepted the unwritten law. The silence attached to the coverage of such a proposition could be interpreted as an acknowledgement that the premise behind the unwritten law was an accepted social norm. There was no outrage or objection to such a law because the public always thought of it as an understood tenet. Any objection would have been viewed as a sign of rebellion.

A universal theme that arose from the articles that covered the two tournaments was the acknowledgement that the unwritten law was not a law at all, rather a nod to "tradition." The newspapers mirrored the climate of the world in which they were produced. They often avoided the obvious questions, ignored logical inquiry, and protected the status quo. No journalist other than Carter was willing to call out the hypocritical nature of enforcing a nonexistent law in either of these situations. Through this silent majority, the views and ideals of the Closed Society were not only in place in the avenue of athletics but were supported and enforced by journalists across the state.

Like many issues of race in Mississippi, the events of late 1956 were quickly ignored. Only the *Jackson State Times*, the *Laurel Leader-Call*, and the *Delta Democrat-Times* mentioned of the events surrounding MSC and Ole Miss in subsequent sports articles.[47]

While letters poured into the administrative offices at Mississippi State and Ole Miss, only three letters to the editor appeared in state newspapers on the matter during this timeframe, making the press a flawed barometer of public opinion. Two such expressions of opinion appeared in the *Jackson State Times*, and both claimed that the negative attention generated by the decisions was well deserved. The first letter, from "One Man and Opinion," said on January 2, 1957, that Mississippi State's and Ole Miss's exit "embarrassed the State of Mississippi before the eyes of the nation and represented the type of petty sulking which hampers, not aids, the segregation fight." Two days later, an anonymous Clinton resident called for Mississippians to "grow up," likening the exits to "a little sulking boy picking up his marbles and going home."

The only other publication to publish a letter to the editor was the *Clarion-Ledger*, which in the January 3, 1957, edition, a "State Observer" wrote that MSC's actions were a violation of "sportsmanship, fair-play, good faith and how to act as a guest" and that Noble thought little of these things before he made the decision to remove the Maroons from the tournament to "head back to home base where Negroes are 'untouchable' in matters of education and religion." The anonymous author concluded by pointing out the negative attention the school had received as a result of the withdrawal and called for Hilbun to "know more about what is going on at State in the future."

In the end, the white establishment of Mississippi breathed a sigh of relief. While the MSC-Denver game made history as the first to be played involving the Maroons and an integrated team, the press ignored the social significance of the contest. For a moment, journalists on both sides of the racial debate saw eye-to-eye on the inconsistent nature of the unwritten law and damned the Maroons and the Rebels for their indiscretions. The material published by

Mississippi newspapers, specifically the *Jackson Daily News*, helped fend off the dual attacks to the unwritten law and solidified the closed nature of college sports in Mississippi. Rather than see the participation of these schools in an integrated tournament as a progressive nod towards human and civil rights, the state's reporters attacked the two schools for the inconsistency in "state athletic policy" and a general lack of knowledge. Despite the varying amounts of journalistic attention paid to the occurrences, the paths taken in each instance by the press in the Magnolia State contributed to the enforcement of the principles and ideals of the Closed Society. While in later years, members of the press would advocate the participation of Mississippi State in integrated competition out of a perceived need for cultural reassurance, the initial challenges to the unwritten law did not ignite such a debate. In all likelihood, the stakes involving Mississippi State and Ole Miss in 1956 simply were not high enough. Little validation could come to the Magnolia State based upon the participation of these two schools in the aforementioned integrated, regional tournaments. In laymen's terms, the risk of Mississippi's white dominant ideology was too great for the potential reward offered by on-court success in the early season contests.

With the borders of the Closed Society reinforced against racially progressive threats provided by the sports world, it was almost two years before the traditions and customs of Mississippi would be challenged again from the hardwood. A familiar foe in the form of James "Babe" McCarthy and the Mississippi State Maroons questioned the racial and social standards of the state and, in turn, the journalists and newspapers of Mississippi, led by Jimmy Ward of the *Jackson Daily News*, would protect the white caste system.

Chapter 2

We'll Stay at Home and Tell Everybody We're the Best

In 1959, the Mississippi State University men's basketball team experienced what still ranks as one of the greatest seasons in school history. Under the leadership of the colorful James "Babe" McCarthy and behind the play of All-American and future Basketball Hall of Fame member Bailey Howell, the Maroons finished the season with a record of 24–1 and the school's first Southeastern Conference basketball championship. As the champions of the SEC, the team received the right to participate in the National Collegiate Athletic Association national championship tournament. However, what appeared to be an honor for the team's on-court play turned into a fierce debate about integration and the possible violation of the state's unwritten law. The NCAA tournament fielded mixed teams, making it possible that the Maroons would face black players during the course of the postseason. Despite the team's desires for a national championship, MSU president Ben Hilbun announced that, rather than test the segregated standards of the Magnolia State, the Maroons would honor the gentleman's agreement and abstain from postseason play. When asked by *Jackson Daily News* sports editor Lee Baker about the decision after MSU's title-clinching victory over Ole Miss on February 28, 1959, McCarthy said, "We'll stay at home and tell everybody we're the best."

The emergence of the Maroons as a college basketball power placed McCarthy's squad in the middle of a firestorm that centered on the Closed Society's tradition of segregation. From the perspective of the press, the merits of violating the unwritten law was the subject of countless news articles, columns, editorials, and letters to the editor that, more or less, supported Mississippi's white way of life and gave little credence to the athletic and, more importantly, the social justification for integration. Much like the historic participation of the Jones County Junior College football team in the Junior Rose Bowl, the 1959 Mississippi State basketball team was seen as a legitimate threat to the Closed Society and a possible catalyst for integration. Mississippi's ideological boarders became increasingly real for members of the black community. Historian John Dittmer writes in his book *Local People: The Struggle for Civil Rights in Mississippi* that, between 1956 and 1959, at least ten black men had been killed

THAT'S THE WAY THE BALL BOUNCES!

Similar to Jimmie McDowell's contention that the Maroons were left out of the NCAA tournament because state politicians were wary of supporting such a controversial decision in an election year, the *Jackson State Times* published a political cartoon depicting a crowned Mississippi State basketball player chained to a rock labeled "Election Year" as a player from the University of Kentucky rides off to the NCAA tournament. *Courtesy Mississippi State University Libraries, University Archives.*

by whites, none of whom were ever convicted for their crimes.[1] MSU's flirtation with the NCAA tournament was not the first debate involving integration and one of Mississippi's segregated pillars of higher education. Months before the start of MSU's historic campaign, Clennon King Jr., a former history professor at Alcorn A&M College, attempted to enroll at the University of Mississippi in June 1958 as a graduate student. Met upon his arrive to the Oxford campus by Governor J.P. Coleman, King was denied admission into the university and detained by Lafayette County officials. King was subsequently committed to the

Mississippi State Hospital in Whitfield because he was considered insane. He was released twelve days later.[2] King's social exile was another demonstration of the depths the purveyors of the Closed Society would go to retain the white status quo and maintain their oppressive control over the Magnolia State. The 1958–1959 basketball season for the Maroons came with the Closed Society at optimum power, a fact that was evident in the pages of the state's newspapers. While a minority of journalists, including sports editor Jimmie McDowell of the *Jackson State Times* and Hodding Carter of the *Delta Democrat-Times*, advocated an MSU trek into the integrated postseason, most reporters and editors in the Magnolia State condemned the Starkville-based basketball team for even considering such an opportunity. Led by Jimmy Ward of the *Jackson Daily News*, a segment of the journalistic population professed their belief in the Closed Society, segregation, and the unwritten law and painted the Maroons as an internal threat of sorts to their white way of life. Other reporters, including those on the sports desk, voiced no opinion on the matter, silently throwing their support behind the unwritten law and enforcing the state's segregationist standard. The Maroons and their 1958–1959 campaign were treated no differently from other social threats to segregation and were dismissed by the journalistic purveyors of the Closed Society, thus demonstrating the power and influence of Ward and his comrades.

In total, the Magnolia State's news and sports press served as an extension of the Closed Society and, by exercising ignorance of or outright contempt for the possibility of integrated competition, suppressed any pro-NCAA tournament feelings within its audience or from the journalistic minority. As a whole, rather than consider the likelihood of an NCAA tournament berth for the Maroons, the press in the Magnolia State preserved the oppressive beliefs of the state and helped keep college basketball a white-only venture.

The legitimization of the Maroons' 1959 basketball campaign came in the form of facing the defending national champion and SEC rival—the University of Kentucky Wildcats of legendary coach Adolph Rupp—on February 9, 1959. Both teams went into the contest with an 18–1 record and, as Carl Walters, sports editor of the *Clarion-Ledger* wrote, a win for the Maroons would lead to a degree of prominence on the national college basketball landscape. While references to MSU's national tournament hopes were few and far between at this point in the season, only the Associated Press identified the postseason as a possible outcome to the Maroons' basketball season but did so with caution, writing, "State officials in the past have refused to permit the Maroons from taking part in tournaments where they would have to play against Negroes."[3] A win for the Starkville contingent would have virtually locked up the SEC title for the Maroons as all five of the team's remaining opponents had losing records. Meanwhile, a Kentucky victory would have put the Wildcats in the driver's seat for the conference championship, pushing them past 16–0 Auburn University, which was on probation and ineligible for tournament play.

In a show of their dominance on the hardwood, the Maroons defeated Rupp's charges 66–58 in what the *Clarion-Ledger*'s Robert "Steamboat" Fulton called a humiliating defeat on February 10, 1959. Howell led the Maroons with twenty-seven points and seventeen rebounds as the team shot 53 percent from the floor to Kentucky's 35 percent.[4] The Maroons controlled the contest from the opening tip, taking a one point lead six minutes in the game and never falling behind. McCarthy, who was given a standing ovation at the conclusion of the contest, won his thirty-first game in a row at home and handed his rival Rupp his second loss of the season. "This is simply great. I have to admit, we've got a pretty good ball club," the joyous coach said to Jim Roden of the *Jackson State Times*.[5] McCarthy later boasted to the Associated Press on February 10, 1959, "We think we can beat anyone in the United States at Mississippi State."[6] The win over the Wildcats sowed the seeds for a possible venture into the integrated postseason for the Maroons. While most local reporters ignored the NCAA tournament as a possibility, wire-based accounts from United Press International identified MSU as both a threat to the SEC championship and the NCAA tournament.[7] An anonymous author with the wire service reported that the team had a desire to play in the tournament and went so far as to describe the unwritten law as "an iron clad policy against Mississippi teams playing teams that have members of the opposite race."[8] Howell told the unnamed reporter, "I would want to go. All the boys would want to and we will if they let us."[9]

This trend continued well after the win for the Maroons as many state newspapers used articles from the AP and UPI, a tactic cited by former Associated Press correspondent Douglas Starr as a way to defer any negative attention to the wire news services.[10] The Jackson-based *Clarion-Ledger* published an AP article on February 11, 1959, that identified the Maroons as a likely recipient for an NCAA berth because of Auburn's probationary status. McCarthy declined to comment on MSU's chances of playing in the integrated postseason. The *Jackson State Times* followed suit, publishing a UPI article in which Rupp said he still felt his team was the favorite for the NCAA bid because of Auburn's ineligibility and State's inability to participate in the tournament "for reason which you all know." UPI sports scribe Cliff Sessions, who had an interesting legacy as a journalist in the Magnolia State during the civil rights movement,[11] wrote that MSU had an easy path to the SEC championship and paid particular attention to the unwritten law, which he described as "an unwritten, iron-clad policy against Mississippi teams meeting racially-integrated teams." Sessions quoted State Rep. Russell Fox of Claiborne County, who said, "You can compromise method and manner but you cannot compromise basic principle without sacrifice in the major issue involved. . . . Pride in one basketball team won't change the people's basic belief. There is a principle involved." Fox had been one of the original advocates of the unwritten law in 1956.[12] William J. "Bill" Simmons of the Citizens' Council was also quoted in Sessions's article, saying that state officials had to make the decision and had to face the eventual consequences. Described a "suave sophisticated zealot," Simmons joined the Citizens' Council after the *Brown vs. Board of Education* decision and feared the possibility of a "black-dominated government."[13] Meanwhile, Governor J. P. Coleman attempted to absolve himself of any responsibility in the impending debate, telling the press that he did not have the authority to keep the Maroons out of postseason play.[14]

In the wake of MSU's basketball success, other universities began to take note of the team's enigmatic head coach. UPI reported, per an article in the *Clarion-Ledger* on February 13, 1959, that the University of Texas contacted McCarthy about its vacant head basketball coach position, although he denied having an interest. Both Texas Athletic Director Ed Olle and McCarthy confirmed to the *Jackson State Times*' McDowell that the Longhorns were interested in the Maroons' leader, but McCarthy said, "He would rather wait until the completion of the current season before discussing it."[15] McDowell would conclude his daily musings by logically identifying a chance at a national title as having a part to play in retaining the Maroons' leader.[16] McCarthy would later get a new four-year contract and a raise, a point McDowell believed years later was done to keep the head coach from publicly opposing the unwritten law.[17]

Attention quickly switched to the Maroons' upcoming battle with the University of Florida, whom MSU dominated in a convincing 105–68 win on February 14, 1959.[18] A UPI account of the win, found in the February 15, 1959, editions of the *Jackson State Times* and the *Meridian Star*, placed State in the position of NCAA tournament favorite if the team could win the remaining games on its schedule. After the victory, Ed Wilks of the AP predicted that the SEC's tournament representative would come from either Starkville or Lexington "should Mississippi State pass up the trip because of race problems."[19] The Maroons again dominated, easily defeating the University of Georgia by a final tally of 76–56, pushing its record to 21–1. On the same day State defeated the Georgia five, Berry Reece of the *Jackson Daily News* reported that Coleman again stressed his inability to interfere in the Mississippi State-NCAA tournament debate, deferring to MSU and the State College Board and calling a potential decision "a matter of policy."[20] The segregationist governor pointed to Mississippi's governing body as the determining factor in the debate. "The Legislature has the power of the purse strings. That's obvious," Coleman said to an anonymous AP reporter, referring the state's threat to cut appropriations for any university that participated in integrated competition.[21] The unknown author also explained that there was no state law against integrated athletics, but "the legislature has indicated it would cut appropriations for any school that takes part in them."[22]

Both the *Jackson State Times* and UPI reported that R. D. Morrow, president of the State College Board, said he doubted that the board would take any action or have anything to say about a potential NCAA bid for the Maroons during its upcoming meeting. Morrow reiterated that the decisions in those matters were usually left up to the president of the institution in question.[23]

While the chances of the Maroons engaging in integrated competition remained a hot-button topic in the Magnolia State, the students at Mississippi State "overwhelmingly" voted to play in the NCAA tournament if the team were to receive a bid.[24] Morrow, in a common theme found in the press, put the onus on Hilbun, to which the MSU president said the students' vote would have no impact. The students' approval of the team venture into the integrated postseason caught the watchful eye of the state Citizens' Council as Robert "Tut" Patterson, secretary of the executive committee of the Council, told reporters, "This organization is unalterably opposed to integration of the races whatever may be the disguise. This includes basketball games and all other athletic and scholastic contests."[25] A graduate and former football star with the Maroons, Patterson had founded the Citizens' Council in 1953 after he learned about the various school desegregation cases that would ultimately lead to the *Brown vs. Board of Education* case.[26]

While the *Clarion-Ledger* and *Meridian Star* reported on the student vote, both publications focused more on the total number of students who participated and less on the outcome, attacking the validity of the election. The *Clarion-Ledger* called the student vote of 973 for and 162 against misleading because only 25 percent of the 4,333 students participated in the election.[27] An anonymous source close to Hilbun told the paper, "It was a foregone conclusion that MSU would not attend the NCAA tournament."[28] The *Meridian Star*'s account expressed a degree of surprise on behalf of the anonymous author. "A majority of students at Mississippi State University apparently are not disturbed over the question as to whether the school's high-riding basketball team will be permitted to participate in the racially-integrated NCAA tournament," the article's lead read, violating the journalistic notion of objectivity.[29] The *Star*'s headline also indicated that the election attracted "little interest" and was not well received on campus because "around 75 percent of the students at the university failed to vote."[30] MSU's student newspaper the *Reflector* also seemed to downplay the overall importance of the vote, as student reporter Ray Sadler wrote, "The ballot, which did not deal with segregation or integration, was merely a statement as to whether or not the Maroons should be allowed to participate in the national tournament, something no other Maroon club had accomplished previously."[31] On the other hand, the *Jackson State Times* countered with news that 86 percent of MSU's 1,135 voting students wanted the team to participate in the NCAA tournament if the Maroons were to win the SEC title.[32] "Whether a Mississippi team can participate in integrated sports outside of the state isn't stated in any statute," the anonymous *Jackson State Times* reporter wrote. Other publications, such as the *Jackson Daily News* and the *Starkville News*, did not publish an article on the student vote.

While the bulk of newspapers in the Magnolia State had been engulfed in the debate surrounding the Maroons and the NCAA tournament, members of the national press, specifically *Sports Illustrated*, began to take notice of MSU's successful season. The sports magazine published an article on the team's 1959 campaign and, citing a "strong statewide rumor," reporter Dudley Doust wrote that if the school refused to accept an invitation to the NCAA tournament, McCarthy would resign from his post to take the previously mentioned job at the University of Texas and students on the Starkville campus would march on the capital.[33] In the Mississippi press, there was no evidence of a student protest or of McCarthy's future resignation. "There is nothing further from the truth. I haven't even considered resigning," McCarthy told reporters in response to Doust's claim.[34] McCarthy reiterated his stance in a conversation with McDowell and refuted a number of details in Doust's work, specifically, the presence of student pressure to make a pro-NCAA decision and the coach's vow to resign if MSU declined the bid. "I wouldn't dare make such a statement," McCarthy said. "As far as tournament participation is concerned, that is entirely out of my hands."[35]

On February 19, 1959, the State College Board held a meeting to address the MSU-NCAA tournament debate and, as demonstrated in the pages of Mississippi's newspapers, few questions were answered. State College Board secretary E. R. Jobe reiterated Morrow's comments in the February 20, 1959, edition of the *Jackson Daily News*, telling an unknown author that the board had "no long standing regulation against interracial athletics," but, based on the actions of colleges and universities in the past, there was an understanding that interracial athletics were prohibited. The following day, in an attempt to present a consensus of opinion from the College Board, Reece polled Mississippi's educational governing body with little success. The board declined to answer any questions pertaining to a possible NCAA bid for the Maroons. Jobe, in particular, took issue with the *Jackson Daily News* reporter, saying, "I don't think that is a proper question for you to ask me." S. R. Evans of Greenwood added that he was against the Maroons playing in the NCAA tournament because he had to go with board policy "which was against playing teams with Negroes on them—at least it was the last time it came up." Only Dudley Bridgforth of Nesbitt told Reece that the team should play, although he professed his belief in segregation.

The continued success of the team only fueled the fear that the segregated Maroons would play in the integrated tournament, as echoed by an AP article in the February 21, 1959, edition of the *Clarion-Ledger*. As the unwritten law faced this homegrown barrage from Mississippi State, at least two papers in the Magnolia State chose to educate its audience on the gentleman's agreement. Both the *Delta Democrat-Times* and the *Meridian Star* published a UPI article on February 22, 1959, from John Herbers that explained the origins of the unwritten law. Mississippi House Speaker Walter Sillers told Herbers "there's no doubt in my mind" that the team should not play in the NCAA tournament. In a violation of journalistic balance, Herbers editorialized and claimed that members of the legislature were "passing the buck like a hot potato and Gov. Coleman said the legislature should be polled," a theme found throughout the coverage of the 1959 MSU squad.

While the debate continued, the Maroons successfully played out their remaining basketball docket. As reported on February 22, 1959, the team defeated a 9–13 Louisiana State University squad 75–67, which moved them into a tie for the SEC lead with the ineligible Auburn Plainsmen, who were soundly defeated by Kentucky 75–56.[36] Meanwhile, state journalists continued to ignore the prospects of an NCAA tournament bid for the Maroons, leaving such recognition to members of the AP and UPI. According to AP sports writer Bailey, while the victory left the SEC-NCAA representative up for grabs, "Whether State officials will permit Mississippi State to go is doubtful because of the race issue."[37] An anonymous author for UPI wrote, per the *Jackson State Times*, that a win against Tulane University on February 23, 1959, would clinch the SEC title and a place in the NCAA tournament, but that "the High flying Maroons may have to reject the berth in the national championship despite a strong desire to participate. Mississippi's segregation policies include an unwritten law keeping its teams out of racially-integrated athletic events."

Back on the hardwood, the Maroons defeated Tulane University 65–51 on February 23, 1959, as Howell broke Bob Pettit's career SEC scoring record with thirty-two points. With the win and a 56–55 Auburn loss to Tennessee, the Maroons officially clinched a tie for the SEC championship.[38] While McCarthy told the AP that his team was one of the best in the country, he stopped short of lobbying for permission to play in the tournament.[39] "We are four games from the national championship. I would love to get a chance to play those four games. So would my boys."[40] McDowell covered the SEC-clinched victory for the *Jackson State Times* and, on the February 24, 1959, editorialized in the confines of a news article, arguing that the team was one of, if not the best, in the nation. "No major college team in America has a record to compare to the mighty Mississippians," wrote the *Jackson State Times* sports editor.

On February 25, 1959, the AP reported that, despite MSU's remaining contest with archrival Ole Miss, the team would have the right to be the SEC representative in the NCAA tournament even if they finished tied with 11–2 Auburn and Kentucky, because of the Maroons head-to-head victory over the Wildcats.[41] Vernon Butler of the AP wrote that State, with its clinching of a partial share of the SEC championship, had a berth in the NCAA tournament if officials in Mississippi would let the team play.[42] Despite the promise of being the SEC representative in the postseason quest for the national championship, an unknown AP reporter predicted that the Maroons would likely wear its SEC crown at home as "Mississippi looks with jaundiced eye on its state supported schools playing teams that have Negro players—almost a certainty in the NCAA playoff."[43]

Two days before MSU's season-ending contest with the University of Mississippi, both the AP and UPI reported that Hilbun would make his decision public after the game and it was expected that the MSU president would say no. The UPI article, written by an anonymous author, said Hilbun had reached a decision "but obviously it was a negative one."[44] McCarthy, who in the future would campaign for MSU's participation in the NCAA tournament, told UPI that nothing would be official until after the game, but he was interested in what the average Mississippian thought. "As a real true segregationist bred in Mississippi I would not want to jeopardize the segregation cause of my state," McCarthy said. "If the majority of white Mississippians feel that we should go, certainly I think that the boys have earned the right to go. If the majority of white Mississippians think they shouldn't go, I would be the first to say we would not step foot out of Mississippi to enter a racially-mixed contest." The AP, citing "informed sources" out of Starkville and Jackson, home of the State College Board, also reported that it was expected the State would bypass the NCAA tournament.[45] In the *Jackson State Times*' article, Hilbun said that McCarthy asked the president to wait to make his decision public until after Mississippi State's last game because it could have been "demoralizing to the team," indicating that Hilbun had already decided to keep the Maroons out of the NCAA tournament.[46] The same could be said for the *Jackson Daily News* version, which stated that odds for rejecting an NCAA bid were "extremely high" according to a source close to the administration.[47] When asked what he would do by *Jackson State Times* reporter George Whittington, Rep. Brown Williams of Philadelphia, Mississippi, told the journalist, "We can't be partly integrated and still believe in the Southern way of life. Let's say that I'm no moderate. I think the legislature made it self clear on what it thought of after such contest in 1956," said Williams in a reference to the 1955 Junior Rose Bowl and the original proposal of the unwritten law.[48]

A day before the final contest, McCarthy was awarded with a new four-year contract and a "substantial salary increase" from athletic director C. R. Noble.[49] McCarthy professed his loyalty and admiration for Mississippi State to the press, regardless of Hilbun's opinions on the NCAA tourney. "No matter what decision may be reached with reference to participation in the NCAA basketball tournament, I plan to remain at Mississippi State," the coach said.[50] UPI's

Cliff Sessions wrote that McCarthy received the new contract and pay raise "after toning down public statements about the Maroons playing in the NCAA tournament."[51] McCarthy again reiterated his belief in segregation. "I stand for the same things Mississippians have always stood for," the MSU coach told Sessions. "I am happy to make my stand alongside the people of Mississippi."[52] McCarthy later told UPI he felt that people should be loyal to their employers and thought that the lack of an NCAA appearance would not hurt the team or its prospects for a successful future.[53] According to the unknown author, McCarthy "expressed an intense desire to enter the tournament but after conferences with Hilbun he said he wouldn't want to do anything 'to jeopardize the segregation cause.'"[54]

In his final article before the Maroons battled Ole Miss, *Jackson State Times* sports editor McDowell again editorialized in a news-based account, writing that Kentucky would likely be the SEC representative in the NCAA tournament "thanks to Magnolia State hospitality and a keen desire not to crawl out on a limb," expressing a degree of displeasure with the upcoming decision.[55] McDowell continued his opinion-based script, again defending the embattled MSU president. "It's election year in Mississippi and politicians are frowning on saying anything one way or another about State seeking the national title," McDowell wrote. "In a spectacular game of 'buck passing' President Hilbun was tagged it by the Board of Trustees, State Institutions of Higher Learning, after Governor J. P. Coleman had correctly said it was up to the Board to decide."[56] The article, while appearing to be a legitimate news account of MSU's NCAA hopes, was a forum for McDowell's opinion and, regardless of "Mississippi Red's" nod to social progress on the hardwood, violated the journalistic notion of objectivity.

While MSU had clinched, at worst, a tie for the conference title, there was still hope in Kentucky and Auburn for a State upset at the hands of SEC doormat Ole Miss.[57] Going into the contest, the Maroons were an NCAA best 23–1 and had won fourteen straight games since a January 3, 1959, loss to the Plainsmen of Auburn. The Rebels came into the game with a 1–12 conference record but were led by the SEC's second-leading scorer Jack Walters, who averaged nineteen points per game.

In what was described as a slow, plodding contest, the Maroons defeated Ole Miss 23–16 to win the SEC championship.[58] Ole Miss head coach Bonnie "Country" Graham employed slow-down tactics in response to the high-scoring Howell, who was held to seven points and failed to eclipse the SEC's all-time single season scoring record, which was held by former Mississippi State teammate Jim Ashmore.[59] However, of larger consequence, Hilbun announced that the MSU team would not accept a bid to the integrated NCAA tournament, citing the unwritten law as justification. In his statement Hilbun said that, basketball aside,

"In this situation there are great issues involved, which transcend mere athletic competition. On these issues and where matters of principle are involved, I have and will always cast my lot with, and stand beside, my people—the people who have been good to me and who, as far as I am concerned, are the greatest people in the world."[60]

McCarthy told Baker that he agreed with the decision and confidently proclaimed the Maroons college basketball's top squad. "We'll stay at home and tell everybody we're the best," the MSU head coach said to Baker.[61] Similarly, McCarthy told McDowell, "Well, at least we can always say that we had the best team in the country and I think winning the [SEC] championship was mighty fine."[62] The SEC title would be MSU's first basketball championship since they had won the Southern Intercollegiate Athletic Association title in 1923.[63] Outraged by the president's decision, the student body at MSU reacted by hanging Hilbun in effigy.[64] Hilbun resigned from his post as president of Mississippi State at the end of the 1959–1960 school year. He would die in 1963, well before the 1965 integration of his alma mater.

In the aftermath of the Ole Miss contest, the *Starkville News* omitted any mention of the NCAA tournament, while the *Reflector*, Mississippi State's student newspaper, only referenced the NCAA tournament once during the examined time period. In its March 3, 1959, edition, Hilbun's decision served as the primary focus of Ray Sadler's article, the bulk of which was made up of Hilbun's official statement. Sadler wrote that Hilbun's decision "had been evident for almost a week and McCarthy's team was not surprised. The consensus of opinion among the players was one of no protest."[65] The level of reporting demonstrated by Starkville's news outlets, especially the *Starkville News*, was shocking. For the Starkville and MSU communities, the issue should have had social and personal relevance, yet editor Henry Meyer's newspaper reflected the contrary. Meyer, who owned the *Starkville News* with his brother Morris, eventually sold the paper to *West Point Times Leader* editor and publisher Henry Harris, a staunch segregationist and protector of the Closed Society.[66] Harris would establish the *Starkville Daily News* in 1960.

Only a day later, on March 2, 1959, AP sports writers Vernon Butler and Hugh Fullerton Jr. reported that Kentucky would go on to the NCAA tournament in MSU's place. Butler said that MSU had fallen victim to the integration issue, and Hilbun's decision was based upon his inability to change the unwritten law.[67] In a different sentiment to the one expressed by Butler, Fullerton wrote that State was serving as a steward of Mississippi tradition and decided to "honor" the gentleman's agreement.[68] Earl Wright of UPI made similar comments in his work, writing, "Mississippi State won't enter the NCAA tournament because of the State's unwritten law against whites competing against Negros in sports."[69] In a separate AP account found in the *Jackson Daily News*, McCarthy said, "I

Bailey Howell was a star with the Maroons and played on both the 1957 and 1959 squads that challenged Mississippi's unwritten law. Howell told the press in 1959 that he wanted to partici-pate in the integrated postseason and would eventually play in integrated postseason college all-star games without opposition. Howell went on to the National Basketball Association where he had a Hall of Fame career. *Courtesy Mississippi State University Libraries, University Archives.*

naturally would have liked to have taken the team to the tournament but I won't squawk. I'll do whatever I can for the school."[70]

Howell, a graduating senior, was undaunted by the decision. The future NBA star played in two integrated all-star games in Maryland and North Carolina after the 1959 season. School officials told UPI that Howell could participate because it was an individual decision and he was not an official representative of the university. Howell told UPI that he and his teammates were disappointed, but he said, "We won't make a fuss about it."[71] Howell was the only unanimous selection to the All-SEC first team, was named a first team All-American, and was named most valuable player in the SEC during the 1958–1959 campaign.[72]

MSU finished third in the final AP national basketball poll behind Kansas State University and Kentucky.[73]

Between the two extremes of vocal discontent and significant silence in the journalism on the Maroons and their possibility for an NCAA tournament bid sat the work of Jimmie McDowell of the *Jackson State Times*. A prominent and visible figure on the Mississippi sports scene, McDowell was one of the few sports journalists who expressed an opinion and supported a possible NCAA tournament bid for the Starkville-based Maroons in his self-titled, daily column. McDowell, or "Mississippi Red" as his fellow sportswriters knew him, was the sports editor of the fledging *Jackson State Times*. McDowell never viewed race as a viable justification for not playing another college or university in an athletic contest. In his mind, competition, not social equality, was reason enough to compete against integrated squads.[74] "To me, those teams deserved it," McDowell said in a 2010 interview. "They won the SEC; they deserved a chance to play for a national title." Although McDowell's unwavering support for the Maroons was never justified as opposition to segregation, the fiery redhead never felt the need to proclaim his loyalty to the Closed Society. Regardless of his justification, McDowell's commentary offered a refreshing and potentially progressive voice in opposition of the typical, white journalistic rhetoric found in Mississippi during the late 1950s and early 1960s. McDowell illustrated foresight in his first column on the MSU-NCAA tournament debate on February 10, 1959, calling the issue a loaded question and predicting that many politicians would stay out of the debate because it was an election year, a point the sports editor would make multiple times in his opinion-based work on the Maroons. In a clear nod to the social implications of MSU's possible appearance in the national championship tournament, McDowell wrote that the Maroons "could be a splendid Magnolia State good will salesmen." McDowell would later use his daily column to ask for public opinion on the issue. Calling the 1959 Maroons the best college basketball team in the history of the state, McDowell urged his readers to make their opinions known, arguing that public sentiment could push the hands of the very politicians he would eventually chastise.[75]

McDowell often made the political elite and the State College Board the target of ridicule in his editorial work, a bold move for any journalist during the civil rights era much less a sports editor. After Coleman publicly alleviated himself of any responsibility in the matter, McDowell offered a contradiction of sorts to the governor's contention in the February 17, 1959, edition of the *State Times*, detailing a conversation he had with an anonymous "sports-minded" legislator who told him that the Maroons should participate in the tournament. While McDowell offered no personal perspective or views on integration, the future Mississippi Sports Hall of Famer frequently objected to the position taken by Mississippi political leaders, in particular Coleman. McDowell, openly perturbed with the lack of resolve on the debate, reminded his readers on February 19, 1959, that permission to participate in the NCAA tournament was not necessary as MSU only needed to win the SEC championship to receive an invitation.

In what the fiery redhead often referred to as "buck passing," McDowell took the powers that be to task for putting the onus on Hilbun rather than offering little more than silence on the issue. "Mississippi Red" placed the lack of public and political support on fear of action from the state Citizens' Council and called the issue the most controversial racial problem since Mississippi integrated Veteran's Hospital in Jackson.[76] McDowell would again reference the lack of public responsibility for an NCAA decision from the state legislature and the State College Board and, in an expression of opinion not found in the work of his journalistic sports brethren, called the Maroons worthy challengers for a national championship and claimed that race should have been a non-issue for the decision makers in the Magnolia State. "Personally, this matter, in my opinion, is entirely different from other racial conflicts in that they are not required to sleep and eat with opposing players. As a matter of fact, they aren't even supposed to touch them or else it would be a personal foul," McDowell quipped in the February 22, 1959, edition of his column. "To be a national champion, you have to whip all comers. It is the belief of this writer that Mississippi State's lionhearted gladiators are capable of scaling such heights." He would later challenge the resolve of the State College Board, asking if the state's governing educational body would "display the same sort of courage as this great ball club?"[77] While "Mississippi Red" took his perceived jabs at the political elite in the state, he still devoted a bulk of his editorial content to the merits of McCarthy's Maroons squad. While many in Mississippi's sports writing community focused on the team's ability to clinch the SEC title, McDowell, in a calculated fashion, wrote that the team would clinch the automatic berth in the NCAA tournament, putting the emphasis on the integrated postseason. "If Mississippi officials are having such a difficult time deciding whether the Maroons should go to the national tournament, passing the buck up and down the line, it is suggested by this writer that the buck be passed to Babe and his team. They'll answer the question, pronto," McDowell wrote on February 23, 1959. McDowell would later argue that the MSU contingent could "whip any team, any time, anywhere."[78]

McDowell also used his opinion-based forum to argue for McCarthy, who told McDowell he openly welcomed the opportunity to play on a national stage. The MSU head coach, who stressed his belief in segregation to the sports editor, pleaded for "white Mississippians" to voice their opinions on the issue. McDowell supplemented "Babe's" commentary by adding that none of the correspondence he received favored integration, rather they argued that it would be for the good of the Magnolia State for MSU to pursue and possibly win a national title.[79]

While McDowell's primary area of focus was sports, specifically the MSU basketball team, he was quick to interlace his own personal feelings on the lack of political responsibility on the issue. In a bold, yet, sarcastic statement on February 25, 1959, McDowell called for the state to end participation in all integrated forums including the return of Mississippi's senators and congressmen to the Magnolia State out of fear of their attendance at integrated national conventions. McDowell quipped, "It's election year in Mississippi and political big wigs are walking the chalk line. The utter lack of courage and the sickening fear of a biased and political whip hovers like a menacing shadow over Mississippi State's shoulder. Is there a truly big man in the house?"

McDowell often reserved his more poignant and passionate remarks for his discussions on Mississippi's stifling political atmosphere and its relationship to the Mississippi State Maroons' NCAA tournament hopes. Calling the political practices of the state's government inconsistent, McDowell referred to the political elite in the state as "'string-pullers' of puppet men who fire away at college lads, insisting they are mere children when they express an honest opinion."[80] McDowell also noted the possible social implications of MSU's appearance in the integrated postseason, writing, "The decision to send or not to send Mississippi State to the National tournament is more important than you think. It will be a long, long time before the last of it is heard, and some gentlemen offering their services for re-election will be retired to private life because the people are sick of the way the entire thing has been handled. No one, no one, seeks to change Mississippi's ways of life in believing the Maroons should seek the National title."[81] McDowell had an ideal opportunity to express his own feelings on segregation, but unlike his fellow sports-based supporters of MSU, he did not. McDowell's own omission of his political beliefs, even in an opinion-based forum, showed a degree of ethical care by the sports scribe. Rather than use the opportunity to protect himself from the Closed Society, the opinionated McDowell kept his focus and stressed his belief in Mississippi State and its basketball team. "Mississippi Red" also identified a greater social importance to participating in the national title tournament outside of race relations and took the purveyors of the Closed Society to task for their attack on the students at Mississippi State. McDowell has argued that his vantage on the MSU-NCAA fiasco was always based on his belief that the debate should have centered on sports and all political and social beliefs should have been cast aside.[82] When asked what his own personal feelings were on segregation, the veteran sports writer quipped, "I don't know. I don't remember."[83] McDowell's belief in the competitive aspect of sports was further supported when he wrote, "Race haters, North and South, have twisted the Maroon story to attempt to make the tournament more than a tournament of champions. And that is the unfair thing about the whole business," a clear objection to the political and social debate that saturated the MSU-NCAA affair.[84]

McDowell would also come to the aid of Hilbun, comparing the embattled president to a "western marshal walking down that lowly street on High Noon" and sympathetically writing, "Now Mr. Ben has his toughest decision of all to make with apparently everyone in Mississippi adopting a hands-off attitude."[85] In McDowell's opinion, Hilbun had been put in an unfair and precarious situation but stressed his own personal faith in MSU's president, calling him a fair man who would do what was best for the institution.[86] McDowell placed the blame for the sixty-nine-year-old's embattled state on Mississippi's political elite, writing, "It's election year and politicians aren't going to commit themselves. What the majority of [voters] think or the students or the players or the coach makes absolutely no difference.... The [State College] Board simply dumped the whole business in Ben's lap and Ben Hilbun isn't going to be the scape-goat. He asked for assistance from the Board and received exactly none."[87] After Hilbun made the decision to keep the Maroons out of the tournament, McDowell, MSU's foremost journalistic supporter, continued to lambast the state's political elite, writing that those seeking office who sat in silence would soon "jump on the band wagon and praise Hilbun for his courageous decision," which McDowell argued was made because of the fear that the State College Board would overrule the MSU president.[88] McDowell also lamented the opportunity lost for the Magnolia State and the Mississippi State Maroons. "This shameful denial will be long remembered in Mississippi by true sportsmen who are also 100 percent segregationists, and who realize that the NCAA tournament was a tournament of champions and nothing else. Mississippi State's greatest basketball opportunity—only four games away from the national championship—may never come again," wrote the fiery sports scribe on March 2, 1959.

While McDowell would not go so far as to call himself a liberal in a 2010 interview, the longtime Mississippi sports writer and editor's work during the 1958–1959 MSU basketball season would bravely challenge the white status quo in the Magnolia State and offer opposition to the unwritten law, ranking him in the company of such journalistic luminaries as Hodding Carter of the *Delta Democrat-Times* as an antagonistic element of change in the Closed Society.[89]

McDowell was not the only sports editor to advocate an NCAA tournament appearance for MSU. Dick Lightsey of the *Daily Herald* in Biloxi and *Vicksburg Evening Post* sports editor Billy Ray stood along McDowell in their belief that the opportunity for a national championship would benefit the Magnolia State. However, both Lightsey and Ray stressed their segregationist beliefs and looked at the tournament as a way for the all-white Maroons to extend the Closed Society's dominance to the national hardwood. Lightsey, who wrote a daily sports column titled "Bunts, Boots and Bounces" for the *Daily Herald*, was one of a few journalists who identified the prospects of an NCAA tournament bid after the Maroons' victory over Kentucky.[90] Lightsey would later take an almost somber approach to the issue, writing that it would be a shame for the Maroons to miss out on the integrated postseason. "They should have a fine ball club and could bring a lot of prestige to the Magnolia State if allowed to go for the mythical national championship," the sports editor wrote on February 16, 1959. Despite the positive tone of his work, Lightsey also did his best to tow the line of the Closed Society. On a number of occasions, while he maintained that the Maroons would make a suitable representative of the Magnolia State, he was quick to point out that, due to the unwritten law, it was unlikely the team would participate in the postseason.[91] Lightsey would later take to his opinion-based forum to explain the origins of the unwritten law, writing on February 26, 1959, that while the "gentlemen's agreement" could not be found in any sort of public record, it was a binding understanding applying to all Mississippi-based institutions of higher learning. Lightsey, a segregationist, argued that the borders of the Closed Society would remain intact if the Starkville contingent were allowed to prove its worth on the hardwood. "We are not in favor of integration in Mississippi, but go along with the old saying: When in Rome, do as the Romans do," Lightsey wrote. "Even if they get beat, they will at least have a chance of proving to themselves—and other Mississippians—just how good they really are. Enough said." Lightsey's advocacy of a postseason berth for the Maroons would end there. After the season-ending victory over Ole Miss, Lightsey called Hilbun's decision a mere formality. Rather than continuing to argue for an NCAA bid for the Maroons, Lightsey chose to cheer on Kentucky, hoping that a Wildcat title would improve the public perception of the 24–1 Maroons.[92] Days later, Lightsey defended Hilbun after students on the Starkville campus hanged the MSU president in effigy, writing he had no choice but to denounce the bid.[93] While the Biloxi-based sports editor may have favored an MSU-NCAA tournament appearance, his justification, like that of his fellow sports writers and editors, was a nod to athletic success and not human equality or civil rights. From an examination of his opinion-based articles, Lightsey wanted to have it both ways. He did not want to advocate anything that would lead to integration, thus challenging the Closed Society, yet he wanted Mississippi State to play for a national championship. Regardless, his support for State was a radical notion for the white elite in the Closed Society. The idea that the harmonious white dominated social structure would be temporarily cast aside for a basketball team's pursuit of glory was attacked by other, more traditional segregationist publications in the Magnolia State.

Like McDowell and Lightsey, Ray also devoted the bulk of his editorial work on the success of the Maroons and the potential NCAA bid. Sparked by the Maroons' victory over the Wildcats, Ray predicted that the "segregation question" would have to be addressed if MSU were to win the remaining games on its schedule. However, he maintained that both the team and fans alike should focus on the team's conference foes and not the issue of race.[94] Following the lead of "Mississippi Red," Ray also asked his audience for their thoughts on a possible tournament bid for MSU. In his daily column, "Press Box Views," Ray identified public sentiment as the deciding factor in the debate and urged his readers to voice their opinions on the matter. Citing 1959 as an election year, Ray insinuated that the political elite in the state could potentially be swayed by public opinion thus justifying why "sports editors throughout the state have called upon the general public to express their opinions on the matter."[95] Ray's strongest commentary, however, was saved for his own opinion, in which he argued for both a tournament appearance and the reaffirming of the subservient position of blacks in the Closed Society. On February 19, 1959, Ray contended that a MSU tournament appearance would generate "good will and beneficial national recognition" for the Magnolia State and potentially validate Mississippi's white-dominated ideals. "Just by playing against a Negro or two for an hour or so a day in a championship event of this sort wouldn't mean the team had turned integrationists . . . and it would give them a chance to show up these colored boys and show the nation how basketball is played at Mississippi State."

Despite Ray's aforementioned argument, the Vicksburg-based sports editor eventually predicted a grim forecast for the Starkville five. While praising the merits of McCarthy's team and predicting the eventual onset of integrated athletic competition, Ray admitted on multiple occasions that it was unlikely Mississippi State would appear in the 1959 tournament.[96] Poignantly, the sports scribe wrote on February 25, 1959, "It's going to be a shame to deny the Maroons this privilege after producing such a fine record and bringing so much valuable publicity to the Magnolia State. A refusal to let the Maroons try for national recognition will turn this excellent publicity into the kind that's hard on the eyes and heavy on the heart." Ray also came to the aid of Hilbun, calling the MSU president a great man who should be free of criticism for keeping the State team out of the tournament due to the lack of support from politicians or the State College Board.[97] In the wake of Hilbun's decision, Ray attempted to console the competitive spirit of McCarthy and his team. "Everyone knows the 'Babe' [McCarthy] sure wished he could have taken his boys North and showed up those 'other' teams, which we believe he could have done and the only thing that would have actually resulted would have been bushels and bushels of beneficial publicity to the Magnolia State—and possibly the national championship," Ray wrote.[98] While Ray may have been a rare, vocal supporter for MSU and integrated play, his justification for such support was clear. While McDowell's work seemed to give a nod to social equality and journalism ethics, with the omission of his opinion on segregation, Ray did the exact opposite. Ray only advocated MSU's participation because of the allure of a national championship and a possible demonstration of the Closed Society's belief of the subservient nature of whites over blacks. While Lightsey and Ray expressed similar beliefs in segregation, Ray's commentary was different because of his quest to use MSU's possible athletic glory as a means to justify the Magnolia State's belief in state's rights and solidify the political white social structure that gripped Mississippi. Ray may have supported the Maroons, but he clearly supported the cause of white Mississippi as well.

Beyond the work of McDowell and, to a lesser extent, Lighsey and Ray, few editors offered their support to the MSU cause. One of the luminaries of Mississippi journalism, Hodding Carter of the *Delta Democrat-Times*, supported a Mississippi State appearance in the integrated postseason after the Maroons' title-clinching victory. Carter argued that most Mississippians would like to see the Starkville five play for the national championship. Carter claimed that the team's participation in the tournament was of little threat to the state's stand on integration and a rejection of an invitation would be "the fault of a few half-baked politicians and writers."[99] Much like McDowell, the *Delta Democrat-Times* editor urged his readers to express an opinion on the matter, calling for MSU's supporters to follow the lead of the university's student body and publicly support the Maroons. "We also feel that to decline the invitation would be unfavorable publicity for the state," Carter wrote. "But more than that it would deny the team the opportunity it deserves."[100] In the aftermath of Hilbun's announcement, Carter attacked the same public support that he once tried to incite for its lack of inactivity and blamed it for making Hilbun's decision an easy one. "Only a few vocal Mississippi State backers spoke up against the politicians and writers who thrive on picking far-fetched excuses to show what ardent segregationists they are, so President Ben Hilbun didn't have the backing he needed. The ironic thing is that State's All American Bailey Howell will play in All-Star games, possibly on the same team with Negroes," wrote the Pulitzer Prize winning editor.[101] Carter's work added a degree of logic to the debate that certainly was not evident in the storm of commentary that originated from the Hederman papers in Jackson.

Despite the progressive commentary offered by McDowell, the Closed Society's foremost journalistic defender took to the pages of the *Jackson Daily News* and used his editorial forum to combat the internal threat posed by the MSU squad to the state's white way of life. No one struck out in defense of the unwritten law and the Closed Society quite like *Jackson Daily News* editor Jimmy Ward. Considered an apprentice of former *Daily News* editor Frederick Sullens, Ward did his best to follow in his mentor's spiteful footsteps. Ward was the central figure in the Hederman's journalistic Jackson-based monopoly and was a strident protector of the Magnolia State's white dominant social structure. His work, rich with sarcasm and hate, attacked integration at every turn and protected the Closed Society from all threats both white and black.[102] Ward would place himself at the front line against integration and civil rights and used his forum to protect the interests and beliefs of the Mississippi Sovereignty Commission and the state Citizens' Council. As an editor, Ward became known for either ignoring issues of race that might have put a proverbial black eye on the reputations of local whites or publishing material that was racist, inaccurate, and void of all objectivity, minimizing his journalistic credibility outside of the southern United States.[103] Ward's "Covering the Crossroads" column was the domicile of the segregationist's insensitive and often insulting views on topics ranging from race, politics, and even sports.[104] Former Mississippi Associated Press correspondent Douglas Starr described Ward as "an opportunist" who took advantage of the racial strife in Mississippi to make a name for himself in the Magnolia State.[105] Ward's commentary on the Maroons-NCAA issue was no different than the venomous tone the editor expressed on other matters of race and equality in Mississippi. On February 17, 1959, Ward called Mississippi State's possible entry into the NCAA tournament "a sidelight to the integration-segregation issue," deemphasizing the social implications of the team's potential participation, and urged the school to make a decision absent of any emotion. Ward later addressed those who justified a pro-NCAA stance by arguing that "the state should do in Rome as the Romans do." In response, Ward quipped, "Is this a consistent attitude for northern bigots and southern mixers?" and openly asked if it was possible to win a national championship in college sports "without getting involved in pseudo-sociological extra curricular expeditions."[106]

Ever watchful of threats to the Closed Society, no one was safe from the spiteful pen of Ward. In a response to Carter's aforementioned editorial support for the Maroons, Ward wrote that his journalistic counterpart's contention was not surprising, referencing Carter's liberal reputation. While the *Daily News* editor complimented Carter for at least taking a position, he doubted the endorsement would enhance MSU's chances of playing in the tournament calling it "a subject for brief debate. Very Brief debate."[107] He would later chastise the *Delta Democrat-Times* editor, who, when asked about the merits of MSU's participation in the NCAA tournament, told the *Chicago Defender* that gradual integration was upon Mississippi. In response, Ward lashed out, denouncing the prospects of integrated athletics, citing Mississippi's era of white supremacy for justification. "The institution [Mississippi State University] has been done a national disfavor that the subject was ever raised in the first place," Ward wrote. "There is more than a basketball score involved."[108] Ward even extended his racist gaze outside of the boundaries of the Magnolia State, aiming his literary cannon at *Times-Picayune* (New Orleans) sports columnist Buddy Diliberto. Ward called Diliberto's contention that MSU was through as a basketball power if they were not allowed to participate in the NCAA "utterly ridiculous" and "silly."[109] Ward referred to Louisiana's own policy against integrated competition as an "alleged handicap" that contradicted the emerging success of the Sugar Bowl, muting the New Orleans-based sports writer's opinion.

While MSU's intent on playing in the national title tournament may have been for competitive reasons, Ward wrote that Mississippi State's possible entry in the integrated tournament would be "misconstrued in the nation's press as a significant sign the state is cracking. It would be an open invitation to the agitators to come on down and start stirring strife. . . . If clear-thinking people can't see the potential harm in passing this impression along to the nation, then they have sticky film over their pupils. Damage to the sensible, tested cause of segregation has been done. A fine institution of higher learning has been made to suffer. Too much has been said on the subject. The issue should die a swift natural death."[110]

In the aftermath of Hilbun's decision, Ward celebrated State's absence from the tournament, boastfully proclaiming on March 2, 1959, that "the social experiment foisted upon the South by the aforementioned nitwits" was a failure. Ward called the NCAA tournament a minor component to a major issue and that any benefits from playing would have been temporary and fleeting. Liking his resolve to that of a ship captain, Ward praised Hilbun, complimenting the MSU president for his unshakable character and resolve. "Excitable voyagers tug at hemlines to go on wandering joy-rides in the bay of life. But true skippers keep their eyes on the harbor, genuine beacons and bright, unchanging stars," Ward wrote. Ward's work was indicative of the sort of commentary the Closed Society's most strident journalistic supporter was known for. There was never a subject too taboo for the segregationist editor. While the merits of the unwritten law would again be a subject of debate in 1961 and 1962, Ward would remain silent on the issue until 1963, when MSU's basketball team would make its NCAA tournament debut and, in essence, put an end to the gentleman's agreement.

While editorial objections to challenges to the Closed Society were common in the Hederman-owned newspapers, especially the *Jackson Daily News*, most of the commentary that was produced by Hederman sports editors Carl Walters of the *Clarion-Ledger*, Lee Baker of the *Jackson Daily News*, and Fitz McCoy of the *Hattiesburg American* either ignored the debate or denounced any hopes of an NCAA tournament bid as a potential crack in Mississippi's segregationist foundation.

Mississippi State's most outspoken critic from the sports desk was *Clarion-Ledger* sports writer and columnist Carl Walters. Unlike fellow sports journalist and Hederman scribe Lee Baker, Walters used his column "Shavin's" on a number of occasions to denounce the possibility of an NCAA tournament berth for the Maroons and offered support for the Closed Society. On February 11, 1959, Walters dismissed any hopes of an NCAA invite in the aftermath of the team's win over Kentucky, calling the Maroons' chances of appearing in the postseason an "excruciatingly slim-possibility" and justified his contention by citing the unwritten law and "the race problem involved in the NCAA tournament." Walters would again denounced the chances of MSU's postseason possibilities, calling the "hullabaloo" surrounding the NCAA tournament "premature and a little on the stupid side."[111] In a strong and definitive response to those supporting an NCAA appearance by Mississippi State, Walters reiterated the perceived binding power of the unwritten law: "The Maroons will not—repeat N-O-T—be numbered among the entries in the NCAA tournament regardless of what any poll or sampling of public opinion may reveal."[112] Following such a profound statement against integrated competition, Walters would devote considerable space to defuse any possibility of an NCAA tournament appearance for the Maroons on February 23, 1959. Walters referred to the team's post-season hopes as a non-issue, even informing his readers that it would not be a topic of conversation. "The reason we did not mention participation in the tourney by the Maroons is because we do not think they have a chance to get a 'go-ahead' signal from the 'powers-that-be,'" admitted the longtime Mississippi sports writer, casting a shadow of doubt on the team's chances. The following day, Walters cryptically wrote of the MSU-NCAA debate, "It is a dead issue. Actually, it never had the breath of life" and admitted to omitting any commentary pertaining to the tournament because of "the fact that nothing new has been advanced in arguing for either side of the question."[113] Clearly, the longtime *Clarion-Ledger* sports writer was making a journalistic attempt to deemphasize the issue, thus reinforcing the unwritten law and the ideals of white Mississippi.

Walters would later take issue with State's place in both the AP and UPI basketball polls rather than discuss the NCAA tournament, calling the Maroons' absence at the top of both polls "utterly stupid."[114] While Walters identified a number of reasons for the State to be considered the best team in the country, the obvious justification—the refusal to play segregated teams—was never discussed. After briefly discussing Hilbun's impending decision, the veteran sports writer informed his audience that he had grown tired of the issue and that he was going through a self-imposed moratorium on discussing the NCAA tourney.[115] Walters's silence on the issue lasted all of three days as he, begrudgingly, addressed Hilbun's decision and openly questioned the news value of the announcement. "Everybody and his brother knew about the establishment several years ago of the 'policy' and as President Hilbun said, it had not been discarded or revised," Walters wrote in an obvious tone.[116] The *Clarion-Ledger* scribe defended the MSU president and took the State College Board to task for refusing to publicly object to an NCAA appearance by the Maroons long before it became an issue. Perhaps the more interesting aspect to Walters's work came well after the MSU-NCAA debate had run its course. In the March 12, 1959, edition of the *Ledger*, Walters called the MSU squad the "finest in the land for 1959, so far as we are concerned." Two days later, Walters would again anoint Mississippi State the best team in the nation after the number one team in the nation, Kansas State University, lost in the tournament to the University of Cincinnati 85–75, and the University of Louisville defeated Kentucky, the second ranked team in the country, by a score of 88–81. "Poll or no poll, tournament or no tournament, the Mississippi State Maroons proved by winning 24 of 25 starts that they were the best team in the land," Walters wrote in a veil of ignorance.[117] Walters's misguided argument failed to address the obvious answer for MSU's lack of success in the polls: the team's failure to play integrated teams outside of the South. It was this "have your cake and eat it too" mentality that poisoned the editorial work of many of Mississippi's prominent journalists, including Walters. Most wanted the Maroons to be considered the best basketball team in the country; however, they were unwilling to support the team's place in the NCAA tournament. Once the decision was made, journalists like Walters called even louder for MSU to receive the same level of national respect typically reserved for college teams that played all comers, regardless of skin color. In fact, a number of Walters's columns took a very defiant tone. Although Walters's opinions mirrored that of the Closed Society and the Hederman family, he said in a 1974 interview that he was never forced into writing a particular opinion or viewpoint because of the Hedermans' ownership of the *Ledger*.[118]

Jackson Daily News sports editor Lee Baker took a less defiant tone than his fellow Hederman scribe Walters, frequently neglecting to mention the NCAA tournament as a possibility for the Maroons in his "Baker's Dozen" daily column. After the team's landmark victory over the Wildcats, Baker argued on February 10, 1959, that the Starkville team's place in the AP ranking should be reflective of the dominant win but never referenced the obvious reason for such an omission; the lack of integrated teams on the school's schedule. While Baker would, logically, identify the unwritten law as McCarthy's possible attraction to the head coaching position at the University of Texas, the sports scribe called McCarthy's possible exit illogical and dismissed any possible protests pertaining to the rejection of an NCAA bid, writing, "Anyone with a grain of sense knows that students are always available for anything even vaguely hinting excitement and adventure."[119] Continuing to dismiss the team's chances of playing in the NCAA tournament, Baker wrote on February 23, 1959, "Of course, they want to go to the NCAA regional. But that is something off in the future to be decided by someone else." Although the future Mississippi Sports Hall of Fame member would focus on the Maroons in two more columns, he did not discuss the national title tournament or the unwritten law.[120] Despite Baker's shortcomings during the 1959 season and subsequent debates surrounding the unwritten law, McDowell offered nothing but praise for his former colleague, calling him a great writer and journalist.[121]

Meanwhile, *Clarion-Ledger* sports editor Arnold Hederman expressed little opinion on the matter, demonstrating a lack of foresight that was evident in his work during the duration of MSU's 1959 basketball campaign. On February 28, 1959, Hederman wrote that, while the MSU-Ole Miss contest had generated a degree of interest, more eyes would be on Hilbun and the announcement of his decision. Hederman later penned a March 3, 1959, column to congratulate the Maroons on their successful season, but not without one last nod to the NCAA tournament. "We are not going to get into the battle of whether the Maroons should or should not have gone to the NCAA, for that has already been settled," Hederman wrote in a dismissive fashion. Two days later, Hederman wrote in Hilbun's defense, "President Ben couldn't have made any other announcement about the NCAA than he made," he wrote.[122] Hederman added that he was disappointed the issue had taken public interest off of education and that the student body should remember that they were there to learn, an interesting perspective coming from a sports writer. While the sports editor may not have been as vocal as Walters or the venomous Ward, his ignorance of the issue, in combination with a few inferences of opinion, made him an ideal journalistic protector of the Closed Society.

Sports writers and editors outside of Jackson also offered their opinions on integrated competition, some with the same bite and ferocity as their journalistic counterparts. Fellow Hederman sports scribe and *Hattiesburg American* sports editor Fitz McCoy took a similar route, attacking the Maroons' NCAA chances with an edge that made him a perfect fit for the Hederman's journalistic empire.[123] McCoy attempted to temper the Maroons' fan base, not with the shadow cast by the gentleman's agreement, but with a general athletic premise. "Speculation about whether State will go to the NCAA playoffs started immediately after the victory," McCoy wrote. "This is being dangerously presumptuous."[124] McCoy later opposed an NCAA appearance on February 20, 1959, calling the building controversy "sickening and embarrassing because we—meaning you and me and our politicians and all of our people who care about and discuss these things publicly—have committed a grave tactical blunder in ever allowing any doubt about what our college teams would do in this situation." McCoy advocated a "stated policy that is clearly understood by all our people" and opposed any pro-NCAA tournament sentiment, not because there would be some sort of harm to the state's segregationist mission, but because the situation would leave "bitterness and division back home that could undermine us worse than the bitterness and division that will result if the team does not go." McCoy closed out his commentary on the Maroons and the NCAA by offering a degree of perspective to the hanging of Hilbun in effigy, writing that no real harm had been done. "The kids, feeling at the time that they are reshaping the world, get it out of their systems and everyone else soon forgets it

ever happened," he wrote.[125] McCoy's work failed to advocate integrated competition, thus honoring the unwritten law, and chastised both the MSU basketball
team and the political elite of the Closed Society for their individual positions.
Despite McCoy's scathing evaluation of his audience, in the end, he protected
the very individuals he was addressing.

Other journalists and editors from the Hederman empire also made their
opinions known on the MSU-NCAA debate. Andrew Harmon, editor of the
Hattiesburg American, wrote a brief editorial on the issue and directed his discontent to the "south-haters, do-gooders and political hatchet-men" for their
attacks on "Southern people and their long-established habits because of the
No-Mix policy established by law and custom."[126] Harmon claimed that forced
integration was ineffective and pointed to both the MSU-NCAA controversy
and a new Detroit-based policy that required officers of different ethnic background to patrol together. The policy, which Harmon wrote had been met
with protests on the part of the police, was proof that "when forced mixing is
attempted it is opposed in Michigan as well as in Mississippi."[127] Citizens' Council member and *Clarion-Ledger* columnist Tom Ethridge, who sympathized
with the appeal of playing for a national championship, denounced any possibility of an NCAA tournament appearance. "Our Magnificent Maroons would
not be contaminated by 'mixing' away from home," Ethridge wrote, adding that
if the decision were left up to him, he would "hold the line—regretfully, but
none the less positively."[128] Fellow *Clarion-Ledger* columnist Charles M. Hills
also wrote about the Maroons after Hilbun's announcement and argued that
there was a profound difference between Mississippi athletes who go on to play
in integrated competition and state-based teams who are charged with representing the Magnolia State. Hills added that state colleges and universities use
money allocated to them by the legislature, and it had been government policy
to stay out of integrated competition. An NCAA appearance by MSU, in Hills's
opinion, could have led to integration of, not only athletic venues, but of state
schools as well. In Hills's words, by playing, MSU would have "started a lot of
complications and implications, so, why not forget it all? We have the championship we wanted anyway. If we had won the national championship, no one
would have been proud of it but us."[129]

The MSU debate also instigated the opinion of *Jackson Daily News* cartoonist
and Citizens' Council supporter Bob Howie, who drew a Bulldog bearing the
"M" of Mississippi State shredding an article from the student-based *Reflector*
that reported on the student body's vote of support for an MSU appearance in
the NCAA tournament. Howie's cartoon was accompanied by the headline: "It's
Our Bulldog That's Being Kicked."[130] Another Howie cartoon appeared depicting a basketball player with a tag that read "State's NCAA Tourney Chances"
being tossed back and forth between two hands labeled "pro" and "con" with the

headline "Jump Ball!"[131] While the cartoonist failed to express the insensitive commentary typically found in his "Hinny" cartoons, nevertheless, his effort certainly coincided with his segregationist beliefs.

In the same social vein of the Hederman papers was the *Meridian Star* of owner and editor James B. Skewes. The Skewes family was unequivocally against any challenge to the Closed Society in Meridian and Lauderdale County, where 40 percent of the population was black during the mid-1950s.[132] As member of the Citizens' Council, Skewes carried on the racist and segregationist traditions at the *Star* that his father and namesake had established.[133] While Skewes's commentary on the MSU-NCAA debate was noticeably absent, his sports editor, Billy "Sunshine" Rainey, addressed the issue in a number of his daily columns, "Sunshine on Sports." Rainey's editorial writing was more dismissive that it was outlandish. Rainey wrote that, despite the Maroons' victory over the Wildcats, "Mississippi's statewide policy against integrated athletics will keep the Maroons off the postseason tournament trail."[134] Rainey would later state in an emphatic tone, "NO team from Mississippi will compete in the NCAA tourney or in any other event where competition against teams with Negro players is involved. We do not necessarily share the opinion that this is the way it should be done but it is our sincere belief that this is the way it WILL be done."[135] On February 24, 1959, rather than discuss the NCAA prospects for the Starkville squad, Rainey took exception to UPI's latest college basketball rankings, which had MSU as the seventh best team in the nation. "The cold hard fact is that though Mississippi State has the best record in the United States with 23 wins and one defeat, the Maroons will NOT gain the approval of the 35 coaches in the weekly UPI polls," the Meridian-based sports editor argued. While Rainey offered no explanation for his theorized UPI oversight, an obvious justification was MSU's refusal to play integrated teams. Later, despite addressing McCarthy's plea for public opinion, Rainey claimed he would be keeping his opinion on the sidelines, saying he did not feel qualified to make a judgment.[136] Although "Sunshine" would write about the Maroons in his March 3, 1959, column, in particular, the epic season Howell was having, he did not address the NCAA controversy again. Rainey's commentary was not necessarily reflective of a man whose work would go well beyond the sports world and place him at the forefront of one of the more tragic and egregious acts of Mississippi's past. Rainey was the *Star*'s primary reporter on the June 1964 murders of civil rights workers Michael Schwerner, James Chaney, and Andrew Goodman in the Neshoba County-based city of Philadelphia during Freedom Summer. While the search and subsequent discovery of their murders made national headlines, Rainey worked on location for fifty-two days until the bodies were found.[137]

Without the same statewide breadth of their Jackson-based colleagues, other editors also addressed the Maroons' hopes of entering the NCAA tournament, some with the same racist rhetoric as the Hederman empire. *Natchez Democrat* editor James Lambert waited until after Hilbun made his decision to chime in on the debate, congratulating the MSU president in a March 3, 1959, editorial for making "his contribution to the great effort now being made here and elsewhere in the South for the preservation of Our Way of Life." Lambert added that MSU's president had no choice in the matter, citing the state's gentleman's agreement against integrated competition as if it had some sort of legal basis. "The law is clear; the line for the preservation of segregation has been plainly and distinctly drawn. There can be no deviation—no matter under what pretense," he claimed. Lambert closed his commentary by describing MSU's potential participation in the tournament as "the breaking down of all we love and stand for in Mississippi and the Deep South" and took some of his journalistic brethren to task for their support of MSU. "There have been some sports editors throughout the state who have become so enthused over Mississippi having a champion SEC team that they seem to have forgotten that far more important than any other basketball game or accomplishment of any sports team in the state is the preservation of Our Way of Life," Lambert wrote. Joe Mosby, a former sports editor at the *Democrat*, described Lambert as "a fine person with the usual local beliefs on the segregation issue" in a 2009 interview.[138] Mosby explained that the paper's newsroom was influenced more by Natchez's extreme MSU fan base than the ideological position taken by their audience.

Natchez sports editor Don Guin expressed less fervor than his editor and followed the standard set by the majority of his sports journalistic brethren, failing to express a definitive opinion on the matter. Guin, in the February 27, 1959, edition of the *Democrat*, wrote, "We are inclined to think that the higher ups and big-wigs of State College know what's best for the whole team and the state as a whole and that they have taken everything into consideration before they make the final statement." Noting the objections voiced by the *Jackson Daily News* and the support offered to the Maroons from Rainey and Billy Ray of *Vicksburg Evening Post*, Guin was noncommittal on the issue, only offering support for MSU's embattled president. "One final word—WHATEVER THE LAST WORD IS—WE GO ALONG WITH IT—WITHOUT QUESTION."

Another voice of opposition came from *Commercial Dispatch* editor Birney Imes, who called the MSU student vote "childishness" and that "ballots are too dangerous for immaturity."[139] Imes claimed that the students were "hoodwinked by NAACP tactics. It's not unusual for students to have the wool pulled over their eyes." Imes continued to criticize the students, writing that the vote was "just another device for headline grabbing for 'the cause.' . . . Students should stick to painting signs along the side of the road about the game with Ole Miss. They handle a paintbrush much better than the ballot."[140] Imes closed by calling any effort by MSU to play in the tournament a precursor for integration.

Sports editor Charles B. Gordon of the McComb-based *Enterprise-Journal* sided with his Jackson-based peers, predicting in a column titled "Sports Journal" that, despite the Maroons' successful campaign, the team would not venture into integrated athletics. "This prediction can safely be made: There's virtually no likelihood that the State team will be seen in the NCAA tournament," Gordon wrote.[141] The sports editor anointed Kentucky as the likely recipient of the NCAA bid, adding that the Maroons would uphold "one thing or another, depending on how you look at the situation," a clear nod to the unwritten law and the principles outlined in the Closed Society.

Editor Harriet Gibbons of the *Laurel Leader-Call* took a common editorial approach when it came to the MSU-NCAA debate, writing that the biggest problem with the issue was the lack of consistency from citizens and political officials in terms of integration. "Our young people are not willing to forego competition that will bring them into integrated situations," Gibbons wrote. "And their parents who find it easier to agree with their children, than to disagree with them, will not raise their voices. And school authorities, that talk segregated schools out of one side of their mouths, talk integrated sports out the other side."[142] Gibbons continued, asking for Mississippians to make up their minds. "Do we mean what we say or say what we mean? Is integration going to follow the path of prohibition in which we have laws that we don't intend to follow?"[143] Gibbons wrote a similar column when her hometown Jones County Junior College Bobcats played in Mississippi's first integrated sports contest, the 1955 Junior Rose Bowl, and lost the junior college national championship to Compton (California) Junior College 22–13.

Much like their news coverage of the 1959 MSU squad, the *Starkville News* offered little in opinion on the matter. After the team's landmark victory of Kentucky, the anonymously penned column "Athletes' Feats" took a similar approach to that of the *Clarion-Ledger*'s Walters, warning the MSU faithful on February 13, 1959, not to get overconfident in the wake of the Wildcats victory. Editor Henry Meyer would later congratulate the Maroons on their SEC championship but failed to reference the NCAA tournament, the unwritten law, or integrated athletics.[144] The same could be said for the March 6, 1959, edition of "Athletes' Feats," which never mentioned the NCAA tournament. While other newspapers expressed little to no opinion on the matter, the story was a local one for Meyer and the *Starkville News*. To be void of original reporting and commentary demonstrated a degree of journalistic neglect by Starkville's primary news source.

With so many journalists failing to voice a definitive opinion on the matter, especially from sports desks across the state, Mosby, much like McDowell, said many reporters thought the political issues of the day and athletics should have remained separate. "The Mississippi sports writers of the time period had the general opinion that sports were for the playing fields and politics and social issues were for other arenas," he said. "There were some exceptions, and when backed into a corner, they followed the wishes of their employers. I put myself in this category."[145] Mosby contention, while logical for the time, highlights a journalistic mindset that lacked the fortitude to question the beliefs and values of the Closed Society. The journalistic support of the MSU contingent was akin to an inquiry on the social values of Mississippi, which included segregation.

While the various editors and columnists debated the merits of the Maroons' possible participation in the integrated postseason, letters of the editor surrounding the issue began to make their way into the pages of Mississippi's editorial sections. While, logically, the letters may not have been representative of the reading population in total, the commentary provided serves as a convenient barometer of the feelings surrounding the MSU-NCAA tournament debate. Furthermore, since the publication of such letters amounts to an editorial decision, the aforementioned editors may have been inclined to publish material that coincided with their own personal viewpoints on the issue, thus serving as additional journalistic evidence of the publication's prevailing opinion on the matter. More so than any newspaper consulted in this chapter, the *Jackson State Times* offered a number of different opinions for and against MSU and, overall, did the best job attempting to strike a journalistic balance between those two opposing opinions.

The readers of the *Jackson State Times* heeded the pleas of McDowell, as the sports editor discussed or published a number of letters on the Maroons and a possible NCAA tournament berth. After his column's request for public opinion, one anonymous author wrote that a national championship would bring positive publicity to the Magnolia State, while another letter from "a prominent lawyer" and self-professed segregationist agreed, logically arguing that Mississippi's political delegates did not abstain from integrated national conventions. Another segregationist wrote that a tournament appearance by MSU would be acceptable "so long as there is no social contact" between the Maroons and their integrated foes.[146] McDowell would write an article on February 15, 1959, detailing letters received by the *State Times*. "Mississippi Red" indicated that readers supported an NCAA tournament appearance by a 5–1 ratio, and in general "stressed that while Mississippi should preserve its segregation laws, the state should not be expected to abide by laws of the other states when playing in an athletic event which could bring national recognition to the Magnolia State." As for the correspondence found in McDowell's article, a member of the Citizens' Council wrote that he found no harm in State's participation, as it would "prove to the nation that we are not race bigots." Another letter from a "lifelong Mississippian, a segregationist, and a good Southern Baptist" called the efforts against MSU "childish, stupid, and utterly ridiculous." However, not all of the letters approved of State's postseason hopes. One letter, identifying blacks as "them," said that Mississippi should abstain from integrated competition "until we are made to." Another reader followed suit, writing, "If our athletic teams play on an integrated basis we may as well abandon our past history, the memory of our valiant ancestors and go whole hog for race-mixing." Perhaps the most interesting perspective came from a Hazlehurst resident who noted that public opinion might be in favor of a Maroons tournament bid but put the responsibility of such debate squarely on the press, specifically McDowell. "I can't help but feel that you are doing them an injustice in writing about their going to the tournament. I believe you would do them a favor to drop the subject." In total, fifteen of the nineteen letters published in McDowell's article supported a Mississippi State appearance in the NCAA tournament.

As the debate persisted, more *Jackson State Times* readers took to the publication's editorial section to weigh in on the impending controversy and, to the newspaper's credit, represented multiple perspectives on the issue. Jackson resident John Cook damned the MSU student body for its vote of approval, writing that men of character existed in the Magnolia State and they would uphold the principles on which the state was founded.[147] L. G. Patterson of Jackson opposed any threats of integration, including those on the basketball court. Patterson wrote, "They may want to intermarry and equally as bad the Maroons might lose and that would be mighty embarrassing."[148] Harrison Saunders, a member of Mississippi State's 1925 freshman basketball team, wrote a personal appeal to Hilbun, asking for the team to be allowed to play in the NCAA tournament while deemphasizing the racial controversy surrounding the issue. "This is no way a battle of the KKK and the big brother mouth organ called the Citizens' Council against any group of people. PRESIDENT HILBUN WE ARE TALKING ABOUT AN ATHLETIC CONTEST."[149] The *State Times* also published letters from Citizens' Council member D. A. Hegwood and MSU graduate Buddy Graves. Hegwood, a "die-hard segregationist" and an active member of the Flowood chapter of the Citizens' Council, approved of a Maroon appearance in the tournament because the team was not "incapable of conducting itself when thrown into interracial athletic events. Some of the best friends I have are colored people and I can proudly say I am respected accordingly."[150] Another letter, from alumnus Graves, also supported the Maroons. "This is not comparable to local integration race relations. Let us not focus the colored races of people of the world down on Mississippi by refusing our boys the privilege to participate, if the team so desires," Graves wrote via telegraph.[151]

While a nod to journalistic balance could be found in the letters published in the *State Times*, the *Jackson Daily News* featured a number of letters to the editor that condemned the Maroons and, like Ward, sought to protect the Closed Society from this internal attack. In a letter from "Our Readers' Viewpoint," Shirley Kempinska of Natchez placed the blame for student support for an NCAA bid on what was being taught in the classroom. "Better check your son or daughter's college required subjects instead of blaming the students for agreeing to compete in non-segregated tournaments," Kempinska concluded.[152] Another reader, Byron De La Beckwith of Greenwood, wrote that, "If parents of students at Mississippi State and the faculty of Mississippi State haven't already explained to the students why they can't play ball with Negro students then it is high time for the taxpayers of the state to tell them why not. Even if your children want to integrate we know the folly of their wishes."[153] The Beckwith name is a familiar one in the dark history of the Magnolia State as the Ku-Klux-Klan member was convicted in the murder of Medgar Evers.[154] A final letter published in the section from L. B. Goodwin of Lexington, Kentucky, claimed that residents of the Bluegrass State also wanted segregated athletics and supported the cause of the Closed Society.[155] On February 28, Ward also published a letter from MSU students Marlyn Sanifer, Herman Cooper Jr., and Bill Hodnett that expressed displeasure with any pro-NCAA tournament sentiment. The letter claimed that the poll held on campus was not publicized and that many of the students who voted did not think about the consequence and repercussions of such a vote. "When the state lets down in any small way on our segregation beliefs then there will be increased pressure from outside trying to break us down forever. Participation in an integrated tournament would go against everything our state stands for," the letter read.[156] Also published in the same edition of the *Jackson Daily News* was a letter from Fayette resident W. M. Drake, president of the Jefferson County Citizens' Council, who praised the paper for its stand on integration and athletics."[157]

The Hederman's other Jackson-based newspaper, the *Clarion-Ledger* published two letters that hailed Hilbun's decision and offered continued support for a segregated Mississippi. The first, written by Ella Perry of Jackson, offered three cheers for Hilbun for "putting those foolish children at State U. in their place.... It was down right indecent for children of former slaves to play around with children of their former masters in basketball or anywhere else."[158] Perry further wrote that integration would lead to "intermarriage or misconception" and attacked MSU students for supporting a tournament appearance for the Maroons.[159] A second letter came from A. S. Coody of Jackson, who said the state should be proud of both the basketball team and Hilbun for abstaining from the postseason. Coody wrote that Hilbun's decision "would be clear when the evil days come upon us and attempts are made by the NAACP and the Commies to enroll Negroes in our Universities. We can then say that we have been consistent and have steadfastly stood against mixing and mongrelizing the races."[160] Although the fellow Hederman newspaper published one letter that advocated an NCAA tournament appearance for MSU, the bulk of the material reflected the *Jackson Daily News* and protected the Closed Society through public opinion.

Skewes's *Meridian Star* only published a single letter during the Maroons' season on the NCAA tournament, from A. M. Shirley of Meridian, a 1928 graduate of Ole Miss, which interestingly enough, contradicted the race-based viewpoints of the newspaper. Shirley called for a tournament appearance by the Starkville team because of the past opportunities lost as a result of the Closed Society. "Petty bigotry which divides and isolates us should have neither place nor part in our problem solving," Shirley wrote.[161]

The close of Mississippi State's 1959 season would not be the last time in the calendar year that a challenge to the unwritten law would occur. In April 1959, the University of Mississippi's baseball team would win the SEC championship only to proudly reject participation in the College World Series. Many in the Mississippi press, including Ward, who hailed the Oxford team for honoring the unwritten law, viewed the actions of Ole Miss as positive. Meanwhile, Mississippi State would suffer a setback during the 1959–1960 season but would again win the SEC title in 1960–1961, 1961–1962, and 1962–1963 and foster subsequent debates about the merits of an NCAA tournament bid for the Maroons.

MSU's efforts did little to change the social climate surrounding Mississippi's segregated colleges and universities. In September 1959, only months after MSU's historic season would come to a close, Clyde Kennard attempted to integrate Mississippi Southern College in Hattiesburg. His application was rejected and, after meeting with college president William McCain, he was subsequently arrested by Forrest County officials for driving recklessly and illegal possession of whiskey, a charge the Hattiesburg native denied. Sovereignty Commission files later revealed that the officers placed the illegal alcohol in Kennard's car. Less than a year later, Kennard and nineteen-year-old Johnny Lee Roberts, were arrested for the theft of five bags of chicken feed. The arrest occurred soon after it was rumored that he would again attempt to enroll at MSC. Kennard, who professed his innocence, was sentenced to serve seven years at Parchman Prison Farm, a place synonymous with punishment and brutality.[162] While in prison, Kennard discovered he had stomach cancer and died in a Chicago hospital in 1963.[163] In December 2005, Roberts told Pulitzer-Prize-nominated journalist Jerry Mitchell of the *Clarion-Ledger* that Kennard was innocent of the burglary charges.[164]

The 1959 Mississippi State University basketball season stood out for a number of reasons; however in the annals of Mississippi history, those reasons had little to do with the Maroons' play on the court. For weeks, journalists and editors debated the merits of an NCAA tournament berth for MSU and, for the most part, debated the social implications of the possible participation of one of its own college teams in integrated competition. The journalistic defenders of the Closed Society took to the front pages of Mississippi newspapers to defend their way of life and denounce any and all arguments for the Maroons. Unlike previous athletic brushes with integration, the 1959 debate involving MSU, for the first time, had both support and opposition from the journalists in the Magnolia State. While the majority of editors followed the lead of Ward and the Hederman-owned newspapers out of Jackson, others such as Carter from the news desk and sports editor McDowell identified the Maroons' prospects for a national championship run as a positive for the state and challenged the segregationist cloud that hovered over the state. Others who argued for an MSU-NCAA bid, such as Lightsey and Ray, openly voiced their support for the Closed Society yet saw only positive repercussions for the very opposition that kept MSU from playing. In fact, both sports editors stated that MSU's participation would only help support Mississippi's white dominated ideology and potentially serve as a physical sign of the dominance of the Closed Society outside of the South. These minor differences of opinion would grow in the coming years to become cracks in the foundation of the Closed Society, culminating in the 1963 participation of MSU in the NCAA tournament. However, based upon the evidence presented in this chapter, the journalists in the state played an important part in the enforcement of the unwritten law in 1959. For the most part, the bulk of journalists denounced the notion of integrated play and almost mocked those who held out hope. Across every turn and win for the Maroons, writers used their work to reaffirm their belief in the Closed Society and honored the premise of the unwritten law, despite its lack of legal legitimacy. In the back and forth wrangling between members of the State College Board, Hilbun and Coleman, it was the press in Mississippi that took issue with the lack of a definitive voice and called for a single individual to enforce the unwritten law. Once Hilbun made his decision, most in the press instinctively flocked to protect the MSU president, despite their position on the issue. Rather than criticize their very way of life, in hindsight, most in the press simply wanted the Closed Society to be protected. The various differences expressed by members of the press in terms of protecting and enforcing the principles of the Closed Society would, over time and with advancements in civil rights, become debates over the legitimacy of their very own white-dominated ideology.

Despite the social impact of the commentary of the Mississippi sports writer, Mosby, who left Nachez and Mississippi in early 1959, said the sports scribes of the day had little to no understanding of the social impact of their work. "I covered games, wrote stories and columns and worked to satisfy my bosses. Outside of that, I worried about having enough money for the rent and the car payment and for groceries," Mosby said. "Social issues were not priorities for me. But I was aware of what was taking place in my community and on a wider scene. Integration in athletics was a sometimes painful and stressful growing process. Maybe this is from left field, but integration in athletics was the teenage years for sports. They struggled, made it through and went on to bigger and better things."

Chapter 3

The Less Said, the Better

While the press in Mississippi debated the merits of the 1958–1959 Mississippi State University basketball team's potential entry into the NCAA tournament and subsequent violation of the unwritten law, the Maroons flew under the sports and political radar during their 1959–1960 campaign. McCarthy's team would finish with a 5–9 record in the SEC and resided in ninth place after the loss of graduating senior Bailey Howell. While the purveyors of the Closed Society were spared the inconvenience of validating and defending the unwritten law during the Maroons' 1959–1960 season, the same could not be said for the 1960–1961 MSU basketball team. Behind standouts such as Jerry Graves, W. D. "Red" Stroud, and Leland Mitchell, the Starkville contingent made another rise to prominence in the difficult Southeastern Conference. On February 27, 1961, the Maroons defeated the University of Tulane 62–57 to win their second SEC championship in three seasons and the right to participate in the NCAA tournament. However, citing the unwritten law, MSU declined, sending the second-place University of Kentucky Wildcats into the national title tournament. When asked about State turning down another postseason opportunity, a dejected McCarthy told John Garcia of UPI, "We've accepted it and that's it. The less said the better."[1]

The events of the 1960–1961 season coincided with a bevy of student-based civil rights activism that had not yet been seen within the Magnolia State. On March 27, 1961, nine students from Tougaloo College participated in a sit-in at the white-only Jackson Municipal Library. The students, all members of the NAACP, were arrested and charged with "intent to provoke a breach of the peace."[2] That evening, in response to the arrest of the anointed "Tougaloo Nine," over seven hundred students at Jackson State College gathered near the campus library, despite the efforts to defuse any sort of mobilization against white supremacy by college president Jacob Reddix. The following day, fifty JSC students, along with other local blacks, marched through the streets of Jackson in an effort to protest outside of the city jail. Their efforts were met with violent consequences as local police used blockades, billy clubs, tear gas, and attack dogs to disperse the crowd.[3] Reddix was so enraged with the student

HINNY

The *Jackson Daily News'* Bob Howie congratulated Mississippi State head coach James "Babe" McCarthy for wining the SEC's Coach of the Year award in a "Hinny" cartoon from 1961. Despite winning the conference in advance of MSU's season-ending contest against Ole Miss, Howie referred to the match-up as McCarthy's biggest test. *Courtesy Bob Howie/Jackson Daily News.*

body's part in the demonstration that he dissolved the JSC Student Government Association.[4] NAACP field security Medgar Evers, who was attacked in the police action, called the scene "indescribable."[5] 1961 also saw the national Freedom Ride effort come through the Magnolia State. The Freedom Rides was an initiative of the Congress of Racial Equality, or CORE, that sent integrated groups on public buses from the North into the Deep South in an effort to test the Supreme Court decision banning segregated facilities for interstate travelers.[6] Passengers on two separate Freedom Rides, originally destined for New Orleans, were met by members of the Mississippi National Guard upon their arrival to Mississippi, escorted to Jackson, and were arrested upon entering the white-only section of the bus station.[7] Even after the two buses were stopped in Jackson, hundreds of college students from the North continued their integration-based efforts, filling bus stations and terminals in the state capital. By the end of the summer, over three hundred participants in the CORE initiative spent time in the Jackson jail.[8] However, the most damning blow to the Closed Society came in the attempted enrollment of James Meredith at the University of Mississippi and subsequent desegregation of that institution. Meredith followed in the footsteps of Clennon King Jr. and Clyde Kennard, who attempted to enroll at the University of Mississippi and Mississippi Southern College, now known as the University of Southern Mississippi, in 1958 and 1959. King was subsequently committed for psychiatric treatment, while Kennard was sentenced to serve seven years in prison for a crime he did not commit. While Meredith's entry in Ole Miss would not happen until September 1962, his initial inquiry in January 1961 and subsequent denial would ignite a powder keg of opposition to the Closed Society. Meredith's addition to the school would strike a damning blow to the foundation of racial discontent on which the Closed Society sat. In response, journalists and editors in the state banded together and, for various reasons, opposed the integration of state schools. While a similar argument existed for journalists in terms of the merits of the unwritten law, in total, the passion and commentary from Mississippi State's 1958–1959 season was lacking as only a select few supported MSU's possible participation in the postseason, much less acknowledge the opportunity lost. Meanwhile *Jackson State Times* sports editor Jimmie McDowell continued to emerge as a progressive voice in Mississippi's journalistic community, arguing for MSU to play in their national championship tournaments and advocating the elimination of the unwritten law, a bold statement for a journalist in the Closed Society. However, as in 1959, a united front emerged in the press, again led by Carl Walters of the Hederman-owned *Clarion-Ledger*, which protected the Closed Society through expressed opposition towards integrated competition or editorial silence. The events in Starkville fueled debate within the state as to the merits of the unwritten law, and the firm establishment of the gentleman's agreement led to the press's overall rejection of any sentiment that supported the team's NCAA tournament bids where the Mississippi contingent would have faced integrated foes. It is that difference of opinion, as expressed by McDowell, which set the *State Times* editor apart from his fellow sports writers and earned the Mississippi native a rightful place with some of the state's more progressive journalists, such as Hodding Carter and J. Oliver Emmerich.

Like the 1959 season, the debate for an NCAA tournament berth for the Maroons emerged in the press in February after the team's yearly, late-season match-up with the University of Kentucky. As of February 2, 1961, the Maroons sat deadlocked atop the SEC standings with the upstart University of Florida Gators.[9] Many newspapers reported that the 13–3 Maroons could wrap up the SEC championship if the team had a successful weekend home stand that featured the likes of Louisiana State University, Tulane, Tennessee, and Kentucky before playing its remaining games on the road.[10] After a sound beating of the LSU Tigers 77–61 in Starkville, coupled with Florida's 89–68 loss to the Wildcats, the Maroons found themselves alone in first place with an upcoming match up against Tulane.[11] Sophomore W. D. "Red" Stroud paced the Maroons with twenty-one points, while fellow sophomore Leland Mitchell and senior Jerry Graves scored fifteen each.[12] An unknown author for the *Starkville Daily News* wrote on February 6, 1961, that "Babe McCarthy has some sensational sophomores of its own to counter with and they were in remarkable form Saturday night," citing the standout performances of Stroud, Mitchell, and senior guard Jack Berkshire. MSU was now a conference best 6–0 and 14–3 overall.[13] Despite State's first place status in the "Dixie Dozen," many sports writers failed to note the possibility of a postseason berth for the Starkville contingent.[14]

The Maroons went on to defeat Tulane 73–59 for McCarthy's one hundredth victory as Mississippi State's head coach.[15] Behind Graves's twenty-eight points, the Maroons increased their lead in the SEC to a full game over Florida and moved to 7–0 in conference play.[16] During Mississippi State's various challenges to the unwritten law, McCarthy was often forced into the spotlight and made the focal point of most inquiries about the team and the potential of integrated competition. James Harrison McCarthy, who was affectionately known as "Babe," never played college basketball. A former member of the U.S. Air Force, McCarthy was in active duty during both World War II and the Korean Conflict. A former high school basketball player, McCarthy picked up his coaching skills while he was in the Air Force coaching base basketball squads. A native of Baldwyn County, McCarthy returned to Tupelo after his Air Force days were behind him and took a job coaching basketball at a local middle school and served as a basketball referee for the SEC. McCarthy then worked with an oil firm in Clarksville until he interviewed and received the position of head coach at Mississippi State College.[17] As of 1961, McCarthy's record at State was 100–42 with a .704 winning percentage.

The Maroons were heading toward the final stretch of its home schedule with a February 11, 1961, match-up against the University of Tennessee before a battle with Kentucky two days later. McCarthy's troops had won nine straight and were still undefeated in conference play.[18] While the Maroons' unexpected, yet successful trek through the conference was gaining attention from multiple corners of the Magnolia State, a number of sports reporters wrote off the Starkville team's hopes for an NCAA berth, citing the unwritten law as evidence of the conference's second-place finisher as the SEC's tournament representative. David M. Moffit of UPI identified the 14–2 Vanderbilt University squad as the only team with a chance to catch MSU and the conference's likely NCAA representative, citing the same "segregation feelings" that prevented the Maroons' participation in 1959.[19] Moffit would later tab the Wildcats, who were at 10–7, as a contender to the NCAA berth without referencing State's place atop the SEC standings.[20] Similarly, the Associated Press's Vernon Butler called the Maroons the conference favorite, but due to "the state's position on racial matters," the team was unlikely to play in the integrated postseason.[21] Another AP sports reporter, Ed Tunstall, profiled McCarthy and, while discussing the thirty-seven-year-old's coaching success in Starkville and the chances of an NCAA tournament berth, the writer quickly told his audience, "There aren't any," which appeared in the *Clarion-Ledger* on February 9, 1961, under the bold-face heading "NO CHANCE," clearly expressing an opinion on behalf of the Hederman-owned newspaper. Don Weiss of the AP also painted a grim picture for the Maroon faithful, proclaiming that the team would not play in the postseason tournament well before a decision had been rendered.[22]

The Maroons would go on to defeat the Volunteers 72–67 for their tenth victory in a row in preparation for its showdown with Kentucky. Robert "Steamboat" Fulton of the *Clarion-Ledger* wrote on February 12, 1961, that the Maroons "strided within smelling distance of their second SEC title in three years" with the victory. McCarthy's team had a 39–28 halftime lead thanks to the physical play of the Volunteers, who sent Graves to the charity stripe for eleven points, Mitchell for ten, and sophomore Joe Dan Gold for eight before the intermission. MSU had a fifteen–point lead at one point during the contest before McCarthy emptied his bench. Mitchell, Gold, and Stroud each finished with seventeen points against the Volunteers.[23] After the win, most writers focused on the Maroons' contest against the Wildcats but continued to identify other teams as positional representatives for the NCAA tournament. In previewing the week ahead in the SEC, an anonymous Associated Press reporter wrote in the February 13, 1961, edition of the *Clarion-Ledger* that the Commodores, not the Maroons, were looking for an NCAA bid and failed to explain State's inability to play on the national stage despite identifying the team as the SEC leader. Fulton's pregame work for the *Ledger* took a similar approach, making no mention of the NCAA tournament for either State or Kentucky.[24] In Scotty Hargrove's account for the *Starkville Daily News*, MSU was identified as "being within striking distance of its second Southeastern Conference title in two years," but NCAA tournament prospects for either team went ignored. Hargrove described the contest with Kentucky as a grudge match of sorts between McCarthy and Rupp, who took issue with the fans' use of cowbells and MSU's strength of schedule, to which the Kentucky leader said, "We can't go around playing a bunch of patsies like Mississippi State does."[25] Bobby Lollar's article for the *Commercial Dispatch* also overlooked any championship or postseason hopes for either team and served, more or less, as an ode to Kentucky's Adolph Rupp, who Lollar called "The Man who built basketball in the South" before he referenced "The Barron's" various accolades and awards.[26]

James "Babe" McCarthy, center, with Baily Howell, left, and Jerry Keeton, right, brought Mississippi State to the forefront of college basketball in the South during the Civil Rights era. The winner of four Southeastern Conference Championships from 1959 through 1963, McCarthy was a advocate of State's possible ventures into integrated athletics if, for no other reason, to win a national championship. *Courtesy Mississippi State University Libraries, University Archives.*

Other media accounts of the upcoming battle with the Wildcats, such as those from the Associated Press, failed to mention the NCAA tournament.[27]

The Maroons suffered a setback on their road to conference dominance when they lost to the Wildcats 68–62 in Starkville on February 13, 1961. The first half of the game was closely contested, with Kentucky taking a 33–31 lead after the Wildcats' Larry Pursiful hit two free throws. State began the second half cold as Rupp's charges sped out to a 54–46 lead with 7:45 to play. State closed it to 64–62 with two free throws from Graves with six seconds left, but Pursiful hit two more free throws to close the scoring for both teams. An unknown AP reporter likened the Maroons' loss to the Wildcats to "a jaded star stealing the scene from the leading character," while *Jackson Daily News* sports editor Lee Baker wrote on February 14, 1961, that Kentucky smashed MSU's "myth of invincibility." In the aftermath of the Maroons' defeat, Butler wrote that Kentucky had a viable shot at the NCAA tournament because, "Mississippi State, the likely SEC winner, won't participate in the postseason competition because of the state's racial feelings."[28] Graves led the State with twenty-seven points in the senior's last home contest and the team's first 1960–1961 SEC loss.[29] The Maroons still seemed to have a firm grip on the top spot in the SEC. While the Maroons fell to 8–1 in the conference, there was a three-way tie for second place between Vanderbilt, Florida, and LSU, all of which had three conference losses.[30]

MSU's attention then turned to the final five games, all on the road, against Florida, Georgia, LSU, Tulane, and Ole Miss. Sports writer Jack Wardlaw of the *Meridian Star* wrote that Kentucky "was still in the race for a NCAA tourney berth, since State will not enter the meet in any case."[31] In similar fashion, both the Associated Press and UPI called MSU the likely winner of the conference but cited the unwritten law as the team's primary NCAA roadblock.[32]

As the Maroons marched towards another conference championship and a possible NCAA debate, McCarthy was rewarded on February 15, 1961, with a new four-year contract and a pay raise from the State College Board, just as he had been two years earlier.[33] The *Jackson State Times'* McDowell wrote that the extension was "a token of appreciation for the wonderful job he has done at Mississippi State in making the Maroons a national major basketball power."[34] McDowell later noted MSU's first place status in the SEC but referred to Florida, Vanderbilt, and LSU as challengers to the conference NCAA tournament bid.[35] The news of McCarthy's new deal overshadowed the Maroons upcoming contest against second-place Florida. As UPI's Moffit reported, the Gators hoped for a second-place finish and a bid to the NCAA tournament because they held little chance of catching and overtaking the Maroons. The UPI sports reporter claimed that State was "prohibited by an unwritten law from playing in tournaments which include Negro players and this would keep the Maroons out of the NCAA playoffs as it did in 1959."[36] Moffit continued to stress the existence of the unwritten law and the probability that the Maroons would skip the NCAA tournament in his article on MSU's February 20, 1961, contest against the University of Georgia and in his preview of the Maroons' title-clinching win over Tulane.[37]

In other previews of the Florida contest penned by anonymous authors, the NCAA tournament or State's chances for tournament play were not discussed.[38] However, per the February 18, 1961, editions of the *Daily News* and the *Daily Herald*, Butler noted that Florida, LSU, Vanderbilt, and Kentucky had a chance at the NCAA tournament as MSU "won't represent the conference in tournament activity because the state has an unofficial policy against competing with teams having Negro players."[39] Much like his UPI counterpart Moffit, Butler often stressed the likelihood that MSU would be kept out of the NCAA tournament due to the unwritten law.[40]

As for the game, a desperation shot from Florida center Cliff Luyk with four seconds left in the contest handed the Maroons their second conference defeat 59–57 on February 18, 1961.[41] The win gave the Gators a 7–3 conference record, keeping Florida in the running for the conference's NCAA tournament bid because of the unwritten law. Soon after the loss, the Associated Press reported that Mississippi State had fallen out of favor as the potential champion of SEC play because of its two-game losing streak.[42] The *Jackson Daily News'* Bob Howie reiterated that point in a cartoon for the February 20, 1961, issue. Howie's work, titled "Athens Cliff Hanger," depicted a State basketball player hanging on to a cliff as a Georgia Bulldog stood over him with a piece of the player's shorts in its mouth.[43] In previewing the Maroons' next contest against the aforementioned Bulldogs, the *Clarion-Ledger's* Scotty Hargrove ended his article by assuming MSU's absence from the postseason was a foregone conclusion. "All eyes in the conference are on the Maroons, for if they should come out on top, the second place team gains the right to represent the SEC in the NCAA tournament as State would probably turn the bid down because of the racial situation."[44]

The Maroons snapped their two-game losing streak, as they beat Georgia 99–77 behind Graves's thirty-four points. State moved to 9–2 in the conference and 17–5 overall, still ahead of Florida by one game. Regardless of the victory, MSU was never mentioned in most media accounts of the game as a viable NCAA contender and only one writer, Hugh Fullerton Jr., of the Associated Press, acknowledged MSU's potential abstention from the national championship tournament.[45]

The following day, Kentucky defeated Vanderbilt 60–59 on center Ned Jennings's basket with twelve seconds left in regulation to give Rupp's charges "a chance for the Southeastern Conference berth in the NCAA tournament."[46] Kentucky was 7–4 in the conference, but the Wildcats had a head-to-head edge over the Commodores, who were also 7–4 in conference play behind the 8–3 Gators. In UPI accounts of the game, MSU was not mentioned as a potential NCAA participant or SEC champion. A February 23, 1961, AP article by Ross M. Hagen claimed that Kentucky stood the best chance of representing the SEC in postseason play because "the Maroons have barred themselves from NCAA tournaments because of their refusal to compete with Negroes."[47] Martin Lander of UPI made a similar statement, writing, "Although Mississippi State is expected to win the Southeastern Conference title and an automatic bid to the NCAA, it is believed the Maroons will pass up the invitation because of segregation problems."[48]

Following the victory over Georgia, the Maroons were faced with the task of going to the Bayou and playing both Louisiana State and Tulane. In an article published by multiple Mississippi newspapers, including the *Clarion-Ledger*, the *Jackson Daily News*, and the *Daily Herald*, an anonymous author looked towards the February 24 contest between MSU and LSU with only a nod to the team's chances of winning the SEC.[49] No mention of the NCAA tournament was made.

Despite trailing for the majority of the game, MSU would go on to beat LSU 56–54 on February 25th behind a Mitchell jump shot with three seconds left, securing a share of the conference championship for the Maroons.[50] MSU moved to 10–2 in the SEC, yet it was still assumed by many journalists, including Hugh Schutte of the Associated Press, that MSU would not "participate in the NCAA's racially integrated tournament."[51] Fellow AP sports scribe Butler wrote that, while the Maroons had won a share of the title, the conference representative to the NCAA tournament was still in question.[52] While the presentation of Butler's work in the *Starkville Daily News* may have supplied some false hope to the MSU faithful, utilizing a subhead that read, "NCAA Entry for Group Undecided," Butler claimed that the Maroons "won't take part in postseason doings because the tournaments are integrated."[53] While a UPI account of the MSU-LSU contest never mentioned the NCAA tournament and only referenced the SEC title, an article on Vanderbilt's victory over Florida from the wire service called the Commodores the likely recipient of an NCAA tournament invitation because MSU was "unwilling" to play integrated foes.[54] Despite Fulton's claims to an MSU championship, the NCAA tournament was never mentioned in his account of the victory over LSU.[55]

The Maroons were two games ahead of the second place Wildcats and Commodores with two games left to play, beginning with their late February contest in New Orleans against Tulane. A win would lock up the SEC title for MSU, yet it was clear from the perspective of journalists, McCarthy's squad would go no further than the SEC crown. On February 27, 1961, the Maroons defeated Tulane 62–57 to win the SEC title. Fulton called the team "a gutty, courageous bunch" who overcame a twelve-point deficit to defeat the Green Wave, yet the Jackson-based sports writer failed to reference the NCAA tournament.[56] The *Clarion-Ledger* also included a brief sidebar to Fulton's work that indicated segregationist Governor Ross Barnett wired the team a telegram to congratulate it on its conference title. Rather than explain Barnett's views on an NCAA bid, the article irrelevantly focused on the governor's love for basketball, explaining that Barnett "was a pretty fancy basketball player in his college days, with a mean hook shot."[57]

The *Jackson State Times* published an article from an anonymous UPI reporter that claimed the Maroons would skip the NCAA tournament "because of a ban on racially-mixed games."[58] Other accounts from UPI took a similar route, conceding the NCAA tournament berth to the conference's second-place team as MSU was barred due to "the state policy against playing teams with Negro players."[59] Phil Wallace of the *Jackson Daily News* penned two articles on the Maroons' conference championship after the win over the Green Wave but neither referenced the NCAA tournament.[60] The same could be said for an article in the *Starkville Daily News* by an anonymous author.[61] Butler reported that, because of Florida's 52–50 loss to Georgia Tech, Kentucky and Vanderbilt would participate in a playoff game to determine the conference's representative to the NCAA tournament because "Mississippi State won't go to the NCAA meet at Louisville next month because the tournament is racially integrated."[62] Similar material could be found in an article from UPI journalist Gary Kale indicating that Kentucky "may sneak into a postseason playoff berth" because of the unwritten law.[63] Despite MSU's SEC championship win, UPI did not consider the Maroons one of the top twenty-seven teams in the nation as the team was absent from the wire service's weekly coaches poll.[64] SEC runners-up Kentucky and Vanderbilt came in at seventeen and eighteen, respectively.

Although a majority of journalists wrote as if the rejection of an NCAA bid on behalf of MSU was a foregone conclusion, UPI's Berry Reese reported that Barnett was opposed to playing in the NCAA tournament if it meant violating the unwritten law.[65] Barnett told Reese that racially integrated athletics could lead to social integration in the Magnolia State. "If there were half a dozen Negroes on the team, where are they going to eat? Are they going to go to the dance later and want to dance with our girls," Barnett explained.[66] McCarthy also chimed in, telling UPI, that he and his team had "no hopes of playing for a national title." Reese also quoted star Maroons Graves, Stroud, and Mitchell, who said they thought they would not go. "I don't find anything wrong with [Negroes]. I played baseball and basketball with them in Texas. But if I thought it would encourage them to want to come to our school, I wouldn't want to go," Mitchell told the UPI reporter. The last paragraph of the article explained that there was no law prohibiting state teams from competing in integrated contests, "But it was agreed in 1955 that they would not after Jones Junior College touched off disapproval among segregation leaders by playing an integrated football team in the Junior Rose Bowl."[67] Of all the newspapers examined, only the *Jackson State Times* published the article on the front page of its newspaper on March 1, 1961. The *State Times* also published the UPI article with a letter from MSU student G. J. Pope, who requested that Barnett use his executive powers to allow the Maroons to participate and, ultimately, win the NCAA tournament in an effort to physically demonstrate the dominant nature of the Closed Society for the rest of the nation. "The time has come for Mississippi to show the nation by action—rather than words—that we are indeed superior: that we are second to none: and that we are willing and able to prove this superiority. During these days, when Mississippi is being assaulted from all corners, and accused of isolationism, I urge you to encourage the Maroons to win this honor for the great sovereign state of Mississippi," the student wrote.[68] While the placement of the Barnett article and the publishing of Pope's letter seemed like a socially progressive decision by the Jackson-based newspaper, Pope's letter was a plea for Barnett to show the rest of the nation that Mississippi's belief in states' rights and the Closed Society was correct. What better way to demonstrate the effectiveness of a caste system that placed blacks in a subservient position to whites than to have an all-white basketball team enter an integrated tournament and win the national championship? The work of the *Jackson State Times* was advanced from an equality standpoint versus other newspapers in the state; however, the publication of Pope's letter was a contradiction of sorts for the primary competitor to the Hederman's Jackson-based journalistic monopoly.

The *Jackson Daily News*, the *Starkville Daily News*, and the *Commercial Dispatch* reported that over four thousand students greeted the Maroons upon the team's return to Starkville.[69] However, none of the articles made any mention of the NCAA tournament. Previews for the MSU-Ole Miss contest overlooked any NCAA tournament talk and, for the most part, focused more on Ole Miss as the Maroons had already clinched the SEC championship.[70] The *Jackson Daily News* featured two previews of the final contest, one from each school's perspective. Although the Maroons' status as conference champions was prominent in the MSU-based article, neither account mentioned the NCAA tournament.[71] The same could be said for previews that appeared in the *Clarion-Ledger*, the *Jackson State Times*, the *Commercial Dispatch*, the *Starkville Daily News*, and the *Daily Herald*.[72] An anonymous account from the Associated Press that previewed the entire slate of SEC contests for March 3, 1961, focused more on the open NCAA tournament spot, which could have been won by Kentucky, Vanderbilt, or Florida. MSU was identified as the conference champion, but the school had "rejected a chance to play for national honors due to its policy of not competing against Negroes."[73] On the same day, John Garcia of UPI reported that McCarthy was named SEC Coach of the Year by the wire service. While the majority of Garcia's article discussed McCarthy's accomplishments during the season, the UPI reporter noted, "The state's 'unwritten law' regarding segregation will keep the Maroons out of the NCAA playoffs this year and probably for years to come."[74] McCarthy, in response to the NCAA tournament, told Garcia, "We've accepted it and that's it. The less said the better."[75]

The Maroons would lose to Ole Miss in the season finale 74–70.[76] Baker described the contest in a March 5, 1961, article in the *Jackson Daily News* as "an ambush."[77] The Rebels' Jack Walters scored twenty-two points and helped orchestrate a 37–22 lead at halftime. The Maroons, who were led by Graves's twenty-two points, mounted a furious comeback in the second half, cutting the lead to 72–70 with just twenty-four seconds left. Reserve Maroons guard George Oakley's shot with seconds left drew iron, and the Rebels closed out the scoring on a lay-up by Sterling Ainsworth, which pushed the final count to 74–70.[78] Both Kentucky and Vanderbilt won their respective games and would have to face each other in a playoff game for the right to appear in the NCAA tournament.[79]

The Maroons finished their championship season with an 11–3 record in the SEC, 19–6 overall, and a glaring absence in the NCAA tournament. In the season's aftermath, Garcia of UPI wrote that State could be on its way to replacing Rupp's Wildcats as the predominate basketball power in the SEC due to the team's two conference titles in three seasons.[80] While writing of MSU's potential conference dominance, the UPI scribe failed to reference the Maroons' inability to play for the NCAA championship. Kentucky would go on to defeat Vanderbilt 88–67 in a playoff game to determine the conference's NCAA tournament representative, which was eventually won by the University of Cincinnati.[81]

While the Closed Society dealt with State's challenge of the unwritten law, what was lacking from the press during the 1960–1961 season as opposed to the 1958–1959 slate was the *Jackson Daily News'* Jimmy Ward and his strident protection of the Closed Society. While Ward's commentary was prominently featured in MSU's first conference championship season for his furious defense of the unwritten law, Mississippi's most notorious journalist chose to sit on the sidelines during the 1961 debate. No issue of the *Jackson Daily News* examined from February 8, 1961, through March 3, 1961, featured Ward's comments on the threat of integrated athletics, placing the segregationist with his journalistic brethren who simply assumed that the Maroons would bow to the unwritten law. While there is no known record of the Sovereignty Commission or the Citizens' Council explicitly asking Ward or any other editor to ignore MSU's chances at an NCAA bid in 1961, Robert "Tut" Patterson of the Citizens' Council did send Ward a letter commending him on the lack of coverage on a 1962 visit from Martin Luther King Jr. to Mississippi. Patterson told Ward he thought "the silent treatment" was an effective strategic move to counter the work of civil rights activists.[82] Ward's derogatory commentary aside, his absence meant that some of the passion and debate from February 1959 was missing. Furthermore, notable journalists from Mississippi's past, including the *Delta Democrat-Times'* Hodding Carter, *Clarion-Ledger's* Tom Ethridge, the *Hattiesburg American's* Andrew Harmon and Fitz McCoy, *Meridian Star* editor James B. Skewes, *Natchez Democrat* editor James Lambert, and sports editor Charles B. Gordon of the *Enterprise-Journal*, all of whom commented on the Maroons' postseason hopes in 1959, failed to supply any commentary during the debate that engulfed the end of the 1960–1961 season.[83] The lack of editorial work from the news desk indicated that most of Mississippi's prominent editors and, with the exception of Carter, strident defenders of the Closed Society and the unwritten law no long saw the Maroons as a legitimate threat to their way of life. Additionally, unlike the 1959 debate, public opinion in the form of letters to the editor was, for the most part, absent in 1961. Because of the sheer numbers of letters and correspondence sent to newspapers during the 1959 and 1963 seasons, it was possible that these newspapers received letters, but the editors simply chose not to publish them.

Despite the absence of some of the Magnolia State's more historically prominent journalists, a few editors and reporters, including Billy Ray of the *Vicksburg Evening Post*, the *Jackson Daily News*' Lee Baker and the *Clarion-Ledger*'s Carl Walters, would again roll up their sleeves and dive into the debate surrounding integrated athletics. However, no journalists, sports or otherwise, stood out like "Mississippi Red."

While Hodding Carter of the *Delta Democrat-Times* and J. Oliver Emmerich of the *Enterprise-Journal* have received praise for their brave stands against the Closed Society, and rightfully so, one reporter who has yet to receive such recognition is Jimmie McDowell. McDowell wrote with a fiery mix of truth and passion that was indicative of the red hair that became his trademark. While McDowell was never an open advocate of integration, the Mississippi Sports Hall of Famer's work was never the less impactful. A native of Brookhaven and a graduate of the University of Mississippi, McDowell's media-based career took him through Hattiesburg as the director of public relations and athletic publicity at Mississippi Southern College from 1951 through 1955 before he would move to the Hederman-owned *Jackson Daily News* where he worked under Frederick Sullens. After a year, McDowell moved to the rival *Jackson State Times* as the paper's sports editor. At every turn during the debates surrounding the unwritten law and Mississippi's abstention from integrated competition, McDowell served as opposition. In his mind, the fields of competition should have been free and clear of the political and social issues of the day. By his own admission, McDowell felt that any debate surrounding Mississippi's potential participation in mixed competition should have excluded any conversation about integration. McDowell proved to be, not only one of the more outspoken sports writers in the Magnolia State, but one of the more socially progressive journalists in Mississippi as he served as the primary voice of opposition against the unwritten law.

McDowell's initial commentary during the 1961 debate began in a mundane manner, focusing solely on the surprising exploits of Mississippi State and McCarthy's sophomore-laden lineup. While the charismatic McDowell discussed the Maroons' successful season in multiple editions of his daily column, the spoils of the NCAA tournament and the SEC championship were never mentioned.[84] However, after the team's early February victory over Tulane, "Mississippi Red" was quick to advocate an NCAA appearance for the Maroons in the February 7, 1961, edition of his self-titled column. McDowell argued that, if MSU were to win the conference championship, it was simply time for teams in the Magnolia State to have a chance to prove themselves on the national level. "Mississippi should not cut off its nose to spite its face when the national scene is involved," McDowell wrote. "Let's not build a brick wall around Mississippi."

Despite McDowell's early advocacy for State's participation in the integrated postseason, the *State Times* sports editor quickly shifted his attention to the Maroons' trek through the SEC gambit. With the same fire that he addressed state politicians and the State College Board in 1959, McDowell mocked Rupp and his comments from the 1960 season when he referred to MSU as a "Cow College."[85] In a more serious tone, McDowell stressed McCarthy's respect for the coaching legend and would later detail a conversation he had with Rupp going into the Maroons' early February battle with the Wildcats. The colorful and, at times, perturbed Rupp told McDowell that MSU was "not invincible" and, referring to Kentucky's thirty-one-point victory over the Maroons in 1960, Rupp said, "We could have really poured it on but we really didn't want to embarrass Babe."[86] After Kentucky's victory, McDowell addressed the issue of an NCAA tournament bid with the Kentucky legend in the February 14, 1961, edition of his column, to which Rupp replied, "The conference should be represented by the best team. If you're not going to participate in the conference's championship playoffs, you ought to get out of the league." While McDowell did not explicitly express an opinion on the merits of MSU's possible inclusion in the postseason tournament, his publication of Rupp's commentary inferred a common ideological ground between the *State Times* sports editor and the Kentucky coaching legend.

After Luyk's last second basket in Gainesville gave his Florida Gators the final second win over the Maroons, McDowell wrote on February 20, 1961, that the team had to refocus for its upcoming game against the University of Georgia. While McDowell called MSU the front-runner to take home the SEC crown, he said its hold on the top spot was shaky at best. In terms of the NCAA tournament, McDowell looked at Rupp's Kentucky team as the likely selection, despite his written support for the Starkville contingent. "Baron Rupp may have the hole hard and may yet wind up as the SEC's representative in the NCAA tournament in Louisville," he wrote.

After the Maroons clinched at least a tie for the conference title with their victory over LSU, McDowell wrote on February 22nd that there was still life in a national championship opportunity for MSU. The Jackson-based sports editor said that MSU's SEC peers should hope that the Starkville contingent would be "denied permission to compete in the District NCAA duel in Louisville, throwing the national invitation wide open." While McDowell's belief in integrated athletic competition was clear, his presentation of said belief during the 1961 campaign was, at times, confusing. On multiple occasions, he implied that an NCAA bid was out of reach for MSU because of the unwritten law, yet he proudly claimed that the Maroons should be allowed to play in the integrated postseason tournament. While there is was no doubt the trailblazing McDowell objected to the gentleman's agreement, it is not clear if he ever viewed a chance for MSU to win the national championships as feasible.

Despite the mixed signals of McDowell's earlier musings, there was no denying where he stood on an NCAA tournament berth after the Maroons claimed the SEC championship. Citing the work of *Atlanta Journal* sports editor Furman Bisher, who wrote that despite winning the SEC title, the team had done little to advance basketball in the South because of "tradition, custom, prejudice, politics and other such factors," McDowell agreed in his March 2, 1961, column and argued that the Maroons had earned a chance at the national crown. "If ever a Cinderella team, a never-say-die group of basketball players deserved a shot to bring the national championship to Mississippi, the 1961 Maroon hoop unit is such a team," he wrote. Furthermore, in an attempt to relate to Mississippi's segregationist governor, McDowell compared the Maroons' quest for a national title to Barnett's failed attempt to secure a presidential nomination from the Democratic Party at the integrated Democratic National Convention in Los Angeles in 1960. According to McDowell, both efforts were done to garner positive publicity and attention to the Magnolia State. Despite his logical argument, the fiery McDowell seemed almost offended at Barnett's objections to MSU's participation in the racially integrated tournament and the line of commentary offered to the press by the segregationist governor. "Barnett clouds the issue by saying 'If integrated teams played in Mississippi where would they eat? Are they going to dance later and want to dance with our girls?' Mississippi State's basketball team isn't interested in going to a dance. They're not interested in playing footsie with anyone. They're interested in whipping the daylights out of any opponent they play, that's all." McDowell's comments not only diffused the governor's objections to integrated competition but did so logically, making Barnett look foolish. While it was clear that McDowell supported a MSU berth in the NCAA tournament, the justification for such support was not necessarily expressed in his writing. In a 2010 interview, "Mississippi Red" said he thought sports should have been treated separately from politics. Additionally, unlike his sports writing brethren in Vicksburg, Biloxi, and Meridian, McDowell never felt the need to offer a definitive stance on segregation. In his mind, the merits of the unwritten law had little to do with debate.

McDowell's last editorial commentary on March 6, 1961, on the 1961 MSU team came in the aftermath of the team's upset loss to Ole Miss. While McDowell used the bulk of his daily column to focus on the effort of Bonnie "Country" Graham's Ole Miss team, the opinionated McDowell attributed the Maroons' defeat to human emotion. "The Maroons had the championship won, which Babe McCarthy admitted earlier in the week was probably a blessing in view of the upcoming invasion in Oxford," McDowell wrote. "The champions also had been denied the right to represent the SEC in national regional competition in Louisville. Any group of American-born champions couldn't help but be disappointed at not getting the opportunity to try and win the national title."

McDowell left Mississippi abruptly in January 1962 after the *State Times* was purchased and closed by the Hederman family. "I didn't even get a final column," McDowell quipped in a joking manner.[87] The need for a job took the legendary sports scribe to the *Trenton Times* as the paper's sports editor. Despite his exit from the state, "Mississippi Red" was still honored as Mississippi's Sportswriter of the Year in 1962. McDowell would return to the South in 1964 as sports editor of the *Memphis Commercial Appeal*. From 1964 until 1991, McDowell worked as director of public relations for the National Football Foundation and Hall of Fame. A southeastern representative of the Heisman Trophy Trust, McDowell was inducted into the Mississippi Sports Hall of Fame in 1999.

As for McDowell's impact on the sports writing community in Mississippi, a number of the editors in the state would go on and write complimentary columns on "Mississippi Red," despite their differences of opinion. McDowell's counterpart at the *Vicksburg Evening Post*, Billy Ray, congratulated the former *State Times* sports editor as the recipient of the 1962 Mississippi Sportswriter of the Year by the National Sportscaster and Sportswriting Award Committee.[88] Charles B. Gordon of the McComb-based *Enterprise-Journal* went further, admitting in the following passage of his "Sports Journal" column on March 20, 1962, that he missed the work of "Mississippi Red" despite their philosophical differences of opinion. "In the case of McDowell, I liked the fact he worked hard at his trade and turned out a lot of stuff—the bigger part of it eminently readable and correct. There is simply nothing else in Mississippi that gives or even pretends to give, the kind of scope of the information McDowell dished out day after day."

Although McDowell's work in 1961 was not as consistent in terms of disdain for the unwritten law, overall, his work was just as defiant and thought-provoking as his previous efforts discussed in Chapter 2. His opinion on the unwritten law not withstanding, McDowell said he would not categorize his writing as liberal. Furthermore, his years of defiance in the face of the Closed Society never subjected the former Navy veteran to any of the scare tactics employed by organizations such as the Citizens' Council. "If they disagreed or were unhappy with my opinion, no one ever said anything to me," McDowell said in an August 12, 2010 interview. "I was never pressured or influenced to writing anything or change my opinion on an issue. [And] I really didn't think about it. I figure if I could handle the Navy, then I could deal with just about anything." While McDowell's support for the MSU cause might have been for the betterment of athletics and in turn the social climate of Mississippi, Kurt Kemper writes in his examination of the 1962 Rose Bowl that "few white southerners actively called for integrated sporting events and publically professed a desire to participate along blacks just as few claims they wanted their children to attend integrated schools. But to actively suppress integrated play often meant the loss of sporting opportunities for both spectators and participants. . . . To do so demanded that southerners deny themselves the cultural satisfaction and validation that sporting contests often provided."[89] Due to the cultural validation that comes with sporting events, or the lack there of in Mississippi, McDowell may have simply tired of watching others validate individual community values through their success on the playing field. Regardless, this explanation should not diminish the original, inquisitive, and brave commentary supplied by "Mississippi Red." McDowell objected to the premise of the unwritten law, and his support of integrated athletics for the sake of competition was as progressive in terms of human and social rights as any other reporter in Mississippi. McDowell's frequent challenges of the unwritten law and, in turn, the Closed Society, should place "Mississippi Red" in the state's annals as one of the more progressive journalists of the civil rights era.

While McDowell led the way in opinion-based commentary supporting the 1961 Maroons and a possible appearance in the NCAA tournament, his sports writing brethren took a more conservative route and, in total, lacked the definitive expressions of opinion that was featured in their 1959 efforts. Biloxi-based *Daily Herald* sports editor Dick Lightsey, who was an outspoken critic of the unwritten law in 1959, took a step back in 1961, maintaining a degree of silence when it came to whispers of a postseason appearance for the Maroons and, when he did express support for McCarthy's squad, did so well after a decision had been rendered. While Lightsey referred to the Maroons as the favorites for the SEC championship and detailed subsequent wins over conference foes, his first reference to the NCAA tournament came when he conceded the national berth to the conference's second place team, citing the unwritten law as justification.[90] He would later call MSU's potential absence from the national tournament "a shame" but offered no argument in defense of the Maroons. Lightsey, who stressed his status as a segregationist in 1959, seemed to take a passive approach to the NCAA tournament issue, a stark contrast to his previous columns, which advocated a tournament berth for the Maroons. Rather, Lightsey had already dismissed any chances of a Mississippi-based national basketball championship. After conceding the tournament bid to the SEC's second place team, Kentucky, Lightsey focused his opinion-based work on State's hopes for the conference championship. Going into the team's matchup with the Wildcats, Lightsey predicted a victory for McCarthy's charges and again christened the Maroons as the "odds-on choice to win the SEC crown" but never referenced the NCAA tournament.[91] The same could be said for his work after the Maroons' 68–62 loss to Kentucky and in the aftermath of State's last second defeat at the hand of the University of Florida.[92] Lightsey continued to neglect postseason hopes for the Maroons and anointed the second-place University of Kentucky, the conference's NCAA tournament representative, writing that "[Kentucky] has a good chance of representing the loop in the NCAA playoffs—even if State should win the crown."[93] Lightsey later addressed McCarthy's contract extension, claiming it was well deserved but, even when discussing MSU's 1958–1959 and 1960–1961 seasons, no reference to the NCAA tournament was made.[94] During the 1958–1959 campaign, sports writers in Mississippi wondered in unison if McCarthy would look to leave Starkville because the school would refuse an NCAA tournament bid, denying the competitive MSU coach a chance to prove his worth on a national stage. While McCarthy eventually was given a new contract that season, the absence of any such commentary a mere two seasons later was perplexing.

Fresh off the Maroons' title-clinching victory over Tulane, Lightsey made an interesting journalistic decision in his "Bunts, Boots and Bounces" column. Rather than discuss the obvious topic, MSU's SEC title, Lightsey began his column by focusing on MSU's chief basketball rival Kentucky and hailed the Wildcats, as the team was a victory away from an NCAA tournament berth.[95] While he later complimented McCarthy's sophomore-laden squad, Lightsey's writing lacked the resolve he displayed just two years earlier when he advocated an NCAA appearance by the Maroons for the sake of a national championship for Mississippi. While he hailed the efforts of MSU, Lightsey put the emphasis on Kentucky and its efforts to lock up the NCAA bid, never once acknowledging that the Maroons, as the SEC champion, were a worthy and just selection. The same could be said for Lightsey's March 2, 1961, work going into the season finale against Ole Miss. While Lightsey again praised the title-winning campaign for the Starkville contingent and noted the dominance of Mississippi's SEC members in football, basketball, and baseball, he made no reference or comment towards an NCAA appearance for MSU. Rather, he wrote that the "grudge match" against Ole Miss was no longer under the "must-win category" due to MSU's title-clinching victory days earlier.

Only after editor J. Oliver Emmerich of the McComb-based *Enterprise-Journal* voiced his support for Mississippi State's participation in the NCAA tournament did Lightsey address the matter in the *Daily Herald*. On March 9, 1961, Lightsey published verbatim Emmerich's column, who wrote that there would be nothing wrong with the MSU contingent playing against integrated teams out of state. "There is a strong force of public opinion in Mississippi that we should insist that others respect our own internal affairs but that we cannot attempt to change the concepts, of people, in other states," Emmerich wrote. "These Mississippians feel that the proposition of integration in Mississippi has nothing whatsoever to do with the way people in other states handle their athletic events." Not surprisingly, considering his editorial approach during the 1961 MSU debate, Lightsey revisited his argument from 1959 and supported a national title run for the Maroons. "Although State's current basketball team may not be great, we feel it has the right—and should be allowed—to take part in the national tournament," Lightsey wrote. "A couple of years ago when Bailey Howell led the Maroons to their greatest season it was a shame the team had to stay home. That team, we felt, would have won the national title. And this year's addition could probably make quite a good showing."

At the conclusion of the NCAA tournament, which was won by the University of Cincinnati, Lightsey would lament for the Maroons' lost opportunity at national prominence. "It's a shame that Mississippi State, as champions of the SEC, did not get a chance to participate in the NCAA event," he wrote in the March 27, 1961, edition of the *Daily Herald*. "The Maroons had a sound ball club." While Lightsey's commentary seemed progressive, his timing and relative silence in comparison to his work only two years earlier emphatically said otherwise. In both 1959 and 1961, Lightsey's work came on the heels of another journalist in the Magnolia State taking a stand. In 1959, it was Jimmie McDowell, and in 1961, it was J. Oliver Emmerich. In 1961, while any progressive voice or commentary in the Closed Society was a rarity, Lightsey's support of an NCAA tournament berth came well after any decision could be made, negating its potential significance.

Another vocal supporter of a Maroon 1959 tournament appearance was Billy Ray, sports editor of the *Vicksburg Evening Post*. Like Lightsey, Ray's commentary in his daily column, "Press Box Views," was tempered to some extent from 1959. While there were opportunities to argue for MSU's place in the integrated postseason, Ray followed many of his colleagues, focusing only on the conference championship for the Maroons.[96] Ray did not address the NCAA tournament until after the Maroons' defeat at the hands of Rupp's Kentucky squad. Citing the unwritten law and the events of 1959, Ray argued on February 15, 1961, that, regardless of the regular season outcome, Mississippi State would not appear in the NCAA tournament because the "NCAA certainty does not prohibit the use of Negroes. . . . The next best thing is winning the SEC title and that's what the Maroons are going after." While his commentary may have been his most extensive on the unwritten law during the 1961 season, at no point did Ray advocate an NCAA appearance by MSU, a noticeable difference from his work in the 1959 season when he argued that the Maroons should have been allowed to play in the tournament. Ray's work painted an NCAA tournament berth as a nonexistent goal for the MSU team. Much like Lightsey, Ray also missed the opportunity to make a case for the Maroons, therefore making a supportive statement for the unwritten law.

Despite the lack of breadth in his commentary on the NCAA issue, Ray wrote with a sense of remorse for MSU's absence from the national championship tournament after the Maroons' title-clinching victory over Tulane. On March 1, 1961, Ray admitted that, in his opinion, the SEC champions were not the best team in the country and were inferior in comparison to the 1959 Mississippi State team. However, he still wondered how the Maroons would perform on a national stage. "It's too bad McCarthy won't be able to take his fine bunch of boys to the NCAA tournament, which they automatically won a bid to for winning the SEC, but are forced to stay home because of the 'unwritten law,'" he wrote. "We'd just like to see how this young bunch would fare with the real 'veterans.'" Ray also touched upon the impending battle for the SEC NCAA bid between Vanderbilt and Kentucky and, rather than advocating an Maroon entry into the tournament, simply acknowledged that MSU was not "allowed to play for national championships."[97]

Other sports writers and editors in the Magnolia State took a conservative approach to the 1961 Maroons and its chances for an NCAA tournament bid. Sports editor, Billy "Sunshine" Rainey of the *Meridian Star*, who in 1959 expressed a combination of wishful hope for the Maroons' participation in the postseason and his own expectations of the team's compliance with the gentleman's agreement, published only two columns on the Starkville contingent, and neither referenced the NCAA tournament as an opportunity for the SEC champions.[98] *Delta Democrat-Times* sports editor Charles Kerg also neglected to mention the NCAA merit of the Maroons in his daily "Kerg's Korner" column. Perhaps the only noteworthy commentary to come from the Greenville-based editor's opinion-based musings focused on Rupp and his derogatory commentary on the behavior of MSU's student body.[99] While Kerg may have made a valid point in illustrating the hypocrisy of Rupp's criticisms of MSU, a more pertinent news item would have been the NCAA chances of the Maroons. In Columbus, the *Commercial Dispatch* also published little editorial commentary on the Maroons and the plight of the 1960–1961 basketball campaign. Sports writer Herb Phillips in his daily, "'N in This Cornah!" column only referenced the postseason once in a discussion of McCarthy and his coaching prowess. Phillips wrote that MSU's head coach should have greater prominence in college basketball's coaching ranks but, due to the unwritten law, "State can never be 'Number One.'"[100] In Phillips's effort to praise McCarthy, the sports writer missed an opportunity to support a tournament bid for MSU and, in turn, a chance to denounce the unwritten law. While many in Mississippi's sports writing ranks addressed the merits of the 1961 Maroons, few spoke out in opposition of the unwritten law and advocated the team's place in the integrated postseason, assuring that the ideological borders of the Closed Society would stand firm.

While the venomous commentary of Ward was missing from the 1961 debate, the writers and editors of the Hederman-owned newspapers in Jackson did their best to protect the Closed Society by enforcing the unwritten law through omission. During the course of the Maroons' run to another SEC championship, the possibility of an NCAA title was rarely mentioned, negating any legitimacy to MSU's possible participation in integrated play and giving credence to the gentleman's agreement.

Clarion-Ledger columnist Carl Walters neglected to mention the integrated postseason for the majority of his editorial work during the Maroons' 1961 campaign. His early columns during MSU's run to the SEC championship ignored any chance at a postseason berth for the Starkville contingent.[101] However, going into the team's contest with Kentucky, the dean of Mississippi's sports journalists focused on Rupp's comments to *Sports Illustrated* concerning the current state of SEC play, to which Rupp told the magazine, "Hell, we could do well in the conference if we warmed up against a bunch of teacher's colleges. We can't go around playing a bunch of patsies like Mississippi State."[102] Walters then addressed Rupp's argument that many of the better teams in the South were using segregation as a way of avoiding tougher competition and, while he attempted to refute the coaching legend's commentary, supported Mississippi's segregated ideals. "On the off chance that Rupp was to include Mississippi State when he insinuated that some SEC schools are 'hiding behind segregation to keep from playing worthy opponents' we would simply remind him that no Mississippi team—because of 'established policy'—can compete against Negroes at home, away, or anywhere and [Rupp] is well aware of that fact," he wrote.[103] Walters went on to point out that the only reason Rupp's charges made it to the 1959 NCAA tournament was because MSU "COULDN'T enter it because of that previously mentioned established state policy against integrated athletic competition," and that Kentucky's 1961 hopes hinged on MSU winning the conference so the second-place Wildcats could take their place in the tournament.[104] Despite his pro-Maroon stance, Walters's depiction of the unwritten law as ironclad only reiterated the state's policy on segregated athletics and offered support to the Closed Society. In a later edition of his column "Shavin's," the veteran sports scribe confidently predicted an SEC title for the Maroons; however, any discussion of a national championship was reserved for the second place team. "We're not going to try to guess which one of the runner-up squads will be designated as the Dixie Dozen entry in the NCAA national championship tourney," Walters wrote, missing an opportunity to argue for the merits of MSU's place in the NCAA tournament, thus protecting the Closed Society from another public debate.[105] Walters would again skirt the issue, identifying Kentucky and Vanderbilt as the probable conference representatives in the NCAA tournament in multiple editions of his column.[106] Rather than seizing the moment to address MSU's place in the tournament or the unwritten law, Walters identified the 11–11 LSU Tigers as State's biggest upcoming obstacle. Walters's neglect of the issue was obvious, as he debated the national championship merits of the other conference members rather than the Maroons. After MSU captured the SEC title, Walters offered McCarthy and his team congratulations but, ever neglectful, Walters focused more attention on MSU's basketball future and the school's mascot switch from the Maroons to the Bulldogs than the team's hopes for an NCAA opportunity.[107] Towards the end of his column, Walters did discuss, in a brief fashion, MSU's tournament hopes, calling the team's absence unfortunate but the lack of a definitive opinion on the matter was obvious.[108] Based on his past commentary, both from 1959 and from 1961, Walters's words echoed a hollow tone. The segregationist and supporter of the Closed Society, at no time, voiced any sort of support for the Maroons and a national championship with his trend of journalistic condemnation and neglect. For Walters to call MSU's tournament absence "unfortunate" made the veteran journalist look hypocritical.

Fellow Hederman sports scribe, *Daily News* sports editor Lee Baker, followed the lead of Walters, writing multiple times on the MSU contingent and its trek to the SEC championship but failing to mention the possibilities of an NCAA tournament bid in his daily sports column, "Baker's Dozen." In fact, on a number of occasions, Baker proclaimed the Maroons as the best team in the conference but never addressed the possibilities of post-season play.[109] In the aftermath of the team's title clinching win over Tulane, Baker hailed the "Cinderella Maroons" for its unexpected conference success, but he never specifically mentioned the NCAA tournament. Making a vague reference to any postseason possibilities, Baker wrote on February 28, 1961, "While this presumably is just as far as the kids will go in 1961, there is reason for great pride and rejoicing throughout Mississippi that the Maroons were able to achieve such a pinnacle with a team so young." Despite ignoring the postseason possibilities for MSU, the Jackson-based sports editor took United Press International to task for the news service's ranking of the Maroons, who, despite the SEC win, were not ranked in the UPI top ten poll. Baker claimed that members of the UPI voting committee, including Rupp and Wells, were responsible for "downgrading the Maroons," thus leading to the team's exclusion from the rankings.[110] Baker went on to write that the SEC title "means a whole lot more than any national rating ever could anyway, particularly since it's performance, not prejudice, that earns it."[111] Baker ignored the obvious reason for State's less-than-stellar reputation outside of Mississippi: the team's refusal to play integrated foes and participate in the NCAA tournament.

Baker's neglectful commentary took a considerable change in the March 1, 1961, edition of "Baker's Dozen" when he dismissed any sentiment of an NCAA berth. "Mississippi State's biennial problem has cropped up again," Baker wrote in a dismissive tone, referring to the unwritten law and the allure of the NCAA tournament. Baker noted that either Kentucky or Vanderbilt would go to the tournament in State's place but added that neither school had "any respect or our way of life." Baker claimed that missing the tournament was nothing new for

MSU and attacked proponents of integrated competition, writing, "At least all of the troublemakers who think that all segregation barriers would not crumble if a Mississippi athletic team would participate against an outside opponent with Negroes, are decently quiet this time around."

Despite the racist connotation of his last name in the annals of Mississippi journalism, the opinions of *Clarion-Ledger* sports editor Arnold Hederman were somewhat mute during the Maroons' season. Like Walters and Baker, Hederman rarely referenced the NCAA tournament in his opinion-based work and never in relation to the efforts of Mississippi State, conceding the postseason berth to the conference's second place team.[112] Hederman would later write about the Magnolia State's emerging dominance in multiple sports on the SEC circuit but again ignored any chance of a Maroon appearance in the NCAA tournament.[113] Unlike Walters, Hederman refused to shed crocodile tears for McCarthy's club. While the *Ledger's* sports editor did congratulate the team for its conference championship, Hederman did not reference the NCAA tournament. Rather, he minimized the importance of the team's match-up with rival Ole Miss and predicted conference championship opportunities for the Maroons in the future.[114]

While his coverage of the Maroons filled the pages of both the *Clarion-Ledger* and the *Jackson Daily News*, Robert Fulton did not publish a column on the Starkville contingent until the March 1, 1961, issue of the *Clarion-Ledger*. While the sports writer recapped MSU's SEC title-winning campaign, Fulton also painted the Maroons as a miracle team of sorts because of the previous year's poor performance. Despite the presence of a new voice in the *Clarion-Ledger's* realm of athletic commentary, Fulton followed in the neglectful footsteps of his fellow Hederman sports scribes, never acknowledging the NCAA tournament or expressing an opinion on the matter. While offering little during the 1961 season, the journalist known as "Steamboat" would become a frequent contributor to the editorial debates surrounding Mississippi State and the NCAA tournament during the 1962 and 1963 campaigns.

Ben Lee Jr., the sports editor of the Hederman-owned *Hattiesburg American*, also followed suit, never expressing a clear opinion on the matter. Lee penned only one editorial on the Maroons during the examined period and, much like his peers, wrote about the team's upcoming banquet and McCarthy's laurels as SEC Coach of the Year.[115] He simply stated that the team had won the conference title and offered little commentary on the season at all, let alone anything resembling an opinion on an NCAA berth.

The sports writers of the Hederman empire were not alone in their failures to offer any definitive commentary on the Maroons and their chance to enter the NCAA tournament. While Bob Howie, a member of the state Citizens' Council and a segregationist, would use his artistic forum as the *Jackson Daily News'* cartoonist to express his opinions on MSU and its title-winning season, his work only advocated compliance by McCarthy's squad. Howie commented on the Maroons' success in a cartoon that depicted a smaller University of Kentucky player overshadowed by an MSU player, with the words "Current SEC Power" prominently displayed next to the Maroon.[116] Going into the contest with the Rebels, Howie used his editorial cartoon, "Hinny" to congratulate McCarthy for winning SEC Coach of the Year. In the cartoon, Hinny told readers that McCarthy's award meant little because "he don't face his biggest test until the game tonight," a point that was made by Howie's coworkers on the sports desk.[117] While the rivalry between the Maroons and the Rebels was the most heated in Mississippi college sports, the notion that in an SEC championship-wining season, the last place Rebels posed as MSU's biggest test was absurd. Contests that would have tested MSU's real worth awaited in the NCAA tournament, yet the editors of the *Jackson Daily News* and the *Clarion-Ledger* would have its audience believe that it was the in-state Rebels that could put a blight on the Maroons' season. If anything, Kentucky, not Ole Miss, proved to be MSU's biggest test. Howie, in a nod to MSU's refusal to play in the NCAA tournament, penned a final cartoon on the Maroons, depicting an MSU player wearing a crown labeled "SEC Champ" putting away his basketball equipment, while two other players, each labeled Kentucky and Vanderbilt, fight one another for second place. The Maroon was shown saying, "Aw, those guys don't know when to stop!"[118]

In total, the various members of the Hederman's newspaper monopoly essentially dismissed the potential legitimacy of MSU's participation in integrated athletics and, clearly, served as another cog in the Closed Society.

As the local paper in Starkville, it was expected that the *Starkville Daily News* would have its fair share of editorial content, especially with opinionated editors and journalists like Sherrill Nash and Henry Harris at the helm. The *Starkville Daily News* was established in 1960 after Henry and Morris Meyer sold the *Starkville News* to segregationist *West Point Times Leader* editor and publisher Harris, who appointed Nash editor of the Starkville-based newspaper, but published his daily musings in both the *Times Leader* and the *Starkville Daily News* while Nash composed all other editorial content.[119] The bulk of articles published in the *Starkville Daily News* were from wire accounts; however, original writing came in the form of a daily column titled "Time Out for Sports" with the byline, "By the Daily News Sports Staff." However, despite the editorial voice present in the Starkville-based publication, little to no attention was paid to the possibility of an NCAA tournament berth, arguably the biggest news in the college town at the time. In one of the first columns published during State's season, an anonymous writer claimed that a conference championship would give the Maroons the opportunity to "pick its tournaments next season," a reference to regular season tournaments rather than the year-ending NCAA joust.[120] While the weekly publication featured columns addressing the Maroons' victorious season, few ever referenced the NCAA tournament.[121] Only after the team's last second loss to Florida did the *Starkville Daily News* staff acknowledge the NCAA tournament and, like other publications, conceded the conference postseason berth to the second place squad.[122] Such an acknowledgment demonstrated that the *Starkville Daily News* had already assumed that, if MSU were to win the conference title, the Maroons would yield to the unwritten law. Plus, the opportunity for the national championship was placed in a secondary position to the SEC title, theoretically making it less likely that Starkville readers would take issue with MSU's adherence to the unwritten law.

The sports staff of the *Starkville Daily News* later predicted a conference title for the hometown team but, in an interesting twist, cited the aforementioned work of the Atlanta-based Bisher, publishing excerpts of his column on the on-court abilities of the Maroons. However, likely due to some strategic editing, Bisher's opposition to the unwritten law and his argument that the team belonged in the integrated postseason was noticeable absent from the column.[123] In a later edition of "Time Out for Sports," the NCAA tournament debate surrounding the Maroons was acknowledged but quickly dismissed as the anonymous author wrote that an appearance in the national title tournament was never a serious consideration. "There has been little talk on the campus of the playoffs since, following the considerable debates of two years ago, everyone has accepted all along that the team wouldn't be allowed to go," the column concluded.[124]

Starkville editor Nash chimed in during State's run to the conference title, but his initial work defended the behavior of MSU's student body during the team's game against Kentucky. Nash attributed the negative attention on the Maroon faithful to members of the sports press, claiming that journalists had blown the situation out of proportion.[125] Nash would again write on MSU's title-winning season; however, the segregationist never referenced the NCAA tournament or made an argument for or against a Maroon national championship. Rather, Nash boldly claimed that Starkville was "the center of the finest collegiate and high school basketball in the entire nation" with State's SEC title win and Starkville High School's successful 29–4 season and upcoming appearance in the state high school championship game.[126]

In total, the editorial commentary from the 1960–1961 season was, with the exception of the work of McDowell, far less impactful in terms of the amount of contributing opinions to the debate and support for the Maroons. While Ray and Lightsey both offered support for the Maroons, their comments came well after a decision by the powers at State had made a decision. Others, such as Walters, openly denounced the Starkville contingent's hopes for a postseason opportunity. With the exception of the work of McDowell, most of the editors simply ignored the chances of integrated competition by a team from the Magnolia State, offering support to the unwritten law and the Closed Society.

The 1960–1961 season for the Maroons of Mississippi State ended in the same manner and with the same lingering questions as past challenges to the unwritten law. Regardless of whether or not it was written opposition to Mississippi State or an objection through silence, in total, Mississippi's journalists did little to challenge the gentleman's agreement and, again, acted as an extension of the Closed Society. Of greater significance to the history of the sports scribes in the Magnolia State was the continued emergence of McDowell as a progressive voice in state journalism. Regardless of his motives or beliefs, "Mississippi Red" tried to give his readers a perspective counter to that of the Closed Society, often leaning on logic and reason as justification. While McDowell never fought, specifically, for integration, his commentary and opposition to the unwritten law still merits a greater historic place in the annals of the Magnolia State for "Mississippi Red."

Mississippi was on the verge of entering a very tumultuous time in U.S. history as the impending challenge of James Meredith and his admission to the University of Mississippi would force a gradual social and ideological change in the white-dominated state. All the while, Mississippi State would again challenge the unwritten law and the Closed Society. While McDowell would leave the state in 1962, other sports scribes would take up his fight and, again, pose a legitimate threat to the Closed Society.

Chapter 4

Is There Anything Wrong with Five White Boys Winning the National Championship?

The year 1962 proved to be one of the more turbulent in the history of Mississippi as James Meredith, with the support of the U.S. government, attempted to integrate the University of Mississippi despite the objections of the state's leaders, specifically Governor Ross Barnett. As Meredith battled Barnett and the Closed Society in the legal arena, the renamed Bulldogs of Mississippi State University were on the heels of another debate that would challenge the validity of the unwritten law, as James "Babe" McCarthy's team finished the 1961–1962 season with a remarkable 24–1 record and a second consecutive Southeastern Conference championship.[1] However, like in the SEC title seasons of 1958–1959 and 1960–1961, MSU rejected an NCAA tournament invitation in accordance with the state's athletic standard against integrated competition. In turn, the sporting press of Mississippi again argued as to whether or not the Bulldogs should have the right to participate in the integrated tournament for a chance at the state's first national basketball championship. While many within Mississippi continued to stress the state's belief in segregation, the debate seemed to become a tired one for some residents of the Closed Society. Rep. Butch Lambert of Lee and Itawamba Counties informally polled his colleagues in the state legislature about relaxing the unwritten law to allow the Bulldogs to play in the tournament. While professing his belief in the continuation of segregated athletics in Mississippi, Lambert told the Associated Press, "It seems foolish to pass up national honors when not playing in Mississippi. . . . Is there anything wrong with five white boys winning the national championship?"[2] Citizens also began to display a degree of attrition in terms of accepting the seemingly ironclad unwritten law as MSU alumni, specifically in Meridian, circulated petitions urging the acceptance of an NCCA tournament bid, arguing that the gentleman's agreement "in no way upholds our southern customs or traditions."[3]

Reflective of the minority of support developing in both the social and political ranks of the Closed Society, the faction of MSU's journalistic supporters began to grow. Although the unwritten law's foremost critic, Jimmie McDowell

After Mississippi State's season-ending victory over the Ole Miss Rebels, the *Jackson Daily News'* Bob Howie acknowledged the Bulldogs' accomplishments in an editorial cartoon depicting an MSU basketball player barreling over an Ole Miss Rebel. *Courtesy Bob Howie/ Jackson Daily News.*

of the *Jackson State Times*, left Mississippi for Trenton, New Jersey in 1961, reporters such as Herb Phillips of the *Commercial Dispatch,* Dick Lightsey of the *Daily Herald* in Biloxi, Billy Ray of the *Vicksburg Evening Post*, and Jimmie Robertson of the student-based *Daily Mississippian* at the University of Mississippi argued for the Bulldogs' place in the integrated postseason and the elimination of the unwritten law, all the while stressing their own belief in segregation. Even sports editor Lee Baker of the *Clarion-Ledger* began to express a supportive sentiment for the Bulldogs, shunning the journalistic neglect he had shown in the past and openly questioning the need for the unwritten law. "It already has been costly to the future of basketball at Mississippi State—and the state's other schools as well, one must realize—and quite possibly will become increasingly so," Baker wrote on March 5, 1962.

Despite the emergence of this supportive minority, the unwritten law was observed and the Bulldogs were kept from the integrated postseason. The majority of reporters in the Magnolia State once again retreated to the comfortable confines of silent support for the Closed Society and failed to express an opinion on the issue. Like the 1960–1961 debate, a number of notable journalists abstained from arguing the validity of a Bulldog venture into integrated athletics. Such luminaries as Jimmy Ward of the *Jackson Daily News,* Hodding Carter of the *Delta Democrat-Times,* and J. Oliver Emmerich of the *Enterprise-Journal,* all of whom had made past arguments either for or against an NCAA title run by McCarthy's troops, failed to publish any opinion-based commentary on the merits of State's 1961–1962 conference title-winning season.

However, the foundation of support for the unwritten law that had been established in past MSU campaigns through derogatory commentary and silence began to weaken. While the majority of the aforementioned reporters failed to identify or advocate State's entry into the tournament as a nod to civil rights, the sheer questioning of the unwritten law was, nevertheless, a bold statement. In combination with the impending integration of Ole Miss, the emergence of doubt in the unwritten law signaled a slow change. While most identified the possibility of an MSU national championship as the justification for the elimination of the unwritten law, the idea that the white dominated standards of the state would even be questioned was a radical one. While the press in Mississippi would unite in its support of Barnett and his objections to the U.S. government's support of Meredith's September 1962 admission on to the Oxford campus, that notion of solidarity was not evident months earlier as the validity of the unwritten law was put to the test.

Much like previous seasons, the MSU faithful and, for that matter, the Magnolia State press, began to take note of McCarthy's Bulldogs before a late-season battle with their rival the University of Kentucky. As of February 1, 1962, MSU was 15–1 and was ranked tenth in the Associated Press college basketball poll. Despite the improving national perception of the defending SEC champions, the team remained in third place in the conference behind the Wildcats and the Green Wave of Tulane as they prepared to face Louisiana State University.[4] Overall, the Bulldogs were led by the stellar play of juniors Leland Mitchell and 1962 SEC Most Valuable Player W. D. "Red" Stroud, who both averaged 17.2 points per game, and future Bulldog head coach Joe Dan Gold, who scored 12.3 points per game.[5]

Despite the absence of guard Jack Berkshire due to the flu, the Bulldogs dominated the Bayou Bengals in Baton Rouge on February 3, 1962, by the score of

87–66, keeping their hopes for a conference title intact.[6] Stroud and Doug Hutton led the Bulldogs with twenty-two and twenty points respectively. The Bulldogs led by nineteen points nine minutes into the game and never looked back, moving to 16–1 on the season and 5–1 in conference.[7] State would then have to play the Green Wave of Tulane in New Orleans in a battle for second place on February 5, 1962. [8] The Bulldogs had to answer the play of Tulane's Jim Kerwin, who was coming off of a forty-one-point performance against the University of Mississippi and led the conference in scoring at 23.8 points per game.[9] Despite MSU's outstanding season up to that point, matching the Bulldog's record of 16–1, an unknown writer with the Associated Press still considered the Wildcats the more likely team to win the conference.[10]

Led by Mitchell, whom the *Clarion Ledger's* Fulton said was "possessed with the agility of a ballet dancer and the nerve of a brain surgeon," the Bulldogs beat the Green Wave 70–59, knocking Tulane out of second place in the conference.[11] Mitchell scored twenty-nine points in the victory, which had to be stopped late in the second half when the 5,600 fans in attendance began throwing garbage on the court.[12] State led 40–28 at halftime and was never threatened as Kerwin finished with twelve points.[13] The win kept MSU "very much in contention for the SEC title," according to a February 6 article by Bob Hartley of the *Starkville Daily News*. Despite not playing Kentucky for another week, UPI wrote that the game would essentially decide the SEC championship. The unknown author gave little chance to the Bulldogs, writing, "You have to go with Kentucky as the favorite for the big game. The Wildcats are playing at home where they seldom lose."[14]

After State moved into the second spot in the SEC, the team travelled to Knoxville to play the University of Tennessee, which had a 4–11 record and was viewed by some journalists as an afterthought.[15] The Vols were coming off of a 100–86 victory over Vanderbilt and were led by center Orb Bowling, who scored 15.3 points per game.[16] From the perspective of an unknown UPI sports writer, who previewed both the Bulldogs' games against Tennessee and Kentucky in the February 9 edition of the *Commercial Dispatch*, a successful road trip was crucial to the team's conference title hopes, however, "Even if State should win, it is likely that Kentucky will represent the SEC in the NCAA playoffs and thus make their bid for their fifth national title. State does not play in interracial tournaments." The unknown author's commentary was the first in a newspaper used in this chapter to reference the NCAA tournament and the Bulldogs. Vernon Butler of the Associated Press would make similar statements in future accounts on the MSU squad during the 1961–1962 season.[17]

McCarthy's troops defeated Tennessee soundly 91–67. According to *Jackson Daily News* sports editor Baker, the Bulldogs were unable to build a big lead in the first half but, as the Volunteers began to have shooting woes, MSU was able to easily move into a lead they would never relinquish.[18] Mitchell led the Bulldogs with twenty-eight points, while Gold added twenty-one and Stroud sixteen.[19] After the win, the Bulldogs had to quickly regroup for its contest with the first-place Kentucky Wildcats in a match-up that the AP called "a clash of the Southeastern Conference's two basketball giants."[20] The two teams were separated by a single conference game, as Kentucky went into the contest with a 17–1 record and as the second-ranked team in the nation, while the Bulldogs were 18–1 and were ranked ninth in the country.[21] Tennessee head coach John Sines told *Clarion-Ledger* correspondent Scotty Hargrove on February 12, 1962, that, if the Bulldogs could get a lead on the Wildcats, MSU had a good chance at winning the game.[22]

The Bulldogs would go on to upset the Wildcats on their home court 49–44 on February 12th.[23] Fulton of the *Clarion-Ledger* wrote of the game, "They said no team could beat Kentucky on its home floor when it meant something. . . . It meant something here Monday night and Mississippi State did."[24] Baker called the win the greatest in the school's basketball history.[25] The Bulldogs held the Wildcats to only fifteen field goals in forty-five attempts and hit 69.2 percent of their shots in the game. Kentucky never led during the contest. Stroud paced State with seventeen points, while Kentucky star Cotton Nash led the Wildcats with twenty-three points. The Bulldogs, in celebration of its first ever victory over the Wildcats in Lexington in thirty-eight years, cut down the nets as they moved into a first-place tie with Rupp's charges.[26] Despite the win, Jim Hackleman of the AP assumed the postseason was an unattainable goal for the Bulldogs, writing on February 13th that McCarthy said "his Bulldogs again will pass up on the NCAA tournament if they repeat as champions because of the school's policy against playing racially integrated teams."[27] The win moved the Bulldogs up one spot in both the AP and UPI national basketball polls.[28]

While the *Starkville Daily News* depended on wire-based material for its coverage of the Bulldogs' win, what was more telling was the placement of those articles. On the front page of the February 13 edition, a brief account about the "celebrations by the deliriously happy state students" in the aftermath of the victory could be found under the banner headline, "Court Rules Meredith Can't Enter Ole Miss," as according to the AP, "The U.S. Court of Appeals refused to issue an injunction which would have permitted Negro James Meredith to enter the University of Mississippi." Henry Harris, the segregationist publisher of the Starkville-based *Daily News*, and the paper's editor Sherrill Nash, who was cut from the same ideological cloth as Harris, were both outspoken critics of the integration of Ole Miss and wrote damning attacks on the pioneering Meredith.[29] The simple placement of these articles on the front page of the *Starkville Daily News* served as a subtle reminder of the role of Harris's paper in the Closed Society and tempered any anti-unwritten law sentiment in the reading audience as a result of the Bulldogs' landmark win. Despite the pertinent news value of the Meredith case, with a simple design decision the *Starkville Daily News* made an editorial statement and solidified its place as a supporter of the Closed Society and the unwritten law.

The Bulldogs were met back in Starkville by a horde of four thousand students in celebration of the team's victory. Sports editor Herb Phillips of the Columbus-based *Commercial Dispatch* wrote on February 14th that MSU "thoroughly outclassed the nation's number two-ranked Kentucky Wildcats" and that the spoils of the victory were for both the student body and the team. Per the *Starville Daily News*, McCarthy told the audience, "This was the greatest night of my life and by far the greatest thrill. That doesn't mean I want to quit however. . . . The race isn't over yet, we've still got five games to go."[30]

Fulton continued to write about the Bulldogs' victory over the Wildcats but began his February 14 sports-based news account with what seemed to be a shocking statement from a reporter from the Hederman-owned *Clarion-Ledger*: "[The] Mississippi State Maroons earned themselves a trip to next month's NCAA finals" with the equally shocking headline, "State Won Trip to NCAA Cage Finals." Fulton would later clarify his statement, writing in the third paragraph of the article, "About the trip to the NCAA, the Maroons will only go to spectate," citing a promise MSU coaches made to the team that a victory over the Wildcats would earn them tickets to the NCAA finals in Louisville on March 24, 1962. Fulton's play on words served as a red herring for the reading public as his article, on the surface, indicated that the team would be playing in the NCAA tournament.

Putting Kentucky in the rearview mirror, State moved on to their contest against the 8–9 University of Florida Gators in Starkville.[31] At 19–1, the Bulldogs would have to pay close attention to star Florida center Cliff Luyk, who averaged twenty-one points per game and scored the game-winning basket during the Gators' 59–57 victory over MSU during the 1960–1961 season. UPI's preview of the week's upcoming SEC action called the Bulldog team "a solid favorite to defend its title" but focused on Kentucky and Auburn's battle for second place as the determining factor in the conference's postseason tournament berth.[32] The Bulldogs would run away from the Gators 67–45 on February 17, 1962, after building a 24–14 halftime lead. McCarthy's troops used the coach's slow-down style in the first half after failing to make the majority of its shots but then starting to run in the second half, building a 42–19 lead.[33] The Bulldogs only hit 37.8 percent of their shots for the game but coasted to the win.[34] Mitchell led State with seventeen points, while Gold had fourteen. Luyk, the Gators' primary offensive weapon, scored only nine points in the loss.[35] State moved to 20–1 on the season and was becoming the talk of the SEC circuit.[36]

In the continued hunt for its third SEC title in four seasons, MSU defeated the University of Georgia 83–74 on February 19, 1962, to move to 21–1 on the season. According to the *Starkville Daily News*' George Anderson, "It was a rough, hel-ter-skelter type ball game with The Babe's men running their fast breaks most of the way but lacking their usual form and style."[37] Mitchell led State with sev-enteen points, but fouled out with 11:12 left in the game.[38] The Bulldogs were tied with Kentucky in the SEC standings and had moved up to fifth in the country in both the AP and the UPI polls.[39] Needing three wins to close out the season and clinch another SEC title, Mississippi State prepared for rematches with LSU and Tulane in Starkville before finishing with in-state rival Ole Miss. LSU was 6–4 in conference and had a 13–8 overall record. The Tigers had already faced the Bulldogs twice during the season and lost both battles.[40] In David M. Moffit's preview of the week's SEC action, the UPI sports scribe began by focusing on Auburn's surprising 16–5 record and challenge to the conference NCAA tour-nament bid. In regards to the Bulldogs' postseason hope, Moffit wrote per the February 23, 1962, edition of the *Meridian Star*, "This is an old story in the SEC," dismissing any notion of State's participation in postseason play. Moffit would reference the existence of the unwritten law in a number of articles during the remainder of the Bulldogs' season, all of which correctly assumed MSU would not participate in the NCAA tournament.[41]

MSU defeated the Tigers on February 24th by a final score of 58–48.[42] State held a slim 30–27 lead at halftime, but LSU would take a one-point lead with 11:12 left in the game. MSU's Doug Hutton hit a jump shot to put the Bulldogs up by one, and State would never trail again. Gold was the statistical leader for the Bull-dogs, scoring twenty-two points and grabbing thirteen rebounds. The "McCar-thymen" were now 11–1 in the SEC and 22–1 overall with two games remaining.

State welcomed Tulane and another match-up with SEC scoring leader Ker-win.[43] While Hedrick Smith referenced MSU's match-up with the Green Wave, the UPI sportswriter paid particular attention to the game between Auburn and Kentucky, which would essentially decide the conference's second-place team and possible NCAA tournament representative as MSU was likely to "oppose tournament teams with Negro players."[44] McCarthy's team would easily defeat the Greenies 83–62 to move within one game of the SEC title, but the Bulldogs remained tied with Kentucky based upon the Wildcats' narrow 63–60 victory over Auburn. Stroud led the way for MSU with twenty one points, seventeen of which came in the decisive second half, which saw the Bulldogs move to a sixteen–point lead only two minutes into the frame.[45] McCarthy would later clean out his bench as the Bulldogs pushed the lead to twenty-one points with four minutes left. Kerwin, who scored twelve points in the previous match-up with the Bulldogs, was held to nine in the rematch. With the win, the Bulldogs remained in fifth place in both the AP and UPI national basketball polls.[46] Both Stroud and Mitchell were also named to the AP All-SEC team, while Mitchell was named to the UPI version.[47] In the aftermath of the win, sport writers Anderson of the *Starkville Daily News*, the *Clarion-Ledger*'s Fulton, and Phil Wallace of the *Jackson Daily News* all anointed the Wildcats as the recipient of the SEC's postseason bid.[48] An anonymous AP reporter made a similar claim, writing that "MSU has said it will not enter NCAA tournament competition because it is racially integrated," despite the fact that no formal announcement from the university, MSU President Dean Colvard or McCarthy, had been made.[49]

State, which needed one more win to clinch the conference championship, moved on from its win over the Green Wave and began to prepare for its March 3 showdown with in-state rival Ole Miss. The Rebels had won four out of their past five games going into the contest with the Bulldogs and were led by Donnie Kessinger, who scored 21.7 points per game. Another victory would match MSU's 1959–1959 SEC title team for most wins in a single season with 24.[50] MSU had a 12–1 conference record versus the 11–1 record of the Wildcats, which had also lost a game out of the SEC.[51] In their previous meeting, MSU beat Ole Miss by four points in a 61–57 Bulldog victory.[52] Much like the local sports writers, AP's Ross M. Hagen called the Wildcats the likely NCAA tournament entry "because Mississippi has an unwritten law forbidding its athletes from competing in integrated sporting events."[53]

While a number of Mississippi-based journalists ignored the chances of an NCAA tournament berth for the Bulldogs, both AP and UPI reported on March 1st that Rep. Butch Lambert of Lee and Itawamba Counties said he got little feedback from talking to members of the state legislature about the possibility of allowing MSU to play integrated teams in the NCAA postseason tournament.[54] In some versions of the wire article from the AP, the lead paragraph acknowledged the existence of some political support for the Maroons: "Nobody wants to talk about it, but there is quite a bit of behind-the-scenes maneuvering in this segregation-conscious state to get approval for fifth-ranked Mississippi State's participation in the NCAA basketball tournament."[55] However, the anonymous author stressed the state's belief in athletic segregation and the unwritten law.[56] In the UPI version, the gentleman's agreement was described as "an unwritten but strong policy against state teams competing in racially integrated events."[57] Lambert, who also moonlighted as an SEC basketball and football official, acted on the request of SEC commissioner Bernie Moore, who wanted to find out if there was any level of support in the state's political elite for a possible MSU national title opportunity. Lambert told the Associated Press that only the State College Board could make a decision concerning the NCAA tournament but added that the 1962 MSU team may have the best chance of not meeting integrated teams in a possible postseason run. Lambert confirmed both his belief in segregation and argued for the Bulldogs' place in the postseason tournament, telling AP, "I'm not for playing on a regularly scheduled basis with integrated teams but it seems foolish to pass up national honors when not playing in Mississippi and when they might not meet an integrated ball club. If it were definite we knew who state would play and it was an integrated club, that would be a different matter. . . . Is there anything wrong with five white boys winning the national championship?"[58] The *Clarion-Ledger* published the article on the inside page of its March 1 sports section with the headline, "No Playoffs for Bulldogs," despite the fact that nowhere in the account was an NCAA tournament bid ruled out.[59] Some newspapers, specifically the *Starkville Daily News*, did not publish anything on Lambert's investigation.

Along with Lambert's support, the *Meridian Star* reported that local residents had joined in with a statewide trend of State alumni circulating petitions urging school officials, specifically MSU president Dean Colvard, to accept the bid to the NCAA tournament. The article, which appeared on the front page of the March 1 edition of the *Meridian Star* without a byline or any sort of wire affiliation, explained, "There is no law barring athletic participation against integrated teams but the policy in Mississippi has been to refuse to play against teams with Negro players."[60] The petition, which was addressed to Colvard and published verbatim in the article, called the absence of MSU in the postseason tournament "unjust; it is harmful to our state and to the Southeastern Conference." Furthermore, the petition stated that the gentleman's agreement only insured that the state would produce "mediocre athletic teams. No southern state except Mississippi has such a policy. It in no way upholds our southern customs or traditions."[61] Despite the author's claim that the petitions were being circulated throughout the state, no other newspaper consulted in this volume published an article on the efforts by MSU alumni.

MSU would go on to defeat the Ole Miss Rebels 63–58 for their third SEC title in four seasons, but "the NCAA bid, the big prize that goes along with winning the SEC title will not be taken by the Bulldogs."[62] State trailed the Rebels by nine points at halftime, 37–28, but, led by Gold's sixteen points, the Bulldogs stormed back to take a 50–49 lead with 10:50 left in the contest. According to Fulton's March 4 account for the *Clarion-Ledger* and the *Jackson Daily News*, MSU "earned the right to accept—or refuse—a trip to the NCAA Regional Finals," despite the fact that a postseason berth for the Bulldogs had been ignored or assumed impossible by most of the sporting press. The same could be said for Tom Gregory of the *Meridian Star*, who wrote in his article covering the game that the win "landed the once-beaten Maroons a trip to the NCAA national championship tournament—if they could take it." Gregory, citing the unwritten law, would later write that a trip would be "highly unlikely." *Commercial Dispatch* sports editor Phillips similarly wrote that the Bulldogs won the right to play in the NCAA tournament but "they will probably have to bow out from the honor because of Mississippi's 'unwritten law' against playing integrated competition as would be the case in the NCAA viewing. Thus, no possible way left for national honors and recognition for MSU's championship squad." State finished the season with a 24–1 record and the conference championship.

In the aftermath of the Bulldogs 63–58 win over Ole Miss, McCarthy told the press he preferred a "relaxation of Mississippi's unwritten rule against sports competition with integrated teams, but he would abide by the decision."[63] The *Clarion-Ledger*'s Baker would go a step further, writing on March 4, 1962, "There is no ruling of the MSU administration or the state college board that would bar competition with integrated teams outside of the state. But there is on record a resolution of the Mississippi legislature, which is considered to cover the situation. The joint resolution calls on all state agencies and institutions to resist integration moves by all legal means." Baker's commentary was interesting, considering that the original 1956 proposal of a state law banning integrated competition was never formally presented to the Mississippi legislature and was essentially a hand-shake agreement between state politicians and college administrators that had no real legal basis. His explanation of the merits of the unwritten law served less as a presentation of fact and more of a reminder of the strict observation by Mississippi's elite of the enforcement of the fictitious law.

The following day, SEC Commissioner Bernie Moore announced that Kentucky would receive the SEC conference invitation to the NCAA tournament that was originally granted to Mississippi State.[64] In a March 5, 1962, article in the *Commercial Dispatch* with no wire affiliation or byline, the unknown author acknowledged Kentucky's place in the NCAA tournament after McCarthy "announced they would not accept the NCAA bid they had won. McCarthy indicated he objected to Mississippi's unwritten policy against its public college playing integrated teams out of state, but he said the Bulldogs would abide by it." Kentucky would go on to defeat Tennessee 90–59 in its season finale to clinch a share of the SEC title and a trip to the NCAA tournament.[65]

Gold, who played on the 1961, 1962, and 1963 SEC title-winning MSU teams, said in a 2009 interview, while he wanted to participate in the tournament, he and his teammates did not consider it a feasible opportunity. "We wanted to go play [every year]; we just didn't have a whole lot of hope to do so," Gold said. "In 1961, I just understood that we wouldn't go. But in 1962, Jack Berkshire, who was from Iowa, was the team's captain. I went home with Jack during a school break and we attended the NCAA regional that was being played in Kansas. It then hit home. At that game, I realized that we were really missing out."[66]

For his work during the season, UPI named McCarthy the SEC Coach of the Year. The March 6, 1962, wire article on McCarthy's award referenced State's absence from the NCAA tournament due to "segregation policies."[67] The

Joe Dan Gold, W.D. "Red" Stroud, and Leland Mitchell, all played an integral part in Mississippi State's multiple Southeastern Conference title wins from 1961 through 1963. Stroud was named the SEC Player of the Year in 1962 while all three Bulldogs occupied sports on the ALL-SEC squad at some point during their three years on Mississippi State's varsity roster.

Courtesy Mississippi State University Libraries, University Archives.

Bulldogs finished the season as the fourth-best team in the nation in both the AP and UPI polls.[68] A version of Norman Miller's UPI article that appeared in the March 12 edition of the *Meridian Star* indicated that of the top 10 teams, only Mississippi State declined a bid to play for the NCAA championship.[69] In an article reviewing the Bulldogs' magical season found in the *Jackson Daily News*, the *Starkville Daily News*, and the *Clarion-Ledger*, the anonymous author never mentioned the NCAA tournament and State's absence from the national championship race.[70] Despite the obvious objections on integrated athletics and an NCAA tournament appearance for the Bulldogs from the political elite in the Closed Society, the State Senate passed a resolution congratulating McCarthy on his Coach of the Year honors.[71]

Weeks after the conclusion of the season, Lewis Lord of UPI wrote a profile of McCarthy and ascribed biblical status to the Mississippi native, calling the head coach "almost—but not quite—a Moses for Mississippi State."[72] Lord's work, which focused more on McCarthy's opinion of the unwritten law and his team's absence from the NCAA tournament, was perhaps the most insightful in terms of the coach's opinion of the gentleman's agreement. While Lord predicted that the Bulldogs would be one of the top teams in the nation during the 1962–1963 campaign, he explained that MSU would likely have to stay home again due to the unwritten law, "a policy formed by legislative leaders, though not written into law, [that] threatens a reduction of state money to any white school which allows its athletes to compete with Negroes." In a direct nod to McCarthy's feelings on the matter, Lord wrote that, "It galls McCarthy, but there is little he can do about it. He has led state to three Southeastern Conference championships in four years. But bringing about a policy change in the state capital—especially when it regards race—apparently requires much greater powers of persuasion. . . . McCarthy says 'the boys should be allowed to play against integrated teams away from home' and he feels most Mississippians agree with him."[73] In response, Barnett told the UPI scribe, "If we play them up there, they will want to come down here. Where would they eat? Where would they stay? And wouldn't they want to go to the dance after the game?"[74]

While the outspoken McDowell was no longer in Mississippi to lead the charge against the unwritten law, other sports reporters and editors surprisingly stepped up to challenge the principles surrounding the gentleman's agreement even if they were motivated more by the allure of a national championship and less by social or civil equality.

One such newspaper was the Columbus-based *Commercial Dispatch* and sports editor Herb Phillips, who would both question the legitimacy and need for the unwritten law while proclaiming his devotion to the Closed Society's segregationist lifestyle. Early in the debate surrounding the 1962 NCAA tournament and the Bulldogs, the *Dispatch*'s place in that argument was unclear. The first opinion-based material to appear in the *Dispatch* came in the February 12, 1962, edition as Wayne King, a sports writer with the *Dispatch*, previewed the game between the Bulldogs and the Wildcats in his column "Sports Off the Cuff." While King's commentary differed little from his journalistic contemporaries in Mississippi, he did call out Kentucky leader Rupp for his recruitment of black athletes to the Wildcat basketball team. "Another Mississippi institution which Rupp has threatened to tear down is segregated athletic contests," King wrote, citing Rupp's open recruitment of black athletes. King's attack on Rupp for threatening the sanctity of the unwritten law was somewhat surprising considering that the *Commercial Dispatch* would eventually take a stance against the gentleman's agreement. By King's work, one could logically deduct that the sports writer believed in the unwritten law and the principles of the Closed Society. Despite Rupp's recruitment, a black athlete would not appear in the SEC until 1966.

Conservatively enough, Phillips began his work on the MSU contingent shortly after the team's victory over the Wildcats, referring to the Bulldogs as the front-runner for the SEC title in the February 14 and 15 editions of his column "'N in This Cornah!" Despite the conservative nature of his early work, Phillips would later criticize the unwritten law, a rarity in the Closed Society, after State ran its record to 21–1 in the February 21, 1962, edition of the *Commercial Dispatch*. Phillips questioned the need for the gentleman's agreement and held out hope for a change of heart by the university and defenders of the Closed Society, while lamenting for an MSU appearance in the integrated postseason.

"Perhaps the 'unwritten law' that keeps teams from the Magnolia State at home while every other outstanding club in the U.S.A. is after the highest plums in sports will be lifted this time—just perhaps." Phillips's commentary, while not particularly scathing, was shocking nonetheless because very few writers spoke out in favor of an NCAA tournament berth and against the unwritten law. Even Phillips's simple questioning of the ban indicated that at least some in the sports journalism community had become tired of the seasonal debate involving integrated athletics and MSU. Phillips later addressed the Bulldogs' head coach and made another bold editorial statement, writing, "Memo to Babe McCarthy: It's not important that you win the Southeastern Conference championship this year or ever," Phillips sarcastically quipped. "For you too, 'cannot participate in any sectional bowl (let's substitute tournament for bowl) where there is integration.'"[75]

Phillips would again make his feelings on the unwritten law known in the February 25 edition of the *Commercial Dispatch* as the sports editor professed to randomly discussing the gentleman's agreement with four individuals he met on the street. Phillips wrote that three of the four favored the elimination of the unwritten law, although all four claimed to be segregationists. Phillips claimed that he agreed with the abolishment of the gentleman's agreement, writing, "This 'unwritten law' regarding the participation of state schools in integrated competition is certainly a handicap, and growing more meaningful all of the time." Before continuing with his argument, Phillips made it a point to clarify that his position was based on athletic merit and not civil rights. "I, like 95 percent of all other white Mississippians, am and always have been a 100 percent racial segregationist. This statement cannot be intelligently challenged by anyone! After making that point perfectly clear allow me to state that all of Mississippi's native athletes who go into the service and play ball there or who advance in a professional athletic career, compete against, as well as with, negroes. This doesn't mean they personally have to socialize with them, for I'll wager 99 percent of them don't. . . . Why can't our athletes, who are consistently so magnificent on the field of play and who bring so much genuine admiration and publicity to our Magnolia State, deal in the same way OUT from our borders with mongrelized teams as other Southern fieldings have been forced for sports' sake into doing?" Phillips added that it was inevitable that integrated play would come to the SEC, citing Rupp's initial recruitment of black athletes but sympathized with the enforcement of the state's segregationist athletic standard, writing that the issue "goes deeper than sports" and identified the prevailing fear that integrated play would lead to the end of segregation in Mississippi. "The nation's courts, politics and big business all seem hell-bent on forcing a curtailment of the Southern way of life at any rate," Phillips wrote. "Folks who only a few years ago boasted 'It'll [integration] never come—never be allowed in Mississippi!'

are now saying 'It's coming!' The time to decide on the matter is now. The grief that would come about with the fall of the nation's finest and mightiest athletic systems, per population, would be tremendous—especially if the reason for the toppling proved negligible." While Phillips's proposed elimination of the unwritten law seemed on the surface as a nod toward the progression of equality in the state, the racist rhetoric utilized in his work negated the potential impact of his writing. While asking for the lifting of the ban on integrated athletics, the Columbus sports editor dismissed blacks as mongrels lacking the ability to function socially. It is clear in his work that his justification was only for the chance at a national championship.

Phillips, who also hosted a weekly broadcast of his opinion-based forum on WCBI-TV in Columbus, used the February 26 edition of "N in This Cornah!" to detail the televised conversation between himself and fellow sports writer Robert "Steamboat" Fulton of the *Clarion-Ledger* on the MSU squad and its chances at the integrated postseason. Phillips wrote that "Steamboat" agreed with his contention that playing integrated foes outside the Magnolia State "could only be beneficial to us and our way of life, and would not have any adverse, undesired effects." News of Phillips's and Fulton's televised comments on the unwritten law appeared in the *Starkville Daily News* via the AP. The article indicated that both men thought the unwritten law should be eliminated, but Fulton said it was highly unlikely—a contradictory statement of sorts for the Jackson-based sports writer.[76]

Phillips's March 1 effort focused on a letter from fellow Mississippian and U.S. Air Force airman O. J. Lawrence Jr., who voiced his support for MSU's appearance in the playoffs "no matter who the opposition may be." Lawrence questioned native Mississippians' pride in their state, especially in light of its denial at opportunities for college national championships, and felt that little harm would come to "the principles the people of Mississippi are trying so desperately to uphold." In response, Phillips agreed with Lawrence and sarcastically marveled at his change in ideology. "Perhaps his liberal wisdom vanished in the light of cold, hard facts and intelligent argument," Phillips quipped.

Prior to the season-ending battle against the Rebels, Phillips again discussed the unwritten law in detail, calling for state politicians to be consistent in their views on race relations. Phillips wrote on Mach 2, 1962, that MSU "was being cheated out of their rightful reward for superiority. Again they are the sufferers of a ridiculous 'enforced for some, lifted for others' ruling like one found in no other Southern state." Phillips opined that all extracurriculars should be subject to the unwritten law for consistency, which would eliminate Miss America candidates, college quiz and debate groups, 4-H organizations, and civic and church clubs, to name a few. "What's fair for one segment should be fair for all. So be fair or else lift the bonds that bind and let our athletes go," Phillips concluded. Again, while Phillips's work was opinionated, based upon his stand against integration, he only wished for athletic superiority for Mississippi and not equality.

Despite Phillips's logical rationale for the elimination of the unwritten law, at least in an athletic context, he still used his March 4 column to express a degree of outrage over the Bulldogs' AP and UPI national poll rankings behind Kentucky. While Phillips used the rankings and Stroud's absence on any of the AP's All-American squads, the Columbus-based editor acknowledged one of the more logical justifications for MSU's poor reputation in the eyes of the nation's sporting press: the lack of integrated teams on its schedule. However, Phillips painted the Magnolia State as a victim of sorts and attacked both polls on their validity. "We Southerners and especially we Mississippians, who are daily pictured by outsiders as 'discriminators' are being discriminated against by some of those same depicters—and that's one reason," Phillips wrote. "The other is that those polls are a lot of hooey so packed with political maneuvering and pressuring that they're no where near accurate, representative or honorable." While Phillips may have objected to the unwritten law, the professed segregationist believed in the principle behind it and supported and defended the Closed Society. On March 6th, Phillips would again lament over the Bulldogs' ranking in the national basketball polls and blamed the national perception of MSU on the state's gentleman's agreement. "This state's 'unwritten law' against playing integrated competition outside of the state is responsible for this, and will continue to plague Mississippi sports of every season," Phillips argued. "Perhaps State has got the best cage team in the country—but we and especially the pessimistic fans outside the Mid-South will never know whether they have or not because the Bulldogs are given no chance to play the other top teams in the NCAA playoffs. . . . It's a shame."[77] While Phillips' argument against the unwritten law was for the sake of State's dominance on the hardwood, his viewpoints demonstrated the slow change in Mississippi's press. While, indeed, his professed belief in segregation muted, to some extent, the potency of his commentary, his advocacy for the elimination of the gentlemen's agreement was nonetheless a progressive statement in the white-dominated Closed Society.

Past State advocate, *Daily Herald* sports editor Dick Lightsey, began his commentary on the Bulldogs' season on February 1, 1962, in his daily column, and the professed segregationist spent his early work on the Bulldogs focusing on the team's chances for a conference title with little to no mention of the NCAA tournament.[78] It was not until February 14, 1962, after MSU's upset victory over the Wildcats that the Biloxi-based sports editor addressed the integrated postseason, giving the advantage to the Lexington-based squad due to the unwritten law despite advocating a tournament appearance for the Starkville contingent in 1959 and expressing a degree of regret over the team's tournament absence in 1961. He soon returned to his conservative ways, addressing only the conference prospects for the McCarthy-led squad and failing to reference the NCAA tournament in subsequent columns.[79] Lightsey finally offered a glimpse of his 1959 form when, in his February 28 edition of "Bunts, Boots and Bounces," the sports editor wrote that the Bulldogs deserved a chance to play in the national title tournament; however, he considered the opportunity and "a possible chance at glory" a lost one because of the unwritten law. While Lightsey spent considerable time being noncommittal about the unwritten law and the chances of an MSU postseason appearance, he would use his March 2nd column to make his strongest editorial statement concerning the gentleman's agreement, as he argued for its elimination. "Since 1956, the Magnolia state has not allowed any of its athletic teams to compete against teams with Negro players. We see no reason for such an 'unwritten law,' especially when Mississippi teams go outside of the state to play against other squads," Lightsey wrote. Interestingly, Lightsey argued that any inquiry into a possible postseason berth for the Bulldogs was "premature" despite publishing his column days before the Bulldogs would conclude the SEC regular season.

Four days after the Bulldogs wrapped up the SEC title, Lightsey called for MSU to move up in the AP and UPI national basketball polls and named the Bulldogs the best team in the country. Because of State's fifth place status in both polls, Lightsey called efforts to rank the nation's best teams "futile" and said it was merely a "popularity contest." Lightsey questioned why the Bulldogs were ranked behind Kentucky even though MSU defeated the Wildcats in Lexington. Despite the logical nature of Lightsey's argument, the obvious justification for MSU's less-than-stellar national profile, the lack of integrated teams on its schedule, was never mentioned. In closing, Lightsey wrote, "People who have seen them in action regard the Maroons as the best collegiate team in the country and, if not, certainly no worse than second."[80]

Lightsey again stressed his opposition to the unwritten law in his March 12 column following Kentucky's regular season finale against Tennessee. Lightsey told his audience that he would cheer for the Wildcats to win the NCAA title but, "[It] seems a shame that State has to stay home after qualifying for the NCAA event. . . . Maybe Mississippi's 'unwritten law' will be tossed out the window if enough pressure is brought to bear on the powers that be." Lightsey would later write, "Sure would like to see Mississippi State competing in that NCAA event!" after previewing the national title tournament.[81] While Lightsey did not express the same level of opposition to the unwritten law as Phillips or, for that matter, McDowell, the Biloxi-based sports editor was one of the few in the Mississippi sports journalism community to speak out against the gentleman's agreement. Lightsey would remain at the *Daily Herald*, which would become the *Sun Herald* in 1982, for forty-three years before his death in 1994 at the age of 68. Lightsey continued writing for the *Herald* even after his retirement in 1991 under the title of sports editor emeritus. His then-executive editor, Mike Tonos, said of Lightsey in his obituary, "Dick was dedicated.... He worked hard for his family, his newspaper, and his community. He's going to be missed by a lot of people."[82]

Another of the more outspoken critics of the unwritten law was *Vicksburg Evening Post* sports editor Billy Ray. As detailed in the previous chapter, Ray argued that the then-Maroons should have been allowed to play in the 1961 NCAA tournament after winning the SEC, although Ray's justification was based on athletic merit and not social equality. Unlike his sports reporting brethren, Ray wasted little time commenting on the unwritten law, using the victory over the Wildcats as a catalyst for the subsequent debate. After writing on the finer points of MSU's win in Lexington, Ray identified the Bulldogs as the frontrunner for the conference title. As for the integrated NCAA tournament, Ray wrote that the Starkville contingent was bound to suffer an injustice at the hands of the unwritten law. "Is it fair to Mississippi State's fine basketball team? Mississippi's lawmakers undoubtedly think so," Ray wrote on February 14, 1962. Only a day later, Ray added to his pro-tournament commentary, citing McCarthy's promise that an MSU win would earn the team a trip to Louisville for the NCAA tournament finals as spectators. "Probably the best team in the country won't be playing, they'll be sitting in the stands," Ray quipped.[83]

Ray's commentary became somewhat tame after the Bulldogs' win over Florida, as he only focused on McCarthy's overall success in Starkville and the SEC title aspirations for the current squad.[84] After a string of relatively mundane columns, Ray again tackled the unwritten law on March 6, 1962, this time addressing the possibility that McCarthy would leave Starkville because of the inability to play for a national championship. "Now that Mississippi State has at least a tie clinched for the 1961–1962 SEC basketball title and another NCAA bid staring them in the face.... Bullie fans are getting a little uneasy that James 'Babe' McCarthy may be a little dissatisfied and will pull up stakes for better treatment elsewhere," Ray wrote. Perhaps, what was more significant was the Vicksburg-editor's explanation of the unwritten law. While citing the lack of a decision out of Starkville in regards to playing in the integrated postseason, Ray incorrectly referred to the unwritten law as "a resolution of the Mississippi legislature, which is considered to cover the situation. The joint resolution call on all state agencies and institutions to resist integration moves by all legal means and to violate this resolution could hurt the school doing the violating quite a bit, especially financially." While he did not express an opinion in this column on the gentleman's agreement, Ray hoped that McCarthy's tenure in Starkville would continue for the foreseeable future. "We hope Babe stays at Mississippi State as long as he lives, but hoping and actually doing it under present conditions vary as much as daylight and dark," he wrote.

Despite Ray's commentary on the unwritten law and the future of the Bull-dogs' leader, he never explicitly denounced the gentleman's agreement; rather his commentary often inferred a philosophical difference between his opinion and that of the Closed Society. In the March 7, 1962, edition of the *Vicksburg Evening Post*, Ray cited Phillips of the *Commercial Dispatch* as being in opposi-tion to the unwritten law and published his aforementioned March 1 column verbatim, but the sports editor never offered a definitive opinion on the mat-ter. Ray would later defend the publication of Phillips's work to local resident James L. Coleman, an alumnus of MSU, who wrote a letter to the sports editor disagreeing with Phillips's proposed elimination of the unwritten law. Ray, who did not publish the local citizen's letter, defended Phillips's contention, writing that his Columbus-based colleague had a point. "What's fair for some should be fair to others . . . or put a damper completely on all out-of-state activities where a possibility of competition between the races exists," Ray wrote. While Ray did not express an opinion on Phillips's work at the time he published it, it is clear from his comments to Coleman that he agreed with Phillips's general premise. The same could be said in regards to Ray's March 11 work, which used McCarthy's SEC Coach of the Year award to make a backhanded, yet profound, statement against the unwritten law, arguing that the team's inability to play for the national title would eliminate "Babe" from consideration from any national coach honors. "It's a shame . . . an injustice if there ever was," Ray wrote in regards to State's absence from the tournament. Ray would later remark, in a show of frustration over MSU's absence from the integrated postseason and the lack of Bulldogs on the AP All-American team, "We could say a few more words, but it wouldn't help any." In one last nod to the debate surrounding the NCAA tournament, Ray addressed the unwritten law and the merits of MSU's basketball team on March 20th in the aftermath of Ohio State's vic-tory over Rupp's Wildcats. In the wake of the Buckeyes' win over Kentucky, Ray wrote that it was logical to question whether or not Ohio State could beat Mississippi State but, "That question will never be answered, thanks to Missis-sippi's 'unwritten law' that prevented Babe McCarthy's Bullies from trying for national basketball honors."

While Phillips, Lightsey, and Ray would debate the merits of the unwritten law but publicly maintain their belief in segregation, *Meridian Star* sports edi-tor Billy "Sunshine" Rainey took a decisively conservative approach to his work. Much like he did during MSU's 1960–1961 run at the conference championship, "Sunshine" only wrote on the Bulldogs once during the examined time period. In his February 13, 1962, edition of "Sunshine on Sports," Rainey hailed McCar-thy as the new "Mr. Basketball" in the SEC in the wake of the team's victory over Rupp's Wildcats, but the Meridian-based Rainey did not address or reference the unwritten law or the NCAA tournament. Fellow sports editor, Charles S.

Kerg of the *Delta Democrat-Times*, did not discuss the Bulldogs' SEC title hopes until the final week of the season and, even then, Kerg's March 2, 1962, commentary simply explained that State needed to defeat Ole Miss in order to win the conference championship.

One of the more progressive voices in terms of racial equality in Mississippi sports came from an unlikely source. Jimmie Robertson, the editor of the student-based *Daily Mississippian* at the University of Mississippi, condemned the unwritten law and painted the gentleman's agreement as a hindrance that was holding the state of Mississippi back. Robertson's ascension to the editor's desk was in itself inauspicious. His only adversary in the election for editor, Billy Barton, became a target of the Citizens' Council and the State Sovereignty Commission after it was discovered he served an internship at the *Atlanta Journal* with liberal publisher Ralph McGill. The Council's William J. Simmons called Barton "a left winger" and claimed the Ole Miss student had participated in several sit-ins while he was in Atlanta. With Simmons's help, the Sovereignty Commission worked in conjunction with the administration at Ole Miss and Barton never took on the role of the newspaper's editor. He eventually stopped actively campaigning for the position although friends of the defamed student continued to campaign for him with no success.[85] Sovereignty Commission publicity director Erle Johnston later admitted that the claims against Barton were false.[86]

Robertson was elected on April 18, 1961, and the junior history major turned out to be an editor and columnist the school's administration and the various organizations within the Closed Society feared. During his time as editor, Robertson advocated the admission of Meredith into the university, condemned the work of the Hederman-owned *Jackson Daily News*, defended Pulitzer Prize-winning editor Hazel Brannon Smith of the *Lexington Advertiser* and the *Northside Reporter* and attacked the Sovereignty Commission for the possible violation of her civil rights, and mocked the racist *Rebel Underground*, likening the newspaper to a comic strip.[87] Robertson took a special interest in athletics, first writing about the unwritten law in November 1961 after Ole Miss's second ranked football team turned down an opportunity to play the nation's number-one ranked and integrated Michigan State Spartans. In response, Robertson sent a letter to the *State News*, the student newspaper of Michigan State, which generated criticism and ridicule from the segregated elite in Mississippi. Robertson would again write about the unwritten law in the January 11, 1962, edition of the *Daily Mississippian,* calling the gentleman's agreement a "death knell for sports in Mississippi." Furthermore, Robertson cited the integration of neighboring southern conferences, specifically the Southwest Conference and Kentucky's public support for the SEC's addition of black athletes, and argued that the unwritten law would have a negative effect on the viability of Mississippi athletics.

In the throes of MSU's run to the SEC championship, Robertson again attacked the unwritten law. While Robertson said that he opposed integration, he wrote that the state's segregationist athletic standard was the only one like it in the South and the principle behind the policy was violated every time a Mississippi congressman participated in an integrated Congress. Robertson cryptically predicted the demise of college sports in Mississippi because of the gentleman's agreement.[88] The controversial work of the outspoken Robertson was picked up by both the AP and UPI and published in papers across the state.[89] Some newspapers, like the Hederman-owned *Clarion-Ledger* and the *Hattiesburg American*, did not publish any content on the work of Robertson.

Robertson later wrote on Mississippi State's hopes for an NCAA tournament appearance in the March 2, 1962, edition of the *Daily Mississippian*, claiming that he was "encouraged by growing discontent" with the unwritten law, which he referred to as "ridiculous and unnecessary." However, in a nod to his professed belief in segregation, Robertson wrote that, at the least, the loyal followers of the Closed Society would want to see "five white boys win the tournament over a score of teams which were integrated," again stressing his opposition to integration. Only days later, Robertson penned another column on the unwritten law, opposing the notion that the elimination of the controversial gentleman's agreement would lead to the integration of the Magnolia State. Perhaps a more shocking notion for the Magnolia State than eliminating the unwritten law was Robertson's argument that if the gentleman's agreement was going to stay in place, then Mississippi State and Ole Miss should withdraw from the SEC. "The time has come for these two schools to quit leaching off the conference, to quit proclaiming the superiority of the SEC while refusing to help prove it," Robertson wrote. "If we know that we are not going to participate in national competition if we are the conference champions, we should gracefully bow out so the SEC may once again be able to send its champion to represent it before the nation. If we are to follow the 'unwritten law,' resignation from the conference is our only honorable recourse."[90]

Robertson even published the work of the *Reflector* from Mississippi State, as a column from the MSU student paper's staff appeared in the March 7, 1962, edition of the *Daily Mississippian*. The *Reflector* staff argued that the unwritten law placed the college sports teams of the Magnolia State on a "second rate level" and asked for the state legislature to examine the policy against playing integrated teams, claiming, "It should not be a dead question" in regards to MSU's possible appearance in the NCAA tournament. However, the column did not go so far as to advocate an elimination of the gentleman's agreement, calling for state politicians to take into account "their way of life." The *Daily Mississippian* would repeat this practice on March 20, 1962. In a column credited to the *Reflector*'s staff, the decision to forgo the tournament was called an injustice and placed the blame on lawmakers who "refused to pass a resolution concerning the matter." The author even challenged the legislature's political resolve, writing, "*The Reflector* has maintained a policy of conservatism throughout the year, but it has been because of a strong belief in those practices which retain patriotism to our state and national government. . . . Liberals have their good points and their bad ones; so do conservatives. The latter group has hit home." While the *Reflector*'s questioning of the unwritten law certainly fell in line with a number of the more progressive journalists, professional or otherwise in the state, the student paper of MSU clearly was hesitant in endorsing the elimination of the gentleman's agreement due to their self-professed conservative approach.

Robertson's work continued to be of a controversial nature during his tenure as the editor of the *Daily Mississippian*, but his stance on the unwritten law was on par with the professional journalists of the time. At every turn, Robertson's work was attacked by the *Rebel Underground* and its racist rhetoric and, without blinking, the student editor fired back at the very caste system that helped him ascend to the top position of power at the *Daily Mississippian*. While he refused to let go of the customs and traditions of segregation and the Closed Society, his support for Mississippi State and constant calls for the elimination of the unwritten law put his commentary on a similar level as Phillips, Lightsey, and Ray.

Much like MSU's previous runs to SEC laurels, sports journalists for the Jackson-based *Clarion-Ledger* and the *Jackson Daily News*, both owned by the segregationist Hederman family, opposed the Bulldogs' opportunity to play in the NCAA tournament. Veteran sports columnists such as Lee Baker, Arnold Hederman, and Carl Walters spent the vast majority of their opinion-based work either neglecting the Bulldogs' chances of playing in the integrated NCAA tournament or stressed the binding nature of the unwritten law. Another Hederman sports scribe, Robert Fulton, expressing little to no opinion on the matter and, when the merits of the unwritten law were a topic of conversation, yielded to the work of his sports reporting brethren from inside the Magnolia State. Like past instances discussed in this volume, the Hederman sports desk did little to contribute to the opinion-based debate and, by spending the bulk of the time on the sidelines, helped enforce the unwritten law and served as a journalistic cog in the Closed Society.

Like in past years, Baker frequently ignored the Bulldogs' building championship resume, initially neglecting both the SEC title and the NCAA tournament. Baker, in the aftermath of MSU's win over LSU, wrote that he did not see Kentucky losing again, in essence conceding the conference title and the tournament bid to the Wildcats.[91] He made a similar point going into State's upset win over Rupp's charges but, while ignoring the Bulldogs' chances at an NCAA invitation, called the State team a credible challenger to the nation's top basketball powers.[92] Baker even argued that pundits should be aware of the constraints Mississippi State faced due to various issues including the unwritten law, writing, "They little appreciate the inability of State to schedule such outside powers, both from the standpoint of Negro players and from the financial end."[93] On February 13, 1962, Baker would again argue for State's place among the top college basketball teams in the land after the victory over the Wildcats and addressed the national championship aspirations of the Bulldogs. However, in a misleading twist, the Hederman sports reporter told his readers that State had earned a trip to the NCAA tournament, referring to McCarthy's pregame promise to his team to purchase tickets to the NCAA tournament if they defeated the Wildcats, giving the perception that the team would participate in the postseason. Baker would follow his misleading comments by writing that the "assumption has formed rather solidly that the Maroons will pass a third time, even if they win the title unless some remarkably changed thinking comes in high places back home." Baker acknowledged that the unwritten law had kept the two-time SEC champions from the national championship tournament, but he never explained that the team would make the trip as spectators. Rather than making a case for the Bulldogs to participate in the tournament, regardless of justification, Baker's statements incorrectly gave the perception that a tournament bid would be accepted. Baker's misleading commentary did little to change his role as a protector and proprietor of the unwritten law and appeared to be a reckless offering to the reading audience.

In the aftermath of his comments on the Bulldogs and the NCAA tournament, the *Jackson Daily News* sports editor returned to safer harbors, continuously ignoring the NCAA tournament and more often than not, a conference title for the Starkville contingent perhaps in an effort to control any pro-tournament sentiment for McCarthy's squad.[94] In the February 20 edition of "Baker's Dozen," Baker suggested, due to likelihood of another SEC championship for the Bulldogs, a state-recognized day to honor the Bulldogs' head coach and Mississippi native. While a day celebrating McCarthy's tenure as MSU head coach may have been a worthwhile suggestion, if attention was what the Bulldogs truly deserved, Baker could have suggested playing for the national title. Like many of his fellow sports writers in the Closed Society, Baker often ignored or simply neglected to make or identify logical reasons and justifications for their opinions and arguments.

Going into MSU's final three games of the season, Baker initially focused on the on-court match-ups between the Bulldogs and LSU, Tulane, and Ole Miss.[95] After the team's win over LSU, Baker wrote on February 25th that the schedule featured rare match-ups of Magnolia State foes and thoughtlessly explained: "Our teams show great reluctance to play one another, based greatly upon fear of a prestige loss. . . . Sometimes it seems that Mississippians worry more about losing face than Orientals, particularly in the world of athletics." Other than

Baker's racist commentary, the SEC title and any postseason hopes for the Bulldogs was absent in his work. Days later, Baker would write that a win over Ole Miss was needed for the conference crown.[96] In the same edition of the *Jackson Daily News*, Bob Howie's latest cartoon depicted an MSU basketball player stepping into a bear trap labeled "Ole Miss," under the heading, "One Last Hazard," a clear nod to the acceptance of conference dominance by Mississippi's press rather than progressing into segregated competition. [97]

Rather than advocate an NCAA tournament appearance for the Bulldogs, Baker and a number of other sports reporters put more stock into the national perceptions of the team through the AP and the UPI polls. In his March 1 column, Baker wrote that he was befuddled by the fifth-place status of State in both national basketball polls, considering that Kentucky remained ahead of the Starkville contingent as the fourth best team in the country. Baker called the participating voters "stubborn" and cited the Bulldogs win over the Wildcats as justification. Baker's argument ignored the absence of integrated and nationally recognized foes on the Bulldogs' schedule, a logical justification for the low regard others had for MSU outside of Mississippi. On the eve of the season finale against Ole Miss, Baker identified the conference title, national recognition via the AP and UPI polls, and the best record in the school's history as obtainable goals with a win over their in-state rivals but, again, neglected any national championship hopes for the school.[98]

Baker's constant neglect of the Bulldogs and the integrated national championship tournament ended on March 5th in the pages of the *Jackson Daily News*. Baker addressed the pro-NCAA sentiment expressed by McCarthy and pondered a future of segregated basketball in Mississippi. In the aftermath of the Bulldogs' title-clinching win over the Rebels, Baker wrote, "The discontent of being left at home while all other conference champions elsewhere about the land prepare for NCAA tournament competition was heavy in the air." Baker questioned the accuracy of McCarthy's belief that most citizens of the Magnolia State wanted MSU to play in the tournament, writing that it "could hardly be determined for it is one thing sure to never end up on a ballot. And with such sentiment unable to be precisely determined, those who control the decision on such a question maintain the stay-at-home policy for Mississippi athletics." Baker also theorized that the result of foregoing three NCAA tournaments in a four-year span would affect recruiting and the sustainability of the program's success. Pointing to the then-freshmen team's record of 9–11, Baker claimed that many of McCarthy's out-of-state recruits failed to come to MSU because of the lack of an opportunity to play for a national title. Baker wrote that the MSU head coach was troubled by the unwritten law. "This situation is one which has brought considerable division of opinion to the state and one which apparently is not going to be resolved anytime soon," Baker wrote, without calling the gentleman's agreement by name. "It already has been costly to the future of basketball at Mississippi State—and the state's other schools as well, one must realize—and quite possibly will become increasingly so."[99] Baker then addressed the future of McCarthy, wondering if the Baldwyn native would follow the lead of former Southern Mississippi head coach Fred Lewis and leave the Magnolia State in order to have the chance to win on a bigger stage. "Can Maroons fans expect a man of McCarthy's drive and ambition to accept year after year the staying at home when the likes of Kentucky goes off to represent the SEC in NCAA play?" Baker asked. "This is the thing that State folks are pondering seriously today as they consider the unwritten law in Mississippi."

While Baker failed to express a definitive opinion on the unwritten law, he clearly addressed the merit of the segregationist agreement and the overall effect it had on Mississippi's athletic landscape. Baker's commentary was a progressive step forward for the Jackson sports editor despite his attack on McCarthy's commentary and his failure to express a true opinion on the matter. Nevertheless, Baker essentially asked the Closed Society if the enforcement of the unwritten law had become a handicap to the betterment of their hallowed athletic institutions, a shocking notion for one who spent considerable time ignoring or denouncing the threat of integrated athletics since 1955. Baker's commentary toed a middle ground that would safely keep him from opposing the Closed Society yet offered enough opposition to, at least, question the observance of the unwritten law. He expressed a definitive opinion only in cases where State's status as a major college basketball power came into question and, despite his pondering of the merit of the unwritten law, kept opinions that may have hurt the mission of the Closed Society to himself. Whether or not Baker supported the elimination of the gentleman's agreement was unknown, and the lack of any real expression of opinion or opposition in his work during the 1961–1962 season did not help.

Carl Walters, another sports-based protector of the Closed Society, began his commentary on the Bulldogs' 1962 run to the conference championship in a defeatist tone, anointing Kentucky as the eventual league champion.[100] Walters would later change his tone after the school's victory over Tulane in his February 7, 1962, "Shavin's" column in the Clarion-Ledger, calling MSU the one and only threat to Kentucky's bid for the Dixie Dozen title. However, Walters would ignore the chances for postseason play.

Walters would be the first writer to reference the integrated NCAA tournament and the unwritten law in one of the Hederman-owned newspapers in his February 11 edition of "Shavin's." Walters, while previewing the evening match-up between the Bulldogs and the Wildcats, wrote that the Rupp-led Wildcats were "making a strong bid for SEC and national laurels" and conceded the NCAA tournament bid to the Wildcats, painting a grim postseason picture for MSU.

"The Cats are a certainty to represent the SEC in the NCAA tournament. . . . The Bulldogs would have to pass it up because of 'established policy' in Mississippi against teams that have Negro players," Walters wrote. Walters would go on to pick the Wildcats to defeat McCarthy's team and take the SEC title. While Walters's commentary on the NCAA tournament and the unwritten law failed to express a definitive opinion on the legitimacy of the agreement or State's claim to the berth, the *Clarion-Ledger* sports columnist still supported and defended segregated athletics with his assumption of an NCAA tournament bid for the Wildcats. Theoretically, with the SEC title still up for grabs, the NCAA conference representative had yet to be decided, thus making both Kentucky and State viable options. Yet Walters's explanation of the unwritten law defied that logic and presented postseason play as an unattainable goal for the Bulldogs. On the day of the KU-MSU game, Walter wrote that "the duel to the death" would decide the SEC conference championship and called it not only the top contest in the Southeast but the "nation's premier attraction," a tough feat indeed for a Mississippi State team that Walters had already eliminated from the national championship picture.[101] In his preview, Walters made no reference to the NCAA tournament.

Walters addressed the Bulldogs' triumph over the Wildcats in the February 14 edition of the *Clarion-Ledger*, calling the win "one of the all-time great sports accomplishments by a Mississippi team." Walters admitted that he did not give the MSU contingent much of a chance going into Lexington, and the win would boost the team's national reputation. "It will prove to be the biggest prestige boost-sports-wise, in Mississippi State history," he wrote. Walters would go on to urge the Bulldogs to "finish the job" and win the SEC title, but he avoided referencing the NCAA tournament.

Walters moved on from the Bulldogs' battle with the Wildcats and previewed the team's upcoming game against the University of Florida on February 16, 1962, but the veteran sports scribe made a greater case for Auburn University as opposed to the Mississippi-based Bulldogs. According to Walters, if the Plainsmen were to defeat Kentucky and win their remaining games, they would be tied with the Wildcats for second place in the conference and win the head-to-head tiebreakers, sending the Alabama-based university to the national championship tournament. As for the Bulldogs and a national title, Walters wrote, "Mississippi State has already let it be known that the Bulldogs will pass up the national tourney because of 'established' policy as regards the race problem, so the Bulldogs are out. But that doesn't necessarily mean the Wildcats are in." While Walters's comments may have been accurate, there was no record of MSU's making any public statement validating his claims in the Mississippi press. Due to Walters's past support of the unwritten law, it was more likely that Walters had simply assumed the Bulldogs would not play in the tournament because of past precedent.

Walters next took issue with an article in the February 19 edition of *Sports Illustrated* by Ray Cave that profiled Rupp before the Wildcats lost to MSU.[102] Using the Bulldogs' victory as justification, Walters wondered if McCarthy was more worthy of such attention from the national sports-based magazine. "Maybe *Sports Illustrated* will wake up to the fact before too many more years pass that the days when Adolph Rupp and his Cats ruled the roost in the South—with little to no competition—are over and done with," the sports writer mused.[103] While McCarthy may have deserved some sort of national attention, Walters ignored the fact that McCarthy's MSU teams had never played in an NCAA tournament and still refrained from scheduling integrated foes, something that could not be said about Rupp and his Wildcats, thus contradicting Walters's criticism of the lack of competition for Rupp's squad.

Like many of his colleagues, Walters addressed the UPI and AP rankings and the perception of the Bulldogs from the national point of view. In his February 21 column, after the Bulldogs had moved up to fifth place in both polls, Walters wrote, "The characters who cast ballots in the basketball ranking polls finally took some notice of the Mississippi State Bulldogs this week, with Babe McCarthy's crew being chosen for the No. 5 spot on both lists." Kentucky was the third-ranked team in both polls, a point that Walters disagreed with. "Kentucky has no business being rated above State, either. . . . The reason the pollsters put 'Tucky ahead of State was because the Cats have played a tougher schedule, which recalls—once again—the difficulty the Ole Miss Rebels encounter in attaining high ranking in football, with too many weak foes among their victims." Again, Walters ignored that Kentucky played integrated foes and in the NCAA tournament, something that MSU had yet to do. Walters would also write that, "State's fifth-place ranking among all the nation's major college cage combines is something to be proud of, however, and the school—and the State of Mississippi—will benefit from this publicity fine," indicating that the veteran columnist put more stock into the polls than in the obvious national stage provided by the NCAA tournament and a possible national championship.

On February 26th Walters wrote that the Bulldogs were two games away for the SEC title and, with an Auburn win over Kentucky, State would "rule the SEC roost alone. . . . The McCarthymen have absolutely no intention of faltering in the stretch with the big prize now just two victories away." Walters, again did not reference the NCAA tournament. The same could be said for his March 1 column that previewed the game between MSU and Ole Miss. Walters predicted an MSU victory and the SEC title but stayed away from any postseason aspirations for the ball club despite the AP reporting on the same day that Lambert had been asking his constituents about the possibility of the Bulldogs playing in the NCAA tournament. Walters predicted a hard-fought victory for the Starkville five and hoped for a Kentucky loss at the hands of Tulane, which "would push the Maroons into the first place standings without any doubt."

After the Bulldogs clinched the conference championship, Walters wrote that MSU "proved they are genuine champions and worthy of all the plaudits coming their way when they rallied in the second half Saturday night to turn back a scrapping band of Ole Miss Rebels, 63–58."[104] After covering the spoils of the Bulldogs' season, the veteran sports reporter addressed MSU and the NCAA tournament, writing that the team's conference championship "also earned them the right to represent the SEC in the NCAA national championship campaigning, a privilege that will be passed up because of 'state policy' which forbids athletic competition between teams of state institutions and other teams that number Negroes among their players . . . not only brought honor to themselves and Mississippi State University, but have also brought honor and national recognition to the State of Mississippi."[105] Although Walters expressed no opinion on MSU's right to participate in the integrated postseason tournament, in the wake of the University of Wisconsin's upset victory over the top-ranked Ohio State Buckeyes, the future Mississippi Sports Hall of Famer wrote, "Thousands of Mississippi basketball fans will always wonder just how Mississippi State's Bulldogs would stack up against the top teams from other sections of the country." Walters also reprinted segments of *Sports Illustrated*'s Mervin Hyman's article, which claimed the Bulldogs were the best team in the southern United States. Hyman wrote that most teams that win the SEC participate in the NCAA's postseason "except when that team is Mississippi State. When the Bulldogs win, they have to beg off because state policy does not permit them to compete in integrated competition."[106]

In the wake of neighboring Memphis State's loss of head coach Bob Vanatta to the University of Missouri, Walters wrote that there were many Tiger fans in Memphis who wanted the school to offer the vacant position to McCarthy. Walters wondered if the Mississippi native would be willing to turn down a chance at a third straight conference title with the bulk of his roster remaining the same for the 1962–1963 season. Walters predicted that McCarthy would remain at MSU but added that the desire for national success could be a determining factor in the viability of the coach's relationship with Mississippi State. "We're simply 'guessing' that a year or two from now, if recruiting problems prove to be a real handicap, if Mississippi teams are still barred from competing for national honors, and if a good offer comes along from a top school that does not pass up NCAA or NIT events, McCarthy—in justice to himself and his future—will be moving along," Walters wrote. "We certainly hope that things DO NOT work out that way, but it's logical to assume that they could."[107] The statement was as daring as it got for the segregationist Walters. While the sports scribe often defended the unwritten law with his denouncement of tournament opportunities for Mississippi collegiate sports teams or with his silence on the issue, his March 14, 1962, commentary was, more or less, a plea to prevent the potential departure of McCarthy. Walters would later take issue with the absence of any MSU Bulldogs on both the United States Basketball Writers National and Southern All-Star squads. Walters admitted that the scoring averages of Mitchell and Stroud, roughly seventeen points each, was less than the other ten players selected and that "State's schedule was strictly sectional," an indirect nod to the absence of northern and, more importantly, integrated teams on the Bulldogs' schedule.[108]

Much like Baker and Walters, fellow segregationist Arnold Hederman also neglected MSU's chances at the postseason. Throughout the Bulldogs' championship campaign, the *Clarion-Ledger*'s sports editor demonstrated little foresight in his discussions on the Bulldogs, taking a game-by-game approach and commenting on the school's chances for a conference title, not surprising considering the conservative Hederman's allegiance to the Closed Society and his previous efforts during MSU's previous title-winning seasons. While the sports editor, on multiple occasions, identified State as a primary contender for the SEC championship in his daily column, "Highlights in Sports," he never made a reference to the NCAA tournament for the Starkville five.[109] Hederman even used one of his daily musings to examine the future prospects for both State and Kentucky and, while identifying both teams as title contenders for years to come, never referenced the integrated postseason or a national championship for either ball club.[110] Hederman, again, played it safe in the March 6 edition of "Highlights in Sports," congratulating McCarthy and his troops on their SEC conference title and discussing Kentucky's final two contests, never referencing the Wildcats's place in the tournament. Hederman closed his commentary by taking a neglectful route to express a degree of disappointment in the Bulldogs' final place in the AP and UPI polls, respectively. While MSU finished in fourth place in both national rankings, Hederman disagreed with the third place status of Kentucky. "What we are wondering about is 'how in the cat's hair' can Kentucky finish in third place after the Maroons had defeated the Wildcats?"[111] While Hederman's point did follow simple sports logic, he overlooked the obvious justification of the presence of integrated foes on Kentucky's schedule and the Wildcats' status as a willing NCAA tournament participant.

Clarion-Ledger sports writer Robert Fulton also got into the act of supplying opinion-based material to the Jackson-based newspaper in his column "High 'N Inside." A new voice to the MSU-NCAA tournament debate, Fulton only wrote one column the previous season discussing the then-Maroons and their plight in any detail. Fulton began his work on the 1962 Bulldogs by certifying the Starkville contingent as a viable contender to the SEC title.[112] Despite his contention, Fulton avoided any discussions on the postseason during the bulk of the 1962 season despite misleading his audience by declaring that the Bulldogs were going to the tournament after the team was promised tickets in exchange for a win over Kentucky.[113] Although the breadth of commentary from "Steamboat" on the Bulldogs and the integrated postseason was absent, the *Clarion-Ledger* sports writer would pen one of the more thought provoking columns on the issue in his March 3 edition of "High N' Inside." Appearing before State's final contest against Ole Miss, Fulton predicted that a Mississippi State win and subsequent SEC title would leave basketball fans in the Magnolia State waiting for "someone to make a decision" as to whether or not the Bulldogs could play in the tournament, which in Fulton's words "would result in the most buck-passing since the day Confederate money was ruled worthless." While Fulton had made a point of avoiding all conversations on an NCAA berth for the Bulldogs and failed to express his own opinion on postseason basketball for MSU, he clearly predicted another episode of political and social debate on the merits of integrated play within the Closed Society. Much like Jimmie McDowell of *Jackson State Times*, Fulton referred to said debate as "buck passing," putting the responsibility of upholding the unwritten law on the shoulders of the political purveyors of the Magnolia State.

Fulton would later use his March 6 edition of "High N' Inside" to focus on a letter from *Jacksonville Journal* sports editor Jack Hairston, a native Mississippian who denounced the unwritten law in his correspondence. Fulton printed Hairston's letter verbatim and the Florida-based sports editor, who identified Mississippi as the "only state in the union whose teams have not competed against Negro athletes" lamented for an athletic opportunity lost rather than a step towards social equality. "My interest is not in crusading for integration. As a former resident of Mississippi, I'm still interested in Mississippi and I hate to see them deprived of their chances at national recognition," Hairston wrote. Fulton expressed no opinion on the matter although his publication of the letter could have been interpreted as the Jackson sports writer's support for Hairston's commentary.

Fulton would conclude his commentary on the Bulldogs' season, writing about a campaign by "supporters of Mississippi State University" to purchase McCarthy a brand-new car. Fulton looked at the effort as a consolation prize for the Bulldogs' head coach, writing, "This will probably tend to sweeten the bad taste left in McCarthy's mouth by his not being allowed to take his Maroon basketball team to the NCAA regional play-offs." Fulton's remarks were the first to allude to the Bulldogs' leader as harboring some resentment for the binding nature of the unwritten law. To that point, the *Clarion-Ledger* had only described McCarthy as being disappointed.

The third and, historically, more conservative Hederman newspaper, the *Hattiesburg American*, also took the same route as its Jackson-based contemporaries, offering little to no commentary on the NCAA tournament or the unwritten law. Paul Morgan, the paper's sports editor, admitted that he doubted the championship legitimacy of McCarthy's squad in the February 7, 1962, edition of his column, "The Sports Hub," identifying the team's dominate win over Tulane as justification for his change of opinion but never explicitly cited the conference title as a possibility. Morgan also took issue with the ninth-place status of State in the AP national polls but quipped, "These rankings don't mean a thing to us," establishing, early in the debate, the editor's journalistic dismissal for any sort of national prominence for the Starkville-based basketball team. Morgan's subsequent columns neglected to reference the conference championship or a national title opportunity for the Bulldogs, even in the aftermath of their victory over Kentucky, despite calling the win "among the greatest cage upsets of modern times. . . . [MSU] showed us that perhaps, indeed, they are one of the best basketball teams in the nation."[114] Despite his sentiment, Morgan ignored the logical argument for State's place in the national title tournament. Morgan would eventually acknowledge MSU's building challenge to the SEC title but never referenced in NCAA tournament. [115] In total, Morgan's work did little to push the sociological and dated views of his readers and expressed no opinion on the merit of integrated athletics or State's right to play for the national title—not surprising considering the sports editor's journalistic allegiance to the Hedermans.

Despite the hometown appeal and proximity of the Bulldogs' challenge to the SEC championship and an NCAA tournament berth, the *Starkville Daily News* published little editorial material on the hometown Bulldogs during the 1961–1962 season. In fact, the first opinion-based material to reference the "McCarthymen" was published on February 15, 1962, in the aftermath of the win over Kentucky. The editorial, presumably written by editor Sherrill Nash, disputed a report in the *Birmingham News* that claimed the students on the Starkville-based campus rioted after the victory. Sports-based opinions and commentary was reserved for the anonymously penned "Time Out for Sports" and did little to advocate a postseason berth for the Bulldogs.[116] In the March 6 edition of the *Starkville Daily News*, Harris and Nash featured a small letter to the Bulldogs on the front page, congratulating them and thanking them for a wonderful season. In a nod to go to the NCAA playoffs, the letter stated "regardless of tournaments, we think you are the greatest basketball team in the Nation." Inside, the paper featured a full-page ad paid for by various local sponsors congratulating the Bulldogs and McCarthy on winning the conference championship.[117] In the same issue, the segregationist Harris congratulated the victorious Bulldogs on its share of the SEC championship in his column, "Pencil Shavings," but the controversial publisher was quick to temper any thoughts or discussion of an NCAA tournament invitation, writing, "Let's not compromise with principles.

Let's not even consider it. Some of our young friends in college may not agree with our views on this subject right now—but some day they will. And we are willing to wait. Being old enough to leave home or to go into the military service, or even vote, doesn't always signal the arrival of full and mature judgment. There is far more to this business of playing integrated basketball teams than can be confined to the walls of a gymnasium." In a nod to his belief in segregation, Harris then quipped, "Once action is underway, few players could tell by the shape of the court or the size of the baskets whether they are playing in Mississippi or Michigan," an obvious attack on the lack of intelligence held by State potentially integrated foes.

While public opinion on the issue could be measured, to some extent, by the presence of letters to the editors, in the case of the Bulldogs' 1961–1962 campaign, published statements of opinion from the reading audience were few and far between. In fact, outside of any references to letters that were used in columns from various Mississippi newspapers, only a single letter appeared in any Mississippi newspaper consulted in this chapter concerning the 1962 NCAA tournament debate.

The first and only letter to the editor in the Jackson-based *Clarion-Ledger* was published on March 20, 1962, sixteen days after the team's title-clinching victory over Ole Miss. Johnny Nikolic, a student at Mississippi State, asked for additional justification as to why the Bulldogs were forced to sit out of the national tournament, citing Mississippi's political elite's permission for "Congressmen to go and participate in an integrated Congress . . . white teachers to teach in a Negro school and . . . Mississippi's most beautiful women to participate before integrated crowds at Miss America Pageants." Nikolic argued that MSU should have been allowed to compete for the title in order to prove the legitimacy of the Closed Society and its segregationist way of life. "I think our boys could prove that our principle of segregation is just as capable of winning an NCAA tournament or any other type of competition as an integrated one," the Jackson resident wrote. "I don't mean we will or would win, but I believe we could use our principle in fighting for what we believe while competing. What's wrong with an all-white team winning the tournament! Nothing, and why don't we prove it?"[118]

The justification for the lack of published commentary from the reading audience is speculative. Like the print-based discussion of the 1961 title-winning Maroons, it was somewhat illogical to think that a single letter to the editor was submitted during the debate surrounding the merits of the unwritten law, considering that MSU President Dean Colvard received his fair share of correspondence on the Bulldogs. As previously established in this text, public commentary was subject to the gatekeeping role of the editors of Mississippi's daily newspapers and it is possible such correspondence were submitted but, due to the contradictory nature of the letters, were never published. Furthermore, the efforts of MSU's basketball team came during Meredith attempts to integrate Ole Miss, making it possible that the editors of the Magnolia State chose to take a conservative approach when it came to public commentary and issues of race. Letters advocating integration or MSU's participation in the NCAA tournament would have supported the idea that the Closed Society and its social beliefs were flawed.

It would still be another year before Colvard would give McCarthy the green light to participate in an integrated postseason. The North Carolina native, who would come under fire from various state entities that promoted and protected the segregationist way of life in Mississippi, would receive letters arguing both for and against the Bulldogs' participation in the NCAA tournament.

In the midst of the racial and social turmoil that engulfed the Magnolia State due to the ongoing and eventual admission of Meredith to Ole Miss, it would be understandable if some journalists overlooked the contributions of Mississippi State's basketball team in weakening the iron-fisted reign of the Closed Society. However, it was clear that the constant challenges to the unwritten law pushed Mississippi's journalists, specifically sportswriters, into a position of support. While almost to a man every supporter of an MSU venture into integrated basketball expressed their segregationist status, in turn they were in opposition of the Closed Society, thus contributing to the weakening of the racist foundation on which it sat. In terms of social progress, no one supported the Bulldogs for the sake of equality and civil rights, but a progressive ideological switch was beginning in the Magnolia State, which was represented in the work of the press. When MSU violated the unwritten law in 1956, the team and the school were met with universal outrage over its participation in an integrated contest. Roughly six years later, some journalists were calling for the elimination of Mississippi's segregationist athletic standard. Even the Hederman papers, while opposing McCarthy's crew, offered subtle hints at such a change, especially in the musings of Baker who surprisingly questioned the merits of the unwritten law. Others, such as Walters, continued to hold on and defend the Closed Society, but more journalists were offering opinions that were noncommittal in content and tone, a progressive step indeed. While Meredith's September 1962 arrival on the Oxford campus would unite the state's press against the Federal Government, the Closed Society and, specifically, the unwritten law faced a final test from the Starkville contingent that would put reporters and editors across the state at ideological odds and leave the gentleman's agreement in shambles.

Chapter 5

This Is the Biggest Challenge to Our Way of Life Since the Reconstruction

The night of March 15, 1963, was one never before seen in the annals of Mississippi State University. The air was thick and contentious in East Lancing, Michigan, as the Bulldogs of James "Babe" McCarthy made their historic debut in the NCAA National Championship basketball tournament. After a successful campaign in the Southeastern Conference that netted the squad their fourth title in five years, the Starkville-based quintet would, on this night, tackle a foe so crippling and intimidating that the contest itself would be the subject of debate for weeks. For the first time in school history, the MSU contingent would participate in an integrated postseason. Behind the vicarious McCarthy and embattled university president Dean W. Colvard, the Bulldogs accepted an invitation to the tournament, violating Mississippi's long observed unwritten law. As *Delta Democrat-Times* editor Hodding Carter quipped on March 13, 1963, "The people decided they were sick of stupidity—no matter under what guise it travelled." While State would lose to the integrated Ramblers 61–51, their participation was a victory over Mississippi's staunch segregationists and protectors of the Closed Society. When asked by reporters how he and his team would be received upon returning to Mississippi's segregated boarders, McCarthy said, "I don't know. I hope they don't bomb the plane."[1]

MSU's decision was the subject of a heated debate in the tense, volatile air of the Magnolia State between the conservative white ideals of the Closed Society and the progression of civil rights in the South. While many of the journalistic stalwarts of Mississippi's oppressive way of life held true to form and supported the unwritten law through their writing or via silence, opposition to the gentlemen's agreement began to swell, infesting the Magnolia State's journalistic community, especially those allocated to the sports section. The debate supporting the 1962–1963 Bulldogs brought forth new support for integrated athletics and demonstrated a slow but progressive change in Mississippi's press that refused to blindly damn any and all notions towards integration and social equality.

The stage had been set, socially, for the Mississippi State contingent to oppose the Closed Society. Only months prior to the start of Mississippi State's

JUMP BALL

In response to the news of the State College Board's meeting concerning Mississippi State's possible participation in the 1963 NCAA tournament, the *Jackson Daily News'* Bob Howie published this editorial cartoon depicting a State basketball player being tossed between two hands, labeled pro and con. *Courtesy Bob Howie/Jackson Daily News.*

1962–1963 season, James Meredith, a transfer student from Jackson State College, was allowed to enroll at the University of Mississippi, marking the beginning of integration for the Magnolia State's previously segregated colleges and universities. Meredith admission to the school was supported by the federal government, which drew the ire of many members of the Mississippi press.[2] On September 30, 1962, Meredith was escorted on the Oxford campus, much to the chagrin of segregationists statewide. That evening, the campus, littered with U.S. marshals and members of the Mississippi National Guard, erupted with riots that left two dead, many injured, and seventy-five people arrested. The incident put a black eye on the university and the state. Flags in Jackson were flown at half-staff; however, as historian Susan Weill writes, "Whether the flag was lowered to honor the two men who were killed or to mourn the loss of segregation at the university was not officially designated."[3] This ideological attack on the Closed Society helped pave the way for MSU's challenge to the unwritten law, leading to the eventual demise of the gentlemen's agreement. From February 26, 1963, when the Bulldogs clinched the SEC championship through March 20, 1963, after the MSU contingent returned to Starkville from the NCAA tournament, editors and reporters in Mississippi debated the legitimacy of the unwritten law. That December, Mississippi State University's basketball Bulldogs would begin its 1962–1963 season, one that would aggravate the already exposed cracks in the racist foundation of white Mississippi. As the Bulldogs mounted the final challenge to the unwritten law, those same journalists and editors were fragmented on their opinions of MSU's desire to play in the integrated tournament, signaling a significant weakness in the Closed Society. The slow but evolutionary change occurring in Mississippi's press was apparent by the number of both sports reporters and editors who expressed a change in opinion from previous debates involving the state's once sacred unwritten law.

The change in journalistic perspective, especially from the vantage point of sports reporters, is not easily explained. While editors in the state were united in their distained over the forced integration of Ole Miss, the participation of Mississippi State in integrated athletics fueled varying responses from the press. The justification in such a change could be found in the social significance of athletics. Even in the Closed Society, athletic endeavors served as a point of pride. As noted earlier in this text, values of a society are often projected within the context of their preferred athletic endeavors. With the Closed Society teetering on the brink of revolution, the support for the Bulldogs could have easily been justified by a desire for reassurance in regards to their own cultural distinctiveness. A successful appearance by one of their own, an all-white MSU basketball team, in the shark infested waters of the segregated NCAA tournament would have provided a degree of validation for their segregationist society. While many of Mississippi's journalistic luminaries were strident voices in the quest for civil rights in the state, the swift ideological change as it pertained to MSU's entry into the NCAA tournament could be attributed to this quest for validation, which could only come by way of an integrated endeavor.[4] Further validation for the newfound support from sports journalists and the search for cultural identity can be seen in the reaction to the Bulldogs' loss to Loyola. Rather than identify the social and cultural relevance of the integration of athletics within the state and the Southeastern Conference, most Mississippi newspapers disregarded the team's appearance in the tournament after the Bulldogs were eliminated from the postseason. To acknowledge the defeat in the same manner that the issue of integrated athletics was debated would be a kin to a reexamination of the pervading cultural identity within the Closed Society, a painful proposition to say the least, considering the value placed on segregation. It was clear that the opportunity to validate the values of the Closed Society, from an athletic perspective, was lost. However, despite the perceived social step backwards, the damage to the Closed Society had already been done. In total, the 1963 MSU-NCAA debate served as a sign of things to come in Mississippi as the press continued in this process that had originally been spurred by Meredith's entry into Ole Miss.

Like in past years, MSU's desire to play in the integrated national championship tournament was well known even before it became an argued norm in the pages of Mississippi's newspapers. As early as January 25, 1963, McCarthy told members of the press that he hoped for the elimination of the unwritten law so his team could have a chance to play for the national championship. McCarthy explained that the purveyors of the Closed Society could no longer look at the Bulldogs as a threat to all out integration in the Magnolia State because that line had already been crossed by Meredith.[5] The Bulldogs would stake their claim to conference supremacy on February 25th with a victory over Tulane University 78–67, clinching the school's third straight SEC basketball championship. The two teams exchanged the lead twenty-one times before State pulled away in the first half. Senior W. D. "Red" Stroud led the Bulldogs with twenty-eight points, while fellow senior Joe Dan Gold added twenty-six in the win. Robert "Steamboat" Fulton of the *Clarion-Ledger*, who just a year earlier called for the elimination of the unwritten law, foretold of the pending controversy, writing, "It is the hour of decision for the officials who have for three years kept championship Miss. State teams at home while less worthy clubs represented the league in the NCAA. If those officials show the guts and courage displayed last night by the Bulldogs, their chances of going will be greatly improved."[6] Others journalists were not as supportive. Fellow Hederman-based sports reporter Phil Wallace of the *Jackson Daily News* wrote that, while the SEC title was in the Bulldogs' sights, the NCAA tournament was still in doubt due to the unwritten law.[7] In an almost universal fashion, most articles that appeared in Mississippi newspapers on the win quoted McCarthy lamenting for a national title opportunity. "I wish the boys, by some means, would have the opportunity to play," the State head coach told the press. "It breaks my heart."[8] McCarthy did not mince his words with the *Starkville Daily News*, telling an anonymous reporter, "It makes me sick when I have to tell friends I don't think we'll get a chance to go. . . . I don't see why they should have to pack their uniforms and let an Alabama or Georgia team represent the SEC when they have the same problem we have. To a man, my boys want to play in the tournament."[9]

Despite McCarthy's public appeal and the team's success, sports reporters such as Jim Hackleman, Tom Dygard, and Robert Davenport of the Associated

Press and David M. Moffit of United Press International either downplayed the team's chances of entering the tournament due to the unwritten law or stressed that conference runner-up Georgia Tech would be the SEC's representative.[10] Carter's *Delta Democrat-Times* even published such an account with the misleading headline, "State Clinches Tie in SEC—Tech Earns NCAA Berth," indicating that the editors at the *Times* assumed that MSU would succumb to the unwritten law.[11] With the win, State moved into the seventh spot in both the AP and UPI national basketball polls.[12]

In the aftermath of MSU's victory over the Green Wave, the Magnolia State's litany of politicians began to appear in the pages of the state's newspapers voicing their opinions on a Mississippi State NCAA tournament appearance. Republican gubernatorial candidate Rubel Phillips told the AP that McCarthy's squad should play in the NCAA tournament, proposing that the reach of the unwritten law remain within Mississippi's borders.[13] In articles from both the AP and UPI, the State College Board athletic committee chairman S. R. Evans said MSU was not likely to accept the bid unless the team had political support within the state.[14] Sen. Billy Mitts of Enterprise, a former MSU cheerleader and a strident defender of the unwritten law during its eight-year duration, went before the state Senate and asked that legislative measures be taken against MSU to prevent them from going to the NCAA tournament. Mitts's request was tabled and sent to committee.[15]

Before MSU's last game against in-state rival Ole Miss, McCarthy spoke to sports editor Bill Ross of the Tupelo-based *Daily Journal* and said he thought the prospects of playing in the NCAA tournament were better than in the team's past SEC title-winning campaigns. In a show of optimism, the Baldwyn native said that he felt there was more general interest in the issue and that prevailing opinion in the state had changed since the team's first conference championship in 1959.[16] Despite McCarthy's positive commentary, MSU athletic director Wade Walker told Ross that it was unlikely the team would violate the unwritten law.[17] Although it was reported in a number of wire-based articles that officials with MSU feared possible punishment from the SEC or the NCAA if it were to reject the bid, SEC commissioner Bernie Moore refuted such a claim in a March 7, 1963, article from UPI per the *Daily Journal*.

Despite all of the public commentary on the chances of MSU playing in the integrated national title tournament, Gold, who was a senior and the team captain of the 1963 squad, said there was little discussion on the matter in the Bulldogs' locker room. "We were aware that McCarthy wanted to go and we were aware that Dr. Colvard was receptive to go, but I don't think we ever got our hopes up because of the unwritten law," said Gold in a July 2009 interview. "As a team, we never really had any discussions on that. We had several Mississippi guys on the team and several from out of state that had played integrated teams

Behind President Dean W. Colvard, the Mississippi State team accepted an invitation to the 1963 NCAA national basketball championship tournament effectively ending Mississippi's unwritten law. *Courtesy Mississippi State University Libraries, University Archives.*

before. I first played against black players in 1957 when I was in high school. We did have some who had never played against black players but I don't think it was an issue for any of us."

On March 2nd, before the Bulldogs were to play their final game of the 1963 regular season against the Rebels of Ole Miss, Colvard surprisingly announced that he would allow McCarthy's team to go to East Lansing, Michigan to play in the NCAA tournament, calling it the "right thing to do." The university president, who received both scorn and praise for his decision, questioned the validity of the unwritten law and noted the enormous amount of support the team received from faculty, alumni, students, friends, and fans, as justification for his decision. "My conviction is that the well-trained young people of Mississippi can compete on a favorable basis, athletically and intellectually, with the best in other parts of the country," Colvard said in his announcement. "I am further convinced that the spirit of fair play on the part of all concerned at the scene of the NCAA play-offs will transcend whatever prejudice or bias may obtain and transmute all participants into their essential roles as champions competing for the crown." [18]

No president in the history of Mississippi State had to confront the issue of race more frequently than Colvard. The North Carolina native replaced Ben

Hilbun at the conclusion of the 1959–1960 school year and was in essence an outsider to the Magnolia State. As historian Michael Ballard notes, Colvard came to MSU with "a wider worldview than some of his predecessors."[19] Furthermore, the issue of race and integration was a dated one for MSU's president. Prior to journeying to Starkville, Colvard served as the Dean of the School of Agriculture at North Carolina State College. While Jim Crow was alive and well in North Carolina, the Tar Heel state was, seemingly, more progressive than their Mississippi brethren, integrating their colleges and universities during the mid to late 1950s, well before Colvard arrived to Starkville in 1960.[20] Even before MSU's basketball team successful 1962–1963 campaign, Meredith's entry in the University of Mississippi brought a tense environment to the Starkville campus. Colvard had a legitimate fear that MSU students would go to Oxford to participate in the demonstration and, while fifteen MSU students were arrested during the riots, his efforts to keep the students in Starkville were successful. However, this was of little comfort to Colvard in the tense air of the Magnolia State. So fearful that atrocities similar to that of the Oxford riots would happen on his campus, the North Carolina native considered leaving State to allow a Mississippian to take the role of president.[21] Despite his concerns, Colvard stayed the course due to the ample support he received from the MSU faculty and student body. [22] While many viewed Colvard as a hero in MSU's long history, at the time, the embattled president's permission to play in the tournament made him one of the more disliked individuals in the Closed Society. [23] With the impending controversy and subsequent decision to allow the Bulldogs to play in the tournament, the MSU president was bombarded with inquiries both supporting and denouncing his decision. According to the president's personal correspondence, a number of journalists contacted MSU's embattled leader to offer their support. Jackson news director Dick Sanders of WJDX and WLBT Channel 3 wrote to Colvard to express his "appreciation and admiration" for allowing the Bulldogs to play in the integrated tournament.[24] J. Oliver Emmerich showed his support for Colvard by writing the president to tell him that most of the *Enterprise-Journal's* reading audience had accepted his decision.[25] Owens F. Alexander, manager of the Capital Broadcasting Company and WJTV Channel 12 in Jackson followed suit, telling Colvard that, in a poll conducted by the CBS affiliate, 85 percent of local residents were "overwhelmingly" in favor of MSU's appearance in the NCAA tournament.[26] Jocko Maxwell, sports director of radio station WNJR in Newark, New Jersey, the self-professed "America's Most Experienced Negro Radio Chain," called the idea that the Bulldogs would miss the tournament due to integrated foes a "silly, un-American view. This is 1963 and we feel that all races in the USA should join together to build a happier world by good sportsmanship, clean politics, and clean living."[27]

Jackson Daily News cartoonist Bob Howie celebrated Mississippi State's win over the Ole Miss Rebels and acceptance of the NCAA invitation in a cartoon published at the conclusion of the 1963 season. *Courtesy Bob Howie/Jackson Daily News.*

The majority of newspaper accounts covering Colvard's announcement published the university president's statement verbatim.[28] *Meridian Star* sports editor Billy "Sunshine" Rainey, who offered little support to the Bulldogs during previous challenges of the unwritten law, wrote in a hesitant tone that the team would "apparently play in the event this year."[29] An anonymous reporter for the Associated Press opened their article on the decision by writing, "Segregationist elements remained silent today on Mississippi State's decision to permit the Maroons to play in the NCAA basketball tournament" in a nod to the bevy of no comments that came from staunch segregationists like Barnett and William J. Simmons of the Citizens' Council.[30] It was also reported that the Mississippi State Student Senate unanimously voted for the team to play in the tournament and offered a public show of support for Colvard, indicating that the decision was well received on the Starkville campus.[31]

Knowing that a chance at a national championship was in their immediate future, the Bulldogs would go on to defeat the Rebels 75–72 as Gold scored twenty-four points and Stroud chipped in nineteen. MSU finished the regular season with a 21–5 record and 12–2 mark in the SEC.[32] After the win, McCarthy told the press he was pleased with Colvard's decision. "It's great," the joyous coach said. "I'm happy we can go. The boys deserve it."[33] With the win, Mississippi State remained the seventh best team in the nation according to the rankings in the AP and UPI national basketball polls.[34]

The day after Colvard's announcement, suspicion grew within the press in regards to the reaction from Mississippi's more stringent supporters of segregation. Moffit noted as such in his article for UPI, writing that "joy, tempered by caution, is today's mode at Mississippi State."[35] The political elite of the Closed Society soon took to the press, attacking MSU and defending the unwritten law. In a UPI article featured in the *Clarion-Ledger* and the *Delta Democrat-Times*, Rep. Russell Fox, who was cited as helping create the gentleman's agreement in 1956, told the anonymous author that Colvard's decision would be misinterpreted as a sign of weakness from other states in Mississippi's stand for segregation.[36] Mitts called the decision a "low blow to the state of Mississippi" and questioned the College Board, telling the unknown author, "It should place native sons of Mississippi in college presidencies and not risk a similar tragedy like this from happening in the future," a swipe at Colvard's North Carolina roots. Representative Walter Hester of Natchez claimed that MSU was opening the doors for all-out integration. "It is no safer to mix with Negroes on the ball courts than it is in the classroom," Hester said. "The liberal press will have their way with this and how can you blame them. We are being sold out by our own people."[37] The Rev. W. E. Gamble of Jackson concurred with Hester's remarks, predicting that MSU's participation would compromise future efforts to maintain segregation in Mississippi schools.[38] Governor Ross Barnett told the press he had no comment.[39]

On March 5, 1963, a number of news outlets reported that the State College Board, led by Hattiesburg-based attorney and segregationist M. M. Roberts, would hold an emergency meeting on March 10th to decide whether or not to override Colvard's decision and prevent the Bulldogs from playing in the NCAA tournament.[40] Cliff Sessions of UPI wrote that a few anonymous members of the board wanted to not only keep the MSU contingent in Starkville but also adopt an official policy against any state-supported institution playing in integrated events.[41] The colorful McCarthy responded to the news of the State College Board's impending meeting in a somber yet defiant manner, telling the *Laurel Leader-Call*, "We've been staying home because of an unwritten law. There is no such thing in my book. . . . If we lose our ability to compete, we lose everything."[42] While Colvard made the decision, it was evident that the media savvy McCarthy served as the primary spokesperson and advocate for the Bulldogs' tournament bid.

Rainey and fellow *Meridian Star* sports writer Howard Beeland took to the streets of Meridian to check the pulse of local Mississippi State graduates and discovered that most of the alumni interviewed supported Colvard and the Bulldogs. Former MSU football player Thomas "Shorty" McWilliams told the *Star*'s duo, "We can't isolate ourselves in the state of Mississippi. If we do, it may come to a point where Mississippi schools are only playing state schools. We need to branch out."[43] Fellow Meridian resident James Garnett said that he was happy to see Colvard accept the invitation, and he did not think the state's segregationist policy would be affected. The only objection to the postseason venture by MSU came from Wayne Anders, who told Rainey and Beeland, "This is opening the door to the NAACP to put Negroes in Mississippi schools at a fast pace."[44] While Rainey's work from MSU's past title-winning campaigns failed to address the debate surrounding the unwritten law, his article in the March 5, 1963, edition of the *Meridian Star* showed a legitimate attempt by "Sunshine" to present a fair and accurate depiction of public opinion on a controversial topic, a bold move for the typically conservative Rainey.

Despite the announcement of the State College Board's meeting, Fulton reported in the March 6 edition of the *Clarion-Ledger* that the Bulldogs were moving ahead with preparing for their trip to East Lansing. In the same edition of the *Clarion-Ledger,* an article from the AP detailed the festering controversy surrounding MSU and the unwritten law. McCarthy was quoted at the conclusion of the piece, telling the reporter, "I think we have a real good chance to go and we'll carry through our plans to make the trip until notified by college authorities to forget it." Fellow Hederman publication, the *Jackson Daily News*, published the same article with McCarthy's closing remarks noticeably absent. Meanwhile, it was reported that both the faculty at Mississippi State and the Oktibbeha County Chamber of Commerce supported Colvard's decision to play and offered votes of confidence for the embattled president.[45]

Barnett broke his silence on the matter on March 7th, as the governor told Charles M. Hills of the *Clarion-Ledger* that the team's participation would bring undue harm to all citizens of Mississippi. "Personally, I feel that it is not for the best interest of Mississippi State University, the State of Mississippi, or either of the races," Barnett said.[46] The AP's account on Barnett's commentary also discussed the possibility that State would encounter an integrated team, such as eventual foe Loyola of Chicago, which had four blacks in its starting lineup, and the defending national champions University of Cincinnati Bearcats, which had three.[47]

Meanwhile, Roberts, who would serve as one of MSU's primary adversaries in the NCAA tournament debate, used the press to call out his colleagues on the State College Board, urging them to "do its full duty to its constituents and to the Southern Way of Life."[48] Roberts, one of the more powerful propitiators of the Closed Society, called the debate "the greatest challenge to our way of life since the Reconstruction," a questionable contention to say the least. [49] The *Jackson Daily News'* William Peart wrote that the segregationist attorney from Hattiesburg "scorched speculation that a quorum would be present at the Saturday meeting," a reference to a rumor reported by the AP and UPI that Colvard's supporters would simply skip the meeting in order to prevent the board from voting.[50] In regards to the State College Board, historians have pointed out that, as the social climate in Mississippi began to shift and integration began to become an inevitable conclusion, most board members were unable or unwilling to accept the changes taking place around them. Segregationists such as Roberts, Ira "Shine" Morgan of Oxford, Ray Izard of Hazelhurst, Williams O. Stone of Jackson, and Leon Lowery of Olive Branch, all of whom were appointed to the board by Barnett, passionately fought against integration and looked out for their own political beliefs and those of the Closed Society.[51] "I look back now, and I am ashamed of the way I voted sometimes," said fellow board member Verner Holmes to historian David Sansing. "I think back in those days we all, in our hearts, we were a little racist."[52]

Peart was one of the few staff writers who reported on Roberts's commentary as the majority of Mississippi's press depended on AP and UPI accounts of the segregationist's statements. Perhaps what was more interesting about the account of Roberts's statements was the placement of James Saggus's article for the AP in the pages of the *Clarion-Ledger*. While Saggus's work was featured on the front page of the March 8, 1963, edition, above the article was an editorial by editor Tom Hederman Jr. that predicted the systematic disintegration of segregation in the Magnolia State if the Bulldogs were to play in the tournament. In combination, the content of the two accounts sent a powerful message to the *Clarion-Ledger's* audience rife with support for the Closed Society and the unwritten law.

Rainey, in another bold journalistic step for the conservative sports editor, penned a brief history of MSU's multiple battles with the unwritten law in the March 8, 1963, edition of the *Meridian Star*. Rainey wrote that either the state's traditional policy of allowing colleges and universities to make decisions on such matters would be broken or the Magnolia State's unwritten law, a nod to the historical precedent that was eventually set. Rainey concluded his article by identifying the precarious nature McCarthy's team was in. Rainey's work, which offered no hint of opinion, was a nod to the civic nature of "Sunshine's" role as a journalist, and his efforts on State's history with the unwritten law was a sound journalistic decision.

Recognizing that the Bulldogs' NCAA tournament fate could have been significantly altered by the State College Board, Fulton began his March 8 article for the *Clarion-Ledger* on the team's preparation for the tournament by stating, "If Mississippi State's basketball team doesn't go to the NCAA Regional next week, a lot of sweat and preparation will have been in vain." Fulton asked McCarthy if he had discussed the possibility of encountering black athletes during the course of the tournament, to which the MSU head coach boldly said, "We won't consider them as being black or white, but as being just another bunch of players." On March 9th, the *Vicksburg Evening Post* and the *Clarion-Ledger* reported that the majority of the board would be present to determine the fate of McCarthy's Bulldogs. The article, which did not have a byline in either newspaper, was the first to identify Loyola as having "four Negroes in its starting lineup" and called the third ranked team in the country a heavy favorite to battle MSU in Michigan.

On March 9, 1963, the State College Board voted by an 8–3 margin to allow MSU to play in the tournament.[53] The *Clarion-Ledger's* Bill Simpson, who called the vote a violation of the unwritten law, reported that Roberts told his fellow board members that State's participation in the tournament would end Mississippi's "southern way of life." In defeat, Roberts called for Colvard's removal as MSU president which was met with a 9–2 vote of confidence for Colvard from the board. Roberts, as detailed in the *Clarion-Ledger*, explained that his resentment towards Colvard was due in part to the MSU president's "defiance" of the board's will, hence his request for the MSU leader to resign. Board member Stone told an unknown UPI reporter that, while he did not believe the team should go, interfering with Colvard's ability to make a decision would have set a negative precedent. "Great harm has already been done to the university by the president's announcement," Stone said. "If we repudiate him, it will do greater harm."[54] Barnett, who only days earlier professed his objection to the school's participation in the integrated tournament, said in a statement that he would yield to the State College Board. "I have great pride in our team and I hope they will win the national championship."[55]

Meanwhile, UPI's account of the meeting predicted that the vote in favor of Colvard and the university would "abandon the state's long-standing policy of prohibiting participating against teams with Negro athletes," thus signaling the end of the unwritten law.[56] John Hall of the AP focused more on the scene in Jackson and the social issues surrounding it. "Some say Saturday's decision was a breakthrough for the forces of integration," Hall wrote. "Others deny it, and claim the issue is state's rights—they do it their way there and we'll do it our way here."[57] McCarthy, who was in Jackson at the state high school basketball championship, was quoted in most accounts of the meeting by saying he was grateful for the decision.[58] Hall's article appeared in the Hederman-owned *Hattiesburg American* on March 11, 1963, with the headline, "Is Board's Decision a Blow to Segregation?"

The *Mississippi Free Press*, a radical minority newspaper that was founded in 1961 under the premise of "Social Justice in Mississippi,"[59] focused on the vote as it pertained to the Magnolia State's segregationist governor in the March 16, 1963, edition of the weekly newspaper, stating, "Ross Barnett's advice was ignored last week as the State College Board voted 8–3 to send Mississippi State University's basketball team to an integrated tournament in Michigan." Barnett was a frequent target of editor Charlie Butts, whose paper was designed to be an alternative to the *Jackson Advocate* and the conservative Percy Greene and often featured opinion-based material in the context of news articles. Greene, who had a reputation for taking a moderate approach to issues of race, only addressed the MSU-NCAA issue once during the eight years of the unwritten law's existence.[60]

Many newspapers, such as the *Jackson Daily News*, the *Meridian Star*, and the *Vicksburg Evening Post*, published photos of E. A. Elam, who was at the meeting with a petition signed by 130 people opposing MSU, heavily chastising State College Board Chairman Tom Tubb. Elam told Tubb that blood would be on his hands as a result of the board's decision.[61] On the same day the board's decision was prominently featured on the paper's front page, the *Jackson Daily News* published a photo of the MSU team in the sports section with the heading, "Miss. State's NCAA Bound S.E.C. Champions."[62]

A temporary sense of order reappeared in the pages of Mississippi newspapers, as the athletic exploits of the Bulldogs became the primary focus of journalists in the state. The *Jackson Daily News* reported that the team began its final preparations for the tournament without McCarthy and assistant coach Jerry Simmons, who were in Evanston, Illinois scouting the first round tournament game between Loyola and Tennessee Tech with the winner to face the Bulldogs in Michigan.[63] In light of the decision, Fulton turned his attention back to the hardwood and wrote in the March 13, 1963, edition of the *Clarion-Ledger* that McCarthy was in awe of the Ramblers after watching Loyola's record-breaking sixty-nine-point victory over Tennessee Tech, 111–42.[64] The Bulldogs' head coach called the Chicago-based team the best MSU had ever played.[65] Perhaps in a nod to Fulton's inexperience addressing issues of race, the future sports editor of the *Clarion-Ledger* and the *Meridian Star* identified every member of the Ramblers' starting line-up with accompanying statistical information. When Fulton addressed John Egan, "Steamboat" referred to the Ramblers' guard as the only starter who was white.

On March 13th, only four days after the State College Board's decision, it was first reported in a small article on the front page of the *Jackson Daily News* that "an unidentified group" was attempting to secure an injunction from a chancery court judge to prevent the MSU contingent from venturing to East Lansing to play in the NCAA tournament. The following day, *Jackson Daily News* staff writers Peart and W. C. "Dub" Shoemaker not only verified that such an injunction had been secured, but that the Mississippi State team essentially ignored the decision and had already left by plane for the tournament. Shoemaker also covered the Emmett Till trial for the *Daily News* and, per historians Gene Roberts and Hank Klibanoff, was not as ardent a segregationist as his editors.[66] The injunction, which was obtained by Mitts and B. W. Lawson and signed by Chancery Court Judge L. B. Porter of Hinds County in Brandon, prohibited MSU from spending state money "to travel from the state of Mississippi to engage in any athletic contest when participation is against mixed teams" and claimed that Colvard had unnecessarily raised tensions on the Starkville campus. Due to Ward's political ties within the Closed Society and Mississippi's political elite, the identification of Mitts, a founding father of the unwritten law as "an unidentified group" was suspect at best. Similar information could be found in other articles published throughout the state. [67] Peart and Shoemaker called State's potential violation of the unwritten law, "The most serious crisis in Mississippi since Negro James Meredith was enrolled at the University of Mississippi," indicating a negative editorial position on behalf of the authors. While the *Jackson Daily News* was the first to have a story on MSU's controversial exodus from the Magnolia State, it would be another day before the details of the team's complex departure would be known.

Segregationist editor Sherrill Nash covered the team's exit for Michigan in the *Starkville Daily News* and expressed a degree of shame in the outlaw-like departure of the SEC champions. "The Bulldogs, with the credentials of heroes, departed for their greatest challenge as a criminal escaping from jail," he wrote. "It was a picture not many Mississippians will want to refer to in the future years."[68] Nash, who defended the unwritten law in the past with publisher Henry Harris, valued the athletic accomplishments of the MSU team and used the paper's editorial outlet to express such pride. However, the Starkville editor identified the potential embarrassment for the state and the university in the aftermath of the tournament but failed to ascribe blame to either MSU or the proprietors of the Closed Society, lending a degree of confusion to his commentary.

While the front page of the March 14 edition of the *Jackson Daily News* prominently featured the news of MSU's exit from Mississippi, sports editor Lee Baker wrote in the paper's sports section that the Bulldogs were "due to keep a long overdue date" with the Ramblers in the NCAA tournament, indicating a favorable impression on integrated play. While Baker spent past debates surrounding the merits of the unwritten law expressing little to no opinion on the matter, his slight jab to the gentleman's agreement and the Closed Society may have been his boldest statement to date and was in opposition of the opinions expressed by his editor, the outspoken Jimmy Ward. Much like Baker, the *Clarion-Ledger*'s Fulton allowed his own personal hopes for the Starkville-based Bulldogs to make their way into his news-based accounts. On the day of the team's departure for Michigan, Fulton described MSU as a determined team, unfazed by their underdog status. "The big thing is that Mississippi State is finally getting the chance to represent the SEC in NCAA play," Fulton wrote in an expression of his own excitement. "Win, lose, or draw, the Bulldogs are hellbent on making a good showing."[69]

Others reporters in the Magnolia State wrote on the injunction, but due to the limbo-like status of its enforcement, also indicated that Mississippi State would be leaving for the tournament as planned.[70] *Commercial Dispatch* sports editor Eddie Dean not only acknowledged the legal purgatory of the MSU team, but also used to opportunity to cheer for the Bulldogs. "Only one thing was certain as you watched the party depart, and that was the enthusiasm of the people watching that the Maroons would win!" Dean exclaimed.[71] Fellow sports writer George Anderson of the *Starkville Daily News* called the NCAA tournament the team's "greatest challenge ever" but neglected the injunction and the unwritten law in his account.[72]

The *Jackson Daily News*' Peart and the AP reported the following day that Mississippi State Supreme Court Associated Justice Robert G. Gillespie had suspended the injunction because it was "issued without authority of law and was improvidently issued without notice."[73] Gillespie said an additional hearing would be held in the future to determine whether or not to dismiss the injunction altogether. With at least a temporary reprieve from the efforts of the Closed Society, Mississippi's journalists reported that the Bulldogs and their coaches arrived in East Lansing without any reports of "picketing or other incidents."[74] While the expectation of some sort of incident showed the still present grip of the Closed Society on the press, what may have been a greater journalistic demonstration of the white caste society's influence was the coverage of the Bulldogs' efforts to avoid the injunction from Hinds County.

In anticipation of the injunction, the brass at MSU, including Colvard and McCarthy, employed what many in the press called "cloak and dagger tactics" to avoid the serving of the legally binding court order.[75] McCarthy left in the dark of the night for Nashville, Tennessee on March 13, 1963, while Colvard drove to Alabama for a speaking engagement at Auburn University. That evening, Oktibbeha County Sheriff Tom Cook sent Deputy Dot Johnson to unsuccessfully serve the injunction as McCarthy and Colvard, who were named as the primary parties on the legal document, had already left Starkville. The next morning, assistant Jerry Simmons stayed with MSU's starters on campus while trainer Dutch Luchsinger went to the airport with the remaining players. If the team had been detained or approached by authorities, Luchsinger was to call Simmons so he could make other arrangements to get the team out of Starkville. Johnson became so impatient waiting at the Starkville Airport for any sign of the MSU contingent that he left by the time Simmons arrived with the rest of the team. The AP reported that McCarthy joined his team in Nashville.[76] At his press conference on March 14th, McCarthy said the team's journey was not to escape the injunction, but rather to scout their opponent. "I wanted to get the boys up here to see the fastest breaking team I've ever seen," he said, referring to the Loyola squad.[77] The *Starkville Daily News'* Anderson, who accompanied the team to Michigan, likened the fiasco to "comedy farce scrip."[78] Jerry Liska, who penned the account on State's tournament arrival for the AP, wrote, "Never had a team moved into NCAA competition under stranger circumstances."[79] The presentation of the news indicated that the journalistic patrons of the Closed Society were trying to save face for their fellow segregationists, who were likely embarrassed by their inability to serve the injunction.

Fulton would file his first on-location report for the *Clarion-Ledger* in the March 15 edition of the paper and, in a reference to the team's difficulties arriving to Michigan, quipped "if half the battle has already been won just getting here, Mississippi State's basketball team is all set to tackle high-geared Loyola of Chicago." According to the AP, upon arriving in East Lansing, Illinois head basketball coach Harry Combs led an official cheer for the Starkville-based Bulldogs, saying, "I don't care about the political aspects of this thing. I think it was a brave and right thing that McCarthy's team came."[80] Despite the Bulldogs successful exodus, UPI reported that Mitts and Lawson were still steadfast in their efforts to successfully enforce the injunction and were simply waiting on a hearing before Hinds County Chancery Judge Stokes V. Robertson Jr. Interestingly enough, the UPI article also claimed that the rumored hearing was scheduled to take place after the game. On the Starkville campus, the efforts of the segregationist state senators were met with disdain and anger, as the student body hung each in effigy during a student rally.[81] As for the team and the work of the press, Gold said he and his teammates were cognizant of the controversy staring down the Bulldogs. "We were aware of all that was going on, but we were playing in the NCAA tournament for the first time," Gold said. "We were just so happy to be there. We knew we had a good team, but you just don't know until you play the game."[82]

On March 15, 1963, the Bulldogs would take part in their first NCAA tournament in a match-up with the eventual national champions the University of Loyola of Chicago. The pregame ritual of shaking hands became a landmark moment in Mississippi sports history as Gold greeted one of Loyola's black starters, All-American Jerry Harkness, in front of the capacity crowd. In Gold's own words, the moment drew a chorus of flashbulbs and became forever etched in the MSU great's memory.[83] Both the *Jackson Daily News* and the *Vicksburg Evening Post* published the pregame photo of the two shaking hands.[84] McCarthy's Bulldogs would put up a valiant fight against the highest scoring team in the nation, holding the Ramblers to sixty-one points, well below its average of ninety-five points per game. Led by senior Leland Mitchell's fourteen points, MSU took an early lead but the Bulldogs could not keep up with the Ramblers as Harkness scored twenty points and Vic Rouse added nineteen rebounds in Loyola's 61–51 victory.[85] In the wake of the controversy and debate that engulfed the weeks after the Bulldogs won the SEC title, the team's ground-breaking appearance in the NCAA tournament ended just as soon as it began. The *Jackson Daily News*, which had been at the journalistic forefront of the 1963 debate, did not feature an article on the game on its front page; rather Ward's newspaper published a UPI article that began by stating that MSU had "stumbled Friday night against Negro-dominated Loyola of Chicago" and focused on McCarthy's postgame contention that he would endorse MSU's continued and future participation in integrated athletics. "There'll either have to be a law forbidding us to come or we'll be back," the colorful head coach told the press.[86] When asked about the integrated status of the victors, McCarthy stressed that race played no part in the game. "The color didn't make any difference. I don't even want to talk about that because it wasn't important," he said in a dismissive tone.[87] In the *Meridian Star*, the UPI article on McCarthy's comments appeared with the condescending headline, "'It Was Nice Way to Get Beat,' McCarthy Says of NCAA Loss." [88] The *Starkville Daily News*' Anderson wrote that the loss "made the historic appearance a sad one."[89] Nash's paper also published an article from the AP that claimed the two teams were "tense at the outset" but the teams' starters "genially shook hands before the tipoff and the game was serenely played."[90] The *Jackson Daily News*' Baker penned an account on the game itself for the March 16 edition, but it was featured in the paper's sports section. Fulton wrote that MSU was "less adapt at playing cat-and-mouse with Loyola of Chicago than they were injunction servers enroute," a final nod to the team's elaborate effort to get to Michigan. Fulton described MSU as a weary team that played its best to compete with the eventual national champions. "Although the widely-publicized NCAA tourney was marred, the Bulldogs made a contest of it, much to the delight of the 12,143 Jenison Field House spectators who warmly applauded the Mississippians time and time again," Fulton wrote.

At least two separate accounts from the AP indicated that the reporters expected some degree of violence or tension to be present during the game. In one article by the AP's Jerry Green, the game was described as "surprisingly civilized and mundane" while an anonymous AP reporter, who referred to the

Chicago-based Ramblers as "Negro-bulwarked," wrote that "both teams were playing on best possible behavior and making every effort to avoid scuffling, shoving or bickering," even noting Loyola's Les Hunter, who was black, helping Stan Brinker to his feet after the Bulldogs' forward fell going for the ball.[91] Both McCarthy and Gold praised Loyola for its sportsmanship and hospitality. Ireland returned the favor, telling Fulton, "One of the things that came out of this game was the fact that you didn't see any pushing, shoving or needling among the players. That shows that Miss. State has a good bunch of kids, just like we have."[92]

As for the loss, Gold said the debate and the pressure put on the team by participating in the historical event could have played a part. "We were just so happy to be there. We knew we had a good team, but you just don't know until you play the game. We were very aware of the outside things that were going on," Gold said. "We had one practice before we played. It's hard to look back, but it wasn't something we dwelled on. Our focus was on playing a basketball game. Just playing in the game was enough but the circumstances surrounding the game could have been a distraction. We played fairly well, but it wasn't one of our better games. I was in the NCAA tournament and, for us, there was a significant amount of pressure. [But] you know, they had pressure on them as well. They knew that they were playing a team that never played blacks."[93]

While not drawing the same media attention, MSU defeated integrated Bowling Green and All-American Nate Thurmond 65–60 in the tournament's consolation game on March 16, 1963.[94] Playing without Gold, who broke his hand in the game against Loyola, the Bulldogs raced out to a 34–26 halftime lead by using a fast-break offense to surprise the Falcons. Thurmond scored on a layup late in the game to pull the Ohio-based Falcons at 57–56. But State held the ball and, although they did not score a basket for the final twelve minutes of the game, the team tallied seventeen points from the free throw line to hold on for the win. Mitchell finished his State career by leading the Bulldogs with twenty-three points and was named to the NCAA East Regional All-Tournament Team.[95]

In the aftermath of the school's first venture into the integrated NCAA tournament, the Bulldogs returned home to "a thousand friends and well-wishers" on March 17th. McCarthy told the masses, "People couldn't have been nicer to us on this trip. No one tried to embarrass or humiliate us. . . . I'm proud of the boys although we weren't able to win over Loyola. I'm personally proud of their great effort."[96] The aforementioned story appeared in the *Jackson Daily News* with photos taken by Baker, while Nash's *Starkville Daily News* published a photo of the team exiting the plane upon its return to the Magnolia State.[97]

Fulton summarized the university's inaugural tournament appearance and identified the profound difference in going to East Lansing versus the return to Starkville. "The return trip was much more pleasant and gratifying for several reasons.... State had received more publicity and acclaim prior to the tourney by just showing up than Loyola did by winning. Big, black headlines in the Detroit and Lansing papers heralded the Bulldogs' long awaited and at times uncertain arrival."[98] Fulton added that NCAA officials hailed State for its brave stance against the Closed Society and the unwritten law. MSU Athletic Director Wade Walker, who predicted weeks earlier that an NCAA tournament bid was not a likely endeavor for the Bulldogs, told the *Clarion-Ledger* sports writer, "We were received like champions, we played like champions and our team acted like champions."[99] While appearing as a straightforward news article, Fulton offered some editorial commentary as he praised the Bulldogs and claimed that Mississippians had accepted State's presence in the tournament and others never would.[100]

While it was not necessarily reflected in the press, some Mississippi residents took issue with State's inability to win the national championship and blamed the university and Colvard. After the Bulldogs' defeat at the hands of the integrated Loyola five, the Sons of Mississippi distributed an essay on the Starkville campus that called the loss, "One of the worst defeats in history.... Any citizen of Mississippi who knowingly supports an act to integrate our schools as playing basketball against niggers cannot help but live in shame. A severe blow has been made at our great way of life in Mississippi."[101] Accompanying the essay was another flyer that was distributed on campus with the headline, "61–51 NIG-GERS–NIGGER LOVERS." The rest of the flyer egregiously stated the following: "MSU, BEING THE FIRST MISSISSIPPI SCHOOL TO BE DEFEATED BY A BUNCH OF NIGGERS, HAS CAUSED OUR FOREFATHERS TO TURN OVER IN THEIR GRAVES."[102]

While many Mississippians felt segregation would be the ultimate casualty of the Bulldogs' appearance in the NCAA tournament, the barriers that held the state's athletic teams hostage began to crumble. On March 21, 1963, the State College Board rejected a proposal that would have required the board to grant permission to teams wishing to participate in integrated competition.[103] The motion, which was proposed by Izard, was based upon State's participation in the tournament and, according to UPI, had some support from college administrators, as it would require the board to share the responsibility associated with such decisions.[104] The rejection of the proposal essentially ended the unwritten law, as the gentleman's agreement was no longer observed. The *Mississippi Free Press*, which was one of the few newspapers that carried an article on the board's decision, titled the account, "Trustees Pass Buck."[105] Eight newspapers consulted in this chapter failed to publish an article on the board's vote and the elimination of the unwritten law.[106] On April 2nd, Robertson signed an order dismissing the injunction that was to bar MSU from playing in the NCAA tournament.[107] From a journalistic standpoint, coverage of Robertson's order was minimal. The *Clarion-Ledger* and the *Daily Journal* were the only two papers consulted that published an account of the State College Board's decision, both of which utilized work from UPI. Much like the silence that permeated the press coverage of the Bulldogs' losing effort against Loyola, the acknowledgement of the end of the unwritten law would have been admitting that Mississippi's white way of life was flawed.

Weeks passed without a mention of McCarthy or the 1963 Bulldogs in the sports media. McCarthy coached at MSU for two more seasons, posting a 9–17 record during the 1963–1964 campaign and a marginally better 10–16 in 1964–1965. McCarthy stepped down as head coach on March 1, 1965. The winner of four SEC championships and the man who spearheaded MSU's first NCAA tournament appearance told UPI that, after 10 years, he could no longer do his best at MSU.[108] Suspicious by its absence, most Mississippi media accounts of McCarthy's resignation and his career did not mention the 1962–1963 season and the NCAA tournament.[109] Because of his resignation, a number of Mississippi's sports columnists used the opportunity to reflect on McCarthy's legacy in Starkville. Both Carl Walters and Wayne Thompson of the *Clarion-Ledger* credited McCarthy for making State into a national basketball power but failed to referenced the former coach's groundbreaking NCAA tournament appearance.[110] Fulton, who had moved on from the *Clarion-Ledger* to the *Meridian Star*, briefly referenced the 1963 NCAA tournament but called the team's victory over Kentucky in Lexington as the crowning achievement for the 1962–1963 MSU squad.[111] An editorial in the *Starkville Daily News* also mentioned the NCAA tournament but claimed that McCarthy "was bitter" because he only had one chance to participate.[112]

The colorful McCarthy, who never played college basketball and only coached at the middle school level before Mississippi State College hired him, is still considered one of the greatest coaches in MSU history. McCarthy left Starkville with a 169–85 record, which is third all-time at MSU, and a .665 winning percentage, fourth highest in school history.[113] McCarthy was not away from the hardwood for long, as he became the head coach at George Washington University in 1966 where he finished his only season a pedestrian 6–18.[114] McCarthy returned to the South as head coach of the American Basketball Association's New Orleans Buccaneers in 1967. McCarthy became a visible figure in the ABA, coaching the Memphis Pros, the Dallas Chaparrals, and the Kentucky Colonels, winning the league's Coach of the Year award twice, becoming the first coach in the league to win 200 games.[115] In 1973, McCarthy agreed to return to the SEC as the head basketball coach at the University of Georgia but, five months into the job, resigned to coach the ABA's Kentucky Colonels without coaching a single game in Athens.[116] Roughly a year later, McCarthy became ill with cancer and died in March 1975.[117] The Baldwyn native was inducted in both the Mississippi Sports Hall of Fame and the SEC Hall of Fame.

As for Colvard, he remained an unpopular figure in the state long after the team's revolutionary actions as the venture into East Lansing became more of a nod to the success of the Bulldogs and less about playing integrated competition.[118] Colvard remained in Starkville until 1966 when he returned to his native North Carolina as the chancellor of the University of North Carolina at Charlotte. He held that post until his retirement in 1978. Colvard died in 2007.

Gold, who became the university's freshman head coach after his career ended with MSU's win over Bowling Green in 1963, was named McCarthy's replacement six days after his resignation.[119] While media accounts noted Gold's successful playing and brief coaching career, there was no mention of the 1963 NCAA tournament even after Gold was identified as the captain of that team. The task of following the legendary McCarthy was a difficult one for Gold, who coached in Starkville for five years and compiled a record of 51–74.

"I was very naive. I never really thought I was replacing a legend. When he left, I didn't know what the future was. I had no idea who was going to be coach and I never even applied for the job," Gold said, explaining his ascension to the head coach's position and his relations with McCarthy. "He was good to me personally. He was very good with people and the community, but he use to always say 'I don't know if we're doing this right or wrong, but we're going to do this together.' He was a competitor and he was an innovator with his coaching. I respected him."[120]

While the typical racist rhetoric of years past infected some newspapers in the state, in particular, the Hederman owned *Jackson Daily News* and the *Clarion-Ledger*, a change was evident within the press when it came to MSU's 1963 NCAA tournament aspirations. Unlike the team's previous title-winning campaigns, journalists offered the most supportive editorial commentary for MSU and a venture into integrated athletics in the eight-year existence of the unwritten law and, in many cases, identified the enrollment of Meredith at Ole Miss as justification. Overall, the musings of the reporters in the Magnolia State, especially from sports journalists and editors, was an indication of how things had changed in Mississippi since the inception of the gentleman's agreement. As the debate in Mississippi about the merits of the unwritten law and MSU's potential appearance in the NCAA tournament progressed, new voices of support could be found throughout the Magnolia State's journalistic landscape. This emergent voice of support was most evident in the sports sections of the state's newspapers as *Daily Journal* sports editor Bill Ross, Dick Lightsey of the Biloxi-based *Daily Herald*, and Billy Ray of the *Vicksburg Evening Post* led Mississippi's sports writing fraternity against the unwritten law. Once a collection of silent journalistic benchwarmers, Mississippi's sports reporters finally went into the ideological game and, universally, offered the Bulldogs support for their foray into integrated competition. The success of the MSU basketball team and the possibility of a national championship brought forth the desire for a sense of cultural validity. A successful trek through the integrated gambit presented by the NCAA tournament would offer validation and enforce the principles found in the Closed Society. While the bravery and guile demonstrated by MSU's journalist supporters should not be diminished, logically such validation could only be acquired through some form of integration, hence the newfound support for the Bulldogs.

During the 1963 debate surrounding the MSU contingent, there were few journalists who expressed as bold an opinion as Bill Ross, sports editor of the Tupelo-based *Daily Journal*. Ross addressed the MSU-NCAA issue frequently in his column "Round and About," and while many sports journalists approved of the Bulldogs' entry into the NCAA tournament, Ross's advocacy extended beyond the hardwood, as he noted on multiple occasions that the participation of the Starkville contingent in the integrated postseason would have positive social repercussions in the Magnolia State, ushering in a new era of athletic equality. Ross's work on MSU began on February 27, 1963, when he argued that public opinion should be considered when it came to making a decision on State's possible entry into the NCAA tournament. It was Ross's contention that most Mississippians wanted to see MSU play for a national championship and that the State College Board had lost sight of its purpose, putting "tradition" before the betterment of education in the Magnolia State. "This board was created to serve the public and not to dictate to the public," Ross wrote. Calling the potential absence of the Bulldogs from the NCAA "a cotton-pickin' shame," the sports editor would later warn the Closed Society of an impending ideological change. "You can't forever remain aloof to everyday living—that cutting off the nose to spite the face solves nothing," he wrote on February 28, 1963. Ross continued to identify the historical significance of the team's venture into the NCAA tournament in the March 2nd and 3rd editions of the *Daily Journal*. "Sooner or later somebody will get the real message. For it's more than sending a team to participate in a basketball tournament. It's one of the best opportunities in years to send a group of young men—good will ambassadors if you will—into a section of the country where they can do some good. . . . To continue such an unprogressive attitude will eventually ruin first rate athletic programs at schools all over the state." In his March 5 column, Ross lauded the Bulldogs' entry into the tournament, calling it an important contribution to the state. "Then from this first beginning, a new and brighter day may develop in the field of athletics," Ross mused. "Perhaps the thinking will spread from there, demanding a more realistic role in such matters." Ross's commentary was picked up by UPI and published in newspapers such as the *Clarion-Ledger*, the *Delta Democrat-Times*, and the *Jackson Daily News*.[121] Even in light of the State College Board's decision to review Colvard's decision, the Tupelo sports editor remained steadfast in his contention and hopeful of an NCAA tournament appearance. In the March 8 edition of "Round and About," Ross wrote about the Bulldogs, "There is no negative mindset around here. It's a healthy climate, one that makes you mighty proud of the young people who attend the state's colleges and universities. If adults handled themselves as well as these young men do, everything would find itself in mighty good shape in a lot of other areas other than athletics."

Despite his frequent support for the MSU contingent, Ross failed to write anything on the board's decision, the team's loss, or their subsequent return from the NCAA tournament. However, it is clear that Ross understood the scope of the situation and identified the potential social repercussions of such an event. Ross's commentary showed a progressive tone not seen from Mississippi's sports reporters since Jimmie McDowell left the Magnolia State. Ross, like much of the journalistic elite in the state, was concerned with outside perceptions of MSU and Mississippi, giving credence to the idea that Ross and his journalistic brethren were looking for cultural validation from MSU's basketball persona. Success for MSU's team would validate Mississippi's cultural values and, perhaps, change external opinions on the state for the better. Ross was one of the few in Mississippi who had the foresight to see not only the elimination of the Closed Society's profound influence on the state's athletic scene, but the social good that could come from State's participation in the integrated postseason.

In previous seasons, some of the more forthright opposition to the unwritten law came in the journalistic work of Dick Lightsey of the *Daily Herald* and Billy Ray of the *Vicksburg Evening Post*. While Lightsey and Ray's past advocacy came with their professed belief in segregation, the 1963 debate surrounding the NCAA tournament excluded such validation, a stark contrast from arguments past. In the February 27 edition of his column "Bunts, Boots and Bounces," Lightsey argued that there was a place in the integrated postseason for the Bulldogs, though he believed the team would abstain from the tournament. "The boys deserve the opportunity of playing against other leading teams in the nation," Lightsey wrote. "Even if they lose they will at least have had the opportunity at competing." With the debate surrounding the unwritten law at the front of Mississippi's journalistic docket, Lightsey took the opportunity to use his March 8 column to educate his audience on the origins of the gentlemen's agreement. While remaining supportive of MSU's possible trek into the integrated postseason, Lightsey admitted that he was unaware of who created the unwritten law or when it was implemented, verifying the secretive nature of the agreement. In the aftermath of the State College Board decision, the sports editor expressed excitement and optimism over the team's entry into the postseason despite facing the Chicago-based juggernaut. "We would like to see the Maroons go all the way to the NCAA title, but whether they win it or not, at least they will have had the chance of playing for it against the best teams in the country," Lightsey exclaimed. "Let's get behind the Maroons and wish them well!!!" While the bulk of Lightsey's March 14 work stayed grounded in the sporting aspects of the team's tournament entry, the sports editor concluded by identifying the historical significance of the team's participation in the tournament. "This will be the most important game a Mississippi State basketball team has ever played," observed Lightsey. "And if they win, each succeeding game will be more important than the last one." The following day, Lightsey admitted that he ignored the news of the injunction because he felt the legal ramblings of Mitts and Lawson would be unsuccessful. "It turns out, we were right," Lightsey quipped before predicting a victory for MSU.[122] Lightsey concluded his commentary on the Bulldogs and the NCAA tournament in the March 18 edition of the *Daily Herald* after State's ten-point loss to the Ramblers, again, stressing the significance of State's appearance in the tournament rather than simply focusing on wins and losses. "We're sorry the Maroons were unable to win the tournament, but at least they had a shot at it, and they did a good job representing the state, their school and the Southeastern Conference," Lightsey wrote. Noticeably absent from Lightsey's work were his past professions as a segregationist. While the Biloxi sports editor may have favored a postseason appearance of the Bulldogs for the chance at a national championship rather than a nod to the progression of civil rights in the Magnolia State, his constant defense of Mississippi State's basketball team showed, at the least, that he found nothing wrong with the state's finest competing against integrated teams, a bold statement to say the least.

Similarly, *Vicksburg Evening News* sports editor Billy Ray argued for MSU's inclusion into the NCAA tournament and, unlike seasons past, never included his own professions as a segregationist in his editorial writing. Ray's support was cautionary as the sports editor often balanced his pro-MSU sentiment with a degree of doubt as to the validity of a tournament appearance for the Bulldogs. Much like Ross, Ray would initially begin his support of the Bulldogs in the February 27 edition of his column "Press Box Views" by identifying the positive publicity a tournament venture would offer the Magnolia State. While he found little harm from MSU's participation, Ray doubted that the team would go to the tournament based upon the enforcement of the unwritten law and openly feared that another tournament rejection could lead to the "disheartening" exodus of McCarthy from Starkville. Ray's cautionary approach was reinforced the following day, writing that while McCarthy's SEC coaching colleagues wanted to see the Bulldogs in the tournament, the team's fate was in the hands of the "big boys" in Jackson, a reference to political opposition that had formed against the MSU squad.[123] On March 5th, Ray all but admitted that he tackled the subject with kid gloves, calling Colvard's decision "startling" because the Vicksburg sports editor "had given up all hope of the old tradition being broken." Despite his cautionary commentary, Ray wrote that the Bulldogs were deserving of the opportunity and wished the team and its enigmatic coach the best. "We still contend that Dr. Colvard, the university's president, did the right thing. Those folks who are against State participating are speaking out . . . and they are fewer in number as compared to those who want the Bulldogs to go," Ray later wrote. [124] Once the State College Board rendered a positive decision for the Bulldogs, Ray's columns expressed a degree of excitement, free of the tempered tones of his previous efforts. On March 12th, Ray predicted that the MSU contingent would "play like gentlemen and be a great credit to Mississippi, their school and the Southeastern Conference." The following day, Ray wrote that McCarthy was undaunted by the "four Negro starters on its front line. . . . He said he didn't care who he played against. He would play them just as he would anybody else."[125] While Ray offered little in terms of his opinion on McCarthy's comments, he was one of the few sportswriters in Mississippi who noted it in an opinion-based forum, indicating that he found merit in the coach's contention. In the aftermath of MSU's loss to the Ramblers, Ray dispelled any notions that violence and hostility would mar the contest, citing comments made by Gold, who called the Loyola squad "perfect gentlemen." Two days later, Ray reiterated that there was no racial tension between the two teams. "There was no bickering, no intentional shoving, no punching," Ray wrote, "just two top-rated teams playing the game the way it should be played in trying to win."[126] While Ray never expressed any sort of support for integration, the editor felt compelled to dispel any hearsay involving the conduct of both the Bulldogs and the integrated Ramblers. Ray's simple explanation of the way in which the two teams behaved dismissed any such thought and showed that, while he may not have approved of integration, Ray supported the efforts of MSU and, from a journalistic standard, reported the truth. For both Lightsey and Ray, their previous professions as segregationists were no longer apart of the public discourse. For each sports writer, MSU's 1963 trek was a chance for validation as it pertained to their cultural beliefs. Success on the hardwood would have solidified the white ideals of the Closed Society and justified Mississippi's belief in segregation. Thus, the argument for MSU's participation in the national tournament was more about asserting a sense of self and identity than it was about equality. However, this quest for cultural validation should not diminish the forthright manner in which Lightsey and Ray advocated integrate competition, a brave rarity in the Closed Society.

Commercial Dispatch sports editor Eddie Dean also spoke out on behalf of the Bulldogs and advocated a tournament appearance by McCarthy's troops.

Much like his sports writing brethren, Dean took a cautious, almost skeptical tone in his early advocation for the Bulldogs. Dean made his first argument for State in the February 26 edition of the *Commercial Dispatch*, writing that the SEC champions had won the right to play and the rejection of another invitation would put a black eye on the Magnolia State. "We talk about how proud we are of the State and all of that but just one such refusal does more harm than good in the period of one administration in the State Capital," Dean concluded. Cynicism continued to persist in Dean's column as the sports editor called State's tournament chances "slim and none," citing Barnett's objections to integrated competition.[127] Dean later feared that any decision to keep the team out of the tournament could result in penalties from the NCAA and McCarthy's possible exit from Starkville.[128] While Dean failed to express an opinion either way, his fears indicated that the *Commercial Dispatch* sports editor was hopeful that State would participate in the national title tournament.

Dean also addressed *Sports Illustrated*'s coverage of MSU in his March 14, 1963, edition of his column, "Scramblin'," when he objected to the magazine's treatment of the Starkville-based Bulldogs. "Even with Mississippi State winning the SEC basketball championship, this magazine wouldn't even list them among the top three teams in the South until they accepted the bid to the NCAA and now the two-faced editors are giving nothing but praise for the Maroons," Dean quipped. Intentional or not, Dean's scathing evaluation of the editors of *Sports Illustrated* acknowledged what sports writers in Mississippi had failed to admit in the past: the absence of an NCAA tournament appearance and the lack of integrated foes on the Bulldogs' schedule had created a less than stellar national perception of the team. In past debates involving MSU and the unwritten law, the school's place in both the AP and UPI national polls was a topic of conversation yet this obvious absence in the Bulldogs' résumé was never cited as a possible culprit.

While Dean would later write in the March 15 edition of the *Commercial Dispatch* that everyone, including MSU's white detractors, would be listen to the game and "pulling for a win, whether they admit it or not," his most opinionated column would appear after the Bulldogs' loss to the Loyola. The *Commercial Dispatch*'s sports editor defended the MSU contingent in the wake of their defeat, writing that the team was not deserving of "the sharp criticism that is now being heard from people that didn't have the guts to say one way or the other how they stood on the situation. . . . Second-guessers are having a field day with the loss and should State have won, not a word on the contrary would have been heard, only praise."[129] While Dean's skepticism and doubt, at times, overshadowed any pro-NCAA tournament sentiment, the *Commercial Dispatch* sports editor was, nevertheless, a supporter of MSU's venture into the integrated postseason.

Although he was not a consistent voice in terms of the sheer number of editorial statements during the duration of the unwritten law's existence, the opinion of Hodding Carter of the *Delta Democrat-Times* was never in question as the Pulitzer Prize winning editor offered the Bulldogs his journalistic support every time he penned a column on the team's efforts to buck the gentleman's agreement. In the March 4, 1963, edition of the *Delta Democrat-Times,* Carter credited Colvard for exercising a degree of common sense in his ruling. Carter, who quipped that he did not belong to any "extremist segregationist group," wrote that most Mississippians thought the unwritten law was "for the birds" and predicted the inevitable and "inescapable" arrival of integrated sports to the Magnolia State. Despite Carter's complimentary content, he was still fearful of a possible action by the State College Board, even urging readers to offer support to the embattled MSU president. Only days later, Carter took note of the political support for the enforcement of the unwritten law, writing in his March 7 editorial that, "The big guns of the professional haters and their political allies are now being brought to bear on the State College Board" in an effort to end State's bid for an NCAA appearance. Never shy about holding his journalistic brethren responsible for their actions, Carter called out both the *Jackson Daily News* and the *Clarion-Ledger,* writing that the two newspapers "are falling all over each other to prove what good segregationists they are." Labeling those who favored such a ban as "extremist," Carter wondered if the segregationist ideology ran deeper than he initially believed and sarcastically suggested a radical solution for Mississippians in opposition of the Bulldogs. "For if it is bad for five members of a basketball team to 'mix' on the court, surely it is worse for state and local officials and representatives to 'mix' while they ride, eat, and sleep. In short, let's wash our hands of the United States and be done with it," Carter quipped.

The following day, Carter published an editorial from Ira B. Harkey Jr.'s *Pascagoula Chronicle*, which hailed Colvard's decision and said it should "gain the applause of both white supremacists and sportsmen." Harkey explained that white supremacists would have a chance to test their separatist ideology of being superior to blacks, while sports fans would have a chance to watch MSU win a national championship. Harkey was at the forefront of journalistic opposition to the segregationist beliefs of white Mississippians and felt that state residents were "making fools of themselves." Harkey's work, while appearing sarcastic in tone, echoed the social validation that most in Mississippi's journalistic community were looking for via MSU participation in the integrated postseason. Harkey won the Pulitzer Prize in May 1963 for his pro-civil rights work.[130]

Carter's strongest commentary appeared in the March 11 edition of the *Delta Democrat-Times.* In a defiant and confident tone, Carter wrote that the decision of the State College Board to support MSU signaled a new social position in the state. "Decent people of Mississippi are sick of letting the professional haters make all of the decisions and control all the shots. The issue of whether Mississippi State's basketball team should or should not play in the NCAA tournament was obviously not the most significant in the world but the fact that the big-time bigots chose to make it a major issue and were defeated is significant," Carter sternly wrote. In Carter's words, the proprietors of the Closed Society attempted to use every weapon in their "extremist" arsenal, yet to no avail. While Carter recognized the potentially fleeting nature of the impact of the decision, he called it a healthy sign. "We can only hope it was not a passing whim, and that having once discovered that lightning does not strike when the bateists are defied, the people will defy them again and again in the future." Although the amount of original commentary could not compare to other newspapers featured in this volume, the *Delta Democrat-Times* held its own in combating the negative, segregationist ideology of those newspapers. Carter, who was considered a liberal journalist in Mississippi during this time period and an advocate of civil rights, poignantly and powerfully made his opinion known.

While the volume of news-based editorial content in J. Oliver Emmerich's *Enterprise-Journal* was minimal, the longtime supporter of integration backed the MSU contingent in the paper's various opinion-based forums. While Emmerich did support states' rights, he also held a belief in fair journalism and attempted to adhere to those principles, regardless of the issue.[131] In his March 2, 1963, editorial, Emmerich called Colvard's decision "both wise and responsible" and argued that it was time for the Magnolia State to abandon what he called "athletic isolation," claiming that the constant rejection of boycotting national tournaments only hurt the credibility of college sports in Mississippi. Despite the past and frequent enforcement of the unwritten law, Emmerich offered a contradiction to the gentleman's agreement, identifying that there was "no board policy which prevents the acceptance of an invitation to participate in a national tournament." The McComb-based editor, who had long recognized the need for civil rights in Mississippi, argued that the continued observance of the unwritten law would not be superseded by the eventual integration of southern sports, rather it would lead to the degeneration of college athletics as they knew it. Emmerich's supportive commentary was picked up by the AP and could be found in the *Daily Herald* in Biloxi, the Columbus-based *Commercial Dispatch*, and the *Jackson Daily News*.[132]

Emmerich's son, John Emmerich also wrote on the issue for the March 18 edition of the *Enterprise-Journal*, confessing that he did not understand why the acceptance of the NCAA bid generated "so much hoopla," asking his readers, "What great principle will have been sacrificed?" Directing a degree of criticism at Roberts for his Reconstruction remarks, Emmerich claimed that integrated basketball would have little impact on segregation within the state, writing, "I learned long time ago that skin color doesn't rub off." Citing his own childhood experiences, Emmerich made a logical appeal for equality on the court, writing in almost a romantic fashion of his youthful days playing with both white and black children. "I thought it was down here in the South—with a long tradition of casual and friendly relations—that every young white lad had a dark skinned friend with whom he shared many boyhood experiences. So what's all the shouting about just because Mississippi State goes to a tournament and does what southern kids have been doing for as long as anyone can remember—that is until recently when we got so sensitive about what you can't do in a segregated system." While the younger Emmerich did not denounced segregation in any way, his commentary advocated civil rights and attempted to offer his audience with a relatable and seemingly stereotypical scenario with which they could identify.

Following the lead of his sports editor, Harry Rutherford of the *Daily Journal* echoed the sentiments of Ross, writing in the March 6 edition of the Tupelo newspaper that he doubted the team's participation in the postseason would lead to the eventual integration of schools statewide and, that if such barriers were to be broken, federal legal action such as the one perpetuated by Meredith would be the likely culprit. "We repeat: The integration of Mississippi schools will come down only when and if such action is ordered by federal courts and all avenues of escaping such decisions are closed. Let us then not penalize a fine group of Mississippi State basketball players and one of the nation's best coaches by trying to place the blame on them for something which will be decided completely outside the realm of their competition in the national tournament they so strongly desire to enter." Rutherford's commentary pulled no punches and, while he did not advocate integration or the elimination of the unwritten law, his work was a direct challenge to the status quo maintained by the Closed Society.

In the past debates involving the MSU team and its efforts to challenge the unwritten law, sports editor Lee Baker of the *Jackson Daily News* and longtime sports columnist Carl Walters of the *Clarion-Ledger* typically held the white line of the Closed Society by either offering little to no opinion on the matter or by rejecting all notions as unattainable. However, in 1963, while their individual editors continued to serve as the journalist watchdogs of Mississippi's all-white caste system, Baker, Walters, and other members of the newspapers' sports staffs supported and encouraged McCarthy's troops to seek the national championship, while never citing civil rights as their justification.

Baker, while rarely justifying his opinion on the matter, became a clear supporter of the Bulldogs' integrated cause. In the aftermath of the Bulldogs' win over rival Ole Miss and Colvard's public acceptance of the NCAA tournament invitation, Baker wrote that he was grateful State would have a chance at the national championship and called MSU's yearly absence from the postseason a "burial," insinuating that the sports editor had opposed MSU's past ostracism from the integrated postseason tournament.[133] Baker's suddenly bold acknowledgement of the Closed Society's southern-base sequestering of the MSU team was in line with the *Jackson Daily News* sports editor's commentary at the end of the Bulldogs' 1962 campaign. While his editor, Ward, approved of the State College Board's decision to meet on the MSU-NCAA matter, Baker did not express the same enthusiasm, writing that the meeting was only being held in the hopes of developing a "roadblock" to keep the Starkville-based Bulldogs from the tournament.[134] After a positive decision was rendered for the Bulldogs by the State College Board, Baker wrote on March 11, 1963, that, "Athletic folks, chafed in the past by the 'unwritten law' straightjacket, hope the thing is dead." Despite his nod to the public opposition to the unwritten law, Baker's personal opinion of the gentleman's agreement was not present. Baker's editorial approach continued when the Jackson-based sports editor wrote, "Injunctions not applying to such a wretched fraternity as po' ol' sports writers, it is hopefully on to East Lansing this day and whatever fate awaits the Mississippi State basketball team."[135] On the day of the game, Baker again referenced the attempts to keep the Bulldogs in state. Expressing a degree of relief as MSU had successfully made its way to the tournament, Baker detailed the anxious atmosphere in East Lansing, writing, "Panic had been growing in the ranks as each hour brought new bulletins out of Mississippi of Wednesday's last desperate effort to stop the Maroons' participation in the tourney here."[136] While Baker took comfort in the Bulldogs' successful arrival to the tournament, he stopped short of endorsing or opposing the team's presence. In the aftermath of MSU's loss to Loyola, Baker described McCarthy's team as "dejected."[137] While he avoided expressing any sort of definitive opinion on the trip, of greater consequence was Baker's citation of Ireland's assessment of the game in which the Loyola head coach said the game featured "no shoving or bickering or needling," especially in light of many media-based accounts that assumed the game would yield some sort of violent incident.[138] The following day, Baker wrote that Ireland would like to play a future game against the Bulldogs in Chicago, a point the Jackson sports editor found unlikely, not because of race, but because he did not think MSU would be as successful in the 1963–1964 season with the loss of Gold, Stroud, and Mitchell. Baker did not discuss the actual game or his opinion, in closing, on State's violation of the unwritten law and subsequent loss to an integrated foe. In anticipation of any criticism from the stalwarts of the Closed Society, Baker used his final column on the NCAA tournament to show support for the Bulldogs. "The only possible regret for the trip was the loss Friday night to Loyola and in that there can be little to apologize about."[139] While Baker failed to use the opportunity to definitively state an opinion on the matter, he offered support to the Bulldogs and was quick to defend the contingent when they returned from Michigan, a far cry from his work during State's previous SEC title-winning campaigns. In total, Baker's column was not reflective of the values and beliefs held true by his segregationist editor Ward. However, based upon Baker's previous commentary on the matter, one could easily argue that, like Lightsey and Ray, the Jackson-based sports editor was looking for a sense of cultural validation into Mississippi's white dominate ideology through athletics. Baker's new-found perspective on the matter could have been an as a result of an ideological change of heart, however, one could argue that the allure of a national championship for the Bulldogs would have served as physical valida- tion for segregation and solidified Mississippi's belief in its separatist culture. Due to Baker's previous writings and the reputation of the *Jackson Daily News*, it is likely that the veteran sports journalist was looking for such validation.

Like Baker, *Clarion-Ledger* columnist Carl Walters, a past supporter of the unwritten law, appeared to have a change in heart. Going into the Bulldogs' finale against Ole Miss, Walters surprisingly endorsed the MSU contingent's efforts to go to the postseason. Defending his past contentions that MSU should not be allowed to participate in the integrated competition, Walters wrote that he was simply being realistic and that a change in state policy was, in the past, unlikely. "With the Bulldogs being permitted to accept a reward which they, themselves, have earned through hard work, determination, and rare skill, we will be plenty pleased," Walters wrote.[140] While the veteran sports columnist's endorsement was refreshingly odd, his skepticism allowed him to keep favor with the political elite of the Closed Society and, specifically, the Hedermans. Walters's surprisingly supportive tone for the MSU team continued in the March 4 edition of "Shavin's" as the veteran sports writer said he was pleased that he overestimated the power of the unwritten law. "[It is] our pleasure and privilege to commend Dr. Colvard for having the courage and integrity to do what he believes was the right thing to do," Walters wrote. While Walters sup- ported the Bulldogs, he remained vague in terms of his justification. After the loss to Loyola, Walters praised the efforts of McCarthy's troops in the March 18 edition of the *Clarion-Ledger* and credited the coach for "making no effort whatsoever to 'alibi' his team's defeat." Walters admitted that he was "pleased with and proud of the Bulldogs for the way in which they handled themselves in Michigan both on the court and off it." Never known for his sensitivity on issues of race, Walters's support for MSU was surprising. While he never explic- itly offered a justification for his support, making it likely that his motive was fueled by the desires for the national championship to reside in Starkville, his work in 1963 was a progressive step for the Mississippi Sports Hall of Famer.

While Baker and Walters changed their proverbial stripes when it came to MSU and the NCAA tournament, Robert Fulton, the *Clarion-Ledger*'s sports editor, made his feelings on the unwritten law known a year earlier when he called for the elimination of the gentleman's agreement. Although Fulton's commentary on the matter during the 1963 season was minimal and lacked the damning tone of his 1962 argument, the man known as "Steamboat" still supported the Bulldogs' appearance in the NCAA tournament. Like many of his sports-writing brethren, Fulton openly questioned whether a rejected tournament invitation would lead McCarthy to leave Starkville. In the March 2nd edition of his column "High N' Inside," Fulton professed his fondness for the head coach and feared that another rejection of a NCAA tournament invitation could have been the last straw for the Baldwyn native. "When a fence is built around a bull or thoroughbred, the grass is always greener on the other side. . . . Mississippi's 'unwritten law' has built such a fence around McCarthy." Fulton admitted that he was using the potential plight of McCarthy to sway political opinion in favor of a State appearance in the NCAA tournament, making it clear that his advocacy was not in the vein of social progress but an effort to keep his friend in Starkville. While his next edition of "High N' Inside" did little in terms of expressing a definitive opinion on the tournament bid and the unwritten law, Fulton used his editorial forum to write the only account found in the newspapers consulted to capture the thoughts and opinions of each member of the State roster. In Fulton's March 9 column, of the thirteen players interviewed, seven specifically addressed integration and all of them used their SEC championship as justification for accepting the NCAA bid. Mitchell told Fulton that he did not see anything wrong with playing against other races, while Jackie Wolford pointed to the exploits of Meredith as reason for the team's participation. "One college in the state is already integrated so it shouldn't make any difference if we went and played against integrated teams," the sophomore guard said. Perhaps the one player who illustrated the greatest foresight was Gold, telling Fulton that playing in the NCAA tournament could change outside perceptions of MSU and the level of prejudice in the state. Despite the limited nature of Fulton's commentary, his work clearly supported an MSU venture into the national title tournament and his efforts to illustrate the various opinions held by members of the State squad demonstrated a concerted effort by the Hederman scribe to offer a degree of journalistic balance to the debate.

Another member of the *Clarion-Ledger*'s sports staff, Wayne Thompson, also expressed a degree of support for McCarthy's squad but did little to justify his opinion, often making vague references to the possible social implications of State's participation in the tournament in an effort to focus only on the athletic aspects of the Bulldogs. In the March 5, 1963, edition of his column, "Hind Sight," Thompson attempted to comfort those in the Closed Society who took issue with the Colvard's decision, writing, "The earth is still spinning on its axis." While his commentary had a dismissive tone to it, Thompson added that his personal feelings on the matter were irrelevant. The *Clarion-Ledger* sports writer continued to discuss the MSU fiasco without expressing a definitive opinion in subsequent columns on March 8th and March 14th. In the aftermath of the tournament, Thompson lamented for a return to the comfortable confines of sports reporting. "I can remember when sports was sports and the controversy, not counting those blind umpires and other officials, was left up to politicians and crooks who usually inhabit the front pages. No more," the sports reporter wrote.[141] Thompson's diatribe, while not directly attacking the Closed Society, was a swipe at the frequent interference of the state's segregationist politicians, all of whom viewed the tournament and participation in it as a possible gateway for all out integration. Thompson's commentary, while supportive of the Bulldogs, never expressed a definitive opinion when it came to the merits of integrated competition and seemed offended that such a controversy had emerged in an athletic context.

Like his sports writing colleagues at the *Jackson Daily News* and the *Clarion-Ledger*, Billy Rainey of the *Meridian Star* also demonstrated a change in heart and, for the first time in eight years, offered any commentary that supported MSU. The sports editor known as "Sunshine" tried to strike a balance between his beliefs in segregation and offering any sort of congratulatory commentary to the MSU contingent. Rainey, who was noncommittal in terms of his views during MSU's previous SEC title-winning campaigns, wrote his only and most forthright expression of opinion during the various debates surrounding the Bulldogs in the February 26, 1963, edition of the *Meridian Star*. Predicting that Georgia Tech would take MSU's place in the postseason, Rainey surprisingly called for the elimination of the unwritten law due to the future recruitment of high school athletes who would hunger for national recognition as opposed to remaining on a southern stage. "The stand Mississippi has taken may or may not be the right one. I don't know. I do know that it's not a stand that will lead to continued success—on a national level—for the athletic teams of our state," Rainey wrote. "Sunshine" ended his commentary, cryptically predicting that the success MSU had experienced in the past would end, regardless of the unwritten law and its enforcement. While his justification had nothing to do with equality, the proposed elimination of the unwritten law was a shocking contention for the conservative Rainey.

While located in the epicenter of Mississippi State's multiple and controversial challenges to the unwritten law, the *Starkville Daily News* of segregationist editor Sherrill Nash and publisher Henry Harris, on the surface, offered a surprisingly supportive editorial voice to their hometown Bulldogs despite discussing the matter with far less frequency than many of their journalistic brethren. Nash made it clear in his editorial writing that he recognized the political and social ramifications of the Bulldogs' possible appearance in the NCAA tournament and, while he was hopeful for such a venture, he would stand by the university regardless of the decision.[142] Nash later supported the embattled Colvard, writing that MSU's president was "beyond criticism" and the

North Carolina native deserved the public's support due to his tenure as president. "Whether you approve of Dr. Colvard's decision on the basketball team or not, he has earned your support through the progressive and sincere work he is doing as President of State University," he wrote on March 6, 1963. Due to Nash's reputation as a segregationist, it is likely that his editorial support for Colvard and Mississippi State had little to do with equality or civil rights.

Nash's support for Colvard and MSU was echoed in the paper's sports section, particularly in a column titled "Time Out for Sports." In the aftermath of the team's acceptance of the tournament invitation, both the March 5 and 13 editions of column, which featured the accompanying byline "Daily News Sports Staff," applauded the opportunity afforded to McCarthy's club. However, neither column addressed the unwritten law or explicitly expressed an opinion on the merits of integrated athletics. In the aftermath of the Bulldogs' exit from the national tournament, *Starkville Daily News* sports writer George Anderson wrote that the game marked the potential end to one era and the start of another. While on the surface Anderson's commentary identified the historic and social significance of the event, Anderson focused on the graduation of Bulldog standouts Mitchell, Gold, and Stroud rather than the possible end of segregated athletics in the Magnolia State.[143] While Anderson did reflect on the team's play in the tournament and the swell of crowd support for the MSU contingent, the Starkville sports writer went no further. Like his Starkville peers, while Anderson supported MSU's venture into the national title tournament, he did little to validate his opinion. Nash's paper seemed content to remain on the ideological sidelines, neither expressing segregationist beliefs nor supporting integration. Like other journalists in the state, Nash and the *Starkville Daily News* looked towards the MSU contingent for a reflection of their own cultural values and a successful entry by the Bulldogs would have offered validation and a sense of local pride to the Starkville community.

In a contrast to the *Starkville Daily News*, the *Reflector*, Mississippi State's student-based newspaper, contained a litany of pro-NCAA commentary in support of the Bulldogs and was consistently critical of the unwritten law. While the editorial staff of the student paper stopped short of advocating integration, it was the prevailing opinion of the publication that the unwritten law had become dated. On February 21, 1963, student editor Jim Yancey lamented MSU's potential absence from the NCAA tournament and described views to the contrary as "pigheaded." Yancey utilized sarcasm in his editorial, writing, "It would be hard for our boys to place themselves on the same court as the negroid race, since all of their lives our boys have been protected from such close personal contact." Yancey concluded by arguing that the notion of positive race relations in the state rarely, if ever, made it beyond Mississippi's borders and MSU's participation would create a greater sense of goodwill. Yancey would defend Colvard in the March 7 edition of the *Reflector*, asking the political purveyors of the Closed Society, "Should a dynamic university be led by a man with the intelligence to make a decision on the merits of the case, and guts to back it up? Or, should that university be led by a man, who out of fear for his job, would listen to and be persuaded by the politicians who are usually trying to create votes?"

While Yancey may have been the *Reflector*'s editor, it was sports writer Malcolm Balfour who was, perhaps, the paper's standout performer when it came to the 1963 Mississippi State debate. Balfour proved to be, not only a solid college journalist, but held his own with Mississippi's professional scribes when it came to getting the news. In the February 28, 1963, version of his column "Sports Talk," Balfour made a passionate and logical plea for State's presence in the postseason tournament. Using Meredith's entry into Ole Miss as justification, Balfour wrote, "To remain segregated, we had to make sacrifices. . . . Whether we like it or not, schools in Mississippi are now integrated, and those of us who feel that integration has been a burden deserve to reap some benefit by being able to play against integrated teams." While Balfour's commentary clearly offered a degree of support to the Closed Society, the student journalist also acknowledged the changing ideological landscape in the Magnolia State. Such foresight was evident in Balfour's subsequent column, which noted the social significance of Colvard's decision and referred to the MSU president's critics as "those who would like to send Mississippi back to the dark ages."[144] Balfour continued to address the Bulldogs and the NCCA tournament when, on March 14th, the student journalist called State's play in the tournament, "The best advertising that the State has had in a long time." Balfour would conclude his commentary on the Bulldogs in the March 21 edition of the *Reflector*, writing that, "Mississippi State lost that first ball game, but it won the hearts of East Lansing." For a student journalist, Balfour displayed a degree of logic and foresight not found in the opinion-based work of some of his professional counterparts. While he may have supported segregation at one time or another, Balfour's commentary was that of a young man who knew the social landscape in Mississippi was changing.

Others, both staff writers and their fellow students, used the opinion-based forum of the *Reflector* to voice their thoughts on the MSU-NCAA controversy. Sports writer Bill Lunardini wrote that MSU's potential absence from the tournament was "a great injustice" and called the seemingly yearly appearance of the conference's second place team ridiculous.[145] The student newspaper also published the opinions of other students on the Starkville campus through guest editorials. On February 28, 1963, three separate opinion-based articles were published in the *Reflector* with two such accounts featured on the paper's editorial page. The first, which did not have a byline, advocated an appearance by the Bulldogs in the NCAA tournament but as a means of validating the state's belief in segregation. "We have faith in our Mississippi State team that they can prove to the nation the superiority of Southern athletes—and Southern ideals," the anonymous author wrote. On the same page, another opinion piece by an anonymous writer advocated State's place in the postseason but, more importantly, argued that the racial playing field was now level. "The negro has proven himself a strong match for the white man in this area. As a matter of fact, many a negro has surpassed the whites in sports events," the anonymous author wrote. "If in any area, sports is the one area in which negroes are considered equal. If they are not considered so, then it is clearly a case of prejudice." In the pages of the March 14 edition of the student newspaper, another anonymous writer claimed that the vast majority of MSU supporters in the Magnolia State were being opposed by "a small group of legislatures who are apparently fighting for their own personal political gains. . . . If this group wins this struggle, justice will be an obsolete word in the law books of Mississippi."

After the Bulldogs returned to Starkville, the staff of the *Reflector* chose to publish an editorial written in the Ripley-based *Southern Sentinel* that attacked the legitimacy of the unwritten law yet defended Mississippi's belief in segregation. While calling the gentlemen's agreement "useless and far-featched," the anonymous author claimed, "There is not a person, negro or white, in the state who doesn't actually believe in segregation. . . . The negro attends his own schools and churches, as the white people attend theirs, and to save me, I can't see anything wrong with it."[146] Equal parts radical and subservient, the editorial represented a common belief within the Magnolia State that, while the unwritten law may have run its course, MSU's participation against integrated competition would not fracture the Closed Society. The ideological boundaries of the Magnolia State and the white status quo were changing, ever so slightly. In time, the cracks created in the Closed Society's racist foundation by the debates surrounding the unwritten law became the chasms that would help eliminate the white caste system.

Because of the changing times in the Magnolia State, the plight of the Bulldogs generated the same sort of racist rhetoric from some of the Closed Society's stalwart protectors, led by Jimmy Ward of the *Jackson Daily News*. During MSU's previous SEC-title winning seasons, any debates surrounding the unwritten law or the merits of a State appearance in the integrated NCAA tournament were met head on by the staffs of the *Jackson Daily News* and the *Clarion-Ledger*. While the sports reporters at the two papers did little to distinguish themselves in terms of expressing an opinion on the issue, the silent approach employed offered support for the unwritten law and the Closed Society. Teamed with the damning commentary of Ward and Tom Hederman Jr., this combination of racial discontent and silence was an effective way of helping maintain the solidarity and sanctity of the Closed Society. However, 1963 marked the first time in the existence of the unwritten law that the sports desks of the Hederman-owned publications offered different opinions on the matter, demonstrating the ideological wedge that was forming within the ranks of the Closed Society. The unified front of discontent from the paper's editors, specifically Ward, and silence within the sports section was now fractured. While Baker, Walters, Fulton and others supported MSU's participation in integrated athletics, the subject still caught the hateful gaze of Ward, one of the foremost supporters of the Closed Society. Ward, whose commentary on the Magnolia State's basketball scene had been dormant since the 1959 Maroons of Bailey Howell pushed the limits of the unwritten law, returned with a spiteful vengeance, saving some of his more derogatory and racist commentary for the eventual NCAA participants. Ward first voiced his opinion on the MSU-NCAA issue in the March 5, 1963, edition of "Covering the Crossroads," historically, a refuge for the segregationist's spiteful and insensitive commentary. Ward, in a sarcastic tone, wrote that the NAACP, which was "obviously elated over the announcement by President D. W. Colvard of Mississippi State University that the Maroon basketball team would indulge in a 'little' integrating," had filed a lawsuit to force the integration of classrooms in Jackson. Ward's reference to the civil rights-based organization was bewildering since the Jackson editor quickly returned to the Bulldogs and offered no additional commentary on the organization's legal action. Rather, Ward pointed to MSU's decision to enter the tournament and warned of the potential destruction of the Closed Society. "The decision made at Starkville involved more than a Roman lust for another basketball trophy. . . . Athletic fans went nuts and lost their sense of values in the days of Caesar and great was the fall of the Empire." Ward's obsessive protection of the Closed Society continued on March 6th when the racist editor applauded the decision by the State College Board to review Colvard's decision. Damning any notion of support for the Starkville five, Ward wrote that "the glitter of another basketball trophy can blind rabid basketball fans or over-eager sports writers, but it should not be so dazzling as to prompt grown men of grave responsibility to dash off into an experimental expedition that has been found time and time again to produce sordid results. . . . A crack at a mythical national championship isn't worth subjecting young Mississippians to the switchblade knife society that integration inevitably spawns." Ward finished his column by referencing the integrated status of MSU's likely foe Loyola, inaccurately calling the Ramblers' starting line-up "all Negro" and predicting the possible eruption of violence if the two teams were to meet. "It would be a most unfortunate if friction developed during this sports contest," Ward cryptically warned. Ward's racially insensitive commentary continued the following day under the misleading and sarcastic heading "Apology to Mississippi State." Ward addressed, by name, the Bulldogs' second-round foe Loyola of Chicago and apologized, correcting his previous comment that the team's starting lineup was composed of nothing but African-Americans. Ward admitted that he was incorrect, citing a photo from the AP, as only four of the five starters for the Ramblers were black. In a mocking voice, the segregationist editor wrote, "If the *Daily News* said all five were Negroes, it was an honest error based on the best sources of information then available. Or maybe a lucky white boy graduated to the first team." Ward, who published the same photo in the paper's sports section, told his readers to save the image and send it to one of the members of the State College Board. Once again, Ward did not disappoint the zealous members of the Closed Society, using his biting wit and condescending tone to object to MSU's venture into integrated competition. News of Ward's comments also appeared in the *Starkville Daily News* by way of a UPI article.[147]

While Ward often pushed the boundaries of journalistic taste, the segregationist editor began to disseminate racist rhetoric towards State's team and its supporters. Ward expressed nothing but dismay and contempt for the State College Board's ruling in the March 11 edition of the *Jackson Daily News*. Writing with the acidity of a bottle of vinegar, Ward called the decision, "A big, bald-faced blunder, dressed up like a faceless tuxedo bound for a raw-meat banquet to celebrate the debut of 'progressive education and brotherhooding' in Mississippi." Ward then warned his audience that a win over Loyola would not clinch a championship for the Bulldogs, as the team had "yet to engage Tougaloo and the University of Congo. But don't complain. Give them time." Rife with contempt, Ward concluded that he was "not patiently vindictive about the decision" and offered a final, hollow cheer for McCarthy's squad. "Beat the Hell out of them State. We Romans are thirsty."

Ward again attacked MSU's supporters, in particular, Hazel Brannon Smith of the *Lexington Advertiser* and the *Northside Reporter*, on March 14th, writing that Smith and her paper had gone "goo-goo with glee, gushing with joy, and flumed ecstasy" over the State College Board's decision to honor the school's acceptance of the bid. In Ward's words, State was going to East Lansing to "engage in just a little bear hugging under the wicket with Loyola University's famed, sepia-toned, basket-whisking, bucket-poppin' quintet." Once again, Ward's venomous pen attempted to protect the interests of the Closed Society by using ridicule and degradation as a means to an end. "Had the Starkville boys not been granted permission to play in that gosh awfully important tournament, the hysterical, liberal advocates of race-mixing would still be in the middle of the street like Chicken Little screaming in panic that the sky was falling."

In his last nod to the eight years of debate surrounding the unwritten law, Ward would address the April 1963 decision by the State College Board to eliminate the state's segregated standard on integrated competition. Ward claimed that the vote from the board would relieve its members from pressure placed on them by "excited students and rabid sports fans."[148] While the meeting was closed to the press, Ward inexplicitly told his audience how each board member voted, with only strident segregationists Roberts, Lowery, Izard, and Morgan voting to keep the gentleman's agreement in play. Sarcastically, Ward closed his column by writing, "So, in the event of another crisis on the subject, don't bother the board. The fountainhead of policy on this subject rests with the college presidents, athletic directors and cheerleaders."[149] The foremost journalistic protector of the Closed Society, Ward's work was pungent with contempt for those who showed weakness in maintaining the "Southern way of life" and scorn for those who dared to incite change. Meanwhile, in the pages of the *Clarion-Ledger*, editor Tom Hederman Jr. was also in the midst of launching a verbal attack on the Bulldogs and their supporters in an effort to protect both the unwritten law and the Closed Society. While Hederman did not write with the same frequency as Ward, his commentary was nevertheless biting. Upon the announcement that the State College Board would meet to review Colvard's decision, Hederman praised the board and feared that State's presence in the tournament would usher in the systematic destruction of the Closed Society's separatist way of life. "The college board needs to take a long look before it lowers a barrier or opens a door that cannot but mean deterioration in our present preferred position."[150] Days later, Hederman, again fearful of racial equality, quipped, "We play integrated teams abroad, next we play integrated teams at home, next we recruit Negro stars to strengthen our team, and the fast cycle of integration is complete."[151] While absent of Ward's venom, Hederman shared the fear of the collapse of the state's white caste system with his fellow Jackson-based editor, and his commentary objected to the team's venture into the tournament.

From an ideological perspective, perhaps no other newspaper editor had as much in common with the racist and insensitive Ward as James B. Skewes of the *Meridian Star*. Like Ward and Hederman, Skewes tried to protect the Closed Society from the inner threat posed by MSU and had no difficulty expressing his separatist beliefs in, perhaps, the most damning opinion-based article found in this volume. In the March 5, 1963, issue of the *Meridian Star*, Skewes called Colvard's decision "a breach of the walls of segregation," adding that State's participation would compromise the "Southern Way of Life" and give the impression that the Magnolia State was ready for integration. While Skewes argued that State's presence in the NCAA tournament would lead to integrated play in the Magnolia State, in one of the more insensitive and downright asinine comments made, the *Meridian Star* editor insinuated that integrated athletic competition would lead to interracial sexual interaction between black athletes and the white women of Mississippi. "The Negroes will participate in after-game social affairs and so on, one thing leading to another," Skewes wrote. His commentary was picked up by UPI and published in the *Delta Democrat-Times*.[152]

Unlike previous debates involving the Bulldogs, other known segregationists in the Hederman journalistic empire failed to offer any sort of definitive protection of the Closed Society. Surprisingly, Tom Ethridge, another one of Hederman's loyal journalistic minions and a member of the Citizens' Council, used his regular column in the *Clarion-Ledger* to focus on the various opinions that had formed both for and against MSU. While the opinion-based work editors such as Carter, Skewes, Smith, and Rutherford appeared in Ethridge's "Mississippi Notebook," the musings of fellow journalists Mary Cain of the *Summit Sun*, F. A. Parker of the *Prentiss Headlight,* and Thomas Alewine of the *Rankin County News* also appeared verbatim. Smith wrote that the MSU contingent should be allowed to go to the tournament, as she did not "believe that young people in Mississippi should be shackled and hampered by the prejudice, cowardice, ignorance and stupidity of their elders who have been setting the 'stay at home' policy in the past."[153] Along with the work of the progressive Smith, the venomous and spiteful tones of Cain, Parker, and Alewine offered protection to the Closed Society. Cain attacked Colvard's North Carolina background as she stressed her personal desire to keep the state segregated. Parker added that he was shocked that anyone within the state of Mississippi would support such a decision and risk possible integration for "a paltry ball game" while Alewine simply wrote that he found no difference between the NCAA and the NAACP.[154] The only inference that could be drawn about Ethridge's opinion was from the subhead, which read, "We Vote 'Nay,' and Other Say —," a feeble attempt by the opinionated columnist to express his opposition to MSU while putting the onus on his fellow journalists. Ethridge later failed to definitively defend the Closed Society in his March 20, 1963, edition of "Mississippi Notebook," praising the team's effort against Loyola. However, the segregationist took McCarthy to task for his pregame comments on the greatness of the Loyola squad, arguing that the MSU coach's constant praise for the Ramblers contradicted State's tournament purpose, which was to "uphold the prestige of basketball as it is played in Mississippi and the Southeastern Conference." Although he referenced his opposition to MSU playing the integrated Ramblers, Ethridge's columns in 1963 were not reflective of that opposition.

Longtime *Jackson Daily News* cartoonist Bob Howie also chimed in on the Bulldogs' venture into the integrated NCAA tournament. While the debate raged on the entry of State into the NCAA tournament, Howie's cartoons took on a surprisingly mundane tone. Howie first offered an opinion on the MSU team with a cartoon in the March 4, 1963, edition of the *Jackson Daily News* that depicted an MSU basketball player stepping on the foot of an Ole Miss Rebel while reading an invitation to the postseason tournament. Howie, who was as stringent a segregationist as Ward and often opposed State efforts to enter into integrated competition, expressed a degree of support for the Starkville contingent. His next cartoon, in the March 8 edition of the *Jackson Daily News*, simply depicted an MSU basketball player tucked into a ball with the label "State's NCAA Participation Hopes," and being tossed back and forth from two large hands representing the State College Board, one hand labeled "pro," the other "con." Rather than expressing an opinion in his work, Howie simply captured the level of debate within the board and the Magnolia State. Howie later used the March 15 edition of "Hinny" to express a potential opposition to integrated competition, depicting the donkey in a suit and holding a sign cheering on the Bulldogs, saying, "Th' injunction that'ud keep 'em home is what some folks tried usin'/Th' injunction Hinny'd like to get would keep our boys from losin'." While Howie's previous work during the 1963 debate may have been an accurate depiction of the segregationist's feelings on State's NCAA appearance, the March 15 edition of "Hinny" indicated a fear that the all-white Bulldogs may lose to the integrated Ramblers, thus causing a damning blow to the Closed Society and the way of life Howie often used his artwork to protect. In the same edition's sports section, Howie's cartoon, titled "The Last Act?" seemed to strike a familiar cord with Ward's past commentary on the MSU contingent as the SEC champions were illustrated in the form of "Caesar" with the establishing dialogue indicating that the Bulldogs were entering "a public place, a great crowd following, among them a soothsayer." The "soothsayer," dressed in a suit and fedora, was an "oddsmaker" who was telling the MSU squad, "Beware the Ides of March!" In response, the Bulldogs or "Caesar," with a look of panic on his face, said emphatically, "I know!" While Howie's work could have been interpreted as a warning about the upcoming battle with the eventual national champions and the Bulldogs' underdog status, Ward's past commentary utilized the same analogy, likening the Closed Society to the Roman Empire and warning of its eventual demise.

Despite his admitted fear of a Bulldog loss at the hands of Loyola's integrated five, Howie penned one last cartoon in honor of Mississippi State's historic appearance in the NCAA tournament, depicting a proud basketball player saying, "At least I didn't come home empty handed" as he carried a large trophy with the label "3rd Place," a reference to the team's victory over Bowling Green. While the cartoonist expressed a degree of pride in the effort of the MSU team, his pleasure from the team's third place finish also could have had more to do with who they beat, the integrated Falcons. While the bulk of Howie's work reflected a positive aura around McCarthy's team, his segregationist past and ties to the state Citizens' Council were hard to ignore.

Despite the mounting opposition in the Hederman-owned newspapers, Gold said in a 2009 interview that he never had much contact with journalists, much less paid attention to the derogatory comments being disseminated across the state. "Most sports writers were pretty supportive," he said. "I didn't get the impression that the sports world was against us going. It was very different time. I wasn't exposed to those issues as much. At the university, it was an isolated and protected environment. It just didn't have the impact on campus."

While Ward, Hederman, and Skewes were unwavering in opposition to the Bulldogs' participation, an ideological division was developing in their newspapers that would see the sports writers of the Hederman empire, intentional or not, offer a degree of opposition to the editorial protectors of the Closed Society, demonstrating, at the least, a temporary journalistic change in the Magnolia State.

Some journalists stuck to their ever-familiar tendency to stay out of offering any opinion on controversial issues or items that dealt with race. The third of the Hederman journalistic triad, the *Hattiesburg American*, again did little to distinguish itself in the MSU-NCAA tournament debate, expressing no real opinion either supporting or refuting the efforts of MSU. *Hattiesburg American* sports editor Ed Staton first addressed the possibility of an MSU appearance in the integrated postseason in his February 25, 1963, column, titled "Statin' Ideas," when he wrote that McCarthy believed his Bulldogs would play in the integrated postseason. Staton's opinion, however, was notable absent. The Hattiesburg sports editor later wrote that, while MSU was the SEC champion, he thought the conference would be represented by the Atlanta-based Yellow Jackets.[155] While the Hattiesburg sports editor failed to express a definitive opinion on the matter, the presence of his prediction, at best, gave his work a skeptical connotation and, at worst, provided a degree of editorial opposition for the MSU team. After the State College Board made its decision on the matter, the editorial staff of the *Hattiesburg American* acknowledged the tradition-breaking precedent set but devoted more ink to the presence of the press at the meeting, arguing that, "Almost everybody, of course, is familiar with the arguments, pro and con, of whether the team should play," dismissing the issue at hand.[156] Rather than express an opinion on the merits of the MSU team or the unwritten law, the paper ignored the debate from an editorial standpoint, demonstrating a degree of journalistic neglect on behalf of the *Hattiesburg American*. Staton wrote on the MSU contingent for a final time in the March 15 edition of the *Hattiesburg American*, using his column to pen a feature-like account on McCarthy. While Staton spent the majority of his opinion-based forum profiling the Baldwyn County native, he expressed little to no editorial support for the MSU head coach or the team. Staton wrote in an almost poetic tone, "Win or lose, at least the Babe's dream came true." Keeping true to its historic form, the *Hattiesburg American* maintained its silent-like treatment of any issues involving MSU and the unwritten law and, to a greater extent, anything involving race. This lack of voice allowed the paper to support the Closed Society by omission.

Delta Democrat-Times sports editor Charles Kerg, who advocated a Bulldog trip to the 1962 NCAA tournament, did not comment on the Bulldogs until the March 3, 1963, edition of his column, "Kerg's Korner," and offered little in terms of the debate. Kerg simply challenged Fulton's argument that a tournament absence would lead to McCarthy's departure from Starkville, countering that the MSU head coach's love for the Magnolia State would keep him in Mississippi. *Laurel Leader-Call* sports editor Odell McRae took a similar route, using his March 5 column to discuss McCarthy's effect on the level of interest in basketball in the Magnolia State, and McRae claimed that the MSU head coach's success in Starkville had contributed to the state's growing interest in high school basketball. Despite his complimentary remarks on McCarthy, McRae did not reference the NCAA tournament.

While columns and editorials served as a source of both opposition and support of the unwritten law, a more accurate measurement of public opinion could be found in letters to the editor. Because of the prevailing opinions of the newspaper's editors, many of the published letters reflected the thoughts of the newspapers themselves. The primary example came from the *Clarion-Ledger* and the *Jackson Daily News*. The Hederman-owned newspapers were at the forefront of public opinion, with the *Clarion-Ledger* publishing thirty letters and the *Jackson Daily News* printing twenty-six on the MSU-NCAA debate. In combination, the other papers consulted during this time period printed only six. On February 28, 1963, four letters appeared in the *Clarion-Ledger*, all in support of the team. One letter, signed by nine different men, was addressed to Barnett and asked him to do everything in his power to assure that State would play in the tournament. Another letter, from the "third floor of McKee Hall Dormitory" on the campus of MSU, also supported State's efforts but indicated that the authors felt the segregationist status of the university and the state would only be compromised if "little brother Bobby decides to shove it down our throats with the aid of federal troops," a reference to Robert Kennedy and the federal government's involvement in Meredith's integration of Ole Miss. While letters from Buddy Graves of Greenville and T. J. Smith of Florence supported the Bulldogs, Smith's letter offered five justifications for the team to play in the tournament, none of which pertained to integration or the playing of integrated teams.

In the March 2 edition of the *Clarion-Ledger*, T. N. Powell of Greenwood blamed sports writers and politicians for creating the controversy surrounding the Bulldogs and claimed that those who supported playing integrated teams were "prostituting their principles." Another letter, from a Jackson student who claimed an affiliation to the *Rebel Underground*, voiced "fraternal pride" for the accomplishments of MSU but asked that they showed the same courage by "refusing the plum that is being dangled so temptingly before them by a common enemy"—integrationists.

The *Clarion-Ledger* published two more letters, each with split views on MSU's participation on March 7, 1963. The first, written by Rex Barber, suggested the university allow the students to vote on the matter and accept their decision rather than be forced to accept integration. Another letter attacked Colvard; however, the writer, J. B. Collier of Meridian, suggested State should have played a black college in Mississippi before playing in the NCAA tournament. The following day, the Jackson-based paper published a score of letters, the majority of which condemned the possibility of athletic competition with integrated teams. Louis Leman of Brookhaven wrote that the students of MSU were nothing but pawns of the "left wing" that were using them to "weaken the entire state."[157] T. B. Templeton of Natchez called for "enough white men with guts enough to stop the Kennedys and their do-good stooges" in an effort to preserve Mississippi well after "that coach and his players are forgotten."[158] Edwin White of Lexington added, "Surely, as soon as we enter the integrated tournament in Michigan, our many enemies will proclaim that we have given way and yielded," and Thaddie Screws of Bentonia claimed, "I hope the leaders of Mississippi will wake up and see what lies ahead."[159] While these letters, in part, sounded of an apocalyptic conclusion facing the Closed Society, it was evident there was a fear that the MSU tournament bid would change Mississippi forever.

As the state awaited the State College Board's decision, more citizens took their opportunity to voice objections for the NCAA bid in the *Clarion-Ledger*. Tom Barrentine of Greenwood claimed that Colvard and McCarthy were in favor of integration and simply lacked the courage to say so.[160] N. E. Dacus of Tupelo called the decision "disastrous," adding that "only our own people following false leadership" would cause the demise of the southern way of life, a jab at the North Carolina native.[161] In the March 13 edition of the *Clarion-Ledger*, Alan Johnson of State College called the justification to not play in the NCAA "ridiculous" while Ray Henderson of Carthage called Colvard's decision one that would lead a great university down a road of ruin.[162]

While many editorials and letters to the editor viewed the unwritten law as a way to keep Mississippi's superior athletic teams from playing inferior integrated competition, at least one reader saw it the other way around. On March 12th, Massachusetts resident Erich Kronfield identified with a northern perspective of the rule, writing that Mississippians feared that their teams would be dominated by integrated competition. Kronfield argued that MSU should play in the tournament to solidify their views on segregation and to show the "superiority of their way."

While Kronfield's letter seemingly mocked the traditions of the Closed Society, the most damning letter to Barnett's opposition appeared in the *Clarion-Ledger* on March 14th. From a person identified as "Alphonse Cincere" of Jackson, the letter was composed in a manner similar to a stereotypical, racist view of the verbal skills of an African-American. "Cincere's" letter, filled with misspelled words, mockingly attacked the segregationist ideology of Barnett and addressed the MSU controversy by asking, "Can't we blame dis basketball ruckus on dem dirty feds or der commies? We have everyting else, eh Barnett?" "Cincere" ended the letter by calling the situation, "most embarressin to me Barnett. I feel like I been unmasked." While coming across as a criticism of the governor and segregation, the use of a racial stereotype actually supported the state's separatist ideology and painted blacks as being less intelligent than their white counterparts. Along with the letter from "Cincere," four other letters appeared in the same issue, all in opposition of MSU.

The *Jackson Daily News* also featured a slew of correspondents, the majority of which backed up the segregationist views of Ward and the newspaper. The first letter appeared on February 28, 1963, from William Farmer of State College who made a logical appeal to the Bulldogs' participation in the NCAA tournament by noting that the state would not step in if a local athlete were to participate in the integrated Olympics. Charles Wallace of Jackson wrote a sarcastic letter congratulating McCarthy on his success and suggesting the coach find a new job at a university meeting his "specification" rather than appealing for NCAA tournament support.[163] As decision day loomed closer for the State College Board, more letters in opposition began to appear in the *Daily News* in the form of the aforementioned letters from White, Luckett, and Barrentine.[164] In the March 8 edition of the *Jackson Daily News*, Presley Snow of Philadelphia called MSU's tournament play "the most disgusting and shameful thing to happen to our state since the Warren Court made state rights and constitutional government a mockery of this nation," and referred to integration as the "Kennedy-backed cancer." Similar sentiment could be found in the *Jackson Daily News* the following day, as E. W. Anderson of Hattiesburg, William S. Deale of Gloster, Sam Farrington, Harper Foundry and Machine Co., and Herbert Lester, all of Jackson, wrote in opposition of State and cited the fear of state integration as being the eventual outcome.[165]

In the March 11 edition of the *Jackson Daily News*, three letters of support for MSU were published, led by Morris Bloodworth and Billy Boyd of State College who told Ward to "cram" the Loyola photo and asked the segregationist editor why he refused to publish material in support of State. Ward, in an editor's note below the letter, simply wrote, "We do." Harold Unland Jr., also of State College, called the approach by Ward and Barnett "cowardly."[166] Paul Bailey of Ottawa, Illinois also wrote to the paper and argued that Mississippians simply feared that State would be defeated in a rout by a superior team. Despite the varied tones of support in these three letters, Dacus essentially canceled them out. In the letter, rife with racial prejudice and under the heading "Integrations -110, MSU, Ole Miss -0," the Tupelo native wondered if history would still be written 100 years from now in "the American Jungle" that would be inhabited "by a dark brown race of men living in clusters of thatched huts super-imposed upon the ruins of brick and steel." Dacus's correspondence would again appear in the *Jackson Daily News* on March 15th. The segregationist noted the MSU student body's support for the team and wondered if State was offering a class in "how to become a first class moron in only a few lessons." Citing the "adopted North Carolina style," a reference to Colvard's background, Dacus claimed he was not surprised by the supportive expression of MSU students. After the Bulldogs' loss to Loyola, W. P. Pinney of New York wrote the decision by the State College Board tore down the loyalty between that organization and the people of Mississippi.[167]

Outside of Jackson, editorial commentary from the reading public was few and far between. In the *Starkville Daily News*, a letter appeared from Warren Barker of Starkville who asked McCarthy not to change the principles of Mississippi for a basketball game and indicated that the integration of Mississippi would lead to chaos.[168] In the aftermath of State's loss to Loyola, A. R. Ballinger of Appleton, Wisconsin, wrote the Starkville-based paper to commend the efforts of MSU and called it "a step in the right direction." He also noted his new sense of pride in being a native of the state.[169] While Emmerich expressed nothing but support for MSU, even the McComb-based *Enterprise-Journal* featured a letter to the editor that opposed the Maroons' NCAA efforts on March 7, 1963, from Harry Marsalis of McComb, who wrote that he loved the southern morals of the state and would not succumb to Emmerich's notion that the integration of athletics and the state was inevitable. Marsalis's letter was the only one to appear in Emmerich's paper during the MSU-NCAA controversy.

In total, the *Clarion-Ledger* and the *Jackson Daily News* served as the predominant outlets in terms of overall public opinion, continuing the influence and dominance of the Hederman franchise. The content of these correspondents reflected the overall outlook of the Jackson-based publications. While the majority of content in these newspapers was against Colvard's decision, the MSU president received numerous letters and telegrams supporting the Bulldogs' NCAA trip.[170]

Another surprising source for public opinion came in the form of the *Reflector* and letters to the editor published by the university's student newspaper. While college newspapers are not normally seen as a haven for such commentary, the biweekly publication nevertheless featured some of the more supportive public pleas for the MSU faithful. The *Reflector* published two letters to the editor in the March 7 edition of the paper concerning the Bulldogs and the chances of playing in the integrated postseason. The first, from Oscar T. Brookins, congratulated the team and hoped the citizens of the Magnolia State realized that playing in the tournament was necessary to continue on as one of the predominant basketball powers in the South.[171] A second letter, from State

College resident Edward Prisock, questioned the need to play in the tournament, calling it "ironical if not hypocritical" and that MSU's supporters were putting "personal pleasure before moral principles."[172] By publishing two letters of opposite perspectives and arguments, the *Reflector* demonstrated a degree of journalistic balance.

After the team returned to Starkville, the *Reflector* also continued to be a forum for public sentiment, surprisingly, for individuals outside of the student paper's target audience. In the March 21 edition of the paper, Elmo Collins of Toledo, Ohio wrote to both congratulate the Bulldogs and dispel any negative misconceptions about the state. In closing his complimentary letter, the Ohio resident added that he hoped that the loss to Loyola would not "deter them if a chance to go again is present in the future." A week later, Dennis Day of East Lansing wrote that MSU was an excellent basketball team and lamented that it "was certainly unfortunate that the segregation controversy and its publicity clouded the issue at hand—basketball! Even though, your team represented Mississippi State University and her student body, both on the court and off, in such a manner that you may well be proud—their sportsmanship was outstanding as was their brand of basketball."[173]

From an examination of the material presented, the winds of change blew through the Magnolia State during the Bulldogs' 1962–1963 SEC championship winning season. While the debate surrounding the validity of the unwritten law would emerge once again, due to the bravery of Colvard and the swagger of McCarthy, the Bulldogs successfully emerged from the Closed Society and, despite their loss in the integrated tournament, demonstrated the slow but evolutionary change in Mississippi's journalists. While segregationist mavens like Ward and Skewes continued to protect Mississippi's ideological borders and acted like the journalistic police of the Magnolia State, their individual shows of discontent and hate did little to alter the drive of State's administration and change the opinions and views of their journalistic colleagues. Unlike past debates, there was a universal tone of goodwill for the Bulldogs and, regardless of each individual's social and ideological justification, Mississippi's journalists supported State's entry into the integrated postseason. On the heels of Meredith's admission to Ole Miss, the almost radical show of support for MSU and the eventual elimination of the unwritten law was one more step in the direction of integration in the Magnolia State. While it is, perhaps, ambitious to identify Mississippi State's basketball team as the origin of this change in the press, nevertheless, the coverage and the expression of opinion in Mississippi's newspapers exposed the crumbling united front of the Closed Society and, at the least, showed that inroads to equality and the end of racial tyranny in Mississippi were on the horizon.

"In my opinion, what we did was a significant step for both the university and the state," Gold proudly said. "I don't think the team understood the social significance of the event [at the time] When we came back, we had a celebration on campus and we had this huge crowd supporting us. But as far as knowing, I don't think it sunk in."[174]

Chapter 6

I've Made My Last Trip to Places like Mississippi

Years passed before the grip of the Closed Society completely let go of Mississippi's college basketball courts. In the aftermath of Mississippi State's participation in the NCAA tournament and the subsequent elimination of the unwritten law in 1963, one would think that equality and integration were well on their way in the Magnolia State. However, this is an oversimplification of the events that transpired in the following years. Racial harmony did not engulf Mississippi overnight, and the subsequent years would bring additional strife and sorrow to the champions of the civil rights movement. Student activism continued in the Magnolia State as eight students from Tougaloo College participated in a sit-in at a lunch counter in a Woolworth's department store in Jackson on May 28, 1963. The attempt at a peaceful demonstration was met with a three hour barge of violence and degradation at the expense of the Tougaloo students. The hideous behavior of white Mississippians towards the students was captured by the press both locally and nationally and began a grassroots demonstration movement in the state's capital city.[1] Soon after the Woolworth's demonstration, Civil Rights champions across the state would lose one of their own as Medgar Evers, the NAACP field security, was assassinated outside of his home in Jackson on June 12, 1963, by Citizens' Council member Byron De La Beckwith.[2] As noted by historian David R. Davies, notorious *Jackson Daily News* editor Jimmy Ward called Evers murder a "dastardly act of inhuman behavior" but focused more on how the event effected the city's reputation and blamed civil rights workers for the loss.[3] Referred to as the "living symbol of all the hopes and aspirations of Mississippi Negros in their long struggle to throw off the shackles of discrimination" by *Lexington Advisor* editor Hazel Brannon Smith, Evers murder was a damning blow to civil rights efforts in the state. The subsequent trial of Beckwith only caused more harm as the case suffered two mistrials.[4]

A little over a year after MSU's NCAA tournament appearance, the Closed Society was dealt another blow as Freedom Summer commenced in Mississippi. An organized effort by a number of civil rights organizations, Freedom Summer was meant to bring racial equality to the Magnolia State by registering blacks to vote and establishing "freedom schools," which offered blacks classes on subjects such as politics and cultural awareness.[5] The response to the civil rights workers, most of who were white college students, was one of resentment from the white community and skepticism from the black. Within the first two weeks of the summer project, Mickey Schwerner, James Chaney, and Andrew Goodman were murdered in Philadelphia and there were at least seven bombings, four shootings, and numerous beatings.[6] Historian John Dittmer called the summer of 1964 "the most violent since Reconstruction," as the ten-week effort saw thirty-five shootings, the bombing of sixty-five homes and buildings, over one thousand arrests, and eighty beatings.[7] According to historian Charles Payne, the violence may have been worse if not for the government's intervention and visible presence in the Philadelphia murders.[8] The summer project expanded thought the state and the "freedom schools" were considered a success although, as Dittmer pointed out, they did not "save the Mississippi movement."[9] The struggle continued even after the summer of 1964 but, if anything, the events that transpired that summer shed a national spotlight on the local conditions in Mississippi. On July 5, 1964, President Lyndon Johnson signed the Civil Rights Act of 1964. The act barred racial discrimination in public facilities such as the workplace, schools, restaurants and theatres, and reduced voter qualifications. Mississippi Governor Paul B. Johnson Jr. called the act "unconstitutional" and openly advocated noncompliance within the state. The Mississippi Legislature voted 113–0 to fight the bill.[10] The passing of the act, for the most part, generated a negative reaction from the press.[11] A year later, Johnson signed the Voting Rights Act on August 6, 1965, which allowed blacks to register to vote with only a proof of age and residency.[12] Mississippi, in essence, was being forced to change as segregation and racial discrimination were now, for all intents and purposes, illegal. However, that change was still met with resistance. 1965 and 1966 brought more government intervention and, while the Citizens' Council was rapidly losing power, the Klu Klux Kan's profile was rising. Case in point: Vernon Dahmer, a Hattiesburg farmer and president of the local NAACP chapter, died in 1966 after his home had set ablaze by members of the Klan.[13] The killing of blacks involved in the civil rights movement continued in 1966 and 1967 with little to no coverage.[14] The state of Mississippi was in full revolt and, despite the violence and discontent that surrounded them, blacks would continue to integrate into Mississippi's white society.

With Meredith's entry and subsequent graduation from the University of Mississippi in 1963, it was only a matter of time before other traditionally segregated colleges and universities in the state welcomed blacks on their campuses. Due, in part to the lessons learned from the integration of Ole Miss and the school's participation in the NCAA tournament, Mississippi State welcomed their first student of color in July 1965 when Richard Holmes, a Starkville resident, enrolled at the institution. Holmes' enrollment was met with little fanfare or attention, in part, because Colvard was determined not to repeat the tragic events that engulf his Oxford brethren. Colvard publically supported Holmes's admission to the university and, while law enforcement officials were placed on stand-by in case there was opposition, Holmes was, seemingly, accepted on the Starkville campus.[15] Despite Meredith's and Holmes's additions to Ole Miss and MSU, athletics remained untouched by equality until 1968. While the Southeastern Conference integrated its ranks in 1965 with Tulane University's addition of Steve Martin to the baseball team, the gymnasiums in Starkville, Oxford, and Hattiesburg did not welcome a black college basketball player until freshmen Perry Wallace of Vanderbilt University took to the court against Mississippi State on February 27, 1967. Wallace later likened the experience to a trip to hell and, upon graduating, claimed, "I've made my last trip to places like Mississippi."[16] Despite Wallace's integration of SEC basketball, it was another two years before one of Mississippi's historically segregated colleges and universities welcomed a black athlete to its white-only ranks. Wilbert Jordan Jr. walked on to the freshman team at the University of Southern Mississippi in 1968, becoming the first black athlete at Southern Miss, the University of Mississippi, and Mississippi State University, and signaling the end of the segregated era in Mississippi sports. Racial equality was on the horizon in Magnolia State sports whether the purveyors of the Closed Society liked it or not. "It was unusual to them, and odd," Jordan said in an August 2010 interview of the influx of African-Americans to the formally segregated university structure in Mississippi. "It was uncomfortable. But it was a sign of the times. Certain things in Mississippi were designed for white people and integration started to change that."

In the 1963 aftermath of the unwritten law, Mississippi's newspapers continued to support the ideals and values of the Closed Society and ignored the historical and social significance of athletic integration as the appearance of Martin and Wallace on the SEC circuit garnered little attention from the state's sports press. Along those same lines, the 1968 addition of Jordan to the Hattiesburg-based Southerners was met with the same neglectful coverage that once poisoned the journalistic ranks during the era of the unwritten law. Jordan's historical rise through the previously segregated ranks of Mississippi sports was not evident in the press as the local *Hattiesburg American* never identified Jordan's status as the state's first black athlete at USM, Ole Miss, or MSU during his first two years as a member of the "Golden Giants."

However, over time, the views on race in Mississippi began to change. From a historical perspective, events like the passing of the Civil Rights Act in 1964 and Freedom Summer demonstrated that the ideological borders placed around Mississippi could not stop the progression of equality and civil rights. The integration of Southern Mississippi's basketball team occurred during the same calendar year as the implementation of the Civil Rights Act of 1968, which made physical discrimination a federal crime.[17] The continued addition of blacks to the previously segregated ranks of the Magnolia State's basketball rosters seeped into the 1970s, and the fervor that once surrounded issues of race began to diminish. Evidence of this transformation in Mississippi's press was apparent during the basketball-based integration of Ole Miss and Mississippi State with the additions of Coolidge Ball at Ole Miss in 1970 and Larry Fry and Jerry Jenkins at MSU in 1971 to the once segregated universities. Ole Miss's 1970 signing of Ball as the school's first black athlete garnered little attention for the majority of the press. Only two of the newspapers consulted during the 1970–1971 season identified the pioneering forward's race during his first season as a member of the Rebels' freshman squad. However, signs of progress were abounding as the emergence of "Cool-Aid" on Mississippi's basketball land-scape garnered both human-interest articles and photos from the historically conservative *Oxford Eagle* and the *Meridian Star*, a far cry from the era of the unwritten law. Furthermore, the outward expressions of hate and degradation were absent, most notably from the *Jackson Daily News* and the *Clarion-Ledger*. While both newspapers were still in the firm grips of the Hederman family and Jimmy Ward, both supporters of the state Sovereignty Commission, a new tone of temperament began to emerge in the pages of the Jackson-based publications that, in part, could be attributed to the social evolution going on in the state. By 1971, the schools in Jackson were integrated and later, with the 1972 election of Governor William "Bill" Waller, who followed through on campaign promises to put blacks in important positions within the state's political structure and vetoed all political efforts to fund the Sovereignty Commission in 1973, racial equality had slowly made its way through Mississippi's previously Closed Soci-ety.[18] Despite the presence of Ward at the *Jackson Daily News* through the 1970s, even the fiery and once spiteful segregationist tempered his views both in the pages of the newspaper and in his interactions with his staff.[19] By the time Ball, in 1972, and Fry and Jenkins, in 1973, had concluded their first varsity seasons, the press had rarely referenced the ethnicity of the trio, not out of neglect, but as a sign of progress. Newspapers, including local and on-campus publications, found little news value in the history-making addition of Jordan, continuing in the silent tactics that were once approved by the Sovereignty Commission, as a way to combat the Civil Rights Movement. However, by the time Ball, Fry, and Jenkins made their presence known as their individual school's first black basketball players on the formally all-white rosters, the press was actually acting out of respect rather than racial outrage. It must be clarified that not every refer-ence to Jordan, Ball, Fry, and Jenkins necessitated an identification of their eth-nicity. However, an initial nod to race would have been sufficient recognition of their place in history and would have allowed the press to report on an item of public interest.

In total, the anger and debate that had saturated Mississippi's newspapers during the era of the unwritten law was gone and in its place was a Fourth Estate that attempted to find a journalistic balance that, at times, appeared neglectful and awkward. The emergence of Jordan, Ball, Jenkins, and Fry at USM, Ole Miss, and MSU was evidence of a bigger change in Mississippi's press that, slowly but surely, began to view race as a forgotten component of the state's news cycle, so much so that the typical characterization of blacks as "negroes" was no longer evident in Mississippi's newspapers by the appearance of Jenkins and Fry on the MSU roster in 1971. Because of the social change permeating the Magnolia State during the late 1960s and early 1970s, the neglect related to the skin color of these athletes became less of a means to protect the Closed Society and more of a demonstration of the progress made by Mississippi's journalistic community. Rather than being viewed strictly as blacks, the press came to treat these pioneering young men simply as members of their respective basketball teams.

After the Bulldogs returned to Starkville from the NCAA tournament in 1963, rumblings of integration in the Southeastern Conference began to come out of Lexington, as the University of Kentucky inquired into where its conference brethren stood on the recruitment of blacks. At the time, no SEC roster had an athlete of color, but there was no rule in the conference prohibiting a school from making such an addition.[20] On April 13, 1963, the Associated Press reported that Kentucky sent questionnaires to the other schools in the conference and only two, Tulane University and Georgia Tech, indicated that they would play integrated teams both at home and on the road. Furthermore, officials for both the Green Wave and the Yellow Jackets claimed that they would keep the Wildcats on their schedules if the school were to add black athletes. Despite playing the integrated Ramblers from Loyola of Chicago less than a month earlier, Mississippi State indicated that the Bulldogs would only play integrated teams on the road. The school did not respond to the question pertaining to the possible integration of Kentucky's athletics.[21] How Ole Miss officials viewed the possible integration of Kentucky's teams was not referenced in any articles on the questionnaire, but the omission of the Rebels indicated that either the university did not respond or they answered no to all three questions.

Dr. Frank Dickey, president of the University of Kentucky's Athletics Association, issued a formal statement on April 29, 1963, saying that they favored the integration of the university's athletic program but would abide by any ruling the SEC had on the matter. While the Wildcats may have been looking to integrate their sports, Dickey told the press that no timeframe had been established because all athletic scholarships at the school were already committed. Dickey said the school would not begin the possible recruitment of black athletes until the conclusion of 1964.[22]

In 1965, almost two years after MSU's famous trip to East Lansing, the SEC integrated as Tulane added Steve Martin to the Green Wave baseball team, making it inevitable that both Ole Miss and Mississippi State would compete against blacks in the Magnolia State.[23] Media coverage in Mississippi of Martin and the integration of the SEC was virtually nonexistent. When Martin made his first trek through the Magnolia State, none of the newspapers consulted in this chapter had a story on the historical occurrence.[24] After the outfielder was promoted to the varsity in 1966, his addition was reported in the *Jackson Daily News* and the *Vicksburg Evening Post* in the form of a wire-based article, both of which referenced Martin as the first "negro" athlete in the conference.[25] Only a week after Martin's addition to Tulane varsity squad was reported in the press, SEC commissioner Tonto Coleman told the AP that he did not think the integration of athletics was going to be a problem because most of the schools accepted it as an inevitable fact. "I don't know that a lot of people pay attention to it anymore," he said.[26] Newspaper accounts of Tulane's baseball matchup with Mississippi State on April 14 and 15, 1966, in New Orleans and April 29 and 30, 1966, in Starkville, made no mention of the black outfielder. By evidence of accompanying box scores, Martin played one game in each series, going a combined one for seven.[27] While his omission could have been justified based on his statistical output, Martin's skin tone, once a magnet for ire and ridicule in Mississippi, went unnoticed. With Jim Crow laws alive and well in the Magnolia State during the mid-1960s, much like the support for integrated athletics in previous years was out of the need for cultural validation, the acknowledgment of Martin's presence within Mississippi's boarders would have magnified the increasingly dated nature of Mississippi's racist rhetoric.

While Martin's efforts broke the colorline for SEC baseball, it was Vanderbilt University's Perry Wallace who braved the white-dominated hardwood in the conference as the first black athlete to receive a basketball scholarship on April 4, 1966. Much like Martin's historic rise, Wallace's signing was met with little fanfare in Mississippi. The *Jackson Daily News* was the only newspaper in the state to carry an article on Wallace's addition to the Commodores.[28] *Jackson Daily News* sports editor Lee Baker noted the signing of Wallace in his column on April 5th and described the heated competition between southern universities for the forward's services. Wallace played at Nashville's Pearl High School in Tennessee, the same school as 1963 Loyola of Chicago stars Les Hunter and Vic Rouse. In a 2006 interview, Wallace said the duo often questioned his choice in schools. "As a black athlete in the mid-1960s, usually the goal was to go to a predominantly black college or go to a university in the North," Wallace said. "They told me not to do it. Their approach was 'to heck with that pioneering stuff.'"

Wallace and walk-on forward Godfrey Dillard, also an African-American, were relegated to the freshman team by NCAA rules during the 1966–1967 season. The presence of Wallace and Dillard became a source of controversy in Mississippi well before the duo played their first contest in the Magnolia State. Ole Miss canceled its 1967 home game against Vanderbilt's freshman squad due to the presence of the two black Commodores. Because of Ole Miss's decision, MSU assistant athletic director Ralph Brown wrote a letter to Dr. T. K. Martin, the executive vice-president to MSU president William Giles, asking that the school use the student newspaper to stress "the responsibilities of the host school pertaining to student conduct and an appeal from the administration for courteous treatment of all visitors."[29] On February 27, 1967, the Commodores' duo made history, leading an integrated Vanderbilt freshman squad against the "Bullpups" in Starkville.[30] The game would be the first for any MSU basketball team against integrated competition since the 1963 NCAA tournament and the first in school history in Starkville as Wallace and Dillard were the first black basketball players to play on the MSU campus. Despite the historical aspects of the game, media accounts on the groundbreaking event were scarce. Only the *Jackson Daily News* carried a short article on the game, an 84–70 MSU victory. While both Wallace and Dillard were identified by name in the story, their race was omitted. Wallace finished with thirteen points and nineteen rebounds, while Dillard had sixteen points and eleven rebounds.[31] Baker briefly mentioned the game in his February 28 column and dismissed the overall significance of the event, writing that the "presence of two Negroes on the Vanderbilt freshman team created not a ripple," he wrote. Baker then proceeded to belittle the historic occurrence, claiming that MSU's victory would place the matter into the "so what category," a surprising point by the Jackson-based sports editor considering his bold commentary on the 1963 MSU team and its entry into the NCAA tournament. The reflective Wallace took umbrage with Baker's incident-free account in a 2006 interview. "It was hell. The stands were right on top of the court, so we heard everything," the SEC Hall of Famer explained. "It was like a chorus of hate and certain individuals had solo parts and their words would just pierce the air. It wasn't just the 'N' word. I remember they kept yelling 'shoe polish' at Godfrey and me. It was outright bigotry."

Wallace also said he was not surprised by the lack of media attention on the culturally relevant event. "It was the South and newspaper reporters knew that this wasn't what white audiences wanted to read about," he said. "They were in denial and I think they were ashamed of their behavior. There was no way they were going to write about the racist behavior of their own home crowd."

Upon Wallace's graduation, the college basketball pioneer told UPI's Walt Smith that he had "made his last trip to places like Mississippi," citing the University of Mississippi as the worst place to play basketball due to the raucous home crowd, who Wallace said once chanted "we're going to lynch you," at the future SEC Hall-of-Famer.[32]

While Wallace's testimony failed to offer much comfort for the black basketball players of the late 1960s and early 1970s, integration would come to the hardwood in the Magnolia State almost two years later as a walk-on at the University of Southern Mississippi made history.

While Meredith served as the catalyst for integration and the advancement of civil rights in Mississippi's segregated colleges and universities, his athletic equivalent did not face the same pressure and degradation at the hands of the press. Wilbert Jordan Jr., a native of Waynesboro, became the first black athlete to join one of the traditionally segregated college basketball teams of the Magnolia State when the former Riverside High School student walked on to the basketball court at the University of Southern Mississippi in 1968. A point guard from Wayne County, Jordan joined the Southerners after USM head coach Lee Floyd suggested to the freshman to try out for the first-year team after watching him play in a few pick-up games.[33] In a 2010 interview, Jordan said he never intended on being the first black athlete at one of Mississippi's predominantly white schools. "I was there for an education, I wasn't there to play basketball," Jordan explained.

While Jordan's presence on the USM roster was a legitimate news story, the majority of the press in the Magnolia State failed to report on the integration of one of the state's college basketball teams. While the exploits of the Southerners appeared in one hundred and fourty-nine articles during Jordan's first two seasons in Mississippi's Hub City, his race was only referenced once.[34] Perhaps the *Hattiesburg American* committed the most egregious oversight as USM's local news outlet and the only publication outside of Jackson owned by the segregationist Hederman family. Despite publishing forty-nine articles on the Southerners during Jordan's first two seasons, no print-based account acknowledged his race. The first and only reference to the presence of Jordan on the USM squad came during his sophomore campaign in a photo, by Dick Tarbutton, in the February 17, 1970, edition of the *American*. Jordan was pictured in a photo trailing teammate Bobby Jones after the sophomore guard caused a loose ball. The visual image of USM's first black athlete was the only acknowledgement of Jordan's history-making presence on the Southerners' roster. In a similar fashion, the *Student Printz*, Southern Mississippi's student newspaper, also failed to identify the trailblazing Jordan as the school's first black athlete in the twenty-seven articles published during Jordan's first two seasons. The only depiction of Jordan's race appeared in the January 13, 1970, edition of the *Student Printz* when the sophomore was pictured going for a rebound against the University of South Alabama in the Southerners' 104–79 victory.

Outside of Hattiesburg, the efforts of Jordan also went unnoticed. The *Jackson Daily News* published fifty accounts on the USM squad during Jordan's freshman and sophomore years, yet it was not until a February 20, 1970, article by longtime *Jackson Daily News* sports editor Baker on the Southerners' season-ending 77–69 victory over in-state rival Delta State that a journalist in the Magnolia State identified Jordan's race. Baker called the pioneering guard "a quick 6–2 Negro sophomore from Waynesboro." Baker's reference was almost comical, as he had been aware of Jordan's presence at USM since December 1968, yet it took the majority of two full basketball campaigns to tell the *Jackson Daily News*' reading audience that Jordan was black. From a journalistic perspective, it was bewildering that Baker did not find Jordan's status as the first black athlete at USM newsworthy, but almost two full seasons later, his ethnicity was somehow relevant in the context of his ability to defend an opposing player at the conclusion of a 15–11 season. Baker's article also appeared in the *Clarion-Ledger* on February 20, 1970, and was that paper's only acknowledgement of Jordan's race during the guard's first two seasons in Hattiesburg despite publishing twenty-seven articles on the Southerners.

Jordan said that his lack of local media-based exposure, in a way, matched from a social perspective, his time on the Hattiesburg campus. "I don't have any horror stories," he said. "It was USM's culture. It was very low key. I'm not going to tell you it was utopia. Some of the people I played with had never even seen black people. I wasn't recruited so no one had to justify me to anyone. I was already on campus. I was nothing more than a guy at Southern Miss and it was fine with me. I had no problem flying under the radar. . . . We were the anti-Ole Miss."[35]

One could have argued that the lack of press on Jordan came from his pedestrian statistical performance during the course of his first year on USM's varsity. Jordan finished the season appearing in twenty-four games, averaging only 2.2 points and two rebounds per game and, during the course of the season, the second-year guard went scoreless in seven contests. From a team perspective, Jordan's harder years were yet to come. After the 1969–1970 season, Jordan's subsequent USM teams would go 7–19 in 1970–1971 and an abysmal 0–24 in 1971–1972, Jordan's senior year.[36] However, Jordan's presence on the Southern Miss basketball team was about more than statistics and wins. While he was never a star in the annals of Mississippi college basketball, Jordan's trailblazing efforts set the stage for other blacks to venture into the previously segregated gymnasiums of the Magnolia State.

Although Jordan was the first black in Mississippi to play basketball at USM, Ole Miss, or Mississippi State, his average statistics with the Southerners were, arguably, the determining factor in the amount of coverage the Waynesboro native received from sports journalists during his first two seasons in the Hub City. That was not the case in Oxford, as an athlete the likes of which the Rebel nation had yet to see leapt on the Magnolia State sports scene in 1970. Coolidge Ball, a forward from Indianola, was a star at Gentry High School where he averaged twenty-eight points and twenty rebounds per game.[37] The Mississippi native would initially choose to play his college basketball at the University of New Mexico but, after staying on the Albuquerque campus, Ball felt he was too far away from home and decided to sign a scholarship with the University of Mississippi. When asked why he chose Ole Miss in December 1970, Ball said, "Not only the coaches and players were friendly, but the fans were so enthusiastic—it all just made up my mind," a far cry from Wallace's comments to UPI only eleven months earlier.[38]

In his first two years at Ole Miss, the journalistic community in Mississippi presented the SEC Hall of Famer in an inconsistent fashion. While Ball and the Rebels appeared in 249 articles consulted in this volume, his ethnic background was referenced on few occasions.[39] Because of the changing social environment of Mississippi in the early 1970s and how the press in the Magnolia State handled issues of race, the almost flighty manner in which Ball's ethnicity was mentioned was an illustration of how the print media in the state was in a transitional period where an individual's color was slowly becoming less relevant.

Ball's August 6, 1970, signing generated little buzz in the sporting press, as only the *Oxford Eagle* published an article on his addition to the Ole Miss basketball team and did so over a month after he signed his scholarship.[40] The unknown author wrote that Ball was the last player inked by the Rebels but failed to reference the forward as being black, a huge oversight considering the social impact Ball's signing would have on the Ole Miss community. Months later, the *Daily Mississippian*, Ole Miss's student newspaper, profiled Ball identifying him as the school's first black scholarship athlete on November 18, 1970, beating the professional *Eagle* to the preverbal punch. The Oxford newspaper would publish the same article on the December 3, 1970. The article appeared in both papers with a photo of the college freshmen with head coach Robert "Cob" Jarvis and freshman coach Kenny Robbins and was the *Eagle*'s only account that referenced Ball's race. The *Daily Mississippian* would only reference Ball's ethnicity on one other occasion during his freshman year. A letter to the editor printed on December 13, 1970, by "a pleased Rebel," claimed that the standing ovation that accompanied Ball during his thirty-point, sixteen-rebound effort in a 108–96 victory over first-year Auburn Tigers was evidence of the university's "acceptance of a black man." Ball was later featured in a photo that accompanied a profile of the budding star by student reporter Dudley Marble.[41] Interestingly enough, Marble never identified Ball's race in his account.

Outside of Oxford, only the *Meridian Star* identified Ball's race and noted his historic presence on the "Baby Rebs" roster. In Angus Lind's December 8, 1970, article on Ole Miss's season-opening win over Texas, Lind identified Ball in the next to last paragraph as "the first Negro to wear the Ole Miss colors on the hardwood." A photo of Ball wearing number 44 and shooting a jump shot over a defender was prominently displayed on the right-hand side of the page. Much like the *Oxford Eagle*, Lind wasted little time identifying Ball's history-making presence on the Ole Miss roster, giving his audience a fair perception of the events in discussion. His identification of Ball's race also allowed the *Meridian Star* to move forward with its coverage of Ole Miss basketball without having to constantly refer to Ball as black. Lind later wrote a feature on the Ole Miss Rebel basketball teams for the December 13, 1970, Sunday edition of the *Meridian Star* and referred to the future combination of Ole Miss freshman stars Ball and Fred Cox with the varsity's Johnny Neumann as "NBC"—Neumann, Ball, and Cox. In Lind's fourth paragraph, the sports writer again identified Ball's race, writing that the forward was "the first Negro ever to play for the Rebels" a little more than halfway through the full-page feature. A photo of Ball was featured in the *Meridian Star* as the Indianola native was pictured shooting a free throw. Lind's "NBC" triad would never come to fruition. While Ball and Cox would spend the next three seasons on the varsity, Neumann, the nation's leading scorer in 1970–1971, would leave Ole Miss to pursue a career in professional basketball. While the newspaper continued to publish articles that referenced the pioneering Ball and his freshman teammates, his race was not mentioned during the remainder of that season.

Other news outlets did not see the presence of Ball as being significant. In his first season with the Rebels, Ball was never referenced as being black in the *Jackson Daily News* or the *Clarion-Ledger*. More often than not, Ball, who was referenced by name in twenty-two articles in the two newspapers during his freshman season, was described as a "leaper," a description missing from his white teammates. Other publications, such as the *Hattiesburg American*, the *Starkville Daily News*, *Vicksburg Evening Post Daily Herald* in Biloxi or the *Delta Democrat-Times* either failed to reference Ball's race or never published any content pertaining to the freshman Rebels squad.

The 1971–1972 season for the Ole Miss Rebels was one that began with optimism because of the play of Ball and Cox during their freshman campaign.[42] The early and unexpected migration of the nation's leading scorer, Neumann, from the Rebels squad dampened the spirits of some of the Rebel faithful, while others, as pointed out by sports editor Lee Baker of the *Jackson Daily News*, breathed a sigh of relief at the loss of the erratic, free-shooting Neumann.[43] While the press, other than the *Oxford Eagle* and the *Meridian Star*, had ignored Ball's skin color, the coverage of the 1971–1972 season would be marred with inconsistent references to Ball's race and questionable editorial decisions in terms of what constituted news.

"Cool-Aid" finished his season by averaging 16.8 points and 10.3 rebounds per game, both of which led the Rebels and earned the sophomore a place on the AP's ALL-SEC Sophomore Team and the All-SEC second team. Ole Miss finished the 1971–1972 campaign with a record of 13–12, 8–10 in conference. It was the first winning season for Jarvis. Like his freshman season, the local *Oxford Eagle* would have a profound local interest in the exploits of Ball. However, unlike his rookie campaign, the Oxford-based newspaper did not identify Ball as being black or as Ole Miss's first black varsity athlete. The *Oxford Eagle* published three photos of Ball, two of which featured game action and a third, published on February 16, 1972, showed the Rebels' forward buying a light bulb from local members of the Boy Scouts who were in the midst of a fundraising campaign. Because of the *Oxford Eagle*'s identification of Ball's history-making presence on the "Baby Rebs" during the 1970–1971 season, it could have been logically argued that there was no need for the newspaper to continue to identify Ball as black, as it could have been interpreted as an insensitive remark towards the college sophomore. Furthermore, as the newspaper for a distinctly local community, Ball's place on the Ole Miss roster was likely well known within Oxford's city limits. Regardless, it was difficult to fathom that the *Oxford Eagle* never once alluded to Ball's status as the first African-American to play for the varsity Rebels.

While the Hederman-owned newspapers in Jackson ignored Ball's presence on the 1970–1971 freshman Rebels squad, the *Jackson Daily News* and sports editor Lee Baker wasted little time identifying Ole Miss's first black athlete, beginning a trend of inconsistent and, at times, illogical reporting on Ball's race. After publishing two accounts featuring Ole Miss's first black varsity athlete, one of which called Ball a "jumping jack," Baker finally acknowledged the forward's place in Mississippi history. In the December 1, 1971, edition of the *Jackson Daily News*, Baker, while previewing the opening games for a number of the colleges in the Magnolia State, wrote of Ole Miss's trip to Austin to play the University of Texas. Baker, in an attempt to temper any discontent within the Ole Miss faithful due to the professional exodus of Neumann, hailed the arrival of Ball to the varsity squad, writing, "Now they have a basketball player in his place, Coolidge Ball, native Mississippian (Indianola) and the first black grant-in-aid recipient at the University." Baker's identification of Ball was surprising considering that, like his fellow Mississippi sports writers, he usually buried or ignored issues involving race with the 1963 MSU-NCAA campaign serving as the lone exception. While overlooking both Ball and Jordan's addition to the Mississippi sports scene was a case of journalistic neglect, Baker's nod to history was a sign of social progress for the long-time *Jackson Daily News* sports editor and was in line with his work during the 1963 Mississippi State basketball season. Furthermore, Baker's use of the phrase "black" rather than the derogatory "negro" was another sign that the longtime Jackson sports editor had become much more open and tolerant when it came to issues of race.

While issues pertaining to race had often brought out the conservative side of Baker, the sports editor appeared to take a liking to Ole Miss's first black athlete. Despite the paper's inconsistent and, at times, puzzling references to Ball's race, Baker would often write about the star forward in his "Baker's Dozen" columns. Although he never referenced his historical status on the Ole Miss roster, Baker often referred to Ball as "Mr. Cool" and pinned his hopes for a Rebels victory on the All-SEC performer.[44]

After Baker's identification of the sophomore star's race, the *Jackson Daily News* began a trend of illogical references to Ball's ethnicity. In total, the *Jackson Daily News* published fifty-five articles on the Rebels during the 1971–1972 basketball season, and only two identified Ball's race or place in Ole Miss history. In a January 5, 1972, account previewing the Rebels' January 8 match-up against perennial SEC power the University of Kentucky, the paper referred to the star forward as "a 6–5 jumping jack, [the] first Negro athlete in Rebel livery." The same article appeared the following day in the *Clarion-Ledger* and was that publication's first reference to Ball's skin color. A profile on Ball would later make its way around the papers of the Magnolia State on January 28th. Published without a byline or wire affiliation in the *Jackson Daily News* and the *Clarion-Ledger*, the article detailed Ball's statistical contributions to the Rebels. However, the profile fell short of a complete account. Ball was never identified in the article as being the school's first black athlete and, in fact, the only reference to the forward's race was in the lead. The article began with a ball bouncing off the rim before "a long black arm snapped it from the air and whipped it downcourt." Ball was also featured in seven photos in the *Jackson Daily News* during his sophomore campaign.[45]

More than a year after Ball's December 1970 debut on the freshman team, the *Clarion-Ledger* finally identified the forward's ethnicity in the aforementioned article from the *Jackson Daily News* on January 6, 1972, article previewing the Rebels' matchup with the University of Kentucky. While the yearlong omission of Ball's ethnic background was negligent on behalf of the *Clarion-Ledger*, the future use of the forward's skin color was curious at best. Larry Guest, the *Clarion-Ledger*'s sports editor, referenced Ball's ethnic status in the January 8, 1972, edition of his column, "In the Spotlight." Guest wrote that the Rebels had a bright future with sophomore standouts Ball, Cox, and guard Tom Jordan. In describing the trio, Guest identified each athlete by a characteristic of his on-court play, referring to Jordan as a "sharp shooting guard" and Cox as a "towering center." Ball's description, however, was both complimentary to his playing style yet potentially offensive as Guest called him a "liquid-smooth black forward." Guest's comments demonstrated the degree of inconsistency that existed in the coverage of race relations in the state. The paper went roughly thirteen months without identifying Ball's historic presence on the Rebel roster, yet in three days, the paper twice identified him as a "Negro" and "black." The inclusion of Ball's skin color also looked more damning considering that his teammates were not identified as white, thus creating an inequality in Guest's views of the three athletes. Ball's race was again referenced in a descriptive manner in Dabbs's January 27, 1972, account of the Rebels' 92–65 victory over the Commodores of Vanderbilt. Dabbs described Ball, who led the team to victory with a game-high thirty points and eleven rebounds, as a "jumping jack" and a "sophomore sensation." Dabbs then called the budding star "the Black bomber," when discussing his statistical output. Dabbs's use of race in her description of Ball could have been interpreted as insensitive, considering the paper had just revealed Ball's race to its audience early in the month. Furthermore, the use of his race was unnecessary and irrelevant in terms of his ability to play the game. Logically speaking, it was unlikely Dabbs would have described any of Ball's white teammates as "white bombers." In terms of photographs, the *Clarion-Ledger* published its first image of the pioneering basketball star in the January 15, 1972, edition adjacent to an article previewing the Rebels' games against Mississippi State. Under the heading "Rebel Leaper," Ball was described in the cutline by his statistical output, but his status as Ole Miss's first black athlete was not referenced. By comparison, the *Oxford Eagle* published their first photo of Ball on December 3, 1970, roughly thirteen months before the *Clarion-Ledger*.

At the *Meridian Star*, the Rebels were prominently featured during the 1971-72 season under the guise of sports editor Robert "Steamboat" Fulton, formally of the *Clarion-Ledger*. However, Ball's status as Ole Miss's first black athlete was not referenced until March 4, 1972. Justification for such an omission could have come from Lind's December 8, 1970, article and December 13, 1970, feature on the Rebels, both of which identified Ball as black and published a photo of the freshman with each article. However, the history-making Ball would catch the eye of "Steamboat," as Fulton took it upon himself to pen the only opinion-based article in the newspapers consulted in this chapter to deal with Ball and the integration of basketball at any of the three universities. In the March 4, 1972, edition of the *Meridian Star*, Fulton wrote that he had three observations about the sophomore superstar: "(1) He is an exceptionally gifted athlete; (2) He is black and, in fact, the first of his race to play basketball at Ole Miss, and; (3) He came to the Rebel campus not to crash barriers but to play basketball in his home state and, hopefully, contribute to the resurgence of the Ole Miss cage program." After detailing the Mississippi native's winding trek to Oxford, including his brief summer stint with the University of New Mexico, Fulton explained that Ball "had no apprehension about becoming the Rebs' first black signee" and that he had not second-guessed his decision, citing the welcoming reception he received from the Ole Miss faithful. "According to the blossoming young sophomore, there have been no regrets," Fulton wrote. "Fellow students, teammates and coaches alike have shown respect for Coolidge Ball as the fine athlete that he is and as a Rebel. There have been no problems." Fulton closed his column by writing that Ball was "proud to be a Rebel and he likes the future ahead." Ball also appeared in five photos during the 1971–1972 season.[46] Fulton's work coincided with his past advocacy for Mississippi State's venture into the integrated NCAA tournament.

The *Hattiesburg American*'s Rick Cleveland also noted the historic signifi- cance of Ball's presence on the Ole Miss roster, writing that the sophomore was "the first scholarship Negro to play at Ole Miss" in his account of Ole Miss's Feb- ruary 16, 1971, win over the Southerners by a 107–92 tally. *Hattiesburg American* sports editor Mickey Edwards followed suit, writing in his column "They Say" that Ball was "the school's first black athlete . . . and a very good one at that."[47] It was an interesting change for the Hederman-owned *Hattiesburg American*, which failed to acknowledge Jordan's race in his first two seasons at USM from 1968 through 1970. In total, none of the written content on the Rebels or Ball from the *Starkville Daily News,* the *Daily Herald,* and the *Vicksburg Evening Post* addressed the star forward's ethnicity.

During his three years on the University of Mississippi varsity, Ball played in seventy-four games, scored 1,072 points, averaged 14.1 points per game, and led the Rebels to three straight winning seasons. For his career, he grabbed 754 rebounds, eighth all-time at Ole Miss. His career rebounding average of 9.9 per game is the second highest in school history. He would be on the Associated Press All-SEC second team in 1972 and 1973, United Press International's All- SEC team in 1972, 1973, and 1974, and the coaches' All-SEC squad in 1972 and 1973. He was voted the team's most valuable player in his senior year by his teammates—all of whom were white. Ball was inducted into the Ole Miss Ath- letics' Hall of Fame in 1991, the Mississippi Sports Hall of Fame in 2008, and was named to the school's All-Century Team in 2009.[48]

The coverage of Ball's trailblazing efforts at Ole Miss, at times, was under- whelming. Nevertheless, the absence and inconsistent use of racial references, especially by the *Jackson Daily News* and the *Clarion-Ledger*, served as a sign that the racial turmoil that once haunted the Magnolia State was slowly being exorcised from sports sections across Mississippi. While many publications exercised a degree of journalistic neglect by never acknowledging Ball's status as a black athlete, the lack of continuous "black" or "negro" references indicated that many in the sporting press began to view color as secondary, a progressive thought to say the least. While reporters seemingly neglected the historic pres- ence of Jordan and Ball, the state of Mississippi was undergoing an ideological and cultural change in the late 1960s and early 1970s. Race, in anything other than a negative connotation, was alien to the press. The silence that was present was more out of an acceptance, begrudgingly or otherwise, to the athletic addition of blacks than it was in protest. This great unknown in the journalistic world explains the illogical and inconsistent references to race that littered the work on Jordan and Ball and would continue to do so with Mississippi State's additions of Larry Fry and Jerry Jenkins.

In 1971, Mississippi State University was the lone member of the SEC that had yet to field an integrated basketball team, a surprise considering it was the 1963 Bulldogs who essentially ended the era of segregated sports in the Magnolia State. The school integrated its student body with the admission of Holmes in 1965 and other racial inroads were made before blacks were welcomed to the university's hardwood.[49] While Jordan was the first black athlete at USM, Ole Miss, or MSU, there was another potential pioneer who attempted to integrate Mississippi State sports a year prior to Jordan's addition to the Southern Miss roster. Freshman George Pruitt, a native of Starkville and graduate of Harrison High School, joined the Bulldogs' football team in the spring of 1967. So convinced that Pruitt would secure a place on MSU's football team, the *Reflector* proclaimed Pruitt "the first Negro athlete in the history of Mississippi State University."[50] However, after missing three straight practices during the spring, head coach Charles Shira dismissed Pruitt from the team. Pruitt later told the *Reflector* that the dismissal was a misunderstanding and his absences were excused as he was being treated by his family physician for an injured right calf rather than MSU's team doctor. Pruitt added that he intended on returning to the team in August 1967, but he never made another appearance on the gridiron for the Bulldogs.[51]

While Pruitt may have failed in his attempts to join the Bulldogs, the athletic integration of MSU still occurred on the football field. Frank Dowsing Jr., who joined the Bulldogs in December 1968, became the first black athlete to receive a scholarship at any of the three schools in discussion, signing a football pact on December 15, 1968, a mere five days after Jordan made his debut for the Southerners. Surprisingly, the *Starkville Daily News* published an article on all of State's signings that college football-recruiting season and failed to identify Dowsing as being black.[52] In the same edition of Sherrill Nash's newspaper, a brief article announced the signing of tackle Robert Bell, "the second Negro athlete to sign with State."[53] Newspapers outside of MSU's Starkville home base published articles from the Associated Press or United Press International. The AP account, which appeared in the *Jackson Daily News* and the *Vicksburg Evening Post*, lumped Dowsing's signing with that of the acceptance of scholarships for fellow black athletes Willie Jackson of the University of Florida, Larry Howell of Georgia Tech, and James Owens of Auburn University.[54] The *Meridian Star* published UPI's article on Dowsing's signing, which focused on all of the college football scholarships at Mississippi State and Ole Miss. The account, which featured the headline, "State Shatters Tradition by Signing Tupelo Negro," began by calling Dowsing's signing "a tradition shattering move" and identified Dowsing as the first black to receive an athletic scholarship in Mississippi, a point of interest missing from the article in the *Jackson Daily News*.[55] Dowsing, a native of Tupelo, was a three-year starter at defensive back for the Bulldogs and was later inducted into the SEC Hall of Fame.

The recruitment of black athletes at Mississippi State garnered student-based support well before the signing of Dowsing. As early as September 1968, fans were calling for the addition of black athletes to the Starkville-based Bulldogs in the pages of the *Reflector*. In the aftermath of State's football loss to Louisiana Tech in 1968, Gary Weatherly penned a letter to the editor pointing out that the school should recruit black athletes, as "Negroes enjoy the facilities of Mississippi State, however, they are not presently included in the scope of athletics. . . . Why then should our school not concert an honest effort toward recruiting Negro athletes?"[56] In another sign of the changing mindset of Mississippians, Ester M. Thornton asked, in line with "the desire for making satisfactory social adjustment," that the student-based paper stop using the word "Negro" and went with either "Afro-American" or "Black," a request that, at least on the surface, was honored.[57]

In terms of the hardwood, the first black athletes to grace the courts at Mississippi State were Larry Fry and Jerry Jenkins. Fry, a guard from Lexington, Tennessee, led the state in scoring during his senior year in high school, while Jenkins, a guard and forward from Gulfport, had already become a star of sorts in the Magnolia State, having led Gulfport High School to two state tournaments and one state championship.[58] Like their trailblazing colleagues Jordan and Ball, Jenkins's and Fry's addition to the Bulldogs roster garnered little attention from Mississippi press.

MSU's hometown news source, the *Starkville Daily News*, did not seem to find the historic presence of Jenkins and Fry newsworthy. During the high-scoring duo's freshman season, the ethnic status of Jenkins and Fry was never referenced in the Starkville newspaper. While the freshman games on a college campus were not necessarily the highest priority in newsrooms across the state, the *Starkville Daily News* published its fair share of material on the 1971–1972 "Bullpup" squad, which finished the regular season an impressive 14–5 and was tagged by freshman head coach Jack Berkshire as "the best team I have had in my seven years of coaching the Bullpups."[59] The *Starkville Daily News* published sixteen articles on the "Bullpups" during the course of the 1971–1972 basketball campaign, none of which identified Jenkins and Fry as being black. Nash's December 2, 1971, account of MSU's season-opening victory over South Alabama included a brief two paragraph wrap-up of the freshman Bulldogs' 71–66 victory over the first-year team from the University of South Alabama. The segregationist Nash cited Jenkins's twenty-six points and twenty-three rebounds as being a deciding factor in the game, an ideal place to introduce the two black ballplayers to the Starkville audience. However, the Starkville editor failed to do so, undermining the social significance of Jenkins's and Fry's presence on the MSU freshman roster. Of the sixteen articles, Jenkins's name was referenced in all of them and Fry's name appeared in nine as Jenkins averaged 20.9 points per game to lead the freshman MSU squad, while Fry finished third on the team with 16.8 points per game. While some of the articles appeared without bylines, Nash, *Starkville Daily News* sports writer Don Foster, and correspondent Larry Templeton all penned accounts on the first-year team meaning, at any time, one of them could have noted Jenkins's and Fry's history-making status as the school's first black basketball players. The only way the audience would have known Jenkins and Fry were black through the pages of the *Starkville Daily News* was in the March 8, 1972, edition of the paper. The final article to appear in the newspaper during the 1971–1972 MSU freshman season featured a team picture with Jenkins and Fry prominently displayed on the front row.[60]

The *Reflector*, Mississippi State's student newspaper, employed a similar approach. In the anticipation for the start of basketball practice, Nook Nicholson of the *Reflector* detailed the new additions to both the freshman and varsity teams, highlighted by the recruitment of Fry and Jenkins. While Nicholson discussed the aforementioned high school credentials of the freshmen guard and forward, he failed to mention that both men were the first blacks to suit up for the Bulldogs in the school's history.[61] Later, going by Jim Nicholson, the *Reflector* sports writer covered the 1971–1972 season opener for the Bulldogs but only referenced Jenkins's statistical output against South Alabama University.[62] In total, Jenkins, Fry, and their "Bullpup" teammates were featured in the *Reflector* seven times during their freshman season, and the duo's race or historical status in Starkville was never mentioned.

In Jackson, both the *Jackson Daily News* and the *Clarion-Ledger* took note of the duo, but like their work on Ball, the notion of race was inconsistently referenced. In the first article in the *Jackson Daily News* to detail the hardwood exploits of Jenkins and Fry, the unknown author called the Gulfport native "one of the first two blacks to play basketball at MSU." Fellow pioneer Fry added twelve points in the 76–53 win over the freshmen of South Alabama, but, despite appearing a mere two paragraphs after Jenkins, he was not identified as the other black athlete on the MSU squad.[63] While the duo was referenced in eleven articles in the *Jackson Daily News* during the season, the ethnicity of Fry was never mentioned. The same could be said for the ten articles referencing Jenkins and Fry in the *Clarion-Ledger*, which failed to disclose the race of either athlete.

The *Meridian Star* and Fulton published six articles on the "Bullpups," none of which identified either member of the duo as being black. In the January 10, 1972, edition of the *Star*, Fulton penned a column dealing with the controversial NCAA rule preventing freshmen from playing with varsity teams. MSU basketball coach Kermit Davis, who replaced Joe Dan Gold in 1970, told "Steamboat" that Jenkins could contribute to his 1971–1972 varsity squad. Despite the complimentary nod, Jenkins's status as one of the team's first black athletes was not referenced.

The *Daily Herald* in Biloxi, which still featured the talents of sports editor Dick Lightsey and was in close proximity of Jenkins's hometown of Gulfport, published five articles dealing with the freshman Bulldogs, however, none of them referenced Jenkins and Fry as black. It was possible, due to the *Daily Herald*'s proximity to Gulfport, that the Biloxi-based newspaper simply felt that their audience was well aware of Jenkins and his race. Other newspapers, such as the *Vicksburg Evening Post* and the *Hattiesburg American*, both failed to publish anything on the 1971–1972 "Bullpups" or its two new black stars.[64]

By the time the 1972–1973 season started, the Magnolia State had made a complete transformation from the Closed Society that banned the play of integrated teams in 1955. Whereas race was once a pertinent issue that was often egregiously ignored by the press or vigorously attacked, the presence of blacks on the state's college athletic teams barely garnered a mentioned, much less was of primary focus by any sports reporters in the Magnolia State. With both Southern Miss and Ole Miss years into their integration on the hardwood, Mississippi State welcomed Jenkins and Fry to the varsity ranks, the first blacks to occupy such positions in the school's history. Their presence on the Bulldogs roster did little to change the bottom line for Davis, as his team went 11–15 with a 4–14 conference record during the 1972–1973 season. From a journalistic perspective, a degree of neglect could be inferred from the lack of any acknowledgement of the duo's place in school history. However, by 1972, MSU was the last of the Closed Society's educational stalwarts to integrate its basketball team and the last in the SEC, making it a somewhat expected and, perhaps, dated occurrence. For the first time in the history of the Magnolia State and integrated athletics, the press simply found little significance in the presence of blacks on one of their once sacred, all-white basketball courts.

One of the primary examples of this change was Nash's *Starkville Daily News*. Not only would the duo become starters, both Jenkins and Fry excelled from a statistical standpoint for the Bulldogs. Jenkins finished his sophomore campaign averaging 17.6 points per game and 7.1 rebounds, while Fry finished his first varsity season with a 12.5 point per game average and a team-leading 7.7 rebounds per contest.[65] Yet, in the twenty-three articles published in the *Starkville Daily*

News during the course of the season, neither sophomore was ever referenced or identified as being black. The Starkville newspaper also published photos of either Fry or Jenkins on five occasions during the 1972–1973 season, serving as the publication's only nod to the race of the Bulldog standouts.[66]

The other notable Starkville-based news source, the *Reflector*, also identified both Jenkins and Fry as possible contributors to the Bulldogs' varsity, starting with the October 17, 1972, edition of the student-based newspaper. In total, the prolific pair was mentioned in twenty-three articles in the student newspaper during the 1972–1973 campaign, none of which recognized their race. Jenkins and Fry also appeared in three photos in the *Reflector* during the season and, like the *Starkville Daily News*, was the only evidence of the pair's ethnicity. [67]

While both news outlets in Starkville failed to reference the race of MSU's groundbreaking duo, the *Clarion-Ledger* took the initiative to note the historic presence of both Jenkins and Fry early in their first varsity campaign. After MSU's 80–69 win over the University of Texas Longhorns, sports writer Ponto Downing called the duo, "Mississippi State's first ever black starters," while noting the pair's contributions to the victory.[68] Downing's nod to the significance of the two varsity rookies was significant for the *Clarion-Ledger*, considering that, in the limited coverage of the 1971–1972 MSU freshman team, neither Jenkins nor Fry were acknowledged as being black. Downing, who was the *Clarion-Ledger*'s assistant sports editor, even referenced the two in his column, "Wednesday's Special" in the January 17, 1973, edition of the *Clarion-Ledger*, but his commentary remained of an athletic hue, focusing on the poor conference start of the Bulldogs. Once Downing identified the race of Jenkins and Fry, the *Clarion-Ledger* kept to the silo-like confines of sports and, in the twenty-eight articles that referenced the two sophomores, only the December 5, 1972, article on the Texas game mentioned that they were black. The paper's conservative approach to the issue was also evident in the column-based work of longtime *Clarion-Ledger* sports writer Carl Walters, who wrote about the MSU squad on January 31 and February 2, 1973. In both editions of his column "Shavin's," Walters identified Jenkins as the team's statistical leader; however, he did not mention his race.[69]

Like the *Clarion-Ledger*, the *Jackson Daily News* noted the significance of the sophomore standouts early in the Bulldogs' 1972–1973 campaign and, in fact, published Downing's December 5, 1972, work on MSU's game against the Longhorns in the *Jackson Daily News* the same day without a byline. As in Downing's original article, both Jenkins and Fry were referenced as State's "first black starters." While the *Jackson Daily News* did identify Jenkins as the school's first black basketball player during his freshman season, Downing's reference to the historic duo helped give the *Jackson Daily News* a degree of balance between identifying the news-based references of their presence and from potentially exploiting race, an unfamiliar degree of care to say the least from the traditionally segregationist newspaper. In the case of the *Jackson Daily News*, it could be argued that the better place to reference the race of Jenkins and Fry would have been in the December 1, 1972, issue when an anonymous author identified the two as new starters for Davis. The *Jackson Daily News* kept any printed material on Jenkins and Fry to the confines of sports as the race of the pair was never referenced in any article for the duration of the 1972–1973 season. Pictures of the two appeared in the January 11, 1973, edition of the paper, accompanying an article on the Bulldogs' January 13 game against the University of Mississippi. The cutline, which only referenced the then-statistical averages of the budding SEC stars, began with the phrase "sophomore STANDOUTS." Fry would later appear in a photo depicting action from the Bulldogs' victory over the University of Georgia 90–84 in the January 30 edition of the *Jackson Daily News*. In the photo, Fry was battling UGA's Tom Bassett and Steve Waxman for a rebound.

Much like his fellow *Jackson Daily News* sports writers, longtime sports editor Lee Baker also stayed away from the issue of race when writing of the MSU team, as evidenced by his January 15, 1973, edition of "Baker's Dozen." In the aftermath of MSU's January 13 loss to the Ole Miss Rebels 74–61, a game in which Jenkins led MSU with twenty-two points and Fry added fifteen, Baker wrote that the young Bulldogs played well but failed to recognize any members of the team by name.

Perhaps the one journalistic decision that could have been argued in the pages of the *Jackson Daily News* appeared in the March 7, 1973, edition of the paper. A feature on MSU freshman standout Rich Knarr appeared in the paper's sports section and, while Knarr's season of eighteen points per game as a first-year Bulldog was noteworthy, it could have been debated that Jenkins's or Fry's first varsity season was an equally deserving story as the tale of Knarr. Jenkins, who finished the season second to Knarr in scoring with 17.6 points per game, was by no means statistically inferior to the freshman, and his status as one of MSU's first black basketball players would have made his story more relevant on both a social and athletic front.

Other newspapers did little to identify the racial status of Jenkins and Fry. The sports section of the *Meridian Star*, which was under the editorial guidance of Orley Hood, published a number of articles on the MSU contingent during the 1972–1973 season but never referenced their race. The *Meridian Star* featured photos of either Jenkins or Fry on two occasions during their first varsity campaign.[70] The *Vicksburg Evening Post* also failed to reference the history-making presence of Jenkins and Fry during the season, publishing primarily material from the Associated Press. The only editorial reference made to the MSU season by Vicksburg sports editor Billy Ray, who lamented the team's disastrous 11–15 season, failed to reference any of the players by name.[71] The

Evening Post published a photo from the AP of Fry in the January 9, 1973, edition of the paper, but it was the only item in the Vicksburg-based newspaper during Jenkins's and Fry's first two seasons in Starkville to acknowledge that a member of the Bulldogs' roster was black. The *Daily Herald* in Biloxi took a similar approach to the 1972–1973 MSU season, publishing only wire-based material and never referencing the ethnicity of Jenkins and Fry. In one of his daily columns, sports editor Dick Lightsey wrote that the arrival of Jenkins was a welcomed addition to the Bulldogs' lineup, but his race was not mentioned.[72] The same could be said for the *Hattiesburg American*, which published seventeen articles during the season and never cited the duo's skin color. Like the aforementioned publications, the *American* featured three photos depicting the pair, specifically Jenkins, during the season and served as the paper's only acknowledgements of the Gulfport native's race.[73]

Both Fry and Jenkins excelled on the hardwood in Starkville, littering their names throughout the school's basketball record book. In their sophomore seasons on the Bulldogs, despite winning only four conference games, Jenkins finished second on the team with 17.6 points and tallied 6.8 rebounds per contest, while Fry finished with 12.5 points and first in rebounds with 7.7 per contest. In their junior season, the groundbreaking duo finished first and third on the Bulldogs in scoring, with Jenkins averaging 18.1 and Fry at 13.5 points per game. Both chipped in 6.8 and 7.7 rebounds, respectively. Jenkins, the team's captain in his senior campaign of 1974–1975, led the team in scoring at 22.1 points per game, the eighth highest single season average in school history, and averaged 6.9 rebounds per game. Fry was right behind Jenkins at 15.5 points and 8.8 rebounds per game.[74] Jenkins scored 1,503 points in his MSU career, eighth all-time at the school, and his average of 19.3 points per game is fourth all-time. Fry scored 1,079 points during his MSU career with a 13.8 point per game average.

From 1968 through 1973, the previously segregated basketball teams at Southern Miss, Ole Miss, and Mississippi State opened up their ranks to African-Americans, ushering in a new sense of equality in Magnolia State athletics. The 1965 integration of the Southeastern Conference and the impending presence of black opponents, not surprisingly, was ignored by Mississippi's newspapers, a typical journalistic tactic approved by the purveyors of the Closed Society. While Mississippi's journalistic community met the early efforts of Wilbert Jordan Jr. at USM with a degree of neglect, the press was in the middle of an ideological change that justified the lack of coverage found years later in the additions of Larry Fry and Jerry Jenkins to the Mississippi State roster. Jordan was, more or less, the James Meredith of Mississippi sports, serving as the first athlete of color to grace any of the state's previously segregated college rosters. His 1968 addition to the Hattiesburg-based Southerners should have been treated with a greater sense of journalistic importance, especially from the local *Hattiesburg*

American and the campus-based *Student Printz.* The fact that these publications
went two years without mentioning that the Waynesboro native was a member
of the USM squad and the state's first black athlete at a segregated institution
was an egregious journalistic violation that was rife with the racist tactics once
employed by the Closed Society's media-based protectors. However, as civil
rights breeched the ideological walls of the state, the press was in the middle of
an evolutionary change. While integration on any level, much less in the valued
athletic ranks of Ole Miss and Mississippi State, was once met with a degree
of outrage, the press began to accept the presence of blacks in various social
venues, including sports. By the time Coolidge Ball, Jenkins, and Fry made their
way to Oxford and Starkville in the early 1970s, social equality had dissolved the
once impenetrable ignorance demonstrated by Mississippi's journalists during
the adoption of the unwritten law. When Ball made his first appearance with
the Ole Miss freshmen in 1970, the reporters in the Magnolia State were in a
transitional stage where the Fourth Estate was, more or less, learning how to
balance news value with issues involving race. While the press was inconsistent
in referencing the ethnic status of these athletes, most of the newspapers consulted in this chapter, at one time or another, did identify their history-making
presence, signifying the social significance of these athletic additions. By the
time Jenkins and Fry joined the Bulldogs, not only did the press find ethnic status less relevant, but the same derogatory and racist terminology that was once
a hallmark in Mississippi's journalistic ranks had disappeared. While on the surface, the failure to identify the race of these athletes may have been viewed as
an inexcusable oversight, by 1973, it was a sign of social progress. As noted in his
volume, silence within the press, more or less, equated to a level of acceptance.
In the past events involving Mississippi State and the NCAA tournament, that
silence was present in the observance and enforcement of the unwritten law.
Years later, that silence signified that the black athlete and their place in Mississippi, on some level, had been accepted. Rather than fixating on the skin color
of Ball, Jenkins, and Fry, the press treated the trio as mere basketball players, a
refreshing and progressive change in Mississippi's journalistic community.

Conclusion

The civil rights era served as one of the more turbulent and tumultuous times in our country's history, and, without a doubt, a microcosm of that chaos could be found in the Magnolia State. As the South's most strident and forthright defender of states' rights and segregation, the people of the Closed Society dominated life in Mississippi from a political and social standpoint and, until the 1954 *Brown vs. Board of Education* decision, were rarely challenged on their ideology. It was a time of violence and social turmoil. With that said, it would be a gross understatement to give Mississippi State's basketball team credit for the eventual deconstruction of the Closed Society. The monolithic nature of Mississippi's dominant white caste system made it almost impossible for a singular entity or event to bring about its demise. However, it is fair to state that MSU's hardwood success played a part in the slow but evolutionary change that took place in the state during the civil rights movement. The ebbs and flows of MSU's various challenges to the unwritten law and the work of the press was a clear demonstration of the advancing mindset in the Magnolia State and the increasing emphasis placed on the success of the state's college sports teams. Within the cultural context of Mississippi, people looked towards their sports as a means of validation and a reflection of their individual values and beliefs and, within the Closed Society, segregation was such a value. The press's initial reaction to any through of integrated competition was one of outright rejection. With the Closed Society on high alert, the 1955 Junior Rose Bowl appearance of Jones County Junior College and that school's venture into integrated athletics was a natural target of ridicule and scorn. For the most part, the press, both news and sports-based, either united in their opposition of any nod to racial equality or remained silent and ignored the issue, a common and frequently utilized technique when it came to items of race from Mississippi's press. In what would become a seemingly common motive for action in Mississippi, the fear that integration was at its proverbial doorstep led the political elite in the Magnolia State to attempt to make it illegal for their segregated college and university teams to participate in integrated competition. When such efforts were met with a degree of failure, as was often the case in the Closed Society, an undocumented and private meeting between politicians and university and college officials led to the birth of the unwritten law, an agreement that would keep segregation alive and well in athletic avenues, and any potential violators would be subjected to the threat of financial sanctions by the state and would become the subject of public degradation and ridicule in the press. Sports in Mississippi did not exist with a degree of autonomy from the other aspects of life in the Magnolia State. While the harbingers of segregation worked at keeping all aspects of life in Mississippi white-dominated, their efforts were just as prevalent in college sports, particularly basketball.

The united journalistic front that was formed in opposition of Jones County Junior College stayed in place, for the most part, during individual instances involving Mississippi State and the University of Mississippi in 1956. Rarely, if ever, did members of the press support any notion of integrated competition as editors such as Frederick Sullens and Jimmy Ward of the *Jackson Daily News* and Hodding Carter of the *Delta Democrat-Times*, whose views on issues of race in Mississippi were, more or less, at opposite ends of the ideological spectrum, united in their criticisms of the State College Board and college and university officials for allowing such egregious violations of the unwritten law to occur. While exceptions did exist in Mississippi, for the most part, journalists and editors who policed the news desk enforced and maintained the standards of segregation, while sports reporters and editors stayed on the ideological sidelines. Like everything else in Mississippi during the civil rights era, the Closed Society ruled all aspects of life with an iron fist that was rarely opposed by anyone, especially those in the sporting world.

In 1959, things began to change as the 1958–1959 basketball Maroons of Mississippi State University set forth a metamorphosis of sorts in the sporting press that would culminate in 1963. The first Southeastern Conference basketball championship for the Starkville-based team of head coach James "Babe" McCarthy and star Bailey Howell yielded an invitation to the integrated NCAA national championship tournament. The press in the Magnolia State, regardless of beats, universally lived up to past precedent, either choosing to ignore the chances of integrated competition for the MSU contingent or would openly campaign against McCarthy's team because of the possible violation of the unwritten law and the fear that such a venture would welcome integration into Mississippi. The mere thought that an all-white team of Mississippi's finest sons would consider undertaking such a social taboo was both insulting and threatening to the Closed Society.

During the implementation of the unwritten law through Mississippi State's first SEC championship and subsequent invitation to the NCAA national championship tournament, the Closed Society and the various mechanisms of white discourse were at optimum power, as demonstrated in the press during the athletic-based events examined in this book in 1955, 1956, 1957, and 1959. Outside athletic avenues, Mississippi's white way of life was rarely, if ever, challenged and when such a challenge occurred, the Closed Society did everything in its power to fight for its racial dominance so much so that the potential integration of Mississippi Southern College by Hattiesburg native Clyde Kennard in 1958 and 1959 and by Clennon King Jr. in 1958 at the Ole Miss ended in the legal imprisonment of both, verifying the strength of the state's cultural boundaries. While these two pioneers, both outsiders to the Closed Society, met their demise of sorts, the challenges posed by Jones County Junior College, Mississippi State, and the Ole Miss were at the hands of their own white athletes, serving as an internal revolt from the state's closed ranks. While the consequences of their various challenges to segregation and the unwritten law were minimal in comparison to that of Kennard and King, these schools and their athletes questioned the status quo through their performance and, within the confines of Mississippi's press, a select few helped champion their cause and that of racial athletic equality in the Magnolia State.

For some members of the press, MSU's basketball success became a point of pride. One journalist in particular paved the way for a possible ideological change in the sports press. The fiery and charismatic Jimmie McDowell of the *Jackson State Times* advocated Mississippi State's appearance in the integrated postseason during the 1959 season. Motive and social beliefs aside, such a suggestion was not only uncommon in the Closed Society, but it was intolerable. It was that bravery and bravado that made "Mississippi Red" the catalyst for future debates involving the merits of integrated competition and the validity of the unwritten law and opened the door for peers such as Billy Ray of the *Vicksburg Evening Post*, Dick Lightsey of the Biloxi-based *Daily Herald*, Bill Ross of the *Daily Journal*, and the Hederman's own Lee Baker of the *Jackson Daily News* to argue for MSU's place in the integrated postseason in 1962 and 1963. It was believed by many of these journalists that cultural validation could come from the team's success on a larger stage and give credence to Mississippi's way of life. This form of validation could only come from a form of integration, a contradiction of sorts in the Closed Society.

Less than two years later, the same debate revolving around Mississippi State's Maroons would reemerge with the school's second conference championship at the conclusion of the 1960–1961 campaign and, for the most part, some of Mississippi's historically well-known journalists and editors had little to say about the potential violation of the unwritten law. Others expressed a belief and confidence in the ultimate enforcement of the gentleman's agreement, essentially minimizing any pro-tournament sentiment. McDowell, who carved a long and storied media-based career both in Mississippi and nationally, continued to emerge as a progressive voice of support even though he never openly advocated integration. While others in Mississippi's sports press came to share the same views and beliefs as McDowell on MSU, such as Lightsey and Ray, both men continued to harbor a belief in segregation and said as much in their columns. The same could be said for the 1961–1962 campaign, which ended with the 24–1 Bulldogs staying in Starkville due to the unwritten law. While McDowell abruptly left Mississippi for Trenton, New Jersey, others such as Lightsey, Ray, and Jimmie Robertson of the *Daily Mississippian* at Ole Miss took up his fight and continued to support integrated athletics for State's basketball team. Despite such support, the majority of the press condemned or ignored MSU's chances at the integrated postseason. However, a decision by the federal government soon intervened in any racial debates in Mississippi, rocking the Closed Society to its core and setting in motion a change in Mississippi's journalists.

While the 1961–1962 season ended and yielded a similar debate involving the unwritten law, something happened that shook the foundation of the Closed Society. After roughly a year of federal litigation, James Meredith was allowed to enter the University of Mississippi in September 1962. The journalists of Mississippi, seemingly with varying beliefs in human and civil rights, threw their support behind Governor Ross Barnett and his belief in states' rights in opposition of the federally forced integration of Mississippi's crown educational jewel. However, that united front began to wane when it became apparent that Meredith would remain a student at Ole Miss, and integration had finally arrived in the Closed Society. From there, the Closed Society's foundation of degradation and hate seemed to crack and slowly separate. This separation was evident in the press and, a mere six months later, the Mississippi State Bulldogs would demonstrate how those cracks were signs of an ideological change in Mississippi's press.

In February 1963, McCarthy's squad won its fourth conference championship in five years and, unlike the previous seasons of subsequent debate and disappointment; there was no enforcement of the unwritten law despite the few loyal purveyors of the Closed Society and their attempted legal injunction. In a show of support that had not been seen in the pages of Mississippi's newspapers, journalists from both the news and sports desks supported and advocated State's participation in the integrated NCAA tournament with the only real opposition coming from Hederman loyalist Ward and the *Meridian Star*'s James B. Skewes. The general consensus from members of the press was a myriad of well wishes for the Bulldogs and a nod of social progress to the state of Mississippi. Over time, the continued basketball success of MSU only fueled this aforementioned desire for cultural validity, culminating in their 1963 appearance in the NCAA tournament. However, with the team's failure to capture a national championship, those advocates went silent. Rather than becoming a point of pride for the Closed Society, the Bulldogs became an embarrassment. Journalistically, they were ignored upon their return to the Magnolia State and little was written about the 1963 team in subsequent years. However, a changing of the guard began to appear in Mississippi's culturally limited borders. Meredith's enrollment at the Oxford-based university in 1962 ushered in the start of a new era of equality in the Magnolia State. Along those lines, the appeals for Mississippi State in 1961, 1962, and 1963 to participate against integrated foes began to generate support from members of Mississippi's press. The addition of Meredith to Ole Miss and the Closed Society opened the door for a new line of thinking in Mississippi that made inroads, albeit small, to social and racial equality. The introduction of blacks into the Magnolia State's traditionally segregated universities and colleges changed the social landscape in the state and that change, albeit a slow one, also evolved in the press and its coverage of the various challenges to the unwritten law.

The Closed Society had lost some of its luster and power and, while the years following the 1963 season were littered with violence and revolution, Mississippi began an ideological metamorphosis that would eventually welcome blacks to the athletic fold. When integrated basketball finally made its initial trek through Mississippi in 1966 with Vanderbilt's Perry Wallace, only one journalist acknowledged the history-making presence of the SEC's first black athlete and identified the lack of attention paid by both the press and the public to his presence. So conflicted by Wallace's presence, Ole Miss even cancelled his first game in Oxford. A mere two years later, Wilbert Jordan Jr. was the first black athlete in one of the state's previously segregated educational institutions as he joined the University of Southern Mississippi basketball team. Jordan's integration of the Southerners and state athletics came in what has been called the most volatile year in this country's history. While the battle for racial equality had yet to be won, as evident in the assassination of Martin Luther King Jr., the civil rights protest at the 1968 Olympic Games, and the passing of the Civil Rights Act of 1968, Jordan's history-making addition to the Southerner's roster was nevertheless a bold statement for blacks in the tumultuous atmosphere of the latter part of the decade. However, the old habits and customs of the press during the height of the Closed Society were still, to some extent, in place. Jordan's history-making presence went completely unnoticed by the local *Hattiesburg American* and was not acknowledged by the *Jackson Daily News* until the last game of his second season, an inexcusable journalistic decision. However, in the aftermath of these social events, Mississippi's editors and reporters were in a state of flux that was hesitant to reference matters of race as integration was in full swing in the Magnolia State. That notion of equality was a part of the new cultural atmosphere in the state, whether individual journalists liked it or not. The historical significance of Jordan's addition to the USM team was lost on the press because they were still coming to grips with the social changes around them.

Ole Miss's successful recruitment of Coolidge Ball gained more attention from the press, but few articles even identified the star forward's race or history-making presence as Ole Miss's first black athlete. With Ball's addition to the Ole Miss Rebels in 1970, the integration of blacks into the structure of Mississippi's previously segregated social outlets had been accepted, begrudgingly or otherwise. Still, the white journalists who covered topics that had a racial connotation were still evolving, hence the confusing and conflicting manner in which Ball's race was referenced. While some publications, such as the *Oxford Eagle* and the *Meridian Star*, identified his ethnic background early in his tenure on the Rebels' basketball team, others such as the *Jackson Daily News*, still under the guise of the segregationist Ward, treated his race inconsistently, referencing the star forward's skintone without any sort of news-based logic or reason. However, the past expressions of outrage were noticeably absent from the Hederman newspapers and the press in general.

Mississippi State's addition of black athletes Jerry Jenkins and Larry Fry to its ranks in 1971 came after the school integrated its athletic program with the 1968 signing of Frank Dowsing Jr., which generated little coverage in the Magnolia State and yielded some outrage, specifically in the pages of the *Meridian Star*. Subsequently, Larry Fry's and Jerry Jenkins's first two years on the Bulldogs' roster was covered in a similar fashion to Ball's initial plight at Ole Miss. Both athletes went through their freshman and sophomore seasons with little to no acknowledgment of their race. However, of greater significance, was that when they were identified for their ethnicity, the *Jackson Daily News* was the only newspaper to do so and utilized the phrase "black" rather than "negro," the preferred description of individuals of color during the height of the Closed Society. Rather than a sign of neglect, the omission of race had become a demonstration of equality. Whereas silence was used as a means of supporting the unwritten law and protecting the Closed Society's ideological boarders in the 1950s and 1960s, the integration of the athletic programs at Southern Miss, Ole Miss, and Mississippi State brought forth a level of acceptance in Mississippi. Silence now acknowledged that acceptance. By the time these schools began adding black athletes, the reign of the Closed Society was at a virtual end. The various challenges to the unwritten law, the subsequent elimination of the state's segregation-based athletic standard, and the eventual integration of college basketball in the Magnolia State was evidence of the social and ideological evolution in Mississippi's press. While the athletic accomplishments of these colleges and universities may not have served as a direct catalyst for change, there was no doubt that the differences of opinions expressed in the pages of Mississippi's newspapers was evidence of a society in transition from the iron grip of the Closed Society to the eventual acceptance of human and civil rights.

Notes

Introduction

1. Neil R. McMillen, *The Citizens' Council: Organized Resistance to the Second Reconstruction, 1954–64* (Urbana: University of Illinois Press, 1971), 15; David R. Davies, *The Press and Race: Mississippi Journalists Confront the Movement* (Jackson: University Press of Mississippi, 2001), 4; and Charles Bolton, *The Hardest Deal of All: The Battle over School Integration in Mississippi, 1870–1980* (Jackson: University Press of Mississippi, 2005), 65.

2. James Silver, *Mississippi: The Closed Society* (New York: Harcourt, Brace, and World, 1964), 3–10.

3. "Seeks Racial Ban in College Sports," *Clarion-Ledger*, January 19, 1956, 1.

4. Russell J. Henderson, "The 1963 Mississippi State University Basketball Controversy and the Repeal of the Unwritten Law: 'Something More than the Game Will Be Lost,'" *The Journal of Southern History* 63, no. 4 (1997): 830.

5. Patrick B. Miller and David Kenneth Wiggins, *Sport and the Color Line: Black Athletes and Race Relations in Twentieth-Century America* (New York: Rutledge, 2004), 279–283.

6. Mississippi State University, "About Us," http://www.msstate.edu/web/gen_info.htm, accessed April 21, 2008. Mississippi State University was known as Mississippi State College from 1932 until 1958, when it was officially granted university status by the state of Mississippi.

7. "Move Is Started Here to Send MSU to NCAA," *Meridian Star*, March 1, 1962, 1. During Mississippi State's numerous basketball-based challenges to the unwritten law, the University of Kentucky was selected to replace the Maroons/Bulldogs in the NCAA tournament in 1959, 1961, and 1962. Then-SEC member Georgia Tech was in consideration for the NCAA basketball tournament bid in 1963 and replaced SEC baseball champion the University of Mississippi in the NCAA tournament in 1959.

8. Davies, *The Press and Race*, 38–41.

9. Davies, *The Press and Race*, 18.

10. Richard Iton, *In Search of the Black Fantastic: Politics and Popular Cultural in the Post-Civil Rights Era* (Oxford University Press, 2008), 9.

11. Kurt Kemper, *College Football and American Culture in the Cold War Era* (Chicago: University of Illinois Press, 2009), 115.

12. Walter Lippmann, *Public Opinion* (New York: Harcourt, Brace, 1922), 330, 355; Maxwell McCombs and Donald Shaw, "The Agenda-Setting Function of Mass Media," *Public Opinion Quarterly* 36, no. 2 (1972): 176–177; and Richard Lentz and Karla Gower, *The Opinions of Mankind: Racial Issues, Press, and Propaganda in the Cold War* (Columbia: University of Missouri Press, 2011).

13. Dave Zirin, *What's My Name, Fool? Sports and Resistance in the United States* (Chicago: Haymarket Books, 2005), 20–21.

14. Kemper, *College Football and American Culture*, 4–5.

15. Kemper, *College Football and American Culture*, 115.

16. Peter B. Levy, *The Civil Rights Movement: Greenwood Press Guides to Historic Events of the Twentieth Century* (Westport, CT: Greenwood Press, 1998), 62.

17. David Sansing, *Making Haste Slowly: The Troubled History of Higher Education in Mississippi* (Jackson: University Press of Mississippi, 1990), 154.

18. Miller and Wiggins, *Sport and the Color Line*, 235.

19. These scholars have argued that the Civil Rights movement is best studied not as a national phenomenon, but by examining local perspectives and studies, which provides greater detail and contribute to the depth of historiographical examinations of the Magnolia State. Their studies are referenced throughout this volume. For more information, see John Dittmer, *Local People: The Struggle for Civil Rights in Mississippi* (Urbana: University of Illinois Press, 1994); Charles M. Payne, *I've Got the Light of Freedom: The Organizing Tradition and the Mississippi Freedom Struggle* (Berkeley: University of California Press, 1996); Emilye Crosby, *A Little Taste of Freedom: The Black Freedom Struggle in Claiborne County, Mississippi* (Chapel Hill: University of North Carolina Press, 2005); Ted Owsby, *The Civil Rights Movement in Mississippi* (Jackson: University Press of Mississippi, 2013); David R. Davies, *The Press and Race: Mississippi Journalists Confront the Movement* (Jackson: University Press of Mississippi, 2001).

20. Russell Thomas Wigginton, *The Strange Career of the Black Athlete: African Americans and Sports* (Westport, CT: Praeger, 2006), 95 and Peter B. Levy, *The Civil Rights Movement: Greenwood Press Guides to Historic Events of the Twentieth Century* (Westport, CT: Greenwood Press, 1998), 83.

21. John Dittmer, *Local People*, 65.

22. Maryanne Vollers, *Ghosts of Mississippi* (Boston: Little, Brown and Company, 1995), 99; and Davies, *Race and the Press*, 8–9.

23. Julius Eric Thompson, *The Black Press in Mississippi, 1865–1985* (Gainesville: University Press of Florida, 1993), 64–66.

24. Ibid.

25. Flamethrowers," *Time Magazine*, 4 March 1966, 1.

26. Dittmer, *Local People*, 65.

27. Ibid.

28. Gene Roberts and Hank Klibanoff, *The Race Beat: The Press, the Civil Rights Struggle, and the Awakening of a Nation* (New York: Knopf, 2006), 271.

29. Ibid.

30. Dittmer, *Local People*, 179.

31. Roberts and Klibanoff, *The Race Beat*, 84–85.

32. James T. Sellers, *A History of the Jackson State Times: An Agent of Change in a Closed Society*. Thesis (Ph. D.), University of Southern Mississippi, 1992, 244–247.

33. Ibid.

34. Thompson, *The Black Press in Mississippi*, 66–67.

35. Erle Johnston, *Mississippi's Defiant Years, 1953–1973* (Forest, MS: Lake Harbor Publishers, 1990), 396.

36. Dittmer, *Local People*, 66.

37. Johnston, *Mississippi's Defiant Years*, 395.

38. Thompson, *The Black Press in Mississippi*, 69–71.

39. Davies, *Race and the Press*, 62–64, 81.

40. Joseph B. Atkins, *The Mission Journalism: Ethics and the World* (Ames: Iowa State University Press, 2000), 52–53.

41. Douglas Starr, interview with author, July 30, 2009.

42. Miller and Wiggins, *Sport and the Color Line*, 248.

43. Barry Jacobs, *Across the Line: Profiles in Basketball Courage: Tales of the First Black Players in the ACC and SEC* (Guilford: Lyons Press, 2008), xiii.

44. Renford Reese, "The Socio-Political Context of the Integration of Sport in America," *Journal of African American Men* 4, no. 3 (Spring 1999): 9.

45. Jacobs, *Across the Line*, xxi-xxii.

46. Dittmer, *Local People*, 139.

47. Charles M. Payne, *I've Got the Light of Freedom: The Organizing Tradition and the Mississippi Freedom Struggle* (Berkeley: University of California Press, 1996), 7.

48. Dittmer, *Local People*, 143–144.

49. Payne, *I've Got the Light of Freedom*, 153.

50. Kenneth Andrews, *Freedom Is a Constant Struggle: The Mississippi Civil Rights Movement and Its Legacy* (Chicago: University of Chicago Press, 2004), 9.

51. Sansing, *Making Haste Slowly*, 199.

52. Wallace Terry, *Missing Pages: Black Journalists of Modern America: An Oral History* (New York: Carroll & Graf Publishers, 2007), 94.

53. Roberts and Klibanoff, *The Race Beat*, 405–406.

54. Chris Lamb and Glen Bleske, "Covering the Integration of Baseball—A Look Back," *Editor & Publisher* 130, no. 4 (27 January 1996): 48–50; and Chris Lamb, *Blackout: The Untold Story of Jackie Robinson's First Spring Training* (Omaha: Bison Books, 2006), 46–47.

55. William Simmons, "Jackie Robinson and the American Mind: Journalistic Perceptions of the Reintegration of Baseball," *Journal of Sport History* 12, no. 1 (Spring 1985): 62.

56. David K. Wiggins, *Glory Bound: Black Athletes in a White America* (Syracuse, NY: Syracuse University Press, 1997), 61.

57. Kathryn Jay, *More Than Just a Game: Sports in American Life Since 1945* (New York: Columbia University Press, 2006), 36.

58. Charles K. Ross, *Outside the Lines: African Americans and the Integration of the National Football League* (New York: NYU Press, 2001), 51, 96; and John Carroll, *Fritz Pollard: Pioneer in Racial Advancement* (Champaign: University of Illinois Press, 1998), 215.

59. Davies, *Race and the Press*, 271.

60. Reese, "The Socio-Political Context of the Integration of Sport in America," 6–7; David Medina, "Opening Doors," *Sallyport: The Magazine of Rice University* 61, no. 1, (Fall 2004), 13–17; and Miller and Wiggins, *Sport and the Color Line*, 248. In late 1955, it was announced that the Georgia Institute of Technology was to play the University of Pittsburgh in the 1956 Sugar Bowl in January. However, Georgia Governor Marvin Griffin ordered Tech to reject the bowl bid because of the presence of Pitt's black fullback Bobby Grier. President Blake R. Van Leer left the decision to Coach Bobby Dodd, who allowed his players to vote. Tech went on to

accept the bowl bid and win 7–0. In 1956, Louisiana state legislators initiated a bill to prohibit any integrated athletic contests in the state. During Ole Miss's multiple appearances in the Sugar Bowl during the 1960s, its foes Louisiana State University, Rice University, and the University of Arkansas had yet to integrate their athletics. LSU's first black athlete, Collins Temple Jr., enrolled in 1971; Rice did not integrate its student body until 1964 with the admittance of Raymond Johnson, and Arkansas's first black athlete, basketball player, Thomas Johnson, began varsity play in 1968.

61. Charles W. Eagles, *The Price of Defiance: James Meredith and the Integration of Ole Miss* (Chapel Hill: University of North Carolina Press, 2009), 111.

62. MSU's athletic teams were known as the Maroons from 1932 until 1961, when the school received university status and adopted the Bulldogs as the team name. However, the name was slowly adopted and most media accounts still referred to the team as the Maroons.

63. "No Social Problem: Paul Davis," *Jackson Daily News,* December 14, 1963, 2.

64. MSU Athletic Media Relations, *2007 Mississippi State Baseball Media Guide,* 104.

65. Chester Morgan, *Dearly Bought, Deeply Treasured: The University of Southern Mississippi, 1912–1987* (Jackson: The University Press of Mississippi, 1987), 102–103.

66. Susan Weill, *In a Madhouse's Din: Civil Rights Coverage by Mississippi's Daily Press, 1948–1968* (Westport, CT: Praeger, 2002), 254. Weill identified the circulation rate for all of Mississippi's daily newspapers during the 1954 *Brown v. Board of Education* ruling, the 1962 integration of the University of Mississippi, and the 1964 Freedom Summer movement to register blacks to vote. The averages provided are calculated by the author based on Weill's figures. From 1954 through 1964, each newspaper had the following average daily circulation: *Clarion-Ledger,* 53,239; *Jackson Daily News,* 46,030; *Daily Herald* (Biloxi), 27,736; *Meridian Star,* 21,406; *Hattiesburg American,* 15,556; *Delta Democrat-Times,* 12,407; *Laurel Leader-Call,* 12,039; *Vicksburg Evening Post,* 10,207; and *Enterprise-Journal,* 5, 771. The 207,579 issues distributed daily represented 70 percent of the 270,459 issues distributed from all daily newspapers in the state over a ten-year time frame. Weill does not include circulation figures for the *Jackson State Times,* likely because it closed in 1961.

67. Thompson, *The Black Press in Mississippi,* 46, 64, and 119.

68. Silver, *Mississippi: The Closed Society,* 30; McMillen, *The Citizens' Council,* 258, 328; Davies, *Race and the Press,* 27, 31, 42–43; and Weill, *In the Madhouse's Din,* 89, 145. Both Ethridge and Skewes spoke out against all threats to white supremacy during the civil rights movement. Ethridge supported Barnett's objection to James Meredith's enrollment at the University of Mississippi and Skewes was critical of Freedom Summer. Carter has been cited by the aforementioned historians as speaking out for racial equality in Mississippi, while Emmerich is viewed as a more moderate voice in Mississippi journalism history; his commentary was considered liberal for the time.

Chapter 1. Sometimes, Even College Administrators Act Like Freshmen

1. Simeon Booker, *Shocking the Consequence: A Reporter's Account of the Civil Rights Movement* (Jackson: University Press of Mississippi, 2013), 7.

2. Gene Roberts and Hank Klibanoff, *The Race Beat: The Press, the Civil Rights Struggle, and the Awakening of a Nation* (New York: Knopf, 2006), 71.

3. David R. Davies, *The Press and Race: Mississippi Journalists Confront the Movement* (Jackson: University Press of Mississippi, 2001), 10–12.

4. Roberts and Klibanoff, *The Race Beat*, 80–82 and Ted Ownby, *The Civil Rights Movement in Mississippi* (Jackson: University Press of Mississippi, 2013), 66.

5. Roberts and Klibanoff, *The Race Beat*, 85–86 and Ownby, *The Civil Rights Movement in Mississippi*, 68.

6. "Report Compton to Play Negroes In Pasadena Game," *Laurel Leader-Call*, December 3, 1955, 5.

7. "Little Rose Bowl to Again Have Negro Players," *Delta Democrat-Times*, December 4, 1955, 2; "Band Assured California Trip as Jaycees State Pledges and Cash Secured to Pay Expenses," *Laurel Leader-Call*, December 4, 1955, 1, 2; "Jones Raises No Objections," *Laurel Leader-Call*, December 4, 1955, 1, 4; "Race Issue Pops Up in Jones County Jr. Rose Bowl Game," *Meridian Star*, December 4, 1955, 1, 2; and "Tech, Jones J.C. Bowl Bids Okayed," *Jackson State Times*, December 5, 1955, 1.

8. Jason Peterson, "'They Deserve a Stinging Defeat': Mississippi Newspaper Coverage of Jones County Junior College's Appearance in the 1955 Junior Rose Bowl," *American Journalism* 28, no. 2 (Spring 2012): 93–123.

9. Roberts and Klibanoff, *The Race Beat*, 83–85; and Neil R. McMillen, *The Citizens' Council: Organized Resistance to the Second Reconstruction,1954–64* (Urbana: University of Illinois Press, 1971), 258. William J. Simmons and the Citizens' Council presented Sullens with a plaque in 1955 in honor of his work and for his defense of "our Southern way of life."

10. "They Deserve Stinging Defeat," *Jackson Daily News*, December 8, 1955, 1.

11. Ibid and "No Investigation Needed," *Jackson Daily News*, December 10, 1955, 1.

12. Lee Baker, "Compton Wins Junior Rose Bowl Thriller 22–13," *Jackson Daily News* and *Clarion-Ledger*, December 11, 1955, 1B.

13. "Jones College to Bowl over Newspaper Threat," *Delta Democrat-Times*, December 6, 1955, 1; "Jr. College Faces Cuts in Funds Because of Racially Mixed Game," *Meridian Star*, December 6, 1955, 1; "Jones Leaves Today to Play in Bowl Game," *Jackson State Times*, December 6, 1955, 7B; "Jones Deserving of Defeat, Paper Declares," *Vicksburg Evening Post*, December 8, 1955, 1; "Bobcats Deserve Stinging Defeat at Pasadena, Paper Says," *Enterprise-Journal*, December 8, 1955, 1, 8; "Jones Jr. College May Lose State Funds, Paper Says," *Hattiesburg American*, December 6, 1955, 9; and "Daily News Says Ellisville Should Lose Grid Game," *Daily Herald* (Biloxi) December 8, 1955, 35.

14. "Seeks Racial Ban in College Sports," *Clarion-Ledger*, January 19, 1956, 1.

15. Frank R. Parker and Eddie N. Williams, *Black Votes Count: Political Empowerment in Mississippi after 1965* (Chapel Hill: University of North Carolina Press, 1990), 83; and Charles Evers and Andrew Szanton, *Have No Fear: The Charles Evers Story* (Hoboken: John Wiley & Sons, Inc., 1998, 77–78.

16. Introduce Bill to Halt Mixed Sports in State," *Meridian Star*, January 19, 1956, 8; "Iron Out Flaws Holding Up Sheriff Recall Bill, First Major State Legislative Move," *Meridian Star*, January 19, 1956, 1; "Stiff Penalties Are Sought for Mixing Athletic Games," *Jackson Daily News*, January 19, 1956, 1; and "Legislative Digest," *Commercial Dispatch*, January 22, 1956, 6B.

17. Roberts and Klibanoff, *The Race Beat*, 90, 199. According to Roberts and Klibanoff, Herbers never let race dictate whether or not an issue was covered. Rather, he made decisions based on the news value of the topic.

18. Russell J. Henderson, "The 1963 Mississippi State University Basketball Controversy and the Repeal of the Unwritten Law: 'Something More than the Game Will Be Lost,'" The Journal of Southern History 63, no. 4 (1997): 828–830. The State College Board meeting minutes, housed at Mississippi State University, show no record of the proposal and adoption of the unwritten law.

19. Ibid.

20. "Stiff Penalties Are Sought for Mixing Athletic Games," Jackson Daily News, January 19, 1956, 1; "Senate-House Talks Today Work Out Coleman Recall Law Kinks," Delta Democrat-Times, January 19, 1956, 1; "Introduce Bill to Halt Mixed Sports in State," Meridian Star, January 19, 1956, 8; and "Sports Segregation Sought," New York Times, January 19, 1956, 22.

21. Jan Paul, Richard McGee, and Helen Fant, "The Arrival and Ascendance of the Black Athlete in the Southeastern Conference, 1966–1980," Phylon 45, no. 4 (December 1984): 284.

22. Mississippi State University, "About Us," http://www.msstate.edu/web/gen_info.htm, accessed April 21, 2008. Mississippi State University was known as Mississippi State College from 1932 until 1958 when it was officially granted university status by the state of Mississippi.

23. "Mississippi State Defeats Denver," Laurel Leader-Call, December 29, 1956, 9.

24. "State Basketballers Play Mixed Quintet," Jackson Daily News, December 29, 1956, 1.

25. Michael B. Ballard, Maroon and White: Mississippi State University, 1878–2003 (Jackson: Mississippi State University, 2008), 142.

26. Ibid.

27. Ballard, Maroon and White, 143.

28. "Ashmore Sinks 30 But State Loses to Murray, 91–80," Delta Democrat-Times, January 1, 1957, 9; and "State Drops Game 91–80 to Murray," Jackson Daily News, January 1, 1957, 6.

29. "Mississippi Loses 91–80," Natchez Democrat, January 1, 1957, 7.

30. Mississippi Department of History and Archives, Mississippi State Sovereignty Commission files, SCR ID# 1-67-2-20-1-1-1, http://mdah.state.ms.us/arrec/digital-archives/sovcomm (accessed on August 19, 2009).

31. Barry Jacobs, Across the Line: Profiles in Basketball Courage: Tales of the First Black Players in the ACC and SEC (Guilford, CT: Lyons Press, 2008), 304.

32. "Ole Miss Denied Request That Iona Drop Negro Cager," Delta Democrat-Times, January 1, 1957, 9.

33. Ibid.

34. Susan Weill, In a Madhouse's Din: Civil Rights Coverage by Mississippi's Daily Press, 1948–1968 (Westport, CT: Praeger, 2002), 109

35. Yasuhiro Katagiri, The Mississippi State Sovereignty Commission: Civil Rights and States' Rights (Oxford: University Press of Mississippi, 2007) 8–9; and Emilye Crosby, A Little Taste of Freedom: The Black Freedom Struggle in Claiborne County, Mississippi (Chapel Hill: University of North Carolina Press, 2005), 71.

36. Crosby, A Little Taste of Freedom, 70–71.

37. Mississippi Department of History and Archives. Mississippi State Sovereignty Commission files, SCR ID # 99-103-0-286-1-1-1, http://mdah.state.us/arrec/digital_archives/sovcom (accessed on August 16, 2009).

38. Mississippi Legislature. State Concurrent Resolution 571. http://billstatus.ls.state.ms.us/documents/2004/html/SC/SC0571SG.htm (accessed August 16, 2009).

39. John Dittmer, *Local People: The Struggle for Civil Rights in Mississippi* (Urbana: University of Illinois Press,1994); 66.

40. Billy Ray, "Press Box Views," *Vicksburg Evening Post*, December 31, 1956, 8.

41. Carl Walters, "Shavin's," *Clarion-Ledger*, December 31, 1956, 7.

42. "This Was Ill-Advised," *Vicksburg Evening Post*, December 31, 1956, 4.

43. "Bad Publicity Showers Mississippi Because of Apparent Team Hypocrisy," *Jackson State Times*, January 2, 1957, 6A.

44. Joe Mosby, "Sideline Slants," *Natchez Democrat*, January 2, 1957, 7.

45. Joe Mosby, "Sideline Slants," *Natchez Democrat*, January 4, 1957, 7.

46. Ibid.

47. "Rebs Cagers Invade Bama to Play Tide," *Jackson State Times*, January 4, 1957, 3B; "State Falls to Murray Teachers," *Laurel Leader-Call*, January 1, 1957, 6; "Miss. State Loses to Murray," *Hattiesburg American*, January 1, 1957, 7A; Associated Press, "SEC Cage Season Opens with Gators Meeting Bulldogs," *Delta Democrat-Times*, December 3, 1957, 5; and "Ashmore Sinks 30 But State Loses to Murray, 91–80," *Delta Democrat-Times*, January 1, 1957, 9.

Chapter 2. We'll Stay at Home and Tell Everybody We're the Best

1. John Dittmer, *Local People: The Struggle for Civil Rights in Mississippi* (Urbana: University of Illinois Press, 1994), 79.

2. Charles W. Eagles, *The Price of Defiance: James Meredith and the Integration of Ole Miss* (Chapel Hill: University of North Carolina Press, 2009) 88–97.

3. "Game at Starkville Is 'Must' for Both," *Delta Democrat-Times*, February 9, 1959, 5.

4. Lee Baker, "State Maroons Hammer No. 1 Kentucky, 66–58," *Jackson Daily News*, February 10, 1959, 6; Jim Roden, "Howell Leads State over Rupp's Raiders," *Jackson Daily News*, February 10, 1959, 4B; "Mississippi State Romps over No. 1 Kentucky Wildcats 66–58," *Delta Democrat-Times*, February 10, 1959, 5; "State Beats 'Cats; Howell Tallies 27," *Greenwood Commonwealth*, February 10, 1959, 4; "Bailey Howell Fires Thunderous Claim to All American Basketball Honors as State Defeats Wildcats," *Laurel Leader-Call*, February 10, 1959, 9; and "Mississippi State Blasts Kentucky in Monday Contest," *Daily Herald* (Biloxi), February 10, 1959, 15.

5. Jim Roden, "McCarthy Is Elated over Great Victory," *Jackson State Times*, February 10, 1959, 4B.

6. "Mississippi State Clubs Top-Ranked Kentucky," *Hattiesburg American*, February 10, 1959, 1B; "Maroons Can Beat Anyone at State Says McCarthy," *Delta Democrat-Times*, February 10, 1959, 6; "Maroons Toy Around with Kentucky in 66–58 Win," *Vicksburg Evening Post*, February 10, 1959, 8; "Humble Happy McCarthy Praises Team; Lauds Big Bailey Howell," *Greenwood Commonwealth*, February 10, 1959, 4; "Maroon Coach Says His Boys Can Win over Any Team at Mississippi State," *Laurel Leader-Call*, February 10, 1959, 8; and "McCarthy Believes State Best in Nation Following Triumph over Wildcats," *Daily Herald* (Biloxi), February 10, 1959, 14.

7. "Upset Victory of 'Tucky Makes State Title Threat," *Meridian Star*, February 10, 1959, 8; "Maroon Stock Soars after Cat Conquest," *Jackson State Times*, February 10, 1959, 5B; and "Maroons Defeat Mighty Kentucky 66–58 As Howell Stars Again," *Commercial Dispatch*, February 10, 1959, 9.

8. "State Cagers Want to Play," *Jackson State Times*, February 10, 1959, 5B.

9. Ibid.

10. Dr. Douglas Starr, interview with author, July 30, 2009. Starr, who worked for the Associated Press during the aforementioned time period, claimed that local news outlets in Mississippi would publish wire material on issues of race in order to deflect negative attention away from themselves. "That way, they could claim it wasn't us, it was the AP," Starr said.

11. Joe Holley, "Cliff Sessions Dies; Civil Rights-Era Reporter," *Washington Post*, December 29, 2005, 5B; and Gene Roberts and Hank Klibanoff, *The Race Beat: The Press, the Civil Rights Struggle, and the Awakening of a Nation* (New York: Knopf, 2006), 200–202. A native of Bolton, Mississippi, Sessions graduated from Mississippi Southern College in 1955 and became a bureau manager in his home state for the AP from 1957 through 1964. The son of an Episcopal priest, Sessions believed that segregation was necessary, but his years as a journalist began to sway the newsman's beliefs. He would later befriend Medgar Evers, even allowing the civil rights pioneer to stay in his home.

12. Dick Lightsey, "Bunts, Boots and Bounces," *Daily Herald* (Biloxi), February 26, 1959, 22.

13. Curtis Wilkie, *Dixie: A Personal Odyssey through Events That Shaped the Modern South* (New York: Touchstone, 2001), 139; and Orley B. Caudill, interview with William J. Simmons, Mississippi Oral History Program of the University of Southern Mississippi, vol. 372, June 26, 1979.

14. "Board Alone Decides Maroons' NCAA Play," *Jackson State Times*, February 11, 1959, 6B. The same article also appeared in the following publications: "Coleman on State Going to NCAA Meet," *Delta Democrat-Times*, February 11, 1959, 1; and "Coleman Says He Hasn't Any Power to Act," *Commercial Dispatch*, February 11, 1959, 6.

15. Jimmie McDowell, "Texas Courts Babe for Coaching Job," *Jackson State Times*, February 12, 1959, 6B.

16. Jimmie McDowell, "Jimmie McDowell," *Jackson State Times*, February 13, 1959, 4B.

17. Jimmie McDowell, interview with author, August 12, 2010.

18. "Howell Gets 43 as State Wins 105–68," *Clarion-Ledger*, February 15, 1959, B1; "Howell Scores 43 In 105–63 Win over Florida," *Delta Democrat-Times*, February 16, 1959, 5; and "Howell Sinks '43' as State Dumps Florida 105–68," *Vicksburg Evening Post*, February 15, 1959, 11.

19. Ed Wilks, "Auburn Team Seeks Top Spot This Week," *Clarion-Ledger*, February 16, 1959, 12.

20. Berry Reece, "J.P. Leaves NCAA Bid Up to Solons," *Jackson Daily News*, February 16, 1959, 1.

21. "Maroons Need Consent of State's Legislature," *Clarion-Ledger*, February 17, 1959, 13; "Decision on Maroons Must Have Okay of Legislature," *Meridian Star*, February 16, 1959, 1; "Miss. State and the NCAA Tournament," *Hattiesburg American*, February 16, 1959, A8; "State Law Won't Keep Maroons Out of NCAA Tourney," *Enterprise-Journal*, February 16, 1959, 1; "Governor Get Mail on State-To-NCAA Hassle," *Jackson State Times*, February 16, 1959, 1; "Governor Says if MSU Plays in NCAA Tournament It Must First Consult the Legislature," *Laurel Leader-Call*, February 16, 1959, 1, 3; John Herbers, "Coleman Threatens to Campaign in '59 Races," *Delta Democrat-Times*, February 16, 1959, 1; "Legislature Will Have to Be Consulted before State Can Go to Tourney," *Daily Herald* (Biloxi), February 16, 1959, 8; and "to Shun NCAA Hassle," *Jackson State Times*, February 17, 1959, 1.

22. "Maroons Need Consent of State's Legislature," *Clarion-Ledger*, February 17, 1959, 13.

23. "to Shun NCAA Hassle," *Jackson State Times*, February 17, 1959, 1; "Board May Talk NCAA; Capital March Rumored," *Jackson State Times*, February 19, 1959, 1, 2A; "NCAA Tourney Action Unlikely at Board Meeting," *Meridian Star*, February 17, 1959, 8; and "Board Tells State to Decide NCAA on Own," *Delta Democrat-Times*, February 19, 1959, 1.

24. "Opinion Vote on NCAA Trip Today at MSU," *Clarion-Ledger*, February 19, 1959, 31; "State Students Cast Votes on NCAA Tourney," *Meridian Star*, February 18, 1959, 9; "Miss. State Students Voting on NCAA Issue," *Hattiesburg American*, February 19, 1959, 8A; "State Students Will Vote on NCAA Trip," *Jackson Daily News*, February 19, 1959, 4; "Students Vote Feelings on NCAA Tourney Seat," *Enterprise-Journal*, February 19, 1959, 13; "State Students Vote on Team Going to NCAA," *Delta Democrat-Times*, February 19, 1959, 6; "State Students to Vote on Whether Team Should Go to NCAA Tournament," *Daily Herald* (Biloxi), February 19, 1959, 25; State Students Vote 'Yes' for Integrated Tournament," *Clarion-Ledger*, February 20, 1959, 1; "State Students Favor NCAA Tourney Entry," *Hattiesburg American*, February 20, 1959, 1, 2; "State Students Vote 973–162 For NCAA Play," *Delta Democrat-Times*, February 20, 1959, 1, 2; "Most State Students for Play in Tourney," *Delta Democrat-Times*, February 20, 1959, 6; "Mixed Play for Cage Stars Is State Vote," *Vicksburg Evening Post*, February 20, 1959, 1; "State Students Favor Playing in NCAA Tourney," *Greenwood Commonwealth*, February 20, 1959, 5; "Student Vote Favors NCAA Tourney Jaunt," *Enterprise-Journal*, February 20, 1959, 8; "One Fourth of Students Vote," *Commercial Dispatch*, February 20, 1959, 1; "MSU Students Vote Heavily for NCAA Play," *Laurel Leader-Call*, February 20, 1959, 1, 3; and "State Students in Favor of Maroons Going to NCAA," *Daily Herald* (Biloxi), February 20, 1959, 18.

25. "MSU Students Favor Trip to Tourney," *Jackson State Times*, February 20, 1959, 1, 2A.

26. James C. Cobb, *The Most Southern Place on Earth: The Mississippi Delta and the Roots of Regional Identity* (New York: Oxford University Press, 1994), 250; and McMillen, *The Citizens' Council*, 16.

27. "Mississippi State Student Vote Could Be Misleading," *Clarion-Ledger*, February 21, 1959, 1.

28. Ibid.

29. "Campus Election on Integrated Tourney Attracts Little Interest at Miss. State," *Meridian Star*, February 20, 1959, 1, 2.

30. Ibid.

31. Ray Sadler, "Southeastern Champion Maroons Will Not Attend NCAA tournament," the *Reflector* (Mississippi State University), March 3, 1959, 1.

32. "MSU Students Favor Trip to Tourney," *Jackson State Times*, February 20, 1959, 1, 2A.

33. Dudley Doust, "Bouquets for Babe and His Bailey," *Sports Illustrated*, February 23, 1959, 50–52.

34. "McCarthy Denies Rumor," *Jackson Daily News*, February 19, 1959, 12; "Campus Election on Integrated Tourney Attracts Little Interest at Miss. State," *Meridian Star*, February 20, 1959, 1, 2; "Board May Talk NCAA; Capital March Rumored," *Jackson State Times*, February 19, 1959, 1, 2A; and "State Students Might Converge on Capital," *Jackson Daily News*, February 19, 1959, 12.

35. Jimmie McDowell, "Jimmie McDowell," *Jackson State Times*, February 19, 1959, 4B.

36. Lee Baker, "State Tips LSU Tigers in Rugged 75–67 Battle," *Clarion-Ledger*, February 22, 1959, 1B; and *Jackson Daily News*, February 22, 1959, 1B; "Maroons Cagers Score 75–67 Win over Louisiana State," *Meridian Star*, February 22, 1959, 10; W. B. Ragsdale Jr., "Kentucky Humbles

Auburn; State Stomps LSU 75–67," *Vicksburg Evening Post*, February 22, 1959, 13; Maroons Triumph over LSU 75–67," *Commercial Dispatch*, February 22, 1959, 6; and Jimmie McDowell, "State 5 Socks Tigers," *Jackson State Times*, February 22, 1959, 1D.

37. Mercer Bailey, "Maroons, Auburn Tied for Southeastern Lead," *Clarion-Ledger*, February 23, 1959, 9; Mercer Bailey, "State Tied for Lead Going into Tonight's Tulane Game," *Hattiesburg American*, February 23, 1959, 2B; Mercer Bailey, "High Scoring Bailey Howell Goes after Big Record against Tulane," *Greenwood Commonwealth*, February 23, 1959, 4; Mercer Bailey, "Big Bailey Howell Goes Running for Scoring Record at Tulane Tonight," *Laurel Leader-Call*, February 22, 1959, 8; and Mercer Bailey, "State Whips LSU, Grabs Share of SEC Basketball Lead," *Daily Herald* (Biloxi), February 23, 1959, 15.

38. Lee Baker, "Howell Scores 32 In Maroon Victory," *Jackson Daily News*, February 24, 1959, 6.

39. "State Wins 65–51; Howell Scores 32," *Clarion-Ledger*, February 24, 1959, 13; Vernon Butler, "Maroons Clinch Bid to NCAA," *Vicksburg Evening Post*, February 24, 1959, 8; "Howell Sets New Conference Record as Maroons Take over Lead," *Commercial Dispatch*, February 24, 1959, 6; Vernon Butler, "All Mississippi State Needs to Win Conference Crown Is Saturday Victory," *Laurel Leader-Call*, February 24, 1959, 8.

40. "Hilbun Will Announce Decision after Reb Tilt," *Clarion-Ledger*, February 26, 1959, 1B.

41. "No Playoff in SEC Needed if 3 Tied," *Clarion-Ledger*, February 25, 1959, 13; and "No Playoff in SEC; State Is Champion," *Natchez Democrat*, February 25, 1959, 9.

42. Vernon Butler, "State Takes over First Place, Howell Breaks Scoring Record," *Hattiesburg American*, February 24, 1959, 6; Vernon Butler, "Maroons Need One Win for Title; Bailey Howell Sets Scoring Record," *Greenwood Commonwealth*, February 24, 1959, 4; Vernon Butler, "Mississippi State Grabs Lead in SEC Basketball Race," *Daily Herald* (Biloxi), February 24, 1959, 12.

43. "Miss. State Maroons between Two 'Fires,'" *Clarion-Ledger*, February 25, 1959, 14; and "Maroons Caught between Two Fires as Season Ends," *Natchez Democrat*, February 25, 1959, 9.

44. "Hilbun Will Announce Decision after Reb Tilt," *Clarion-Ledger*, February 26, 1959, B1; "State Expected to Turn Down NCAA," *Meridian Star*, February 26, 1959, 8; "State's Coach Asks People," *Jackson State Times*, February 25, 1959, 1A; "President to Reveal It after Ole Miss Game," *Delta Democrat-Times*, February 26, 1959, 7; "Thousands Welcome Maroons, Coach Asks Opinions on Tourney," *Delta Democrat-Times*, February 25, 1959, 1, 2; "Speak Out Cage Coach Says Today," *Commercial Dispatch*, February 25, 1959, 1; and "Mississippians Fail to Answer Call for Opinion," *Commercial Dispatch*, February 26, 1959, 1.

45. "Hilbun Expected to Keep State Out of Tourney," *Hattiesburg American*, February 26, 1959, A8; "State NCAA Play Up in Air; Ben Holds Decision," *Vicksburg Evening Post*, February 26, 1959, 1; "Maroons Fate in Basketball Play Still Unknown," *Greenwood Commonwealth*, February 26, 1959, 5; "Informed Sources Say State Not to Play in NCAA," *Laurel Leader-Call*, February 26, 1959, 16; "Ben Hilbun Will Give NCAA Decision Saturday," *Enterprise-Journal*, February 26, 1959, 12; "State Prexy Says Will Decide if State Can Play," *Natchez Democrat*, February 26, 1959, 11; "Hilbun Will Decide Whether State Can Go to NCAA," *Daily Herald* (Biloxi), February 25, 1959, 14; and "Still Mum at State on NCAA Tourney," *Daily Herald* (Biloxi), February 26, 1959, 24.

46. "NCAA Decision to Come after Game," *Jackson State Times*, February 26, 1959, 3A.

47. "Maroons 'Certain' to Miss Tourney," *Jackson Daily News*, February 25, 1959, 1.

48. George Whittington, "Williams Would Shun NCAA Tournament," *Jackson State Times*, February 27, 1959, 10A.

49. "McCarthy Given 4-Year Pact; Salary Increased," *Clarion-Ledger*, February 28, 1959, 5; "McCarthy Signs New State Pact," *Jackson Daily News*, February 28, 1959, 3; "State Due to Edge Rebels, Wrap Up SEC Title and Reject NCAA Tourney," *Delta Democrat-Times*, March 1, 1959, 9; "State Awards New Contract to McCarthy; Mild Pay Hike," *Natchez Democrat*, February 28, 1959, 6; and "McCarthy Accepts Big Four-Year Maroon Contract," *Vicksburg Evening Post*, February 28, 1959, 3.

50. "McCarthy Signs New State Pact," *Jackson Daily News*, February 28, 1959, 3.

51. Cliff Sessions, "McCarthy Gets New Pact," *Jackson State Times*, February 28, 1959, 7; and Cliff Sessions, "McCarthy Signs 4-Year Contract," *Meridian Star*, February 28, 1959, 6.

52. Cliff Sessions, "McCarthy Gets New Pact," *Jackson State Times*, February 28, 1959, 7.

53. "Howell Is Not Through Yet," *Meridian Star*, March 2, 1959, 8.

54. Ibid.

55. Jimmie McDowell, "Kentucky Seems Cinch for NCAA," *Jackson State Times*, February 28, 1959, 7.

56. Ibid.

57. "Rebels Hope to Knock State Out of SEC Lead," *Clarion-Ledger*, February 26, 1959, 2B; "Kentucky, Vols Vie, State Meets Rebels," *Jackson Daily News*, February 28, 1959, 2; "Reb-Maroon Game Ends SEC Race," *Jackson State Times*, February 26, 1959, 13C; and "Rebels Will Need All Out Effort to Upset Maroons," *Vicksburg Evening Post*, February 27, 1959, 8.

58. Bill Ray, "State Edges Rebs 23–16 For SEC Title," *Vicksburg Evening Post*, March 1, 1959, 3.

59. Lee Baker, "Maroons Beats Rebs 23 to 16 in Deep-Freeze; NCAA Spurned," *Clarion-Ledger*, March 1, 1959, B1; Lee Baker, "Maroons Beats Rebs 23 to 16 in Deep-Freeze; NCAA Spurned," *Jackson Daily News*, March 1, 1959, 1B; "Scores 23–16 Win over Ole Miss in Slow Moving Tilt," *Meridian Star*, March 1, 1959, 10; Jimmie McDowell, "State Nips Rebs for First SEC Cage Title," *Jackson State Times*, March 1, 1959, 1D; and Bill Ray, "State Edges Rebs 23–16 For SEC Title," *Vicksburg Evening Post*, March 1, 1959, 3.

60. Ben Hilbun Presidential Papers, File 6, Athletic Department, Document #340, Mississippi State University Archives. Hilbun's announcement could also be found published in the following articles: "Mr. Ben Says No Trip," *Jackson State Times*, March 1, 1959, 1; "Hilbun Refuses to Give Maroons NCAA Permission," *Meridian Star*, March 1, 1959, 10; "Hilbun Says Miss. State Maroons Won't Make NCAA Play," *Natchez Democrat*, March 1, 1959, 12A; "Maroons Turn Down NCAA Bid," *Vicksburg Evening Post*, March 1, 1959, 3; "State Not to Play in NCAA Meet," *Commercial Dispatch*, February 28, 1959, 1; "Mississippi State Defeats Ole Miss to Win Their First SEC Title," *Commercial Dispatch*, March 1, 1959, 6; Lee Baker, "Maroons Beats Rebs 23 to 16 in Deep-Freeze; NCAA Spurned," *Clarion-Ledger*, March 1, 1959, 1B; Lee Baker, "Maroons Beats Rebs 23 to 16 in Deep-Freeze; NCAA Spurned," *Jackson Daily News*, March 1, 1959, B1; "Scores 23–16 Win over Ole Miss in Slow Moving Tilt," *Meridian Star*, March 1, 1959, 10; Jimmie McDowell, "State Nips Rebs for First SEC Cage Title," *Jackson State Times*, March 1, 1959, 1D; and Bill Ray, "State Edges Rebs 23–16 For SEC Title," *Vicksburg Evening Post*, March 1, 1959, 3.

61. Lee Baker, "Maroons Beats Rebs 23 to 16 in Deep-Freeze; NCAA Spurned," *Clarion-Ledger* and *Jackson Daily News*, March 1, 1959, 1B.

62. Jimmie McDowell, "State Nips Rebs for First SEC Cage Title," *Jackson State Times*, March 1, 1959, 1D.

63. Greg Rosa, *Football in the SEC: Southeastern Conference* (New York: Rosen Publishing Group, 2007), 1–3; and Southern Conference, History of the Southern Conference, accessed on March 18, 2010, http://www.soconsports.com. Mississippi State, then known as Mississippi A&M, joined the Southern Intercollegiate Athletic Association a year after its inception in 1895. The SIAA is considered the first major collegiate athletic conference. In 1920, the thirty members of the SIAA disagreed on whether or not freshmen should be allowed to participate in varsity sports, leading fourteen of the schools, including Mississippi State, to leave the SIAA and form the Southern Conference in 1921. In December 1932, it was announced that 13 of the 23 Southern Conference members were breaking away to form the Southeastern Conference. The decision was based on geographical lines, as the thirteen schools selected were west and south of the Appalachian Mountains. Mississippi State has remained in the SEC ever since.

64. "Fans Hang Hilbun Effigy," *Clarion-Ledger*, March 3, 1959, 1.

65. Ray Sadler, "Southeastern Champion Maroons will not attend NCAA tournament," the *Reflector* (Mississippi State University), March 3, 1959, 1.

66. Susan Weill, *In a Madhouse's Din: Civil Rights Coverage by Mississippi's Daily Press,1948–1968* (Westport, CT: Praeger, 2002),56–57, 86–87, and 226–227. Weill's book details Harris's opposition to *Brown vs. Board of Education*, the enrollment of James Meredith in the University of Mississippi, and the death of Dr. Martin Luther King Jr., voiced in his column "Pencil Shavings." In an example of Harris's insensitivity to King's death, the segregationist openly attacked the status of martyr bestowed on King after his death.

67. Vernon Butler, "SEC's Champs Sit Home While 'Cats Go to NCAA," *Clarion-Ledger*, March 2, 1959, 9; Vernon Butler, "Maroons Win First SEC Title but Kentucky Goes to Tourney," *Hattiesburg American*, March 2, 1959, 2B; Vernon Butler, "Thanks to Miss. State, Kentucky Is in NCAA Again," *Vicksburg Evening Post*, March 2, 1959, 7; Vernon Butler, "Coach Adolph Rupp Takes 'Cats to NCAA Tourney for 11th Contest," *Greenwood Commonwealth*, March 2, 1959, 5; Vernon Butler, "Kentucky Gets 11th NCAA Trip," March 2, 1959, 4; Vernon Butler, "Mississippi State Wins Southeastern Title but Wildcats Go to NCAA Event," *Laurel Leader-Call*, March 2, 1959, 8; and Vernon Butler, "Mississippi State Claims SEC Title, Beats Ole Miss," March 2, 1959, 19.

68. Hugh Fullerton Jr., "Cats 'Given' Chance to Defend NCAA Title," *Clarion-Ledger*, March 2, 1959, 10.

69. Earl Wright, "Kentucky Defends Tournament Title," *Meridian Star*, March 2, 1959, 9; Earl Wright, "Kentucky Will Seek Fifth NCAA Crown," *Jackson State Times*, March 2, 1959, 5B; and "Kentucky Wildcats to Defend Title in NCAA Basketball Tourney," *Commercial Dispatch*, March 2, 1959, 6.

70. "Kentucky Braces for NCAA Action," *Jackson Daily News*, March 2, 1959, 10.

71. Cliff Sessions, "It's OK for Bailey to Play in Star Games," *Jackson State Times*, March 2, 1959, 4B; "Howell Is Not Through Yet," *Meridian Star*, March 2, 1959, 8; "State Star Will Play in Post Season Classic," *Jackson Daily News*, March 2, 1959, 10; and "Bailey Howell Plays Ball with Teamster Squad," *Enterprise-Journal*, March 9, 1959, 4.

72. David M. Moffit, "Howell Heads SEC Stars," *Jackson State Times*, March 5, 1959, 7B; "Bailey Howell on SEC Team," *Clarion-Ledger*, March 4, 1959, 13; Ted Meier, "Bailey Howell, Cox Give SEC Two Slots on AP All-America," *Clarion-Ledger*, March 6, 1959, 20; Murry Olderman, "State Star Bailey Howell Is NEA All-American," *Meridian Star*, March 10, 1959, 9; "Howell

Voted MVP in SEC Basketball," *Jackson Daily News*, March 2, 1959, 11; "Bailey Howell Selected as Most Valuable Player in SEC," *Natchez Democrat*, March 4, 1959, 9; "Bailey Howell Again Voted SEC's Most Valuable Player," *Vicksburg Evening Post*, March 2, 1959, 7; "Bailey Howell Heads 1959 SEC Cage Squad," *Enterprise-Journal*, March 4, 1959, 5; "Bailey Howell Named to All-American Basketball Team in Vote," *Commercial Dispatch*, March 3, 1959, 8; "For 4th Year Howell Voted Best in Circuit," *Laurel Leader-Call*, March 2, 1959, 9; "Howell and Cox Head All Stars in Southeastern," *Laurel Leader-Call*, March 4, 1959, 8; "Bailey Howell Is Named to 1959 AP All American Basketball Lineup," *Laurel Leader-Call*, March 6, 1959, 6; and "Howell Voted Most Valuable," *Greenwood Commonwealth*, March 2, 1959, 5.

73. "K-State Displaces 'Tucky in AP Poll," *Clarion-Ledger*, March 11, 1959, 13; and "Kentucky Wildcats End in First of National Poll," *Laurel Leader-Call*, March 3, 1959, 6.

74. Jimmie McDowell, interview with author, August 12, 2010. A similar sentiment on McDowell's work can be found in Eagles, *The Price of Defiance*, 106–109.

75. Jimmie McDowell, "Jimmie McDowell," *Jackson State Times*, February 11, 1959, 6B

76. Jimmie McDowell, "Hilbun Walks A Lonely Street," *Jackson State Times*, February 22, 1959, 2D.

77. Jimmie McDowell, "Jimmie McDowell," *Jackson State Times*, February 24, 1959, 4B.

78. Jimmie McDowell, "Jimmie McDowell," *Jackson State Times*, February 25, 1959, 4B.

79. Ibid.

80. Ibid.

81. Ibid.

82. Jimmie McDowell, interview with author, August 12, 2010.

83. Ibid.

84. Jimmie McDowell, "Jimmie McDowell," *Jackson State Times*, February 27, 1959, 4B.

85. Jimmie McDowell, "Hilbun Walks A Lonely Street," *Jackson State Times*, February 22, 1959, 2D.

86. Jimmie McDowell, "Jimmie McDowell," *Jackson State Times*, February 26, 1959, 12C.

87. Jimmie McDowell, "Jimmie McDowell," *Jackson State Times*, February 27, 1959, 4B.

88. Jimmie McDowell, "Jimmie McDowell," *Jackson State Times*, March 2, 1959, 4B.

89. Jimmie McDowell, interview with author, August 12, 2010.

90. Dick Lightsey, "Bunts, Boots and Bounces," *Daily Herald* (Biloxi), February 11, 1959, 10.

91. Dick Lightsey, "Bunts, Boots and Bounces," *Daily Herald* (Biloxi), February 20, 1959, 17; and Dick Lightsey, "Bunts, Boots and Bounces," *Daily Herald* (Biloxi), February 23, 1959, 14.

92. Dick Lightsey, "Bunts, Boots and Bounces," *Daily Herald* (Biloxi), March 2, 1959, 18.

93. Dick Lightsey, "Bunts, Boots and Bounces," *Daily Herald* (Biloxi), March 5, 1959, 26.

94. Billy Ray, "Press Box Views," *Vicksburg Evening Post*, February 12, 1959, 10.

95. Billy Ray, "Press Box Views," *Vicksburg Evening Post*, February 17, 1959, 6; and Billy Ray, "Press Box Views," *Vicksburg Evening Post*, February 19, 1959, 10.

96. Ibid; Billy Ray, "Press Box Views," *Vicksburg Evening Post*, February 25, 1959, 8; and Billy Ray, "Press Box Views," *Vicksburg Evening Post*, February 26, 1959, 14.

97. Billy Ray, "Press Box Views," *Vicksburg Evening Post*, February 26, 1959, 14; and Billy Ray, "Press Box Views," *Vicksburg Evening Post*, March 3, 1959, 8.

98. Ibid.

99. "The NCAA Tournament," *Delta Democrat-Times*, February 22, 1959, 4; and "Carter Favors NCAA," *Jackson State Times*, February 23, 1959, 4B.

100. "It's Up to Hilbun and You," *Delta Democrat-Times*, February 25, 1959, 4.

101. "Good Luck Bailey," *Delta Democrat-Times*, March 2, 1959, 4.

102. Weill, *In a Madhouse's Din*, 85, 111, and 222–223; and James Dickerson, *Dixie's Dirty Secret: The True Story of How the Government, the Media, and the Mob Conspired to Combat Integration and the Vietnam Antiwar Movement* (Armonk, NY: M. E. Sharpe, 1998), 23, 30. No threat to the Closed Society was safe under Ward's eagle-like watch. He attacked James Meredith's entry into Ole Miss, defended Barnett's fight to keep Meredith out of the university, claimed the 1964 Civil Rights Act was the work of Communists who would regret supporting such legislation, and wrote after the assassination of Martin Luther King Jr., "It's sickening that Dr. King went to Memphis to fan the flames of racial discord." (Weill, *In a Madhouse's Din*, 222–223). Even the tragic murder of Emmett Till was subject to the sensationalist attacks of Ward and the *Jackson Daily News*, when the editor claimed that Till's father, who was killed in Italy during World War II, was hanged by Italian authorities for murder and rape. Ward's insensitive, inaccurate, and horrific claim was an attempt to counter the outrage aimed at Mississippi and the white social structure for Till's murder.

103. David R. Davies, *The Press and Race: Mississippi Journalists Confront the Movement* (Jackson: University Press of Mississippi, 2001), 85–88. and Joseph B. Atkins and Stanley Aronowitz, *Covering for the Bosses: Labor and the Southern Press* (Jackson: University Press of Mississippi, 2008), 86–87. Davies and chapter coauthor Judy Smith cite 1967 comments from the *Columbia Journalism Review* that called Ward's *Jackson Daily News* "the worst metropolitan newspaper in the United States," as well as *Time* magazine's claim in 1961 that the *Daily News* published "unabashed prejudice." (Davies, *The Press and Race*, 85). Atkins and Aronowitz cited a 1966 speech from Claude Ramsey, president of the Mississippi AFL-CIO, who said, "The press in Mississippi has to be rated as the worst in the nation. This is especially true as far as the Hederman papers in Jackson are concerned. They have probably done more to retard this state than any other single institution." Ward had labeled Ramsey a communist in the past (Atkins and Aronowitz, *Covering for the Bosses*, 85–86).

104. Adam Nossiter, *Of Long Memory: Mississippi and the Murder of Medgar Evers* (Reading, MA: Addison-Wesley, 1994), 84. Perhaps one of the more egregious examples of Ward's editorial content in his column comes from the editor's work during the 1963 civil rights demonstrations in Jackson. Ward wrote, "Agitators who chant the 'freedom song' reminds us of the story about a chap who had just graduated, rushed out of the school shouting, 'I'm free, I'm free.' A little girl standing nearby said, 'So what? I'm four.'" Ward also wrote that comedian Dick Gregory, who was planning to make an appearance in Jackson during the demonstrations, would "parade up Capital Street barefooted. Throw him peanuts and he catches them between his toes."

105. Dr. Douglas Starr, interview with author, July 30, 2009.

106. Jimmy Ward, "Covering the Crossroads with Jimmy Ward," *Jackson Daily News*, February 25, 1959, 1.

107. Jimmy Ward, "Covering the Crossroads with Jimmy Ward," *Jackson Daily News*, February 24, 1959, 1.

108. Ibid.

109. Jimmy Ward, "Covering the Crossroads with Jimmy Ward," *Jackson Daily News*, February 26, 1959, 1.

110. "Damaging An Institution," *Jackson Daily News*, February 26, 1959, 8.

111. Carl Walters, "Shavin's," *Clarion-Ledger*, February 12, 1959, 32.

112. Ibid.

113. Carl Walters, "Shavin's," *Clarion-Ledger*, February 24, 1959, 15.

114. Carl Walters, "Shavin's," *Clarion-Ledger*, February 25, 1959, 22.

115. Carl Walters, "Shavin's," *Clarion-Ledger*, February 26, 1959, 4B; and Carl Walters, "Shavin's," *Clarion-Ledger*, February 27, 1959, 18.

116. Carl Walters, "Shavin's," *Jackson Daily News*, March 1, 1959, 9B; and Carl Walters, "Shavin's," *Clarion-Ledger*, March 2, 1959, 10.

117. Carl Walters, "Shavin's," *Clarion-Ledger*, March 16, 1959, 12.

118. *Orley B. Caudill. An Oral History with Mr. Carl Walters: Eminent Mississippi Sports Columnist*, Mississippi Oral History Program of the University of Southern Mississippi, April 14, 1984, 59–60.

119. Lee Baker, "Baker's Dozen," *Jackson Daily News*, February 13, 1959, 5; and Lee Baker, "Baker's Dozen," *Jackson Daily News*, February 20, 1959, 11.

120. Lee Baker, "Baker's Dozen," *Jackson Daily News*, February 24, 1959, 16; and Lee Baker, "Baker's Dozen," *Jackson Daily News*, February 25, 1959, 10.

121. Jimmie McDowell, interview with author, August 12, 2010.

122. Arnold Hederman, "Highlights in Sports," *Clarion-Ledger*, March 5, 1959, 30.

123. Weill, *In a Madhouse's Din*, 121. In anticipation of Freedom Summer, McCoy, a segregationist, wrote a column for the *Hattiesburg American* that called the Martin Luther King's Congress of Racial Equality, or CORE, "a militant, extremist organization with wild, often stupid, escapades."

124. Fitz McCoy, "Giving 'em Fitz," *Hattiesburg American*, February 12, 1959, 9A.

125. Fitz McCoy, "Giving 'em Fitz," *Hattiesburg American*, March 6, 1959, 8.

126. "Mix, North and South," *Hattiesburg American*, March 4, 1959, 22.

127. Ibid.

128. Tom Ethridge, "Mississippi Notebook," *Clarion-Ledger*, February 19, 1959, 3.

129. Charles M. Hills, "Affairs of State," *Clarion-Ledger*, March 4, 1959, 6.

130. "It's Our Bulldog Being Kicked," *Jackson Daily News*, February 26, 1959, 8.

131. Bob Howie, "Jump Ball!" *Jackson Daily News*, February 27, 1959, 4.

132. Weill, *In a Madhouse's Din*, 6, 54.

133. Davies, *The Press and Race*, 42; and Weill, *In a Madhouse's Din*, 83, 93, 111. The younger Skewes once called the Civil Rights Movement "the Negro Revolution" and wrote that the Civil Rights Act of 1964 was "another step towards mongrelization."

134. Billy Rainey, "Sunshine on Sports," *Meridian Star*, February 10, 1959, 9.

135. Billy Rainey, "Sunshine on Sports," *Meridian Star*, February 12, 1959, 9.

136. Billy Rainey, "Sunshine on Sports," *Meridian Star*, February 25, 1959, 11.

137. Laura Richardson Walton, "In Their Own Backyard: Local Press Coverage of the Chaney, Goodman, and Schwerner Murders," *American Journalism* 23, no. 3 (Summer 2006): 29–51. According to Walton, Rainey, intentionally or unintentionally, made the search seem almost pointless in his copy, and at other times went to great lengths to defend the community at large in an attempt to shield them from national criticism. Rainey also failed on numerous occasions to get comments from family members or civil rights workers who knew the three men giving his work a degree of balance. What was clear was that Rainey never believed that the missing civil rights workers were a part of an elaborate hoax.

138. Joe Mosby, email interview with author, July 23, 2009.

139. "Children in Students Clothing," *Commercial Dispatch*, February 23, 1959, 4.

140. Ibid.

141. Charles B. Gordon, "Sports Journal," *Enterprise-Journal*, February 23, 1959, 3.

142. "Consistent?" *Laurel Leader-Call*, February 21, 1959, 4.

143. Ibid.

144. "Putting the OK on Tibbeha," *Starkville News*, March 6, 1959, 1.

145. Joe Mosby, email interview with author, July 23, 2009.

146. Jimmie McDowell, "Jimmie McDowell," *Jackson State Times*, February 13, 1959, 4B.

147. "Letters from Readers," *Jackson State Times*, February 24, 1959, 6A.

148. "Letters from Readers," *Jackson State Times*, February 20, 1959, 4A.

149. "A&M Frosh Urges Ben to OK NCAA Trip," *Jackson State Times*, February 27, 1959, 6B.

150. "Citizens' Council Officer in Favor," *Jackson State Times*, February 27, 1959, 6B.

151. "State Grad in Favor of Tourney," *Jackson State Times*, February 27, 1959, 6B; and "Local State Ex Urges Tournament Play by Maroons," *Delta Democrat-Times*, February 26, 1959, 2.

152. Shirley Kempinska, "Examine Those Required Subjects," *Jackson Daily News*, February 26, 1959, 8.

153. Byron De La Beckwith, "Spare the Rod, Spoil the Student," *Jackson Daily News*, February 26, 1959, 8.

154. For more on Beckworth and the Evers murder, see Nossiter, *Of Long Memory*.

155. L. B. Goodwin, "State Policies Gain Support," *Jackson Daily News*, February 26, 1959, 8.

156. Marlyn Sandifer, Herman Cooper Jr., and Bill Hodnett, "'Stay Home' Says State Students," *Jackson Daily News*, February 28, 1959, 6.

157. W. M. Drake, "Segregation Stand Was Convincing," *Jackson Daily News*, February 28, 1959, 6.

158. Ella Perry, "Voice of the People," *Clarion-Ledger*, March 4, 1959, 6.

159. Ibid.

160. A. S. Coody, "Voice of the People," *Clarion-Ledger*, March 4, 1959, 6.

161. A.M. Shirley, "The People Speak," *Meridian Star*, February 20, 1959, 4.

162. Neil R. McMillen, *The Citizens' Council: Organized Resistance to the Second Reconstruction, 1954–64* (Urbana: University of Illinois Press, 1971), 15–17; and David Oshinsky, *Worse than Slavery: Parchman Farm and the Ordeal of Jim Crow Justice* (New York: Free Press, 1996), 1.

163. Dittmer, *Local People*, 79–83.

164. Jerry Mitchell, "The Clyde Kennard Story," *Clarion-Ledger*, December 31, 2005, 1.

Chapter 3. "The Less Said, the Better"

1. John Garcia, "Babe Is Coach of the Year," *Jackson State Times*, March 3, 1961, 3B; "McCarthy Again 'Coach of Year,'" *Jackson Daily News*, March 3, 1961, 10; and John Garcia, "Babe McCarthy SEC Coach of the Year," *Clarion-Ledger*, March 3, 1961, 16.

2. Peter Wallenstien, *Higher Education and the Civil Rights Movement: White Supremacy, Black Southerners, and College Campuses* (Gainesville: University Press of Florida, 2008), 123; and Ted Owsby, *The Civil Rights Movement in Mississippi* (Jackson: University Press of Mississippi, 2013), 106–107.

3. Wallenstien, *Higher Education and the Civil Rights Movement*, 125.

4. Ibid.

5. M.J. O'Brien, *We Shall Not Be Moved: The Jackson Woolworth Sit-In and the Movement It Inspired* (Jackson: University Press of Mississippi, 2013), 26.

6. Raymond Arsenault, *Freedom Riders: 1961 and the Struggle for Racial Justice* (New York: Oxford University Press, 2006), 2–3; and O'Brien, *We Shall Not Be Moved*, 22.

7. O'Brien, *We Shall Not Be Moved*, 22

8. Ibid.

9. "Trip of Decision Awaiting Gators," *Jackson Daily News*, February 2, 1961, 10; "Miss. State Could Wrap Up SEC, Florida on Road," *Commercial Dispatch*, February 2, 1961, 2B; "Maroons to Host LSU Tigers on Saturday," *Starkville Daily News*, February 1, 1961, 2; "Tigers Invade MSU on Saturday Night," *Starkville Daily News*, February 3, 1961, 2; and "State Faces Rugged LSU Tigers Saturday," *Jackson State Times*, February 2, 1961, 4C.

10. "State Can Clinch SEC Title at Home," *Meridian Star*, February 4, 1961, 5; "Maroons to Open Final Home Stand," *Clarion-Ledger*, February 2, 1961, 29; "Maroons Open Crucial Home Stand against LSU Tonight," *Clarion-Ledger*, February 4, 1961, 5; "Maroons Hope to Regain SEC Cage Lead Saturday by Beating LSU Tigers," *Daily Herald* (Biloxi), February 2, 1961, 22; "It's a 'Must Win' for State over LSU Tigers Saturday," *Vicksburg Evening Post*, February 2, 1961, 17; Vernon Butler, "Mississippi State and Florida in Key SEC Battles Tonight," *Vicksburg Evening Post*, February 4, 1961, 6; Vernon Butler, "Maroons, Gators Tie for First in SEC Conference," *Greenwood Commonwealth*, February 4, 1961, 8; "Tigers Invade MSU on Saturday Night," *Starkville Daily News*, February 3, 1961, 2; Vernon Butler, "MSU Aims at Tigers 4-Game Win Streak," *Starkville Daily News*, February 4, 1961, 2; "Tigers, MSU Battle It Out Here Tonight," *Starkville Daily News*, February 4, 1961, 2; "Maroons and Rebs Await Louisianans," *Jackson State Times*, February 3, 1961, 4B; and David M. Moffit, "SEC Lead at Stake Tonight," *Jackson State Times*, February 4, 1961, 4A.

11. Lee Baker, "Maroons All Alone Atop SEC; They Win and Gators Don't," *Jackson Daily News* and *Clarion-Ledger*, February 5, 1961, 1B; George Anderson, "Maroons Take SEC Lead, Rebels Lose," *Jackson State Times*, February 5, 1961, 1D; "State Moves Back into Lead in SEC," *Meridian Star*, February 5, 1961, 1; "State Is All Alone in First Place," *Meridian Star*, February 5, 1961, 8; "Maroons Are Out Front in SEC Basketball Race," *Meridian Star*, February 6, 1961, 11; Bobby Lollar, "Maroons Move Step Closer to Conference Title, Rap LSU Tigers 77–61," *Commercial Dispatch*, February 5, 1961, 8; and "Steamed-Up Maroons Cool Tigers," *Vicksburg Evening Post*, February 5, 1961, 13.

12. Lee Baker, "Maroons All Alone Atop SEC; They Win and Gators Don't," *Jackson Daily News* and *Clarion-Ledger*, February 5, 1961.

13. "Maroons Riding High in SEC Cage Chase," *Jackson State Times*, February 6, 1961, 10.

14. Van Savell, "Ole Miss vs. Kentucky State's Top Attraction," *Clarion-Ledger*, February 6, 1961, 11; Bobby Lollar, "Maroons to Face Tulane in Crucial SEC Battle," *Commercial Dispatch*, February 5, 1961, 6; Ross M. Hagen, "Maroons All Alone Atop SEC Standings," *Daily Herald* (Biloxi), February 6, 1961, 18; Ross M. Hagen, "State Meets Tulane Tonight in Big One," *Vicksburg Evening Post*, February 6, 1961, 5; and Ross M. Hagen, "Maroons Rule Conference Lead; Meet Tulane Greenies Tonight," *Greenwood Commonwealth*, February 6, 1961, 5.

15. "Maroons Move Away in Conference Basketball Race," *Starkville Daily News*, February 7, 1961, 2.

16. Robert Fulton, "State Wins Again; Vols Top Florida," *Clarion-Ledger*, February 7, 1961, 11; "State Stretches SEC Lead; Rebels Bow to LSU Tigers," *Meridian Star*, February 7, 1961, 10; Vernon Butler, "Mississippi State Widens Lead in SEC Cage Warfare," *Daily Herald* (Biloxi), February 7, 1961, 14; Vernon Butler, "State Presents McCarthy 100th Victory," *Vicksburg Evening Post*, February 7, 1961, 8; Vernon Butler, "Maroons Hand Coach McCarthy 100th Win; Heads for SEC Title," *Greenwood Commonwealth*, February 7, 1961, 5; and "2nd Division SEC Clubs Battle Tonight," *Jackson State Times*, February 7, 1961, 4B; and Lee Baker, "Maroons Power by Green Wave," *Jackson Daily News*, February 7, 1961, 7, 8.

17. The Daily News Sports Staff, "Time Out for Sports," *Starkville Daily News*, February 8, 1961, 2.

18. "Maroons Seek 10th Straight Win on Home Court Saturday Night," *Meridian Star*, February 8, 1961, 10; "Maroons Reach Crucial Stage," *Jackson Daily News*, February 8, 1961, 10; "Nine-Game Win Streak to Be Placed on Line When Maroons Meet Tennessee," *Daily Herald* (Biloxi), February 9, 1961, 18; "Maroons Close Season at Home," *Commercial Dispatch*, February 9, 1961, 10; "Vols, Wildcats Will Close Out MSU Stand," *Starkville Daily News*, February 8, 1961, 2; and "Maroons Wait on the Vols," *Jackson State Times*, February 9, 1961, 9A.

19. David M. Moffit, "State Cagers End Home Play with Tennessee and Kentucky," *Meridian Star*, February 9, 1961, 7; and David M. Moffit, "Maroons Seek Eighth Straight Win in SEC Play," *Meridian Star*, February 11, 1961, 6.

20. Ibid.

21. Vernon Butler, "Kentucky-Rebs in Jackson; Vols at State," *Vicksburg Evening Post*, February 11, 1961, 3; and Vernon Butler, "Vandy, Florida Take to Road over Weekend," *Starkville Daily News*, February 11, 1961, 2.

22. Don Weiss, "College Basketball Moves into Showdown Week," *Hattiesburg American*, February 13, 1961, 8A.

23. Billy Rainey, "State Maroons Win," *Meridian Star*, February 12, 1961, 8; "State Stops Tennessee 72–67 Maintaining SEC Lead Pace," *Vicksburg Evening Post*, February 12, 1961, 10; and George Anderson, "Rebs Bow to 'Cats; Maroons Top Vols," *Jackson State Times*, February 12, 1961, 1D.

24. Robert Fulton, "Maroons and Kentucky Collide at State Tonight," *Clarion-Ledger*, February 13, 1961, 11.

25. Scotty Hargrove, "MSU Nearing Second SEC Basketball Title," *Starkville Daily News*, February 13, 1961, 2.

26. Bobby Lollar, "Babe vs. Baron Tonight as Maroons Host 'Cats," *Commercial Dispatch*, February 13, 1961, 3.

27. Ross M. Hagen, "State, Kentucky Collide Tonight in Key SEC Cage Contest at State College," *Daily Herald* (Biloxi), February 13, 1961, 15; "'Tucky Gunning for State Tonight," *Jackson Daily News*, February 13, 1961, 10; "State-Kentucky Game Tonight at Starkville Is Tops in SEC," *Delta Democrat-Times*, February 13, 1961, 7; Ross M. Hagen, "Maroons Rule Conference Roost; to Meet Kentucky Wildcats Next," *Greenwood Commonwealth*, February 13, 1961, 5; Ross M. Hagen, "Maroons and Kentucky in SEC spotlight tonight," *Hattiesburg American*, February 13, 1961, 8A; and "Rupp Seeks to Avoid Being Ninth Victim," *Starkville Daily News*, February 13, 1961, 2.

28. Vernon Butler, "'Tucky Wins but State Loses No Ground," *Vicksburg Evening Post*, February 14, 1961, 8; Vernon Butler, "Kentucky Wildcats Beat Maroons; Leaves Conference in Tight

Race," *Greenwood Commonwealth*, February 14, 1961, 7; and Vernon Butler, "Wildcats Hand MSU First Defeat, 68–62," *Hattiesburg American*, February 14, 1961, 11.

29. Hugh Fullerton Jr., "Mississippi State, Kansas State Bow, But Buckeyes Continue Winning Ways," *Daily Herald* (Biloxi), February 14, 1961, 15; Bobby Lollar, "Maroons Bow to Kentucky: District Tourneys Start Wednesday," *Commercial Dispatch*, February 14, 1961, 3; and Scotty Hargrove, "Kentucky Colonels Defeat High Flying Maroons," *Starkville Daily News*, February 14, 1961, 5.

30. "Vandy, LSU, Florida Tied for 2nd in Hot SEC Roundball Race," *Jackson State Times*, February 14, 1961, 5B; and "Maroons Hold Tight Grip on First Despite Defeat," *Meridian Star*, February 14, 1961, 7.

31. Jack Wardlaw, "Wildcat Defense Too Much for MSU Sophs; State Holds Loop Lead," *Meridian Star*, February 14, 1961, 7.

32. "SEC Chase Gets Wilder," *Jackson Daily News*, February 14, 1961, 10; "Wildcats Take First Half Lead to Get Win," *Delta Democrat-Times*, February 14, 1961, 5; "Maroon Touring Starts Saturday," *Jackson Daily News*, February 16, 1961, 12, 13; "SEC's Top Miss. State Begins Long Run," *Delta Democrat-Times*, February 16, 1961, 6; and "No. 2 Team in SEC Gets the NCAA Bid," *Starkville Daily News*, February 17, 1961, 2.

33. "Babe McCarthy Rewarded; MSU Signs Donahue," *Meridian Star*, February 16, 1961, 1; "Babe McCarthy Is Given New Four-Year Contract," *Meridian Star*, February 17, 1961, 8; "Board Boosts Babe's Pact 2 More Years," *Jackson Daily News*, February 16, 1961, 13; "Babe McCarthy Given Two-Year Extension," *Clarion-Ledger*, February 17, 1961, 17; and "McCarthy Gets New Contract," *Starkville Daily News*, February 18, 1961, 2.

34. Jimmie McDowell, "New Contract for McCarthy," *Jackson State Times*, February 16, 1961, 1C.

35. Ibid.

36. David M. Moffit, "State Invades Florida to Play SEC Feature," *Clarion-Ledger*, February 18, 1961, 8; David M. Moffit, "Maroons Set for Crucial Road Jaunt," *Jackson State Times*, February 16, 1961, 5C; and "Maroons Out to Break Gators' Home Win Streak," *Meridian Star*, February 18, 1961, 6.

37. David M. Moffit, "Kentucky Moves Back into NCAA Spotlight," *Jackson State Times*, February 20, 1961, 4B; David M. Moffit, "Strange Bounces Around SEC, Kentucky Contender," *Commercial Dispatch*, February 20, 1961, 3; "Kentucky in the running for NCAA berth," *Meridian Star*, February 20, 1961, 10; David M. Moffit, "Maroons Considered Cinch to Win Crown," *Jackson State Times*, February 27, 1961, 3B; and David M. Moffit, "Maroons Can Win SEC Title Tonight," *Meridian Star*, February 27, 1961, 8.

38. "State Moves Out on Road," *Jackson Daily News*, February 17, 1961, 8; "MSU in Crucial Games with Georgia, Florida," *Delta Democrat-Times*, February 17, 1961, 7; "State Five Hits Road for Crucial SEC Tilts," *Clarion-Ledger*, February 17, 1961, 20; "State Begins Long Season Trip to Wind Up Season," *Daily Herald* (Biloxi), February 18, 1961, 11; "Road Running Maroons Tangle with Tough Gators," *Commercial Dispatch*, February 17, 1961, 6; "Maroons Are Set to Travel," *Jackson State Times*, February 15, 1961, 1C; and "Maroons Face Florida, Georgia in Cage Tilts," *Starkville Daily News*, February 16, 1961, 2.

39. Vernon Butler, "Mississippi State Faces Florida Five in Key SEC Contest," *Daily Herald* (Biloxi), February 18, 1961, 11; Vernon Butler, "SEC Spotlight Tonight on Miss. State-Gator

Contest," *Vicksburg Evening Post*, February 18, 1961, 3; "Uneasy Maroons Invading Gators," *Jackson Daily News*, February 18, 1961, 2; and Vernon Butler, "Uneasy Maroons Play Florida Tonight," *Hattiesburg American*, February 18, 1961, 11.

40. Vernon Butler, "Kentucky Making Big Comeback Bid," *Hattiesburg American*, February 22, 1961, 4B; "Kentucky Eyes NCAA Berth," *Jackson Daily News*, February 22, 1961, 9; "Rupp's Cats Stay in NCAA Contention," *Vicksburg Evening Post*, February 22, 1961, 10; Vernon Butler, "LSU Could Narrow Maroons' SEC Lead with Win Tonight," *Daily Herald* (Biloxi), February 25, 1961, 12; Vernon Butler, "Cold, Cold Road for State and Florida Tonight as Kentucky, Vandy Eye NCAA," *Vicksburg Evening Post*, February 25, 1961, 3; and Vernon Butler, "Top Maroons to Meet LSU," *Greenwood Commonwealth*, February 25, 1961, 8.

41. Ross M. Hagen, "Florida Dumps State in Key SEC Contest; Shakes Up Standings," *Daily Herald* (Biloxi), February 19, 1961, 14; "Mississippi State Takes Second Defeat of Southeastern Season 59–57," *Commercial Dispatch*, February 19, 1961, 8; "Gators Edge State 59–57," *Vicksburg Sunday Post*, February 19, 1961, 12; Ross M. Hagen, "SEC Title Up for Grabs as State Falters," *Vicksburg Evening Post*, February 20, 1961, 6; Ross M. Hagen, "Maroons Lose Second in Row; Race On for Number One Spot," *Greenwood Commonwealth*, February 20, 1961, 5; and Ross M. Hagen, "Maroons Falter against Florida," *Hattiesburg American*, February 20, 1961, 5B.

42. Vernon Butler, "Florida Gators Still Alive in SEC by Topping Maroons," *Clarion-Ledger*, February 20, 1961, 11; "SEC Cage Battle Growing Hotter," *Jackson Daily News*, February 20, 1961, 10; "SEC Race Goes Down to Wire," *Delta Democrat-Times*, February 20, 1961, 8; Vernon Butler, "Maroons protect one-game edge," *Hattiesburg American*, February 21, 1961, 11; and Vernon Butler, "Reports of Gators' Death in SEC Wrong," *Starkville Daily News*, February 20, 1961, 2.

43. Bob Howie, "Athens Cliff Hanger," *Jackson Daily News*, February 20, 1961, 10.

44. Scott Hargrove, "State Maroons Seeking Victory over Georgia," *Clarion-Ledger*, February 20, 1961, 12.

45. Scotty Hargrove, "Maroons Keep Lead in SEC with Victory," *Starkville Daily News*, February 21, 1961, 2; "Maroons Defeat Georgia; Florida Edges Ole Miss," *Meridian Star*, February 21, 1961, 16; Lee Baker, "Maroons March through Georgia," *Jackson Daily News*, February 21, 1961, 9; "Maroons Stay Ahead as Graves Scores 34," *Delta Democrat-Times*, February 21, 1961, 5; Scott Hargrove, "Maroons Run Again; Rout Georgia 'Dogs," *Clarion-Ledger*, February 21, 1961, 32; Vernon Butler, "Florida Bumps Ole Miss in Overtime, Stays Second," *Daily Herald* (Biloxi), February 21, 1961, 18; "Maroons Defeat Bulldogs, Florida Eases by Rebels," *Commercial Dispatch*, February 21, 1961, 7; Vernon Butler, "State Keeps SEC Lead, Trounce Georgia," *Vicksburg Evening Post*, February 21, 1961, 8; Vernon Butler, "Florida Gators Take Top Spot in Conference," *Greenwood Commonwealth*, February 21, 1961, 5; Hugh Fullerton Jr., "Jerry Graves Scores 34 points to Lead Maroons over Bulldogs," *Greenwood Commonwealth*, February 21, 1961, 5; and "Graves Leads State; Florida Edges Rebs," *Jackson State Times*, February 21, 1961, 5B.

46. United Press International, "Kentucky Wildcats," *Meridian Star*, February 22, 1961, 16.

47. Ross M. Hagen, "'Tucky Stands Better Than Even Chance to Represent SEC in Big NCAA Tourney," *Vicksburg Evening Post*, February 23, 1961, 15; Ross M. Hagen, "Kentucky Cats Moves Toward Tourney Play," *Greenwood Commonwealth*, February 23, 1961, 5; and "Kentucky May Be SEC's Team in NCAA," *Delta Democrat-Times*, February 23, 1961, 5.

48. Martin Lader, "Baron May Have Last Laugh Yet," *Jackson State Times*, February 22, 1961, 4B.

49. "Maroons Go into Bayous," *Jackson Daily News*, February 23, 1961, 10; "State Five Plays Pair of Key SEC Road Tilts," *Clarion-Ledger*, February 24, 1961, 14; "State Maroons Need Two More Cage Wins to Claim SEC Title," *Daily Herald* (Biloxi), February 24, 1961, 19; "Maroons Embark on Trip to Determine Loop Play," February 24, 1961, 6; "State Begins Crucial Two Game Trip into Louisiana," *Vicksburg Evening Post*, February 24, 1961, 9; "State Cagers Ready for Louisiana Trip," *Jackson State Times*, February 23, 1961, 3D; and "MSU Needs Two Wins to Clinch SEC Title," *Starkville Daily News*, February 23, 1961, 2.

50. Robert Fulton, "Mitchell's Jump Shot Knocks Off LSU, 56–54," *Jackson Daily News* and *Clarion-Ledger*, February 26, 1961; "Maroons Rally, Edge LSU, 56–54," *Meridian Star*, February 26, 1961, 8; "Lee High Finishes Basketball Play; Maroons Defeat Tigers 56–54," *Commercial Dispatch*, February 26, 1961, 8; "Maroons Nip Tigers 56–54," *Vicksburg Evening Post*, February 26, 1961, 11; "Vandy Tames Gators to Tie for Second Place," *Meridian Star*, February 26, 1961, 8; and "State Nips LSU; Wave Tops OM," *Jackson State Times*, February 26, 1961, 1D.

51. Hugh Schutte, "State Downs LSU, Clinches at Least a Tie for SEC Cage Crown; Faces Green Wave," *Daily Herald* (Biloxi), February 27, 1961, 19; Hugh Schutte, "Maroons Out to Wrap-Up SEC Title Tonight," *Vicksburg Evening Post*, February 27, 1961, 6; Hugh Schutte, "Three-Way Playoff Expected Now for Spot in Basketball Tourney," *Greenwood Commonwealth*, February 27, 1961, 5; and Hugh Schutte, "Maroons Cinch Tie for Championship," *Hattiesburg American*, February 27, 1961, 4B.

52. Vernon Butler, "Mississippi State Grabs Share of SEC Title Saturday," *Starkville Daily News*, February 27, 1961, 2.

53. Ibid.

54. "Vandy Tames Gators to Tie for Second Place," *Meridian Star*, February 26, 1961, 8.

55. Robert Fulton, "Mitchell's Jump Shot Knocks Off LSU, 56–54," *Jackson Daily News* and *Clarion-Ledger*, February 26, 1961, 1B.

56. Robert Fulton, "State Defeats Tulane 62–57 to Clinch SEC Cage Crown," *Clarion-Ledger*, February 28, 1961, 11.

57. "Governor Wires Congratulations to Maroon Five," *Clarion-Ledger*, February 28, 1961, 11.

58. "State Nips Tulane 62–57 For SEC Title," *Jackson State Times*, February 28, 1961, 1C.

59. "Maroons Are SEC Champions," *Meridian Star*, February 28, 1961, 9; "Mississippi State Wins Southeastern Crown by Edging Tulane 62–57," *Commercial Dispatch*, February 28, 1961, 7; and "Battle for Second Gets SEC Spotlight," *Jackson State Times*, February 28, 1961, 5C.

60. Phil Wallace, "All's Gold, Glory on Maroons Now," *Jackson Daily News*, February 28, 1961, 9; and Phil Wallace, "Babe Call Team Real Champions," *Jackson Daily News*, February 28, 1961, 9.

61. "Mississippi State Grabs SEC Championship in 62–57 Win," *Starkville Daily News*, February 28, 1961, 2.

62. "Florida Falters in Bid for 2nd Spot," *Jackson Daily News*, February 28, 1961, 10; Vernon Butler, "Mississippi State Maroons Wrap Up SEC Cage Crown," *Daily Herald* (Biloxi), February 28, 1961, 14; Vernon Butler, "Gallant 2nd Half Effort Gives Maroons Title," *Vicksburg Evening Post*, February 28, 1961, 9; Vernon Butler, "Maroons Take Tulane to Win Conference Title; Florida Loses," *Greenwood Commonwealth*, February 28, 1961, 5; and Vernon Butler, "Miss. State Wins SEC championship," *Hattiesburg American*, February 28, 1961, 13.

63. Gary Kale, "Kentucky May Get Chance at NCAA," *Jackson State Times*, February 28, 1961, 4C; and "'Tucky Could Sneak in NCAA," *Commercial Dispatch*, February 28, 1961, 7.

64. Tim Moriarty, "SEC Champs Not on UPI's Top 27 Teams," *Jackson State Times*, February 28, 1961, 5C. In the article, the top twenty teams in the nation are listed per the coaches' votes followed by schools that received votes from the coaches but not enough to merit a place in the top twenty. Seven schools were listed as receiving votes, hence the top twenty-seven teams.

65. Berry Reese, "Barnett Says He 'Will Oppose' NCAA Play," *Clarion-Ledger*, March 1, 1961, 17; "No NCAA meet for State," *Meridian Star*, March 1, 1961, 14; "Ross Opposes NCAA Playoff Spot for State," *Jackson Daily News*, March 1, 1961, 10; and "Barnett Opposes State's NCAA Cage Participation," *Commercial Dispatch*, March 1, 1961, 7.

66. Berry Reese, "Barnett Says He 'Will Oppose' NCAA Play," *Clarion-Ledger*, March 1, 1961, 17.

67. Ibid.

68. G. J. Pope, "State Student Begs Ross to Let Team Prove Itself," *Jackson State Times*, March 1, 1961, 1A.

69. Scott Hargrove, "SEC Champs Welcomed by Huge Throng," *Jackson Daily News*, March 1, 1961, 11; "Starkville, University Turn Out to Welcome Maroons," *Starkville Daily News*, March 1, 1961, 1, 3; and "SEC Champion Maroons Receive Big Welcomes on Arrival in Mississippi," *Clarion-Ledger*, March 1, 1961, 17.

70. "Win over Maroons Would Add Luster," *Jackson State Times*, March 1, 1961, 4B; "Ole Miss Hosts State Saturday," *Meridian Star*, March 2, 1961, 8; and "Rebels Will Be Gunning for Maroon Scalp Saturday," *Daily Herald* (Biloxi), March 2, 1961, 20.

71. "Maroons Closing Out in Rebeltown," and "Reb Season Nearing End," *Jackson Daily News*, March 3, 1961, 9.

72. "State-Rebels Close Season Tonite," *Clarion-Ledger*, March 4, 1961, 9; "Maroons, Rebs Wind Up Season Saturday," *Jackson State Times*, March 3, 1961, 3B; "Ole Miss, State to Close Out Season," *Daily Herald* (Biloxi), March 4, 1961, 12; "Maroons Close Out Year Saturday with Ole Miss," *Commercial Dispatch*, March 3, 1961, 6; "SEC Champs Hurt in Rebel Game Tonight" *Starkville Daily News*, March 4, 1961, 2; and "Maroons Close Year with Ole Miss Game," *Starkville Daily News*, March 2, 1961, 3.

73. "SEC Cage Season Climaxes Tonite," *Vicksburg Evening Post*, March 4, 1961, 3; "Who Will Get Tourney Berth Still in Doubt," *Greenwood Commonwealth*, March 4, 1961, 8; and "Situation in SEC Odd," *Starkville Daily News*, March 4, 1961, 2.

74. John Garcia, "Babe Is Coach of the Year," *Jackson State Times*, March 3, 1961, 3B; "McCarthy Again 'Coach of Year,'" *Jackson Daily News*, March 3, 1961, 10; and John Garcia, "Babe McCarthy SEC Coach of the Year," *Clarion-Ledger*, March 3, 1961, 16.

75. John Garcia, "Babe Is Coach of the Year," *Jackson State Times*, March 3, 1961, 3B.

76. "State Falls to Lowly Rebs 74–70," *Vicksburg Evening Post*, March 5, 1961, 15.

77. Lee Baker, "Rebs Halt Late Rally to Edge State 74–70," *Jackson Daily News* and *Clarion-Ledger*, March 5, 1961, 1B.

78. Tom Donovan, "Rebs Edge by State, 74–70," *Jackson State Times*, March 5, 1961, 1; and "Maroons End Year in Loss," *Starkville Daily News*, March 6, 1961, 2.

79. "Playoff in SEC for NCAA Berth," *Jackson Daily News*, March 6, 1961, 1B; "State Is SEC Champion; but Big Tilt Remains," *Clarion-Ledger*, March 6, 1963, 1D; "Ole Miss Knocks Off State in Cage Finale Saturday," *Daily Herald* (Biloxi), March 6, 1961, 18; "Rebels Hand Southeastern Conference Champions 74–70 Licking," *Commercial Dispatch*, March 5, 1961, 8; "SEC Play over Except for Vandy, Tucky," *Vicksburg Evening Post*, March 6, 1961, 6; "Kentucky Meets

Vanderbilt in SEC Playoff," *Greenwood Commonwealth*, March 6, 1961, 5; and "Vandy meets 'Cats in playoff game," *Hattiesburg American*, March 6, 1961, 4B.

80. John Garcia, "Maroons Could Replace 'Tucky as League Power," *Commercial Dispatch*, March 7, 1961, 8.

81. "Kentucky Earns Right to Play in NCAA Battle," *Commercial Dispatch*, March 10, 1961, 8; "'Tucky Will Represent State in NCAA," *Vicksburg Evening Post*, March 10, 1961, 8; and "Kentucky Will Challenge Ohio State in NCAA Go," *Hattiesburg American*, March 10, 1961, 10.

82. Mississippi Department of History and Archives, Mississippi State Sovereignty Commission files, SCR ID # 9-11-1-86-1-1-1, http://mdah.state.ms.us/arrec/digital_archives/sovcom (accessed on February 10, 2011).

83. Weill, *In a Madhouse's Din*, 36. All of the referenced editors and journalists were still with the listed newspapers in 1961. Leonard Lowery would replace Harmon in 1962.

84. Jimmie McDowell, "Jimmie McDowell," *Jackson State Times*, February 3, 1961, 3B; and Jimmie McDowell, "Jimmie McDowell," *Jackson State Times*, February 6, 1961, 10.

85. Jimmie McDowell, "Jimmie McDowell," *Jackson State Times*, February 9, 1961, 9A.

86. Jimmie McDowell, "Jimmie McDowell," *Jackson State Times*, February 13, 1961, 4B.

87. Jimmie McDowell, interview with author, August 12, 2010.

88. Billy Ray, "Press Box Views," *Vicksburg Evening Post*, March 14, 1962, 12; and "McDowell and Cristil Receive Top State Awards," *Vicksburg Evening Post*, March 14, 1962, 12.

89. Kurt Kemper, *College Football and American Culture in the Cold War Era* (Chicago: University of Illinois Press, 2009), 89.

90. Dick Lightsey, "Bunts, Boots and Bounces," *Daily Herald* (Biloxi), February 1, 1961, 18; Dick Lightsey, "Bunts, Boots and Bounces," *Daily Herald* (Biloxi), February 2, 1961, 22; Dick Lightsey, "Bunts, Boots and Bounces," *Daily Herald* (Biloxi), February 6, 1961, 14; and Dick Lightsey, "Bunts, Boots and Bounces," *Daily Herald* (Biloxi), February 10, 1961, 18.

91. Dick Lightsey, "Bunts, Boots and Bounces," *Daily Herald* (Biloxi), February 11, 1961, 12; and Dick Lightsey, "Bunts, Boots and Bounces," *Daily Herald* (Biloxi), February 13, 1961, 14.

92. Dick Lightsey, "Bunts, Boots and Bounces," *Daily Herald* (Biloxi), February 15, 1961, 22; and Dick Lightsey, "Bunts, Boots and Bounces," *Daily Herald* (Biloxi), February 22, 1961, 18.

93. Dick Lightsey, "Bunts, Boots and Bounces," *Daily Herald* (Biloxi), February 22, 1961, 18.

94. Dick Lightsey, "Bunts, Boots and Bounces," *Daily Herald* (Biloxi), February 17, 1961, 14.

95. Dick Lightsey, "Bunts, Boots and Bounces," *Daily Herald* (Biloxi), March 1, 1961, 22.

96. Billy Ray, "Press Box Views," *Vicksburg Evening Post*, February 8, 1961, 8; Billy Ray, "Press Box Views," *Vicksburg Evening Post*, February 9, 1961, 16; Billy Ray, "Press Box Views," *Vicksburg Evening Post*, February 16, 1961, 14; Billy Ray, "Press Box Views," *Vicksburg Evening Post*, February 21, 1961, 8; Billy Ray, "Press Box Views," *Vicksburg Evening Post*, February 22, 1961, 10; and Billy Ray, "Press Box Views," *Vicksburg Evening Post*, March 5, 1961, 6.

97. Billy Ray, "Press Box Views," *Vicksburg Evening Post*, March 7, 1961, 12.

98. Billy Rainey, "Sunshine on Sports," *Meridian Star*, February 3, 1961, 9; and Billy Rainey, "Sunshine on Sports," *Meridian Star*, February 6, 1961, 10.

99. Charles Kerg, "Kerg's Korner," *Delta Democrat-Times*, February 26, 1961, 7.

100. Herb Phillips, "'N in This Cornah!" *Commercial Dispatch*, February 16, 1961, 4.

101. Carl Walters, "Shavin's," *Jackson Daily News* and *Clarion-Ledger*, February 5, 1961, 3B; Carl Walters, "Shavin's," *Clarion-Ledger*, February 8, 1961, 15; Carl Walters, "Shavin's,"

Clarion-Ledger, February 19, 1961, 3B; Carl Walters, "Shavin's," *Clarion-Ledger*, February 20, 1961, 13; Carl Walters, "Shavin's," *Clarion-Ledger*, February 22, 1961, 24.

102. Carl Walters, "Shavin's," *Jackson Daily News* and *Clarion-Ledger*, February 12, 1961.

103. Ibid.

104. Ibid.

105. Carl Walters, "Shavin's," *Clarion-Ledger*, February 23, 1961, 38; and Carl Walters, "Shavin's," *Clarion-Ledger*, March 1, 1961, 18.

106. Carl Walters, "Shavin's," *Clarion-Ledger*, February 24, 1961, 14.

107. In 1961, soon after the state of Mississippi granted Mississippi State university status, the school officially changed its school mascot and nickname from the Maroons to the Bulldogs. For a number of years, the press would refer to the teams at MSU as both the Maroons and the Bulldogs. http://www.mstateathletics.com/ViewArticle.dbml?DB_OEM_ID=16800&ATCLID=926236 (accessed on February 10, 2011).

108. Carl Walters, "Shavin's," *Clarion-Ledger*, March 1, 1961, 18.

109. Lee Baker, "Baker's Dozen," *Clarion-Ledger*, February 5, 1961, 4B; Lee Baker, "Baker's Dozen," *Jackson Daily News*, February 7, 1961, 7; Lee Baker, "Baker's Dozen," *Jackson Daily News*, February 14, 1961, 9; Lee Baker, "Baker's Dozen," *Jackson Daily News*, February 15, 1961, 11; Lee Baker, "Florida Edges State, 59–57," *Jackson Daily News* and *Clarion-Ledger*, February 19, 1961; Lee Baker, "Baker's Dozen," *Jackson Daily News*, February 20, 1961, 10; Lee Baker, "Baker's Dozen," *Jackson Daily News*, February 22, 1961, 9; Lee Baker, "Baker's Dozen," *Jackson Daily News*, February 27, 1961, 9.

110. Lee Baker, "Baker's Dozen," *Jackson Daily News*, February 28, 1961, 9.

111. Ibid.

112. Arnold Hederman, "Highlights in Sports," *Clarion-Ledger*, February 7, 1961, 14; Arnold Hederman, "Highlights in Sports," *Jackson Daily News*, February 12, 1961, 5B; and Arnold Hederman, "Highlights in Sports," *Clarion-Ledger*, February 24, 1961, 17.

113. Arnold Hederman, "Highlights in Sports," *Clarion-Ledger*, February 22, 1961, 18.

114. Arnold Hederman, "Highlights in Sports," *Clarion-Ledger*, March 1, 1961, 19.

115. Ben Lee Jr., "Jus' BEN Thinkin'," *Hattiesburg American*, March 7, 1961, 12.

116. Bob Howie, "Times Have Changed," *Jackson Daily News*, February 13, 1961, 10.

117. Bob Howie, "Hinny," *Jackson Daily News*, March 4, 1961, 1.

118. Bob Howie, "Still at It," *Jackson Daily News*, March 9, 1961, 1D.

119. Weill, *In a Madhouse's Din*, 56–57, 86–87, 226–227.

120. The Daily News Sports Staff, "Time Out for Sports," *Starkville Daily News*, February 1, 1961, 2.

121. The Daily News Sports Staff, "Time Out for Sports," *Starkville Daily News*, February 8, 1961, 2; the Daily News Sports Staff, "Time Out for Sports," *Starkville Daily News*, February 10, 1961, 2; the Daily News Sports Staff, "Time Out for Sports," *Starkville Daily News*, February 15, 1961, 2.

122. The Daily News Sports Staff, "Time Out for Sports," *Starkville Daily News*, February 20, 1961, 2.

123. The Daily News Sports Staff, "Time Out for Sports," *Starkville Daily News*, February 24, 1961, 2.

124. The Daily News Sports Staff, "Time Out for Sports," *Starkville Daily News*, March 3, 1961, 2.

125. "Hurrah for A Fighting Spirit," *Starkville Daily News*, February 22, 1961, 4.

126. "Basketball Center of the U.S.A.," *Starkville Daily News*, March 1, 1961, 4.

Chapter 4. Is There Anything Wrong with Five White Boys Winning the National Championship?

1. In 1961, the school officially changed its team name from "Maroons" to "Bulldogs." Many journalists used the two names interchangeable, while others simply switched Bulldogs with Maroons. Because of the switch, the author chose to refer to the Mississippi State contingent as the Bulldogs.

2. Associated Press, "No Playoffs for Bulldogs," *Clarion-Ledger*, March 1, 1962, 2F; Associated Press, "Will State Go to NCAA," *Jackson Daily News*, March 1, 1962, 1F; "'Unwritten' Law Opposition Grows," *Hattiesburg American*, March 1, 1962, 1, 6; "See Possibility of State Playing in NCAA Tourney," *Daily Herald* (Biloxi), March 1, 1962, 18; "A Lot of Folks Want State to Go to NCAA Cage Event," *Vicksburg Evening Post*, March 1, 1962, 12; "Approval Sought for State to Enter NCAA Contests," *Enterprise-Journal*, March 1, 1962, 10; and "Efforts to Send MSU Cagers to US Tourney Failed," *Delta Democrat-Times*, March 1, 1962, 9.

3. "Move Is Started Here to Send MSU to NCAA," *Meridian Star*, March 1, 1962, 1.

4. "State Cagers Hit Road for Action," *Clarion-Ledger*, February 1, 1962, 3D; "MSU Facing Crucial Foe," *Starkville Daily News*, February 2, 1962, 3; "National Ranking to Be Put on the Line by Maroons at Baton Rouge Saturday," *Daily Herald* (Biloxi), February 1, 1962, 21; and "State Maroons Face LSU Tigers Tonight," *Daily Herald* (Biloxi), February 3, 1962, 13.

5. "Bulldogs and Tigers Clash," *Starkville Daily News*, February 3, 1962, 3.

6. Robert Fulton, "State Cagers Blast Tigers," *Clarion-Ledger*, February 4, 1962, 1B.

7. "Stroud-Lead Bulldogs Scatter LSU's Cajuns in 87–66 SEC Rout," *Commercial Dispatch*, February 4, 1962, 7; and "Maroons Rout LSU Tigers for Sixth League Victory," *Meridian Star*, February 4, 1962, 8.

8. Associated Press, "Tulane, Miss. State Game Top Action," *Clarion-Ledger*, February 5, 1962, 11.

9. "Green Wave Lashes at Bulldogs Tonight in Battle of New Orleans," *Commercial Dispatch*, February 5, 1962, 3; and Hedrick Smith, "State Battles Strong Tulane," *Meridian Star*, February 5, 1962, 8.

10. Associated Press, "Kerwin tallies 41 points, takes over scoring lead," *Hattiesburg American*, February 4, 1962, 5B; "Maroons Face Tulane in Crucial SEC Tilt," *Daily Herald* (Biloxi), February 5, 1962, 15; and Associated Press, "Kerwin Sinks 41 Points as Tulane Takes 107–77 Win over Bulldogs," *Greenwood Commonwealth*, February 5, 1962, 5.

11. Robert Fulton, "Maroons Produce Fireworks 70–59," *Clarion-Ledger*, February 6, 1962, 13.

12. Ibid.

13. Vernon Butler, "Bulldogs blast Greenies; Kentucky showdown nears," *Hattiesburg American*, February 6, 1962, 9; "State's Latest Victory Puts Green Wave on Ice," *Commercial Dispatch*,

February 6, 1962, 6; Vernon Butler, "Showdown Looms for SEC Title Monday; State Beats Tulane," *Daily Herald* (Biloxi), February 6, 1962, 15; Vernon Butler, "State Takes on Dream Team Look; Showdown against 'Tucky Coming," *Greenwood Commonwealth*, February 6, 1962, 5; "'On to Lexington' Is State Maroon War Cry," *Enterprise-Journal*, February 6, 1962, 5; and "State Smothers Tulane Greenies," *Meridian Star*, February 6, 1962, 6.

14. "Wildcats Host Bulldogs in Crucial One Monday," *Commercial Dispatch*, February 7, 1962, 8.

15. "MSU Cagers Face Vols," *Starkville Daily News*, February 9, 1962, 3; "State Plays Vols, Cats on Big Trip," *Clarion-Ledger*, February 9, 1962, 7; and "State Maroons Face Tennessee Tonight," *Daily Herald* (Biloxi), February 10, 1962, 16.

16. "MSU Faces Tricky Vols," *Starkville Daily News*, February 9, 1962, 4.

17. Vernon Butler, "Babe beats the Baron at home; tenacious Bulldogs win it 49–44," *Hattiesburg American*, February 13, 1962, 11; Vernon Butler, "Mississippi State Shocks Kentucky in SEC Skirmish," *Daily Herald* (Biloxi), February 13, 1962, 14; Vernon Butler, "Miss. State Beats Second Ranked Kentucky 49–44," *Vicksburg Evening Post*, February 13, 1962, 8; Vernon Butler, "Coach Babe McCarthy Riding High after Toppling Rupp's Wildcats," *Greenwood Commonwealth*, February 13, 1962, 5; Vernon Butler, "State Maroons Stun Kentucky 49 to 44," *Enterprise-Journal*, February 13, 1962, 5; Vernon Butler, "Auburn Risks Title Hopes on Road Trip," *Daily Herald* (Biloxi), February 16, 1962, 22; "Auburn Looms as SEC Dark Horse for NCAA Berth," *Vicksburg Evening Post*, February 16, 1962, 6; Vernon Butler, "Darkhorse Auburn May Be Team to Play in Annual NCAA Tourney," *Greenwood Commonwealth*, February 16, 1962, 5; Vernon Butler, "State, 'Tucky, Auburn Can't Make a Slip Now," *Hattiesburg American*, February 19, 1962, 4A; Vernon Butler, "State Maroons Grab SEC Basketball Lead," *Daily Herald* (Biloxi), February 19, 1962, 12; Vernon Butler, "Babe's Bullies Go after 21st Win Tonite," *Vicksburg Evening Post*, February 19, 1962, 7; Vernon Butler, "State, Kentucky, Auburn Enter into Stretch Drive for Title," *Greenwood Commonwealth*, February 19, 1962, 5; Vernon Butler, "Mississippi State Takes Lead in SEC Cage Race," *Enterprise-Journal*, February 19, 1962, 5; "S.E.C. Leaders Drive to Thrilling Finish," *Jackson Daily News*, February 19, 1962, 9–10; "Reb Soph Is Top Scorer; MSU vs. Georgia Tonight," *Commercial Dispatch*, February 19, 1962, 3; Vernon Butler, "Only Three Hurdles Remain in Path of McCarthymen," *Hattiesburg American*, February 20, 1962, 10; Vernon Butler, "Auburn, Kentucky, State All Post Victories," *Daily Herald* (Biloxi), February 20, 1962, 15; Vernon Butler, "Bullies Claw Georgia 83–74; Vandy Scares Cats but Lose," *Vicksburg Evening Post*, February 20, 1962, 10; Vernon Butler, "Only Three Teams Stand between State and SEC Basketball Title," *Greenwood Commonwealth*, February 20, 1962, 5; Vernon Butler, "Maroons Defeat Georgia 83–74," *Enterprise-Journal*, February 20, 1962, 5; and "3 Games Left for Maroons," *Jackson Daily News*, February 20, 1962, 9–10.

18. Lee Baker, "State Bags Tennessee, Kentucky Next Target," *Clarion-Ledger* and *Jackson Daily News*, February 11, 1962, 1B.

19. "Steady State Blasts Volunteers 91–67; Onward to Kentucky," *Commercial Dispatch*, February 11, 1962, 8; and "Mississippi State Downs Tennessee," *Vicksburg Evening Post*, February 11, 1962, 11.

20. Associated Press, "Cats, Maroons Game Is Week's Highlight," *Clarion-Ledger*, February 12, 1962, 13.

21. "State's Bulldogs vs. Kentucky's Wildcats Up in Bluegrass Tonight," *Commercial Dispatch*, February 12, 1962, 6; Vernon Butler, "Kentucky Faces Mississippi State in Big One," *Daily Herald* (Biloxi), February 12, 1962, 14; Vernon Butler, "Kentucky and State Said in Top Form," *Vicksburg*

Evening Post, February 12, 1962, 7; Vernon Butler, "State Wins over Tennessee 91–67 As Kentucky Beats Ole Miss 83–60," *Greenwood Commonwealth*, February 12, 1962, 5; and "Maroons, Kentucky Tangle in SEC's Top Tilt Tonight," *Enterprise-Journal*, February 12, 1962, 5.

22. Scotty Hargrove, "Tennessee Coach Says State Can Whip Cats," *Clarion-Ledger*, February 12, 1962, 13.

23. "Mississippi State Wins Collegiate Basketball's Game of the Year," *Commercial Dispatch*, February 13, 1962, 7; "Bulldogs Turn Back Kentucky," *Meridian Star*, February 13, 1962, 9; "Says Rupp, 'We Knew It,'" *Jackson Daily News*, February 13, 1962, 11; Bill Neikirk, "State Was Scared but Wouldn't Quit," *Clarion-Ledger*, February 13, 1962, 13; and "Bulldogs Keep Poise for Win," *Starkville Daily News*, February 13, 1962, 3.

24. Robert Fulton, "Mississippi State Shatters Invincible Rule of Kentucky Wildcats, 49 to 44," *Clarion-Ledger*, February 13, 1962, 13.

25. Lee Baker, "Maroons Down Mighty Wildcats," *Jackson Daily News*, February 13, 1962, 11–12.

26. Ibid; and Phil Wallace, "Remember Last Maroon Win at 'Tucky?" *Jackson Daily News*, February 14, 1962, 14.

27. Jim Hackleman, "State in Spotlight but Will Again Turn Down NCAA Bid," *Vicksburg Evening Post*, February 13, 1962, 9; Jim Hackleman, "Bulldogs Beat Mighty Kentucky Tie Wildcats in Conference Play," *Greenwood Commonwealth*, February 13, 1962, 5; and "MSU Bulldogs Defeat Kentucky 48–44," *Starkville Daily News*, February 13, 1962, 3.

28. Associated Press, "Same Old Story with Ohio State Atop Poll," *Clarion-Ledger*, February 13, 1962, 16; "Bulldogs Ranked 8th in UPI Poll," *Clarion-Ledger*, February 14, 1962, 17; "Bulldogs Jump to 8th Ranking," *Commercial Dispatch*, February 13, 1962, 7; Sheldon Sakowitz, "State Moves Up to Eight in AP Poll," *Daily Herald* (Biloxi), February 13, 1962, 15; Sheldon Sakowitz, "State Only 8th This Week, But Wait Until Next!" *Vicksburg Evening Post*, February 13, 1962, 8; "State Is Eight in AP Poll," *Enterprise-Journal*, February 13, 1962, 5; Norman Miller, "State Cagers Rated Eight in UPI poll," *Meridian Star*, February 13, 1962, 8; Sheldon Sakowitz, "State Holds 9th in AP Cage Poll," *Jackson Daily News*, February 13, 1962, 12; and "Maroons Finally in UPI's Top 10," *Jackson Daily News*, February 13, 1962, 12.

29. Susan Weill, *In a Madhouse's Din: Civil Rights Coverage by Mississippi's Daily Press, 1948–1968* (Westport, CT: Praeger, 2002), 88.

30. "1500 Cheer Cage Heroes' Return Home," *Starkville Daily News*, February 14, 1962, 1, 3.

31. Bob Green, "State Can Take over SEC with Win over Fla. Tonite," *Vicksburg Evening Post*, February 17, 1962, 3; and Bob Green, "Eight Ranked State Meets Florida in One of Country's Top Games," *Greenwood Commonwealth*, February 17, 1962, 5.

32. "State Meets Florida Next," *Clarion-Ledger*, February 16, 1962, 20; "Maroons to Meet Florida Tonite," *Clarion-Ledger*, February 17, 1962, 6; "Bulldogs Will Host Florida Saturday," *Starkville Daily News*, February 15, 1962, 3; "Gators and Bulldogs Will Tangle Tonight," *Starkville Daily News*, February 17, 1962, 3; "Bulldogs Look Towards Invading Florida Gators," *Commercial Dispatch*, February 15, 1962, 7; "Mississippi State Entertains Florida," *Daily Herald* (Biloxi), February 17, 1962, 12; "Maroons Could Move Up in AP Rankings by Beating Florida," *Daily Herald*, (Biloxi), February 17, 1962, 13; "Giants Killers from State Primed for Gator Invasion," *Vicksburg Evening Post*, February 16, 1962, 7; "M.S.U. Eyes Florida 5 Saturday," *Jackson Daily News*, February 15, 1962, 1D; and Associated Press, "Maroons Eye Sole SEC Lead Tonight," *Jackson Daily News*, February 17, 1962, 2.

33. Lee Baker, "State Toys with Gators to Close Grasp on SEC," *Jackson Daily News* and *Clarion-Ledger*, February 18, 1962, 1C.

34. Herb Phillips, "State Captures 20th Win; Florida Is 67–45 Victim," *Commercial Dispatch*, February 18, 1962, 5; and Van Savell, "Bulldogs Down Florida 67–45," *Vicksburg Evening Post*, February 18, 1962, 9.

35. "Bulldogs Wallop Florida," *Meridian Star*, February 18, 1962, 8.

36. Vernon Butler, "State Hogs Spotlight as Cinderella Team," *Clarion-Ledger*, February 19, 1962, 9.

37. George Anderson, "Babe's Boys Beat Ga. 83–74; Keep S.E.C. Lead," *Starkville Daily News*, February 20, 1962, 3.

38. Robert Fulton, "Maroons Reduce Magic Number to 3 With Win," *Clarion-Ledger*, February 20, 1962, 17; "Bulldogs Out-Maneuver Classy, Game Georgians," *Commercial Dispatch*, February 20, 1962, 6; "State Gets 21st Cage Win, 83–74," *Meridian Star*, February 20, 1962, 9; Lee Baker, "Maroons Slither by Dogs, 83–74," *Jackson Daily News*, February 20, 1962, 9; and United Press International, "SEC's Top Miss. State Defeats Georgia 83–74," *Delta Democrat-Times*, February 20, 1962, 7.

39. Joe Sargis, "Maroons Advance to 5th in UPI Cage Poll," *Clarion-Ledger*, February 20, 1962, 18; Associated Press, "State Ranked Fifth by AP; 'Tucky 3rd," *Clarion-Ledger*, February 21, 1962, 15; Don Weiss, "Miss. State Moves Up to Fifth Place," *Hattiesburg American*, February 20, 1962, 10; Don Weiss, "Mississippi State Moves Up to Fifth in AP Cage Poll," *Daily Herald* (Biloxi), February 20, 1962, 14; Don Weiss, "Mississippi State Ranked 5th in Nation," *Vicksburg Evening Post*, February 20, 1962, 10; "Mississippi State Fifth in AP Voting," *Enterprise-Journal*, February 20, 1962, 5; Associated Press, "Bucks on Top, Maroons 5th," *Jackson Daily News*, February 20, 1962, 10; "Maroons Up to 5th Place in UPI Polling," *Jackson Daily News*, February 20, 1962, 10; and "Ohio State Holds No. 1 Rating; Miss. State Vaults to 5th Place," *Delta Democrat-Times*, February 20, 1962, 7.

40. "State Cagers Clash with Tigers, Tulane," *Clarion-Ledger*, February 23, 1962, 18; "Pressure-Packed Play Is Slated by Bulldogs," *Clarion-Ledger*, February 24, 1962, 6; "MSU Needs 3 Victories for Crown," *Starkville Daily News*, February 23, 1962, 3; "Bulldogs-Bengals Tangle Tonight," *Starkville Daily News*, February 24, 1962, 3; "Bulldogs after Victories in Final Three Contests," February 22, 1962, 8; "State Gets Ready for LSU Invasion," *Daily Herald* (Biloxi), February 23, 1962, 19; "Bullies Need 3 More Wins to Clinch SEC Title," *Vicksburg Evening Post*, February 23, 1962, 6; "MSU Bulldogs Must Hurdle LSU and Tulane for Big SEC Title," *Greenwood Commonwealth*, February 23, 1962, 5; and "Maroons Driving Towards Crown," *Jackson Daily News*, February 22, 1962, 1D.

41. David M. Moffit, "Rebs, Maroons Meet Bayou 5s," *Meridian Star*, February 24, 1962, 7; "SEC Eyes on Monday," *Jackson Daily News*, February 24, 1962, 3; David M. Moffit, "Mitchell Gains Berth on UPI All-SEC Squad," *Clarion-Ledger*, March 2, 1962, 18; "Kentucky's Cotton Is High-Grade Choice of UPI Poll's Sportswriters," *Commercial Dispatch*, March 1, 1962, 10; David M. Moffit, "Most SEC teams win up Saturday," *Meridian Star*, March 2, 1962, 8; "Bulldogs and Wildcats in Probable Title-Tie," *Commercial Dispatch*, March 2, 1962, 3; and "No. 1 MSU Favored to Down Rebs, Win Title," *Delta Democrat-Times*, March 2, 1962, 9.

42. Robert Fulton, "State Wins by 58–48, But LSU Plenty Tough," *Jackson Daily News* and *Clarion-Ledger*, February 25, 1962, 1B; Herb Phillips, "State Uses Charity Line to Push Back

LSU, 58–44," *Commercial Dispatch*, February 25, 1962, 62, 6; Associated Press, "Stage Is Set for Tonight's Tiger-Wildcat Showdown," *Hattiesburg American*, February 26, 1962, 4B; Associated Press, "Auburn-Kentucky in Showdown Tonite," *Vicksburg Evening Post*, February 26, 1962, 7; Associated Press, "Showdown Battle Slated Tonight as Mighty 'Tucky, Auburn Clash," *Greenwood Commonwealth*, February 26, 1962, 5; "Maroon Foul Shots Down LSU, 58–48," *Meridian Star*, February 25, 1962, 8; Van Savell, "Mississippi State Nips Tigers 58–48," *Vicksburg Evening Post*, February 25, 1962, 13; and United Press International, "MSU Tops LSU 58–49; Rebs Overcome Tulane," *Delta Democrat-Times*, February 26, 1962, 5.

43. "Maroons Cast Wary Eyes at Green Wave," *Clarion-Ledger*, February 26, 1962, 10.

44. Hedrick Smith, "Auburn-Kentucky Showdown Tonight," *Meridian Star*, February 26, 1962, 8.

45. "Bulldogs Bop Tulane Wave for 23rd Win," *Meridian Star*, February 27, 1962, 8.

46. Dick Joyce, "State Maintains 5th Spot in UPI Ratings," *Clarion-Ledger*, February 28, 1962, 17; Associated Press, "State Still Fifth in AP Cage Poll," February 27, 1962, 12; and "State Remains Fifth in AP College Poll," *Daily Herald* (Biloxi), February 27, 1962, 14.

47. Vernon Butler, "Stroud, Nash Voted Unanimous All-SEC," *Clarion-Ledger*, February 27, 1962, 13; Vernon Butler, "Two Maroons Make All-SEC Team," *Hattiesburg American*, February 27, 1962, 12; Vernon Butler, "Stroud-Mitchell Named on First Team All-SEC," *Starkville Daily News*, February 27, 1962, 2; "Stroud, Mitchell Make AP's All-SEC 1st Team," *Commercial Dispatch*, February 27, 1962, 8; Vernon Butler, "State and Kentucky Places Two on All-SEC Cage Squad," *Daily Herald* (Biloxi), February 27, 1962, 15; Vernon Butler, "State and Kentucky Pace All-SEC Team," *Vicksburg Evening Post*, February 27, 1962, 11; and "State Holds 5th in Cage Ratings," *Meridian Star*, February 27, 1962, 8.

48. George Anderson, "MSU Blasts Tulane Five," *Starkville Daily News*, February 27, 1962, 3; Phil Wallace, "Maroon Express Keeps on Rolling," *Jackson Daily News*, February 27, 1962, 8; and Robert Fulton, "State Back on Beam in Romp over Greenies," *Clarion-Ledger*, February 27, 1962, 13.

49. "Kentucky Stops Auburn, May Get N.C.A.A. Berth," *Jackson Daily News*, February 27, 1962, 7–8.

50. "State after SEC Title, Prestige on Saturday," *Clarion-Ledger*, March 1, 1962, 1F; "Red Hot Rebs Invade State," *Clarion-Ledger*, March 1, 1962, 1F; "High Flying State Closes Out Season with Rebels Saturday," *Starkville Daily News*, February 28, 1962, 3; "Bulldogs Preparing to Host Rebels in Regular Cage Season's Closeout," *Commercial Dispatch*, February 28, 1962, 2; "State Closes Out Season Saturday," *Daily Herald* (Biloxi), March 1, 1962, 19; "State Ends Season Tonight When Rival Rebels Invade," *Vicksburg Evening Post*, March 3, 1962, 3; "State, Ole Miss Clash Tonight in SEC Finale to Decide Title," *Greenwood Commonwealth*, March 3, 1962, 5; and "Maroons Close Out after One More," *Jackson Daily News*, February 28, 1962, 14.

51. "SEC Title at Stake in Battle," *Clarion-Ledger*, March 3, 1962, 9; and "Bulldogs and Rebels Clash Here Tonight," *Starkville Daily News*, March 3, 1962, 3.

52. "Rebels Call on Maroons," *Jackson Daily News*, February 28, 1962, 14; "Rebs after Upset Win in Finale," *Clarion-Ledger*, March 3, 1962, 9; "Rebs Ready for Battle with State," *Daily Herald* (Biloxi), March 2, 1962, 16; "Hot Rebels Seek to Cool Off Rival State Saturday," *Vicksburg Evening Post*, March 1, 1962, 13; and "State Set for Rebels," *Jackson Daily News*, March 2, 1962, 8.

53. Ross M. Hagen, "Family Squabbles in SEC Focus Tonight," *Daily Herald* (Biloxi), March 3, 1962, 17; and Associated Press, "Last Big Night for SEC Cagers," *Jackson Daily News*, March 3, 1962, 2.

54. Associated Press, "No Playoffs for Bulldogs," *Clarion-Ledger*, March 1, 1962, 2F; Associated Press, "Will State Go to NCAA," *Jackson Daily News*, March 1, 1962, 1F; "'Unwritten' Law Opposition Grows," *Hattiesburg American*, March 1, 1962, 1, 6; "See Possibility of State Playing in NCAA Tourney," *Daily Herald* (Biloxi), March 1, 1962, 18; "A Lot of Folks Want State to Go to NCAA Cage Event," *Vicksburg Evening Post*, March 1, 1962, 12; "Approval Sought for State to Enter NCAA Contests," *Enterprise-Journal*, March 1, 1962, 10.

55. Associated Press, "Will State Go to NCAA," *Jackson Daily News*, March 1, 1962, 1F.

56. Ibid.

57. "Efforts to Send MSU Cagers to US Tourney Failed," *Delta Democrat-Times*, March 1, 1962, 9.

58. Associated Press, "No Playoffs for Bulldogs," *Clarion-Ledger*, March 1, 1962, 2F.

59. Ibid.

60. "Move Is Started Here to Send MSU to NCAA," *Meridian Star*, March 1, 1962, 1.

61. Ibid.

62. "State Turns Down Bid to Tourney after Win," *Delta Democrat-Times*, March 5, 1962, 5.

63. Lee Baker, "State Coach for Relaxing Ruling," *Jackson Daily News* and *Clarion-Ledger*, March 4, 1962, 1; "McCarthy Wants State in NCAA Tourney Play," *Commercial Dispatch*, March 4, 1962, 6; and "Babe Thinks State Should Go to NCAA," *Meridian Star*, March 4, 1962, 8.

64. Ross M. Hagen, "It's Official Now—Wildcats to NCAA," *Clarion-Ledger*, March 5, 1962, 13; Ross M. Hagen, "Cats Invited to Represent SEC in NCAA Playoffs," *Hattiesburg American*, March 5, 1962, 8A; Ross M. Hagen, "Mississippi State Takes Share of SEC Title, Beats Rebels," *Daily Herald* (Biloxi), March 5, 1962, 14; Ross M. Hagen, "SEC Scoring Leaders to Clash Tonight," *Vicksburg Evening Post*, March 5, 1962, 6; Ross M. Hagen, "Kentucky Faces Tulane Tonight; Top Scoring Aces Battle It Out," *Greenwood Commonwealth*, March 5, 1962, 7; and Associated Press, "SEC Point Title on Line Tonight," *Jackson Daily News*, March 5, 1962, 10.

65. "Wildcats Claim Title-Tie with Victory over Vols," *Commercial Dispatch*, March 11, 1962, 6; and Bill Neikirk, "Cats Win and Tie for Lead," *Jackson Daily News*, March 11, 1962, 2B.

66. Joe Dan Gold, interview with author, July 23, 2009.

67. "Babe McCarthy Named UPI Coach of Year," *Clarion-Ledger*, March 6, 1962, 11; "Babe McCarthy named Coach of Year in SEC," *Meridian Star*, March 6, 1962, 9; "McCarthy SEC 'Coach of Year,'" *Jackson Daily News*, March 6, 1962, 10; "Babe McCarthy's Coaching Has Been Key to Bulldogs' Cage Success," *Commercial Dispatch*, March 6, 1962, 8; and United Press International, "Coach of the Maroons Guided Win over Cats," *Delta Democrat-Times*, March 6, 1962, 9.

68. Norman Miller, "Miss State Ranked 4th in Final National Polls," *Clarion-Ledger*, March 13, 1962, 13; "Final UPI Polling Has Kentucky and State Ranked Third and Forth," *Commercial Dispatch*, March 12, 1962, 3; "Maroons Are Fourth in AP Poll," *Enterprise-Journal*, March 13, 1962, 5; Associated Press, "Buckeyes 1st, Maroons 4th," *Jackson Daily News*, March 13, 1962, 7; and "Bucks Get Unanimous Vote of 35 Coaches," *Delta Democrat-Times*, March 12, 1962, 5.

69. Norman Miller, "State Fourth in Final UPI Ratings," *Meridian Star*, March 12, 1962, 8.

70. "Maroons Equal to Best Team of Previous Years," *Jackson Daily News*, March 7, 1962, 16; "State Had Eventful Cage Season," *Clarion-Ledger*, March 8, 1962, 2B; "Cagers Tie Best Record; Babe Is Coach of Year," *Starkville Daily News*, March 7, 1962, 3; "Mississippi State Cagers Equal Best Record Ever," *Commercial Dispatch*, March 7, 1962, 9; "State Maroons Wind Up Campaign;

Equal Best Previous Mark," *Daily Herald* (Biloxi), March 8, 1962, 30; "State's Cagers Equaled Best Showing in History," *Vicksburg Evening Post*, March 8, 1962, 15; "State Bulldogs Finish Fifth; Record Setters Get SEC Honor," *Greenwood Commonwealth*, March 8, 1962, 4; and "MSU Closes Season to Equal Best Cage Mark," *Delta Democrat-Times*, March 8, 1962, 9.

71. "State Senate Congratulates Babe McCarthy," *Clarion-Ledger*, March 9, 1962, 21.

72. Lewis Lord, "Babe Becomes a Moses for State's Bulldogs," *Starkville Daily News*, March 17, 1962, 3; Lewis Lord, "McCarthy Almost Leads State to Promised Land," *Commercial Dispatch*, March 16, 1962, 6; "Ultimate Beyond Grasp for Babe," *Jackson Daily News*, March 16, 1962, 13; and "Babe Hasn't Quite Led MSU to Promised Land," *Delta Democrat-Times*, March 16, 1962, 8.

73. Lewis Lord, "Babe Becomes a Moses for State's Bulldogs," *Starkville Daily News*, March 17, 1962, 3.

74. Ibid.

75. Herb Phillips, "'N in This Cornah!" *Commercial Dispatch*, February 22, 1962, 9.

76. "Writers Say End Sports Ban," *Starkville Daily News*, February 27, 1962, 3.

77. Herb Phillips, "'N in This Cornah!" *Commercial Dispatch*, March 6, 1962, 8.

78. Dick Lightsey, "Bunts, Boots and Bounces," *Daily Herald* (Biloxi), February 1, 1962, 21; Dick Lightsey, "Bunts, Boots and Bounces," *Daily Herald* (Biloxi), February 5, 1962, 14; Dick Lightsey, "Bunts, Boots and Bounces," *Daily Herald* (Biloxi), February 7, 1962, 19; Dick Lightsey, "Bunts, Boots and Bounces," *Daily Herald* (Biloxi), February 9, 1962, 17; Dick Lightsey, "Bunts, Boots and Bounces," *Daily Herald* (Biloxi), February 12, 1962, 14; Dick Lightsey, "Bunts, Boots and Bounces," *Daily Herald* (Biloxi), February 15, 1962, 17; and Dick Lightsey, "Bunts, Boots and Bounces," *Daily Herald* (Biloxi), February 16, 1962, 21.

79. Dick Lightsey, "Bunts, Boots and Bounces," *Daily Herald* (Biloxi), February 24, 1962, 17; and Dick Lightsey, "Bunts, Boots and Bounces," *Daily Herald* (Biloxi), February 26, 1962, 14.

80. Dick Lightsey, "Bunts, Boots and Bounces," *Daily Herald* (Biloxi), March 7, 1962, 18.

81. Dick Lightsey, "Bunts, Boots and Bounces," *Daily Herald* (Biloxi), March 17, 1962, 10.

82. "Lightsey: A Dedicated Life of Sportswriting," *Sun Herald* (Biloxi), October 25, 1994, 1A.

83. Billy Ray, "Press Box Views," *Vicksburg Evening Post*, February 15, 1962, 14.

84. Billy Ray, "Press Box Views," *Vicksburg Evening Post*, February 18, 1962, 10; Billy Ray, "Press Box Views," *Vicksburg Evening Post*, February 20, 1962, 10; Billy Ray, "Press Box Views," *Vicksburg Evening Post*, February 21, 1962, 10; and Billy Ray, "Press Box Views," *Vicksburg Evening Post*, March 1, 1962, 12.

85. Johnny Gregory, "Robertson Elected 'U' Student Editor," *Clarion-Ledger*, April 19, 1961, 1.

86. Joseph Crespino, *In Search of Another Country: Mississippi and the Conservative Counterrevolution* (Princeton, NJ: Princeton University Press, 2007), 38–40.

87. Jimmie Robertson, "Liberals Often Do More Harm Than Good," *Daily Mississippian* (University of Mississippi), January 18, 1962, 2; Jimmie Robertson, "State Senate Approves Efforts of State Times," *Daily Mississippian*, January 19, 1962, 2; Jimmie Robertson, "Rebel Underground?" *Daily Mississippian*, February 13, 1962, 2. Per the AP, the *Rebel Underground*, which was an anonymous independent newspaper published at Ole Miss, took issue with Robertson and told the *Daily Mississippian* editor to "get off your integration kick and scandal sheet and write about the real problems facing this campus." In addition, Robertson was accused of "being sympathetic" with Meredith's plight and supporting the twenty-nine–year-old's efforts

to enter the all-white school. "An Anonymous Newspaper Blasts Ole Miss Editor," *Greenwood Commonwealth*, February 17, 1962, 1.

88. Robertson's work from page two of the February 22, 1962, edition of the *Daily Mississippian* was missing from the paper's archives at the University of Mississippi. However, the details of his column could be found in a number of wire-based articles that were published in the state, including the following: "Editor Assails Ban on Teams," *Starkville Daily News*, February 24, 1962, 3; "State's Policy against Inter-Racial Sports Hit," *Commercial Dispatch*, February 23, 1962, 3; and "'Mississippian' Protests Racial Athletic Policy," *Jackson Daily News*, February 23, 1962, 7.

89. "Editor Assails Ban on Teams," *Starkville Daily News*, February 24, 1962, 3; "State's Policy against Inter-Racial Sports Hit," *Commercial Dispatch*, February 23, 1962, 3; and "'Mississippian' Protests Racial Athletic Policy," *Jackson Daily News*, February 23, 1962, 7.

90. Jimmie Robertson, "Teams Must Withdraw from Tournament Play," *Daily Mississippian* (University of Mississippi), March 6, 1962, 4.

91. Lee Baker, "Baker's Dozen," *Jackson Daily News* and *Clarion-Ledger*, February 4, 1962.

92. Lee Baker, "Baker's Dozen," *Jackson Daily News*, February 12, 1962, 13.

93. Ibid.

94. Lee Baker, "Baker's Dozen," *Jackson Daily News*, February 14, 1962, 14; Lee Baker, "Baker's Dozen," *Jackson Daily News*, February 15, 1962, 1D; Lee Baker, "Baker's Dozen," *Jackson Daily News*, February 16, 1962, 7; Lee Baker, "Baker's Dozen," *Jackson Daily News*, February 19, 1962, 9; Lee Baker, "Baker's Dozen," *Jackson Daily News* and *Clarion-Ledger*, February 18, 1962.

95. Lee Baker, "Baker's Dozen," *Clarion-Ledger*, February 23, 1962, 7.

96. Lee Baker, "Baker's Dozen," *Jackson Daily News*, February 28, 1962, 14.

97. Bob Howie, "One Last Hazard," *Jackson Daily News*, February 28, 1962, 14.

98. Lee Baker, "Baker's Dozen," *Jackson Daily News*, March 2, 1962, 8.

99. Baker identified the following players from McCarthy's three SEC title teams as coming to Starkville from another state: Bailey Howell (Tennessee), Ted Usher (New York), Jerry Graves (Tennessee), Jack Berkshire (Iowa), and Joe Dan Gold (Kentucky).

100. Carl Walters, "Shavin's," *Clarion-Ledger*, February 5, 1962, 12.

101. Carl Walters, "Shavin's," *Clarion-Ledger*, February 12, 1962, 14.

102. Ray Cave, "The Old Master Has A New Kind of Winner," *Sports Illustrated*, February 19, 1962, 52–53.

103. Carl Walters, "Shavin's," *Jackson Daily News* and *Clarion-Ledger*, February 18, 1962, 4C.

104. Carl Walters, "Shavin's," *Clarion-Ledger*, March 5, 1962, 14.

105. Ibid.

106. Ibid.

107. Carl Walters, "Shavin's," *Clarion-Ledger*, March 12, 1962, 14.

108. Carl Walters, "Shavin's," *Clarion-Ledger*, March 13, 1962, 22.

109. Arnold Hederman, "Highlights in Sports," *Clarion-Ledger*, February 9, 1962, 26; Arnold Hederman, "Highlights in Sports," *Clarion-Ledger*, February 11, 1962, B2; Arnold Hederman, "Highlights in Sports," *Clarion-Ledger*, February 14, 1962, 20; Arnold Hederman, "Highlights in Sports," *Jackson Daily News* and *Clarion-Ledger*, February 18, 1962, 6C; Arnold Hederman, "Highlights in Sports," *Clarion-Ledger*, February 20, 1962, 18; Arnold Hederman, "Highlights in Sports," *Clarion-Ledger*, February 25, 1962, 3B; Arnold Hederman, "Highlights in Sports," *Clarion-Ledger*, March 6, 1962, 13.

110. Arnold Hederman, "Highlights in Sports," *Clarion-Ledger*, February 20, 1962, 18.

111. Arnold Hederman, "Highlights in Sports," *Clarion-Ledger*, March 15, 1962, 12.

112. Robert Fulton, "High 'N Inside," *Clarion-Ledger*, February 10, 1962, 7.

113. Robert Fulton, "High N' Inside," *Clarion-Ledger*, February 24, 1962, 8.

114. Paul Morgan, "The Sports Hub," *Hattiesburg American*, February 12, 1962, 4B; and Paul Morgan, "The Sports Hub," *Hattiesburg American*, February 13, 1962, 10.

115. Paul Morgan, "The Sports Hub," *Hattiesburg American*, February 23, 1962, 13; Paul Morgan, "The Sports Hub," *Hattiesburg American*, March 3, 1962, 10; and Paul Morgan, "The Sports Hub," *Hattiesburg American*, March 5, 1962, 7A.

116. The Daily News Sports Staff, "Time Out for Sports," *Starkville Daily News*, February 17, 1962, 3; and the Daily News Sports Staff, "Time Out for Sports," *Starkville Daily News*, March 8, 1962, 3.

117. "The Best in the Nation," *Starkville Daily News*, March 6, 1962, 8.

118. "Voice of the People," *Clarion-Ledger*, March 20, 1962, 6.

Chapter 5. This Is the Biggest Challenge to Our Way of Life Since the Reconstruction

1. "'They Were Gentlemen' Loyola, Miss. Both Say," *Chicago Defender*, March 18, 1963, 22. McCarthy's almost terroristic fears were not expressed in any articles found in the Mississippi press.

2. David R. Davies, *The Press and Race: Mississippi Journalists Confront the Movement* (Jackson: University Press of Mississippi, 2001), 30–34.

3. Susan Weill, *In a Madhouse's Din: Civil Rights Coverage by Mississippi's Daily Press, 1948–1968* (Westport, CT: Praeger, 2002),79–81.

4. Kurt Kemper, *College Football and American Culture in the Cold War Era* (Chicago: University of Illinois Press, 2009), 115.

5. "Babe Expecting Okay This Time," *Delta Democrat-Times*, January 25, 1963, 1.

6. Robert Fulton, "Bulldogs Defeat Tulane to Clinch Tie for Title," *Clarion-Ledger*, February 26, 1963, 11.

7. Phil Wallace, "'Played It Safe' Says McCarthy," *Jackson Daily News*, February 26, 1963, 9.

8. "Babe Wants Playoff Spot," *Clarion-Ledger*, February 26, 1963, 11; Robert Davenport, "State Clinches Tie for SEC Cage Title," *Daily Herald* (Biloxi), February 26, 1963, 14; "State Tops Waves in 78–67 SEC Tilt," *Natchez Democrat*, February 26, 1963, 7; "Bulldogs Trounce Tulane," *Starkville Daily News*, February 26, 1963, 1; "State Quintet Certain of Least Share of This Season's SEC Laurels," *Daily Journal* (Tupelo), February 26, 1963, 2; and Malcolm Balfour, "State Cagers Cop Third Straight Championship," the *Reflector* (Mississippi State University), February 28, 1963, 1, 8.

9. "Babe Says Boys Want NCAA Berth," *Starkville Daily News*, February 28, 1963, 1. Despite McCarthy's strong commentary, his statements concerning Georgia and Alabama were somewhat inaccurate. By 1963, colleges and universities in both states participated in integrated athletic events on the road. For more information, see Patrick B. Miller and David Kenneth Wiggins, *Sport and the Color Line: Black Athletes and Race Relations in Twentieth-Century America* (New York: Rutledge, 2004), 279–283; and Keith Dunnavant, *The Missing Ring: How*

Bear Bryant and the 1966 Alabama Crimson Tide Were Denied College Football's Most Elusive Prize (New York: St. Martin's Press, 2007), 83.

10. Jim Hackleman, "Tulsa Gives Cincy A Scare," *Hattiesburg American*, February 25, 1963, 17; David M. Moffit, "State Needs but One Victory to Clinch Tie for SEC Crown," *Meridian Star*, February 25, 1963, 9; Tom Dygard, "Bulldogs Win Third SEC title in a Row; NCAA Play Doubtful," *Meridian Star*, February 26, 1963, 8; Tom Dygard, "Bulldogs Trounce Tulane to Win SEC Title," *Starkville Daily News*, February 26, 1963, 3; Robert Davenport, "Georgia Tech Probably Will Play in NCAA Tournament," *Hattiesburg American*, February 26, 1963, 13; Robert Davenport, "Maroons Win but Tech's NCAA Chances Increase," *Enterprise-Journal*, February 26, 1963, 5; Robert Davenport, "State Ride over Wave; Babe Makes Appeals," *Laurel Leader-Call*, February 26, 1963, 8; Robert Davenport, "McCarthy Wants State to Go to NCAA," *Vicksburg Evening Post*, February 26, 1963, 8; United Press International, "State Clinches Tie in SEC—Tech Earns NCAA Berth," *Delta Democrat-Times*, February 26, 1963, 5; United Press International, "Tech Expected to Go to NCAA," *Meridian Star*, February 26, 1963, 8; "Bulldogs Clinch at Least Tie," *Commercial Dispatch*, February 26, 1963, 7; David M. Moffit, "Tech Flexes Muscles for NCAA," *Commercial Dispatch*, February 28, 1963, 8; "Tech Meets Vandy in Final Tuneup before NCAA Meet," *Delta Democrat-Times*, February 27, 1963, 8; David Moffit, "SEC Cage Action to End Saturday," *Clarion-Ledger*, February 28, 1963, 3D; "SEC Basketball Finish on Saturday," *Daily Journal* (Tupelo), February 28, 1963, 5; David Moffit, "SEC Cage Action to End Saturday," *Clarion-Ledger*, February 28, 1963, 3D; and "Curtain Down on S.E.C. Cage," *Jackson Daily News*, March 2, 1963, 2.

11. United Press International, "State Clinches Tie in SEC—Tech Earns NCAA Berth," *Delta Democrat-Times*, February 26, 1963, 5.

12. Ted Meier, "Duke Is Moving Up Fast in AP's Cage Ratings," *Meridian Star*, February 26, 1963, 9; and "State Moves to Seventh in UPI Basketball Poll," *Meridian Star*, February 26, 1963, 9.

13. "Phillips Says MSU Should Play" *Clarion-Ledger*, February 27, 1963, 5; "Rubel in Favor of NCAA Tourney for State Team," *Commercial Dispatch*, February 27, 1963, 2A; "To Go or Not to Go IS Question," *Jackson Daily News*, February 27, 1963, 11; "Rubel Phillips Says MSU Should Play in NCAA," *Delta Democrat-Times*, February 27, 1963, 2; and "Phillips Favors Bulldogs, NCAA," *Starkville Daily News*, February 27, 1963, 3.

14. David M. Moffit, "Ga. Tech Coach Wants State in NCAA Tourney," *Clarion-Ledger*, February 27, 1963, 13; "College Board May Not Okay State's Trip," *Commercial Dispatch*, February 26, 1963, 1; "College Board Official Opposes MSU to NCAA," *Delta Democrat-Times*, February 26, 1963, 1; "State May Be Forced to Reject NCAA Berth," *Delta Democrat-Times*, February 27, 1963, 8; "State Unlikely for NCAA Cage Tourney: Evans," *Jackson Daily News*, February 26, 1963, 9; "To Go or Not to Go Is Question," *Jackson Daily News*, February 27, 1963, 11; Maroons Await Decision on Trip to NCAA Tourney," *Laurel Leader-Call*, February 27, 1963, 11; "State May Know Friday about Playing in NCAA," *Enterprise-Journal*, February 27, 1963, 9; "State's NCAA Hopes Faint," *Tupelo Daily Journal*, February 28, 1963, 2; and "State May Know NCA Verdict in A Few Days," *Vicksburg Evening Post*, February 27, 1963, 8.

15. "Senator Opposes State to NCAA," *Delta Democrat-Times*, March 1, 1963, 1; "NCAA Play Decision is Refused," *Enterprise-Journal*, March 1, 1963, 1; "Senate Declines Resolution for 'Dogs in NCAA," *Natchez Democrat*, March 1, 1963, 2; and "Solons Drop NCAA Stand," *Starkville Daily News*, March 2, 1963, 1.

16. Bill Ross, "Prospects Better for NCAA Trek," *Jackson Daily News*, March 1, 1963, 7; and Bill Ross, "Babe Figuring NCAA Chances Much Improved," *Daily Journal* (Tupelo), March 1, 1963, 3.

17. "Tuesday Deadline on State Decision," *Clarion-Ledger*, March 1, 1963, 19; "Deadline Set on NCAA Bid," *Commercial Dispatch*, March 1, 1963, 6; "Tuesday Deadline on Whether State Will Enter NCAA," *Delta Democrat-Times*, March 1, 1963, 6; "Decision on NCAA Play Must be Made Tuesday," *Meridian Star*, March 1, 1963, 9; and "State Is Given Until Tuesday to Reach Decision," *Vicksburg Evening Post*, March 2, 1963, 3.

18. D. W. Colvard Presidential Papers, Box 2 (Department of Archives Mitchell Memorial Library Mississippi State University) and Box A85-203, Volumes I and II, Colvard Miscellaneous Collection. Athletic Department—1962–1963, NCAA Basketball Tournament, A79-39, Box 9, Statement by D. W. Colvard, President of Mississippi State University, Relative to Participation in National Collegiate Athletic Association Championship Competition, March 2, 1963.

19. Michael Ballard, *Maroons and White: Mississippi State University, 1878–2003* (Jackson: University Press of Mississippi, 2008), 144.

20. Guy B. Johnson. "Racial Integration in Southern Higher Education," *Social Forces* 1956, 309–312. *JSTOR Journals*, EBSCO host (accessed January 30, 2015); and Tom Breen, "University of North Carolina Celebrates 1955 Racial Integration Milestone," *Diverse: Issues in Education*, September 21, 2010, http://diverseeducation.com. A professor at the University of North Carolina, Johnson noted in his 1955 article that the majority of schools in the state had integrated based on the threat of legal action. Furthermore, UNC integrated their student body in 1955 with the admission of undergraduates John Brandon, Ralph Frazier, and LeRoy Frazier.

21. Ballard, *Maroon and White*, 148.

22. Ibid.

23. Ballard, *Maroon and White*, 143, 149–150.

24. Dean Colvard Papers, Basketball Team Participation in N.C.C.A. Tournament, A8, Box 9, correspondence from Dick Sanders, Jackson, Mississippi, March 3, 1963.

25. Dean Colvard Papers, Basketball Team Participation in N.C.C.A. Tournament, A8, Box 9, correspondence from J. O. Emmerich, McComb, Mississippi, March 5, 1963.

26. Dean Colvard Papers, Basketball Team Participation in N.C.C.A. Tournament, A8, Box 9, correspondence from Owens F. Alexander, Jackson, Mississippi, March 6, 1963.

27. Dean Colvard Papers, Basketball Team Participation in N.C.C.A. Tournament, A8, Box 9, correspondence from Jocko Maxwell, Newark, New Jersey, March 9, 1963.

28. "State Is Granted Permission to Play in NCAA Tourney," *Clarion-Ledger* and *Jackson Daily News*, March 3, 1963; "State President Favors Playing," *Daily Herald* (Biloxi), March 4, 1963, 18; "State Gets Permission to Enter NCAA Play," *Commercial Dispatch*, March 3, 1963, 1; "State 'Dogs to Play in NCAA Cage Tourney," *Natchez Democrat*, March 3, 1963, 10A; "Trustees to Meet, Study NCAA Trip," *Starkville Daily News*, March 5, 1963, 1–2; "Mississippi State to Go to NCAA Tournament," *Vicksburg Evening Post*, March 3, 1963, 8; and "Mississippi State Wins SEC Title, Will Get Chance at National Crown," *Daily Journal* (Tupelo), March 4, 1963, 2.

29. Billy Rainey, "President of Mississippi State Okays Play in NCAA Tournament," *Meridian Star*, March 3, 1963, 1, 2.

30. "All Still Quiet on Segregation Front," *Jackson Daily News*, March 4, 1963, 9; "State President Favors Playing," *Daily Herald* (Biloxi), March 4, 1963, 18; "Miss. State 'Repeals Law,' Plans

to Play in NCAA," *Hattiesburg American*, March 4, 1963, 18; and "Barnett Has No Comment on Decision by Dr. Colvard," *Vicksburg Evening Post*, March 4, 1963, 5.

31. "MSU Student Senate Votes to Go NCAA," *Jackson Daily News* and *Clarion-Ledger*, March 3, 1963, 4C; "State Gets Permission to Enter NCAA Play," *Commercial Dispatch*, March 3, 1963, 1; "President Colvard Says State Will Play in NCAA Tourney," *Daily Journal* (Tupelo), March 4, 1963, 2; and Carolyn Williams, "Bulldogs Should Be Allowed to Play in NCAA Tourney," the *Reflector* (Mississippi State University), February 28, 1963, 8.

32. "Maroons Undisputed SEC Champions," *Commercial Dispatch*, March 3, 1963, 6; "Gold Sparks State over Ole Miss, 75–72," *Delta Democrat-Times*, March 4, 1963, 5; "State Wins Third SEC Title in Row," *Meridian Star*, March 3, 1963, 8; "State Beats Ole Miss 75–72 in SEC Wrap-Up," *Natchez Democrat*, March 3, 1963, 11A; Robert Davenport, "SEC Stax," *Natchez Democrat*, March 4, 1963, 5; United Press International, "Mississippi State Wins SEC Title, Will Get Chance at National Crown," *Daily Journal* (Tupelo), March 4, 1963, 2; "Miss. State Edges Ole Miss 75 to 72," *Daily Journal* (Tupelo), March 4, 1963, 2; "State Cage Team Wins Third SEC Crown in Row," *Vicksburg Evening Post*, March 3, 1963, 11; Malcolm Balfour, "State Cagers Cop Third Straight Championship," the *Reflector* (Mississippi State University), February 28, 1963, 1, 8; and "State Edges by Ole Miss," the *Reflector* (Mississippi State University), March 7, 1963, 5.

33. "Babe McCarthy Comes to Laurel," *Laurel Leader-Call*, March 4, 1963, 10; Bob Green, "Jubilant Maroons Await NCAA Play," *Meridian Star*, March 4, 1963, 7; "State Coach Exuberant for Team," *Natchez Democrat*, March 4, 1963, 5; and Bob Green "McCarthy Beaming over Verdict," *Vicksburg Evening Post*, March 4, 1963, 5.

34. Associated Press, "NCAA-Bent State Holds 7th Rank," *Jackson Daily News*, March 5, 1963, 9.

35. David M. Moffit, "Maroons Joyous but Cautious over Trip," *Commercial Dispatch*, March 4, 1963, 3; United Press International, "Joy and Caution Is Today's Mode at State," *Delta Democrat-Times*, March 4, 1963, 5; United Press International, "National Crown, Here Comes State," *Jackson Daily News*, March 4, 1963, 9; and David M. Moffit, "Bulldogs Beat Rebels 75–72 to Win SEC Title," *Starkville Daily News*, March 5, 1963, 5.

36. "Little Opposition Heard to State's NCAA Entry," *Clarion-Ledger*, March 4, 1963, 1, 12; and "Protest, Plaudits on MSU Play," *Delta Democrat-Times*, March 4, 1963, 1.

37. MSU Entry Brings Additional Criticism," *Clarion-Ledger*, March 5, 1963, 1; "Solon Calls NCAA Trek 'A New Low,'" *Jackson Daily News*, March 5, 1963, 10; "Basketball Decision Is Blasted," *Enterprise-Journal*, March 5, 1963, 5; "MSU Decision Is 'New Low,' Lawmaker Says," *Meridian Star*, March 5, 1963, 1; and Wayne Freeman, "5 Members Ask Board to Convene," *Starkville Daily News*, March 5, 1963, 1, 2.

38. "MSU Entry Brings Additional Criticism," *Clarion-Ledger*, March 5, 1963, 1; "State College Board Meets Saturday to Consider MSU Issue," *Meridian Star*, March 5, 1963, 1; and "Hester Charges MSU Action Is Mix Surrender," *Natchez Democrat*, March 5, 1963, 8.

39. "Barnett Has No Comment on Decision by Dr. Colvard," *Vicksburg Evening Post*, March 4, 1963, 5.

40. "Board to Discuss State Cage Play," *Daily Herald*, March 6, 1963, 19; "Board Reviews Colvard's Acts," *Laurel Leader-Call*, March 6, 1963, 1; "Board Will Discuss NCAA Trip," *Enterprise-Journal*, March 6, 1963, 9; "State College Board Meets Saturday to Consider MSU Issue," *Meridian Star*, March 5, 1963, 1; "College Board to Confer on Participation," *Natchez Democrat*, March 6, 1963, 1, 8; "Board of Trustees Meeting May Throw Block at NCAA," *Starkville Daily News*, March 6, 1963, 1; "State Quintet Must Wait Outcome of Board Confab," *Tupelo Daily*

Journal, March 6, 1963, 8; and "Will State Go to NCAA?" *Vicksburg Evening Post*, March 6, 1963, 8.

41. Cliff Sessions, "State College Board to Discuss Tourney," *Clarion-Ledger*, March 6, 1963, 1; Cliff Sessions, "Roadblock for State NCAA Play?" *Commercial Dispatch*, March 5, 1963, 1; "To Ban MSU to NCAA?" *Delta Democrat-Times*, March 5, 1963, 1; and "Maroons' Journey May Be Menaced," *Jackson Daily News*, March 5, 1963, 10.

42. "McCarthy Hopes Nothing Will Prevent NCAA Trip," *Laurel Leader-Call*, March 5, 1963, 6.

43. Billy Rainey and Howard Beeland, "Alumni Happy with State's NCAA Plans," *Meridian Star*, March 5, 1963, 7.

44. Ibid.

45. "Board Reviews Colvard's Act," *Laurel Leader-Call*, March 6, 1963, 1; and "Chamber Directors Back Colvard Move," *Starkville Daily News*, March 6, 1963, 1.

46. Charles M. Hills, "Gov. Barnett Opposes State Playing in NCAA," *Clarion-Ledger*, March 7, 1963, 1A, 12A; "Obstacles Mount before Maroons," *Jackson Daily News*, March 7, 1963, 1D; and "Barnett Throws Weight against Tournament Play," *Natchez Democrat*, March 7, 1963, 13.

47. "State's Bid to Play in NCAA Opposed by Barnett," *Daily Herald* (Biloxi), March 7, 1963, 30; "Obstacles Mount in MSU's Path, *Hattiesburg American*, March 7, 1963, 1; "Ross Decries Decision on Tournament Entry," *Laurel Leader-Call*, March 7, 1963, 1–2; "Barnett Opposes State NCAA Trip," *Enterprise-Journal*, March 7, 1963, 8; James Saggus, "Barnett Seeks Halt to NCAA Journey," *Starkville Daily News*, March 7, 1963, 1, 5; and "Ga. Tech May Still Go to NCAA Event," *Vicksburg Evening Post*, March 7, 1963, 14.

48. James Saggus, "Big Challenge Seen in Tourney Debate," *Clarion-Ledger*, March 8, 1963, 1; "Full Board Expected at Tournament Talks," *Hattiesburg American*, March 7, 1963, 1, 12; James Saggus, "Will Board Reverse Colvard's Action?" *Natchez Democrat*, March 8, 1963, 5; James Saggus, "Controversy Continues over NCAA," *Starkville Daily News*, March 8, 1963, 1; and "College Board Member Hints NCAA Rejection," *Daily Journal* (Tupelo), March 8, 1963, 2.

49. "Board to Decide State's Future," *Biloxi Daily Herald*, March 8, 1963, 15; "Full Board Expected at Tournament Talks," *Hattiesburg American*, March 7, 1963, 1; "Controversy Continues over NCAA," *Starkville Daily News*, March 8, 1963, 1; and "College Board Member Hints NCAA Rejection," *Tupelo Daily Journal*, March 8, 1963, 2.

50. William Peart, "Board Member Says Quorum Will Decide," *Jackson Daily News*, March 7, 1963, 1A, 12A.

51. David Sansing, *Making Haste Slowly: The Troubled History of Higher Education in Mississippi* (Jackson: University Press of Mississippi, 1990), 198–199.

52. Ibid., 213.

53. Bill Simpson, "Board Votes in Favor of Playing in Tourney," *Clarion-Ledger* and *Jackson Daily News*, March 10, 1963, 1A, 10A; Cliff Sessions, "Colvard Tells State to Go to Tournament," *Commercial Dispatch*, March 10, 1963, 1; "Board Gives Nod to State Maroons," *Natchez Democrat*, March 10, 1963, 10; "College Board Rules State's Cage Team Can Play NCAA Tournament," *Daily Journal* (Tupelo), March 11, 1963, 2; "Officials Back State's Move to Play in NCAA Cage Meet," *Vicksburg Evening Post*, March 10, 1963, 1; and "Colvard's Decision Stands," the *Reflector* (Mississippi State University), March 9, 1963, 1.

54. "MSU's Bulldogs Given Chance to Complete in National Tourney," *Delta Democrat-Times*, March 10, 1963, 1; and "Green Light Given MSU Team to Participate in NCAA Play," *Meridian Star*, March 10, 1963, 1, 2.

55. "Governor Hopes Miss. State Wins National Championship," *Clarion-Ledger* and *Jackson Daily News*, March 10, 1963.

56. "MSU's Bulldogs Given Chance to Complete in National Tourney," *Delta Democrat-Times*, March 10, 1963, 1.

57. John Hall, "State Quintet Gets NCAA Green Light," *Daily Herald* (Biloxi), March 11, 1963, 19; John Hall, "Is Board's Decision a Blow to Segregation?" *Hattiesburg American*, March 11, 1963, 10; John Hall, "Decision to Let State Play Presents Hot Arguments," *Jackson Daily News*, March 11, 1963, 14; John Hall, "Decision of Board Promotes Argument," *Laurel Leader-Call*, March 11, 1963, 11; "Argument over Game Rages On," *Enterprise-Journal*, March 9, 1963, 1, 3; and John Hall, "Even Women Couldn't Stop State from Going to NCAA," *Vicksburg Evening Post*, March 11, 1963, 3.

58. John Hall, "Decision to Let State Play Presents Hot Arguments," *Jackson Daily News*, March 11, 1963, 14; "McCarthy's Happy with Board's Vote," *Jackson Daily News*, March 11, 1963, 12; "McCarthy Grateful of Board's Decision," *Natchez Democrat*, March 10, 1963, 10A; "Team Grateful Says Maroon Cage Coach," *Natchez Democrat*, March 11, 1963, 5; and McCarthy Gratified with Go Ahead Vote," *Starkville Daily News*, March 12, 1963, 3.

59. Julius Eric Thompson, *The Black Press in Mississippi, 1865–1985* (Westport, CT: Greenwood Publishing, 1993), 62.

60. "Go…Go…Maroons," *Jackson Advocate*, 16 March 1963, 3.

61. John Hall, "Decision to Let State Play Presents Hot Arguments," *Jackson Daily News*, March 11, 1963, 14; "'You Got Blood on Your Hands,' Tom Tubb Told," *Meridian Star*, March 10, 1963, 1; and John Hall, "Even Women Couldn't Stop State from Going to NCAA," *Vicksburg Evening Post*, March 11, 1963, 3.

62. "Miss. State's NCAA Bound S.E.C. Champions," *Jackson Daily News*, March 10, 1963, 1C.

63. "Maroons Begin Final Practices," *Jackson Daily News*, March 12, 1963, 13.

64. United Press International, "Ramblers Ready for State Friday," *Jackson Daily News*, March 12, 1963, 12; and George Sainsbury, "Babe McCarthy Scouts Loyola, Is Impressed by Great Speed," *Meridian Star*, March 12, 1963, 7.

65. Robert Fulton, "Loyola Best Team State Has Ever Met—McCarthy," *Clarion-Ledger*, March 13, 1963, 15.

66. Gene Roberts and Hank Klibanoff, *The Race Beat: The Press, the Civil Rights Struggle, and the Awakening of a Nation* (New York: Knopf, 2006), 93.

67. "Ask Hinds Court to End Miss. State U. Injunction," *Clarion-Ledger*, March 14, 1963, 1A, 11A; "State Enjoined from Participating in NCAA Basketball Tournament," *Natchez Democrat*, March 14, 1963, 12; James Saggus, "Injunction Issued to Block MSU Trip," *Starkville Daily News*, March 14, 1963, 1; "Court Injunction Seeking to Keep State Five Out of Integrated NCAA Basketball Tourney," *Daily Journal* (Tupelo), March 14, 1963, 2; and Malcolm Balfour, "Mississippi State Maroons Now on the Way to History Making Bout with Loyola of Chicago," the *Reflector* (Mississippi State University), March 14, 1963, 5.

68. Sherrill Nash, "Harassed Bulldogs Prepare for Loyola," *Starkville Daily News*, March 15, 1963, 1.

69. Robert Fulton, "State Leaves for Tourney," *Clarion-Ledger*, March 14, 1963, 1E.

70. "State Team Takes Off for NCAA Event," *Daily Herald* (Biloxi), March 14, 1963, 31; "Miss. State Heads for Tourney," *Hattiesburg American*, March 14, 1963, 1, 2; "Bulldogs Head for

Tournament," *Enterprise-Journal*, March 14, 1963, 9; and "Maroons Enplane for NCAA Despite State Court Order," *Vicksburg Evening Post*, March 14, 1963, 1, 8. "State Flies to Lansing in Face of Injunction," *Laurel Leader-Call*, March 14, 1963, 14; "School Spokesman Says Maroons Will Leave Today as Scheduled," *Natchez Democrat*, March 14, 1963, 12; "Bulldogs Head North to Tourney," *Starkville Daily News*, March 14, 1963, 1; John J. McDavitt, "State Cagers Fly North, Wait for Court to Okay Play," *Commercial Dispatch*, March 14, 1963, 1; "State Team Goes Despite Injunction," *Delta Democrat-Times*, March 14, 1963, 1; "MSU Team on Way to NCAA Playoff," *Meridian Star*, March 14, 1963, 1, 2; and "MSU Team Off to Integrated Tourney," *Meridian Star*, March 14, 1963, 1, 2.

71. Eddie Dean, "Fans Watch 'Dogs Leave," *Commercial Dispatch*, March 14, 1963, 1.

72. George Anderson, "MSU Team Leaves Today for NCAA Tourney," *Starkville Daily News*, March 14, 1963, 3.

73. William Peart, "Legal Barrier Removed for State Team," *Jackson Daily News*, March 15, 1963, 1, 16A; "Injunction Suspended," *Natchez Democrat*, March 15, 1963, 8; "Injunction Is Removed by Justice," *Starkville Daily News*, March 15, 1963, 1; and "Injunction Held Up, State's Cagers Set for Loyola Tilt," *Daily Journal* (Tupelo), March 15, 1963, 1.

74. William Peart, "Legal Barrier Removed for State Team," *Jackson Daily News*, March 15, 1963, 1, 16A.

75. "Mississippi State Tackles Loyola in NCAA Playoff," *Daily Journal* (Tupelo), March 15, 1963, 2.

76. McCarthy Picked Up in Nashville," *Starkville Daily News*, March 15, 1963, 1.

77. "No Demonstrations Mar MSU Michigan Arrival," *Clarion-Ledger*, March 15, 1963, 1, 24.

78. George Anderson, "State Plays Loyola Team Tonight," *Starkville Daily News*, March 15, 1963, 3.

79. Jerry Liska, "Maroons Lauded for Making Trip," *Daily Herald* (Biloxi), March 15, 1963, 27; "Maroons Face Loyola Tonight," *Hattiesburg American*, March 15, 1963, 10; Jerry Liska, "State Has Free Rein to Tangle with Loyola," *Laurel Leader-Call*, March 15, 1963, 15; "Bulldogs Are Ready for Tonight's Clash," *Enterprise-Journal*, March 15, 1963, 9; and Jerry Liska and Robert Fulton, "State's Escape over 'Wall' Well-Planned," *Vicksburg Evening Post*, March 15, 1963, 6.

80. "State Finally Set for State, Loyola," *Jackson Daily News*, March 15, 1963, 13.

81. "Injunctioners Get 'Rope' from State Students," *Jackson Daily News*, March 14, 1963, 1B; "Effigy Hangings on State Campus," *Laurel Leader-Call*, March 14, 1963, 14; and Lewis Jackson, "Students Protest," the *Reflector* (Mississippi State University), March 14, 1963, 1.

82. Joe Dan Gold, interview with author, July 23, 2009.

83. Joe Dan Gold, interview with author, July 23, 2009.

84. "Just Before the Battle," *Jackson Daily News* and *Clarion-Ledger*, March 15, 1963; and "Mississippi State-Loyola Captains Shake Hands," *Vicksburg Evening Post*, March 18, 1963, 5.

85. "State Beaten by Loyola in NCAA Event," *Daily Herald* (Biloxi), March 16, 1963, 16; Jerry Liska, "Loyola Ramblers Best MSU Bulldogs 61–51," *Meridian Star*, March 16, 1963, 7; and "Loyola Crubs Ambitious State 61–51 As Illinois Tags Bowling Green Five," *Daily Journal* (Tupelo), March 16–17, 1963, 2.

86. "Maroons Lead Early but Fall to Ramblers," *Delta Democrat-Times*, March 17, 1963, 10.

87. "State's Coach Counting on Another Shot," *Jackson Daily News*, March 16, 1963, 1, 20A; and "Maroons Lead Early but Fall to Ramblers," *Delta Democrat-Times*, March 17, 1963, 10.

88. "'It Was Nice Way to Get Beat,' McCarthy Says of Loss," *Meridian Star*, March 16, 1963, 1.

89. George Anderson, "Loyola Drops State 61–51; Bowling Green Foe Tonight," *Starkville Daily News*, March 16, 1963, 1, 3.

90. "State Stall Stuns NCAA," *Starkville Daily News*, March 16, 1963, 3.

91. Jerry Green, "No Incidents in State-Loyola Tilt," *Daily Herald* (Biloxi), March 16, 1963, 16; Jerry Green, "'Talk about the Way Loyola Played'—Babe," *Hattiesburg American*, March 16, 1963, 8; Jerry Green, "Ramblers Too Tall for State Maroons," *Laurel Leader-Call*, March 16, 1963, 6; "State Is Defeated by Loyola in First NCAA Appearance," *Hattiesburg American*, March 16, 1963, 8; "State Hoping for Consolation Win," *Vicksburg Evening Post*, March 16, 1963, 2; and "State Bows to Loyola of Chicago," *Natchez Democrat*, March 16, 1963, 4.

92. Robert Fulton, "Miss. Cagers Defeated by Loyola in NCAA Tourney," *Clarion-Ledger*, March 16, 1963, 9.

93. Joe Dan Gold, interview with author, July 23, 2009.

94. Robert Fulton, "State Cage Aces Win Consolation Contest," *Clarion-Ledger* and *Jackson Daily News*, March 17, 1963; Lee Baker, "Maroons Control Charity Tosses," *Clarion-Ledger* and *Jackson Daily News*, March 17, 1963; "Bulldogs Win in Consolation," *Commercial Dispatch*, March 17, 1963, 6; Sheldon Sakowitz, "Ramblers Take Title, Maroons Finish Third," *Laurel Leader-Call*, March 18, 1963, 10; "State Cagers Head Home after Victory," *Meridian Star*, March 17, 1963, 1; Jerry Liska, "Bulldogs defeat Bowling Green 5," *Meridian Star*, March 17, 1963, 8; "State Rolls to 65–60 Win over Bowling Green," *Natchez Democrat*, March 17, 1963, 9A; George Anderson, "State Cagers Win One and Lose One in First NCAA Tourney," *Starkville Daily News*, March 19, 1963, 3; "State Third in NCAA Bid," *Daily Journal* (Tupelo), March 18, 1963, 3; and "Miss. State Holds Off Bowling Green Five, 65–60," *Vicksburg Evening Post*, March 17, 1963, 12.

95. "All NCAA Tourney Selection," *Delta Democrat-Times*, March 18, 1963, 9; and "Mitchell Is Named on All Tourney," *Starkville Daily News*, March 19, 1963, 3.

96. "Return of the Heroes," *Clarion-Ledger*, March 18, 1963, 1C; "Babe McCarthy Proud of Maroons Efforts in NCAA," *Delta Democrat-Times*, March 18, 1963, 9; "McCarthy Proud of Maroons," *Jackson Daily News*, March 18, 1963, 12; "Bulldogs Get Big Welcome Home," *Meridian Star*, March 17, 1963, 7; and "Wants State to Play in NCAA Meet Again," *Daily Journal* (Tupelo), March 18, 1963, 2.

97. Lee Baker, "You Bet, Maroons, We Still Love You, Win or Lose," *Jackson Daily News*, March 18, 1963, 12; and "Champs Return," *Starkville Daily News*, March 19, 1963, 1.

98. Robert Fulton, "Miss. State's NCAA Tourney Debut Memorable, Rewarding, Satisfying," *Clarion-Ledger*, March 18, 1963, 3C.

99. Ibid.

100. Ibid.

101. Dean Colvard Papers, Basketball Team Participation in N.C.C.A. Tournament, A8, Box 9, "Citizens of Mississippi," Sons of Mississippi/The Rebel Underground, date unknown.

102. Dean Colvard Papers, Basketball Team Participation in N.C.C.A. Tournament, A8, Box 9, flyer, unknown author, unknown date.

103. "College Board Will Shun Sports Issue," *Jackson Daily News*, March 21, 1963, 1.

104. "'Mixing' Proposal Refused by State's College Board," *Clarion-Ledger*, March 22, 1963, 1; "College Board Defines Policy," *Delta Democrat-Times*, March 22, 1963, 1; "Board Defeats Plan to Make Them Responsible for Integrated Play," *Commercial Dispatch*, March 22, 1963, 6; and "State College Board Rejects Motion," *Natchez Democrat*, March 22, 1963, 12.

105. "Trustees Pass Buck," *Mississippi Free Press*, March 30, 1963, 4.

106. The following newspapers failed to publish an article on the State College Board's decision to give all power on decisions involving a college or university's potential participation in integrated athletic competition, essentially ending the unwritten law: *Jackson Advocate, Laurel Leader-Call, Hattiesburg American, Daily Herald* (Biloxi), *Enterprise-Journal, Meridian Star, Starkville Daily News*, and the *Daily Journal* (Tupelo).

107. "Injunction against MSU Is Dissolved," *Clarion-Ledger*, April 3, 1963, 12; and "Judge Ends NCAA Suit," *Daily Journal* (Tupelo), April 3, 1963, 2.

108. "Babe Resigns as Coach at Miss. State," *Clarion-Ledger*, March 3, 1965, 15; "McCarthy Leaves State," *Commercial Dispatch*, March 3, 1965, 6A; "Babe Steps Down at Mississippi St.," *Jackson Daily News*, March 3, 1965, 1; "Coach Babe McCarthy Resigns," *Starkville Daily News*, March 3, 1965, 3; and "State Looking for New Cage Mentor," *Vicksburg Evening Post*, March 3, 1965, 10.

109. "Babe Steps Down at Mississippi St.," *Jackson Daily News*, March 3, 1965, 1. Of the noted articles on McCarthy's resignation, only the *Jackson Daily News* mentioned the 1962–1963 Bulldogs and their NCAA appearance.

110. Carl Walters, "Shavin's," *Clarion-Ledger*, March 4, 1965, 5; and Wayne Thompson, "Hind Sight," *Clarion-Ledger*, March 4, 1965, 7.

111. Robert Fulton, "Babe's Resigning . . . Scoop No One Wanted," *Meridian Star*, March 3, 1965, 10.

112. "No Definite Plans for A Successor," *Starkville Daily News*, March 3, 1965, 3.

113. *2009–2010 Mississippi State University Men's Basketball Media Guide* (Starkville: Mississippi State University Athletic Department, 2009), 147–148, 180.

114. Basketball (Men), *The GW and Foggy Bottom Historical Encyclopedia*, Special Collections Research Center, Gelman Library, George Washington University, http://encyclopedia. gwu.edu/gwencyclopedia/index.php?title=Basketball_%28Men%29 (accessed on December 6, 2010).

115. Terry Pluto, *Loose Balls: The Short, Wild Life of the American Basketball Association* (New York: Simon and Schuster, 1991), 75, 247, 272–273, 337–338.

116. "For the Record," *Sports Illustrated*, September 17, 1973, 147.

117. "For the Record," *Sports Illustrated*, March 31, 1975, 85.

118. Ballard, *Maroons and White*, 152.

119. "Joe Dan Gold Named State Basketball Coach," *Jackson Daily News* and *Clarion-Ledger*, March 7, 1965, 1B; Wayne Thompson, "Gold Discuss Coaching Plans," *Jackson Daily News* and *Clarion-Ledger*, March 7, 1965, 1B, 8B; and George Anderson, "Joe Dan Gold Is Named Basketball Coach for Bulldogs," *Starkville Daily News*, March 9, 1965, 9.

120. Joe Dan Gold, interview with author, July 23, 2009.

121. "Tupelo Editorial Says NCAA Play by MSU Is Good Thing," *Clarion-Ledger*, March 6, 1963, 18; "MSU in the NCAA Won't Bring about Integrated Schools," *Delta Democrat-Times*, March 6, 1963, 5; and "Tupelo Paper Defends Maroons' NCAA Rights," *Jackson Daily News*, March 6, 1963, 13.

122. Dick Lightsey, "Bunts, Boots and Bounces," *Daily Herald* (Biloxi), March 15, 1963, 27.

123. Billy Ray, "Press Box Views," *Vicksburg Evening Post*, February 28, 1963, 14.

124. Billy Ray, "Press Box Views," *Vicksburg Evening Post*, March 6, 1963, 9.

125. Billy Ray, "Press Box Views," *Vicksburg Evening Post*, March 13, 1963, 13.

126. Billy Ray, "Press Box Views," *Vicksburg Evening Post*, March 19, 1963, 10.

127. Eddie Dean, "Scramblin'," *Commercial Dispatch*, February 28, 1963, 8.

128. Eddie Dean, "Scramblin'," *Commercial Dispatch*, March 7, 1963, 8.

129. Eddie Dean, "Scramblin'," *Commercial Dispatch*, March 17, 1963, 6.

130. Davies, *The Press and Race*, 174, 196.

131. Davies, *The Press and Race*, 112.

132. "*State Decision to Enter Meet*," *Daily Herald* (Biloxi), March 4, 1963, 1, 8; "Editor Praises Colvard's Move," *Commercial Dispatch*, March 5, 1963, 4; and "Newspaper Commends Colvard," *Jackson Daily News*, March 5, 1963, 9.

133. Lee Baker, "Baker's Dozen," *Jackson Daily News*, March 4, 1963, 9.

134. Lee Baker, "Baker's Dozen," *Jackson Daily News*, March 6, 1963, 12.

135. Lee Baker, "Baker's Dozen," *Jackson Daily News*, March 14, 1963, 2C.

136. Lee Baker, "Baker's Dozen," *Jackson Daily News*, March 15, 1963, 13.

137. Lee Baker, "Baker's Dozen," *Jackson Daily News*, March 16, 1963, 2.

138. Ibid.

139. Lee Baker, "Baker's Dozen," *Jackson Daily News*, March 18, 1963, 12, 15.

140. Carl Walters, "Shavin's," *Clarion-Ledger*, March 1, 1963, 18.

141. Wayne Thompson, "Hind Sight," *Clarion-Ledger*, March 21, 1963, 3D.

142. "Hour of Decision," *Starkville Daily News*, March 1, 1963, 4.

143. George Anderson, "Time Out for Sports," *Starkville Daily News*, March 19, 1963, 3.

144. Malcolm Balfour, "Sports Talk," the *Reflector* (Mississippi State University), March 7, 1963, 5.

145. Bill Lunardini, "Sports Shorts," the *Reflector* (Mississippi State University), February 28, 1963, 7.

146. "NCAA and Colvard," the *Reflector* (Mississippi State University), March 21, 1963, 4.

147. "Paper Slap Decision of Dr. Colvard," *Starkville Daily News*, March 7, 1963, 4.

148. Jimmy Ward, "Covering the Crossroads," *Jackson Daily News*, March 22, 1963, 1.

149. Ibid.

150. "College Board Should Utilize Opportunity to Review Trends," *Clarion-Ledger*, March 6, 1963, 10.

151. "Coaches Seek Negroes, Walls Begin to Fall," *Clarion-Ledger*, March 8, 1963, 1A.

152. Ibid; and "*Meridian Star* Questions Wisdom of MSU in NCAA," *Delta Democrat-Times*, March 6, 1963, 5.

153. Tom Ethridge, "Mississippi Notebook," *Clarion-Ledger*, March 9, 1963, 4, 9.

154. Ibid.

155. Ed Staton, "Statin' Ideas," *Hattiesburg American*, February 27, 1963, 14.

156. "In the Open," *Hattiesburg American*, March 12, 1963, 12.

157. "Voice of the People," *Clarion-Ledger*, March 8, 1963, 2C.

158. "Voice of the People," *Clarion-Ledger*, March 8, 1963, 2C.

159. Ibid.

160. "Voice of the People," *Clarion-Ledger*, March 9, 1963, 4 and 9.

161. Ibid.

162. "Voice of the People," *Clarion-Ledger*, March 13, 1963, 6.

163. "Our Readers' Viewpoint," *Jackson Daily News*, March 5, 1963, 4.

164. "Our Readers' Viewpoint," *Jackson Daily News*, March 7, 1963, 6.

165. "Our Readers' Viewpoint," *Jackson Daily News*, March 9, 1963, 6.

166. Ibid.

167. "Our Readers' Viewpoint," *Jackson Daily News*, 20 March 1963, 5B.

168. "Letters to the Editor," *Starkville Daily News*, February 28, 1963, 4.

169. "Letters to the Editor," *Starkville Daily News*, March 23, 1963, 4.

170. Colvard Miscellaneous Collection, Box 2 and A85-203, Volumes I and II, D. W. Colvard Presidential Papers, the Department of Archives, Mitchell Memorial Library, Mississippi State University.

171. "Letters to the Editor," the *Reflector* (Mississippi State University), March 7, 1963, 4.

172. Ibid.

173. "Letters," the *Reflector* (Mississippi State University), March 28, 1963, 7.

174. Joe Dan Gold, interview with author, July 23, 2009.

Chapter 6. I've Made My Last Trip to Places like Mississippi

1. M.J. O'Brien, *We Shall Not Be Moved: The Jackson Woolworth's Sit-In and the Movement It Inspired* (Jackson: University Press of Mississippi, 2013), 120–144, 152.

2. David R. Davies, *The Press and Race: Mississippi Journalists Confront the Movement* (Jackson: University Press of Mississippi, 2001), 73–74.

3. Davies, *The Press and Race*, 98.

4. Davies, *The Press and Race*, 256–257

5. Davies, *The Press and Race*, 40.

6. Charles M. Payne, *I've Got the Light of Freedom: The Organizing Tradition and the Mississippi Freedom Struggle* (Berkeley, CA: University of California Press, 1996), 301.

7. John Dittmer, *Local People: The Struggle for Civil Rights in Mississippi* (Urbana: University of Illinois Press, 1994), 251.

8. Payne, *I've Got the Light of Freedom,* 301.

9. Dittmer, *Local People*, 257, 260, 264.

10. Susan Weill, *In a Madhouse's Din: Civil Rights Coverage by Mississippi's Daily Press, 1948–1968* (Westport, Conn: Praeger, 2002), 108–109

11. Weill, *In a Madhouse's Din*, 109–113.

12. Dittmer, *Local People*, 390.

13. Dittmer, *Local People*, 391 and Payne, *I've Got the Light of Freedom,* 398.

14. Payne, *I've Got the Light of Freedom,* 398.

15. Michael Ballard, *Maroons and White: Mississippi State University, 1878–2003* (Jackson: University Press of Mississippi, 2008), 153.

16. Perry Wallace, interview with author, April 18, 2006; and Walt Smith, "'I've Made My Last Trip to Places Like Mississippi'—Perry Wallace," *Meridian Star*, February 13, 1970, 10.

17. James P. Marshall, *Student Activism and Civil Rights in Mississippi: Protest Politics and the Struggle for Racial Justice, 1960–1965* (Baton Rouge: Louisiana State University Press, 2013), 172.

18. Nossiter, *Of Long Memory*, 202; and Dickerson, *Dixie's Dirty Little Secret*, 195. Nossiter writes that the integration of the schools in Jackson had gone so smoothly that veteran broadcast journalist Walter Cronkite cited the city and the school system as the ideal model for

implementing integration. Dickerson identified the "surprising" election of Waller as having a social and political impact throughout the state and whose decisions in office helped lead to the end of the Sovereignty Commission in 1977.

19. Alex A. Alston and James L. Dickerson, *Devil's Sanctuary: An Eyewitness Account of Mississippi Hate Crimes* (Chicago: Chicago Review Press, 2009), 329. Dickerson, a former *Jackson Daily News* reporter during the 1970s, writes that Ward was "a personable man with a good sense of humor who never made a racist comment in my presence," despite his sour reputation.

20. Kelso Sturgeon, "Cats Want Negroes Recruited in SEC," *Clarion-Ledger*, March 26, 1963, 13; "Will Negroes Enter S.E.C.?" *Jackson Daily News*, March 26, 1963, 13; and "Kentucky Board to Study Mixing," *Jackson Daily News*, April 4, 1963, 11.

21. "'Tucky Questions SEC on Integrated Athletics," *Clarion-Ledger*, April 13, 1963, 8; "Not at Home Vow Maroons," *Jackson Daily News*, April 13, 1963, 2; "Tech, Tulane, Kentucky Will Break Color Barrier in Athletics," *Meridian Star*, April 13, 1963, 7; "Two SEC Teams Agree to Play against Negroes," *Natchez Democrat*, April 13, 1963, 5; "State Replies 'No' to Mixed Sports Inquiry," *Starkville Daily News*, April 13, 1963, 3; "Three SEC Schools Okay Mixed Athletic Lineups," *Daily Journal* (Tupelo), April 16, 1963, 2; and "Tech and Tulane Okay Integration," *Vicksburg Evening Post*, April 13, 1963, 3.

22. "U.K. Athletic Directors Formally O.K. Mixing," *Clarion-Ledger*, April 30, 1963, 11; "Kentucky Says Negroes 'SI,'" *Commercial Dispatch*, April 30, 1963, 7; "Kentucky Formally Favors Sports-Mix," *Jackson Daily News*, April 30, 1963, 10; "'Tucky Negroes Out This Season," *Jackson Daily News*, April 30, 1963, 16; "'Tucky May Use Negro Athletes," *Meridian Star*, April 30, 1963, 9; "Kentucky Lowers Sports Race Bar," *Starkville Daily News*, April 30, 1963, 3; and "Kentucky Asks to Integrate Athletic Setup Inside Framework of Circuit," *Daily Journal* (Tupelo), April 30, 1963, 2.

23. "Tulane Frosh Win Two Games," *Times-Picayune*, March 14, 1965, 7E.

24. The *Jackson Daily News*, *Clarion-Ledger*, and *Starkville Daily News* were examined from March 1, 1965, through May 1, 1965. No articles on MSU's baseball games against Tulane were found.

25. "1st SEC Negro Athlete Plays with Tulane," *Jackson Daily News*, March 8, 1966, 16; and "Negro Makes Debut with Tulane Nine," *Vicksburg Evening Post*, March 9, 1966, 11.

26. "Coleman to Take SEC Office Today," *Times-Picayune*, April 1, 1966, 5C.

27. The following newspapers were consulted for this information on April 15, April 16, April 30, and May 1, 1966, the dates in which MSU would have been playing Tulane's baseball team in New Orleans and Starkville. None of following newspapers made mention of Martin in their accounts: *Daily Herald* (Biloxi), *Clarion-Ledger*, *Commercial Dispatch*, *Delta Democrat-Times*, *Hattiesburg American*, *Jackson Daily News*, *Meridian Star*, *Natchez Democrat*, *Starkville Daily News*, *Daily Journal* (Tupelo), and *Vicksburg Evening Post*.

28. "Wallace First Negro to Get SEC Grant," *Jackson Daily News*, April 4, 1966, 4.

29. William Giles Papers, A81-25, Box 5, Athletic Department, 1966-67. Letter to Ralph Brown from T. K. Martin, January 4, 1967. University Archives, Special Collections, Mississippi State University.

30. While freshmen games generally did not draw a lot of media attention, when they were covered, the freshman teams of Mississippi State University, the University of Mississippi, and the University of Southern Mississippi were often nicknamed by the press in order to distinguish the rookie team from their varsity counterparts. At Mississippi State, the freshman squad

was often referred to as the "Bullpups" rather than the Bulldogs; at Ole Miss, it was the "Baby Rebs" as opposed to the Rebels; and at USM, and it was the "Baby Southerners" or the "Baby Giants" rather than the Southerners or the "Golden Giants."

31. "Bullpups Hammer Vanderbilt Frosh," *Jackson Daily News*, February 28, 1967, 9.

32. Walt Smith, "'I've Made My Last Trip to Places Like Mississippi'—Perry Wallace," *Meridian Star*, February 13, 1970, 10.

33. Wilbert Jordan Jr., interview with author, August 15, 2010.

34. The newspapers consulted include the *Jackson Daily News*, the *Clarion-Ledger*, the *Vicksburg Evening Post*, the *Hattiesburg American*, the *Student Printz*, the *Daily Herald*, the *Meridian Star*, the *Delta Democrat-Times*, the *Jackson Advocate*, and the *Starkville Daily News* during Jordan's first two seasons as a member of the Southern Miss freshmen and varsity basketball team from November 1968 through the end of his sophomore season in March 1970.

35. Wilbert Jordan Jr., interview with author, August 15, 2010.

36. *2009–2010 University of Southern Mississippi Men's Basketball Media Guide* (Hattiesburg: University of Southern Mississippi Athletic Department, 2009), 134.

37. Email correspondence with Kyle Campbell, Associate Director of Athletics Media Relations, University of Mississippi, September 21, 2006.

38. "'Cool-Aid' Takes Word to the Wise," *Oxford Eagle*, December 3, 1970, 9B.

39. The newspapers consulted include the *Jackson Daily News*, the *Clarion-Ledger*, the *Vicksburg Evening Post*, the *Oxford Eagle*, the *Daily Mississippian*, the *Hattiesburg American*, the *Daily Herald*, the *Meridian Star*, the *Delta Democrat-Times*, the *Jackson Advocate*, and the *Starkville Daily News* during Ball's first two seasons as a member of the Ole Miss freshmen and varsity basketball team from his signing in August 1970 through the end of his sophomore season in March 1972.

40. "Ole Miss Make Final Frosh Player Signups," *Oxford Eagle*, September 10, 1970, 4C.

41. Dudley Marble, "Frosh Cage Star Keeping 'Cool,'" *Daily Mississippian* (the University of Mississippi), February 5, 1971, 7.

42. Harvey Faust, "Between the Foul Lines," *Oxford Eagle*, November 10, 1971, 8A.

43. Lee Baker, "Magnolia State Cagers Go on Display Tonight," *Jackson Daily News*, December 1, 1971, 1E.

44. Lee Baker, "Baker's Dozen," *Jackson Daily News*, February 7, 1972, 18A; Lee Baker, "Rebels Rap Tigers 101–78; Bulldogs Startle Tide 97–91," *Jackson Daily News* (1B) and *Clarion-Ledger* (9B), March 5, 1972; Lee Baker, "Baker's Dozen," *Jackson Daily News*, March 6, 1972, 14A; and Lee Baker, "'Bama Stumbles Past Ole Miss 5," *Jackson Daily News*, March 7, 1972, 11A.

45. "Jump Ball," *Jackson Daily News*, December 2, 1971, 13B; "Tennessee's Late Comeback Barely Nudges Out Ole Miss," *Jackson Daily News*, January 11, 1972, 9; "Nabs Rebound," *Jackson Daily News*, February 17, 1972, 9B; "Vanderbilt 5 Hammers by Ole Miss," *Jackson Daily News*, February 17, 1972, 9B; "Coolidge Keying Ole Miss Drive," *Jackson Daily News*, January 28, 1972, 14A; "Out of Coolidge Ball's Reach," *Jackson Daily News*, February 29, 1972, 10A; and "Interception by Rebs' Coolidge Ball," *Jackson Daily News*, March 7, 1972, 11A.

46. Robert Fulton, "Kentucky Roars Back to Smother Ole Miss," *Meridian Star*, January 9, 1972, 1C; "Rebs Have a Ball," *Meridian Star*, January 27, 1972, 9; Bo King, "Rebs Foul Out of SEC Race," *Meridian Star*, February 8, 1972, 8; and Robert Fulton, "Coolidge Ball Came to Play, Not to Crash Barriers," *Meridian Star*, March 4, 1972, 3B.

47. Mickey Edwards, "They Say," *Hattiesburg American*, December 16, 1971, 11.

48. *2009–2010 University of Mississippi Men's Basketball Media Guide* (Oxford: University of Mississippi Athletic Department, 2009), 112–117, 131–132, 135–139, 142.

49. Ballard, *Maroon and White*, 153.

50. Curt Guenther, "Local Grid Star Shines," the *Reflector* (Mississippi State University), April 25, 1967, 10.

51. George Farr, "Prewitt to Return," the *Reflector* (Mississippi State University), May 5, 1967, 8.

52. "Bulldogs Ink Top Football Prospects," *Starkville Daily News*, December 17, 1968, 4.

53. "Second Negro Signs with State," *Starkville Daily News*, December 17, 1968, 4.

54. "4 SEC Schools Sign Negroes to Grants," *Jackson Daily News*, December 16, 1968, 4B; and "4 Negroes Sign SEC Football Scholarships," *Vicksburg Evening Post*, December 16, 1968, 9.

55. "State Shatters Tradition by Signing Tupelo Negro," *Meridian Star*, December 16, 1968, 9.

56. Gary Weatherly, "Negro Athletes May Bring Victory," the *Reflector* (Mississippi State University), September 24, 1968, 5.

57. Esther M. Thornton, "Black Not Negro," the *Reflector* (Mississippi State University), October 4, 1968, 5.

58. Nook Nicholson, "Courtmen Open Practice Soon," the *Reflector* (Mississippi State University), October 12, 1971, 15.

59. "Bullpup Coach Jack Berkshire Tags Team His Best at Mississippi State," *Starkville Daily News*, March 8, 1972, 3.

60. Ibid.

61. Nook Nicholson, "Courtmen Open Practice Soon," the *Reflector* (Mississippi State University), October 12, 1971, 15.

62. Jim Nicholson, "Bulldogs Open Cage Season with 71–66 Drubbing of South Alabama," the *Reflector* (Mississippi State University), December 3, 1971, 9. While the *Reflector* did not identify Jim Nicholson as "Nook" Nicholson, it is assumed that because both were identified as sports writers during the same semester that they are one and the same.

63. "Bullpups Trample South 'Bama Frosh," *Jackson Daily News*, December 2, 1971, 10B.

64. The *Hattiesburg American* and the *Vicksburg Evening Post* were both examined from December 1, 1971, through March 8, 1972. Neither publication published anything pertaining to Fry, Jenkins, or the freshman Mississippi State basketball team.

65. Larry Templeton, "Michigan State Hands Miss. State First Loss," *Starkville Daily News*, January 3, 1973, 3; Larry Templeton, "Jenkins, Knarr Pace MSU Win over Hawaii," *Starkville Daily News*, January 4, 1973, 3; Sherrill Nash, "Bullies Fight UK All Way; See Change to Triumph Slip," *Starkville Daily News*, January 9, 1973, 2; and Larry Templeton "State Upsets Georgia on Cold Road, 90–84," *Starkville Daily News*, January 30, 1973, 4; Sherrill Nash, "Fry, Knarr Pour in 30 Apiece as MSU Downs Auburn 94–87," *Starkville Daily News*, February 20, 1973, 4; and Lee Baker, "Bulldogs Bother Tide before Bowing 92–87," *Jackson Daily News* and *Clarion-Ledger*, March 4, 1973, 1D.

66. "Bulldogs Hit the Road for Date with South Alabama," *Starkville Daily News*, December 6, 1972, 4; Sherrill Nash, "Miss. State Rally Falls Short in Loss to Tigers," *Starkville Daily News*, February 6, 1973, 2; Sherrill Nash, "Fry, Knarr Pour in 30 Apiece as MSU Downs Auburn 94–87,"

Starkville Daily News, February 20, 1973, 4; and "Miss. State in Season's Final against Vandy Today," *Starkville Daily News*, March 10, 1973, 1.

67. Scoop Bass, "Bulldogs Fall to Florida Gators," the *Reflector* (Mississippi State University), January 30, 1973, 9; "State Takes on Vols Next," the *Reflector* (Mississippi State University), February 9, 1973, 8; and Scoop Bass, "Dogs Win," the *Reflector* (Mississippi State University), February 20, 1973, 9.

68. Ponto Downing, "Bulldogs Down Texas in True Test, 80–69," *Clarion-Ledger*, December 5, 1972, 5B.

69. Carl Walters, "Shavin's," *Clarion-Ledger*, January 31, 1973, 21; and Carl Walters, "Shavin's," *Clarion-Ledger*, February 2, 1973, 3C.

70. "Bullies, Rebs Tonight," *Meridian Star*, January 13, 1973, 2B; and "Brave Bulldogs to Battle 'Bama," *Meridian Star*, February 2, 1973, 2B.

71. Billy Ray, "Press Box Views," *Vicksburg Evening Post*, February 13, 1973, 14.

72. Dick Lightsey, "Dick Lightsey," *Daily Herald* (Biloxi), December 8, 1972, 31.

73. AP Wirephoto, "Big Obstacle," *Hattiesburg American*, January 15, 1973, 27; AP Wirephoto, "Jumper over Jenkins," *Hattiesburg American*, February 6, 1973, 8; and AP Wirephoto, "Putting One Up," *Hattiesburg American*, February 27, 1973, 19.

74. *2009–2010 Mississippi State University Men's Basketball Media Guide* (Starkville: Mississippi State University Athletic Department, 2009), 102–108, 125, 130–133.

References

Primary Sources

Newspapers

Clarion-Ledger, 1955–1973.
Commercial Dispatch, 1955–1963.
Daily Herald (Biloxi), 1955–1973.
Daily Journal (Tupelo), 1961–1963.
Daily Mississippian (University of Mississippi), 1962, 1970–1972.
Daily Times Leader, 1955.
Delta Democrat-Times, 1955–1963.
Enterprise-Journal, 1955–1963.
Greenwood Commonwealth, 1955–1963.
Hattiesburg American, 1955–1973.
Jackson Advocate, 1955–1963.
Jackson Daily News, 1955–1973.
Jackson State Times, 1955–1961.
Laurel Leader-Call, 1955–1957.
Meridian Star, 1955–1973.
Mississippi Free Press, 1962–1963.
Natchez Democrat, 1955–1963.
New York Times, 1957.
Oxford Eagle, 1968–1973.
The Reflector (Mississippi State University), 1955–1973.
Starkville Daily News, 1960–1973.
Starkville News, 1955–1960.
Student Printz (University of Southern Mississippi), 1968–1969.
Vicksburg Evening Post, 1955–1973.

Interviews

Gold, Joe Dan. Interview with author. July 23, 2009.
Jordan, Jr., Wilbert. Interview with author. August 15, 2010.
McDowell, Jimmie. Interview with author. August 12, 2010.
Mosby, Joe. Email interview with author. July 23, 2009.

Starr, Douglas. Interview with author. July 30, 2009.
Wallace, Perry. Interview with author. April 18, 2006.

Special Collections

Colvard, D. W. Presidential Papers. Mitchell Memorial Library, Mississippi State University, Starkville, MS.
Giles, William. Presidential Papers. Mitchell Memorial Library, Mississippi State University, Starkville, MS.
Greene, Percy. Oral History with Neil R. McMillen, December 14, 1972, Mississippi Oral History Program, University of Southern Mississippi, Hattiesburg, MS.
Hilbun, Ben. Presidential Papers. Mitchell Memorial Library, Mississippi State University, Starkville, MS.
Mississippi State Sovereignty Commission Records. Department of Archives and History, Jackson, MS.
Simmons, William J. Oral History with Orley B. Caudill, June 26, 1979, Mississippi Oral History Program, University of Southern Mississippi, Hattiesburg, MS.
Walters, Carl. Oral History with Orley B. Caudill, April 14, 1984, Mississippi Oral History Program, University of Southern Mississippi, Hattiesburg, MS.
Wilson, Harrison B. Oral History with Ervin L. Jordan Jr., October 6, 1978, Special Collections, Old Dominion University, Norfolk, VA.

Books

Andrews, Kenneth. *Freedom Is a Constant Struggle: The Mississippi Civil Rights Movement and Its Legacy.* Chicago: University of Chicago Press, 2004.
Arsenault, Raymond. *Freedom Riders: 1961 and the Struggle for Racial Justice.* New York: Oxford University Press, 2006.
Atkins, Joseph B. *The Mission Journalism: Ethics and the World.* Ames, Iowa: Iowa State University Press, 2000.
Ballard, Michael B. *Maroon and White: Mississippi State University, 1878–2003.* Oxford: University Press of Mississippi, 2008.
Bolton, Charles. *The Hardest Deal of All: The Battle over School Integration in Mississippi, 1870–1980.* Jackson: University Press of Mississippi, 2005.
Booker, Simeon. *Shocking the Consequence: A Reporter's Account of the Civil Rights Movement.* Jackson: University Press of Mississippi, 2013.
Brooks, Dana, and Ronald Althouse. *Racism in College Athletics: The African American Athlete's Experience.* Morgantown, WV: Fitness Information Technology, 1993.
Cobb, James C. *The Most Southern Place on Earth: The Mississippi Delta and the Roots of Regional Identity.* New York: Oxford University Press, 1994.
Crespino, Joseph. *In Search of Another Country: Mississippi and the Conservative Counterrevolution.* Princeton, NJ: Princeton University Press, 2007.
Davies, David R. *The Press and Race: Mississippi Journalists Confront the Movement.* Jackson: University Press of Mississippi, 2001.

Dickerson, James. *Dixie's Dirty Little Secret: The True Story of How the Government, the Media, and the Mob Conspired to Combat Integration and the Vietnam Antiwar Movement.* Armonk, NY: M. E. Sharpe, 1998.

Dittmer, John. *Local People: The Struggle for Civil Rights in Mississippi.* Urbana: University of Illinois Press, 1994.

Eagles, Charles W. *The Price of Defiance: James Meredith and the Integration of Ole Miss.* Chapel Hill: University of North Carolina Press, 2009.

Evers, Charles, and Andrew Szanton. *Have No Fear: The Charles Evers Story.* New York: J. Wiley & Sons, 1996.

Fitzpatrick, Frank. *And the Walls Came Tumbling Down: Kentucky, Texas Western, and the Game that Changed American Sports.* New York: Simon & Schuster, 1999.

Iton, Richard. *In Search of the Black Fantastic: Politics and Popular Cultural in the Post-Civil Rights Era.* New York: Oxford University Press, 2008.

Jacobs, Barry. *Across the Line: Profiles in Basketball Courage: Tales of the First Black Players in the ACC and SEC.* Guilford, CT: Lyons Press, 2008.

Jay, Kathryn. *More Than Just a Game: Sports in American Life Since 1945.* New York: Columbia University Press, 2006.

Johnston, Erle. *Mississippi's Defiant Years, 1953–1973.* Forest, MS: Lake Harbor Publishers, 1990.

Katagiri, Yasuhiro. *The Mississippi State Sovereignty Commission: Civil Rights and States' Rights.* Oxford: University Press of Mississippi, 2007.

Kemper, Kurt. *College Football and American Culture in the Cold War Era.* Chicago: University of Illinois Press, 2009.

Lamb, Chris. *Blackout: The Untold Story of Jackie Robinson's First Spring Training.* Omaha, NE: Bison Books, 2006.

Levy, Peter B. *The Civil Rights Movement: Greenwood Press Guides to Historic Events of the Twentieth Century.* Westport, CT: Greenwood Press, 1998.

Marshall, James P. *Student Activism and Civil Rights in Mississippi: Protest Politics and the Struggle for Racial Justice, 1960–196.* Baton Rouge: Louisiana State University Press, 2013.

McMillen, Neil R. *The Citizens' Council: Organized Resistance to the Second Reconstruction, 1954–64.* Urbana: University of Illinois Press, 1971.

Miller, Patrick B., and David Kenneth Wiggins. *Sport and the Color Line: Black Athletes and Race Relations in Twentieth-Century America.* New York: Rutledge, 2004.

Mississippi State University Athletic Media Relations. *2007 Mississippi State Baseball Media Guide.* Starkville: University Publishing, 2007.

Mississippi State University Athletic Media Relations. *2009–2010 Mississippi State University Men's Basketball Media Guide.* Starkville: Mississippi State University Athletic Department, 2009.

Morgan, Chester. *Dearly Bought, Deeply Treasured: The University of Southern Mississippi, 1912–1987.* Jackson: The University Press of Mississippi, 1987.

Musgrove, Ronnie. *The Mississippi Public Community and Junior College Story: 1972–2002.* Jackson: University Press of Mississippi, 2007.

Nossiter, Adam. *Of Long Memory: Mississippi and the Murder of Medgar Evers.* Cambridge, MA: Da Capo Press, 2002.

O'Brien, M. J. *We Shall Not Be Moved: The Jackson Woolworth Sit-In and the Movement It Inspired.* Jackson: University Press of Mississippi, 2013.

Ownby, Ted. *The Civil Rights Movement in Mississippi.* Jackson: University Press of Mississippi, 2013.

Parker, Frank R. and Eddie N. Williams. *Black Votes Count: Political Empowerment in Mississippi after 1965.* Chapel Hill: University of North Carolina Press, 1990.

Payne, Charles M. *I've Got the Light of Freedom: The Organizing Tradition and the Mississippi Freedom Struggle.* Berkeley: University of California Press, 1996.

Reddix, Jacob L. *A Voice Crying in the Wilderness: The Memoirs of Jacob L. Reddix.* Jackson: University Press of Mississippi, 1974.

Roberts, Gene, and Hank Klibanoff. *The Race Beat: The Press, the Civil Rights Struggle, and the Awakening of a Nation.* New York: Knopf, 2006.

Roberts, Randy and James Stuart Olson. *Winning Is the Only Thing: Sports in America since 1945.* Baltimore: Johns Hopkins University Press, 1989.

Sansing, David. *Making Haste Slowly: The Troubled History of Higher Education in Mississippi.* Jackson: University Press of Mississippi, 1990.

Silver, James. *Mississippi: The Closed Society.* New York: Harcourt, Brace, and World, 1964.

Thompson, Julius Eric. *The Black Press in Mississippi, 1865–1985.* Gainesville: University Press of Florida, 1993.

University of Mississippi Athletic Media Relations. *2009–2010 University of Mississippi Men's Basketball Media Guide.* Oxford: University of Mississippi Athletic Department, 2009.

University of Southern Mississippi Athletic Media Relations. *2009–2010 University of Southern Mississippi Men's Basketball Media Guide.* Hattiesburg: University of Southern Mississippi Athletic Department, 2009.

Vollers, Maryanne. *Ghosts of Mississippi.* Boston: Little, Brown and Company, 1995.

Wallenstien, Peter. *Higher Education and the Civil Rights Movement: White Supremacy, Black Southerners, and College Campuses.* Gainesville: University Press of Florida, 2008.

Weill, Susan. *In a Madhouse's Din: Civil Rights Coverage by Mississippi's Daily Press, 1948–1968.* Westport, CT: Praeger, 2002.

Wiggins, David K. *Glory Bound: Black Athletes in a White America.* Syracuse, NY: Syracuse University Press, 1997.

Wigginton, Russell Thomas. *The Strange Career of the Black Athlete: African Americans and Sports.* Westport, CT: Praeger, 2006.

Wilkie, Curtis. *Dixie: A Personal Odyssey through Events That Shaped the Modern South.* New York: Touchstone, 2001.

Zirin, Dave. *What's My Name, Fool? Sports and Resistance in the United States.* Chicago: Haymarket Books, 2005.

Theses and Student Papers

Sellers, James T. *A History of the Jackson State Times: An Agent of Change in a Closed Society.* PhD Dissertation, University of Southern Mississippi, 1992.

Magazines

Cave, Ray. "The Old Master Has A New Kind of Winner." *Sports Illustrated*, February 19, 1962, 52–53.

"Dixie Flamethrowers." *Time Magazine*, March 4, 1966, 1.

Doust, Dudley. "Bouquets for Babe and His Bailey." *Sports Illustrated*, February 23, 1959, 50–52.

"For the Record." *Sports Illustrated*, September 17, 1973, 147.

"For the Record." *Sports Illustrated*, March 31, 1975, 85.

Medina, David. "Opening Doors." *Sallyport: The Magazine of Rice University* 61, no. 1, (Fall 2004).

Poinsett, Alex. "President's Action Chokes Off." *Jet*, October 26, 1961, 24–27.

"Scoreboard." *Sports Illustrated*, December 20, 1954, 57.

Research Articles

Henderson, Russell J. "The 1963 Mississippi State University Basketball Controversy and the Repeal of the Unwritten Law: 'Something more than the game will be lost.'" *The Journal of Southern History* 63, no. 4 (1997): 827–854.

Lamb, Chris, and Glen Bleske. "Covering the Integration of Baseball—A Look Back." *Editor & Publisher* 130, no. 4 (January 27, 1996): 48–50.

Paul, Jan, Richard McGee, and Helen Fant. "The Arrival and Ascendance of the Black Athlete in the Southeastern Conference, 1966–1980." *Phylon* 45, no. 4 (December 1984): 284–297.

Reese, Renford. "The Socio-Political Context of the Integration of Sport in America." *Journal of African American Men* 4, no. 3 (Spring 1999): 5–22.

Simmons, William. "Jackie Robinson and the American Mind: Journalistic Perceptions of the Reintegration of Baseball." *Journal of Sport History* 12, no. 1 (Spring 1985): 39–64.

Secondary Sources

Books

Alston, Alex A., and James L. Dickerson. *Devil's Sanctuary: An Eyewitness Account of Mississippi Hate Crimes*. Chicago: Chicago Review Press, 2009.

Atkins, Joseph B., and Stanley Aronowitz, *Covering for the Bosses: Labor and the Southern Press*. Jackson: University Press of Mississippi, 2008.

Beito, Linda Royster. *Black Maverick: T. R. M. Howard's Fight for Civil Rights and Economic Power*. Urbana: University of Illinois Press, 2009.

Campbell, Will D. *Robert G. Clark's Journey to the House: A Black Politician's Story*. Jackson: University Press of Mississippi, 2003.

Carroll, John. *Fritz Pollard: Pioneer in Racial Advancement*. Champaign: University of Illinois Press, 1998.

Crosby, Emilye. *A Little Taste of Freedom: The Black Freedom Struggle in Claiborne County, Mississippi*. Chapel Hill: University of North Carolina Press, 2005.

Dunnavant, Keith. *The Missing Ring: How Bear Bryant and the 1966 Alabama Crimson Tide Were Denied College Football's Most Elusive Prize*. New York: St. Martin's Press, 2007.

Evers-Williams, Myrlie, and Manning Marable. *The Autobiography of Medgar Evers: A Hero's Life and Legacy Revealed through His Writings, Letters and Speeches*. New York: Basic Civitas Books, 2005.

Frederickson, Kari A. *The Dixiecrat Revolt and the End of the Solid South, 1932–1968.* Chapel Hill: University of North Carolina Press, 2001.

Howard, John. *Men Like That: A Southern Queer History.* Chicago: University of Chicago Press, 1999.

Leverett, Rudy H. *Legend of the Free State of Jones.* Jackson: University Press of Mississippi, 1984.

Pluto, Terry. *Loose Balls: The Short, Wild Life of the American Basketball Association.* New York: Simon and Schuster, 1991.

Rosa, Greg. *Football in the SEC: Southeastern Conference.* New York: Rosen Publishing Group, 2007.

Rosen, Charley. *The Wizard of Odds: How Jack Molinas Almost Destroyed the Game of Basketball.* New York: Seven Stories Press, 2001.

Ross, Charles K. *Outside the Lines: African Americans and the Integration of the National Football League.* New York: NYU Press, 2001.

Simmons, Charles A. *The African American Press: A History of News Coverage during National Crises, 1827–1965.* Jefferson, NC: McFarland & Co., 1998.

Terry, Wallace. *Missing Pages: Black Journalists of Modern America: An Oral History.* New York: Carroll & Graf Publishers, 2007.

Weiss, Don, and Chuck Day. *The Making of the Super Bowl.* New York: McGraw-Hill Professional, 2003.

Research Articles

Walton, Laura Richardson. "In Their Own Backyard: Local Press Coverage of the Chaney, Goodman, and Schwerner Murders." *American Journalism* 23, no. 3 (Summer 2006): 29–51.

Websites

http://encyclopedia.gwu.edu/gwencyclopedia/index.php?title=Basketball_%28Men%29
http://www.hattiesburgamerican.com
http://www.mstateathletics.com
http://www.msstate.edu/web/gen_info.htm.
http://www.nsu.edu/inauguration/NSUPresidents.html
http://www.soconsports.com/

Index

CPSIA information can be obtained at www.ICGtesting.com
Printed in the USA
BVOW04*0152150816

458623BV00008B/2/P